JEWS IN AN ARAB LAND

Jews in an Arab Land
LIBYA, 1835–1970

By Renzo De Felice

Translated by Judith Roumani

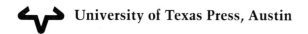 University of Texas Press, Austin

Library of Congress Cataloging in Publication Data

De Felice, Renzo, 1929–
  Jews in an Arab land.
  Translation of: Ebrei in un paese arabo.
  Includes bibliographical references and index.
  1. Jews—Libya—History. 2. Libya—Ethnic relations.
I. Title
DS135.L44D413 1985   961.2004924   84-11851
ISBN 0-292-74016-6

This book has been published with the cooperation and financial support of the Cultural Center of Libyan Jewry.

The preparation of this volume was made possible by a grant from the Translations Program of the National Endowment for the Humanities, an independent federal agency. The views, interpretations, and conclusions contained herein should be understood to be solely those of the author and should not be attributed to the Endowment.

Translated from *Ebrei in un paese arabo: Gli ebrei nella Libia contemporanea tra colonialismo, nazionalismo arabo e sionismo (1835–1970)*, Copyright © 1978 by Società editrice il Mulino, Bologna

Contents

Tables

Translator's Preface

The image that "Libyan Jewry" evokes in many people is a confused one. Some are led to think of the aristocratic demesne of the "pure" Sephardim—those who trace their ancestry to Spain and Portugal. Others conjure up the simple folkways of cave dwellers. For anyone wanting to gain an informed insight into the historical development of Jewish life in Libya, a major obstacle in the past has been the "deplorable dearth of historical accounts of African and Levantine Sephardic Communities" lamented by the American Sephardic scholar M. A. Benardete in 1952.[1] Though the gap has in the meantime been filled for other communities and Libyan Jewry has been the subject of detailed anthropological research, the lack of historical accounts persisted until the appearance in Italy in 1978 of Renzo De Felice's *Ebrei in un paese arabo*—"Jews in an Arab Land." The rich and varied political, social, and cultural life of this community has finally emerged, thanks to De Felice's multifaceted approach to it.

As a distinguished historian of Italian Fascism, Renzo De Felice is skilled in bringing an impartial and balanced mode of analysis to the issues of modern history which otherwise may arouse shrill, impassioned tones. Though his original interest had been in Jacobinism and the French Revolution, he was the first postwar scholar to venture on a critical but detached study of Fascism, and his work set off an extensive debate in Italy. His multi-volume biography of Mussolini, with its careful documentation and measured interpretations, is acknowledged as the major work on Il Duce. De Felice also studied the situation of Italian Jews under Fascism in *Storia degli ebrei italiani sotto il fascismo* (1961). Partly as an extension of that work, particularly Fascist colonial policy, in 1978 he published the present book on the Jews of Libya, a country that was subjected to Italian colonial rule between 1911 and 1945.

De Felice examines Libyan Jewry not only in the context of colonialism, but also in terms of the inner dynamics of this ancient community (established since the time of the Second Temple, 520

B.C.—70 A.D.) and its encounters with Islam and the Ottomans, with the West through Italian colonization and British occupation during and after the Second World War, with Arab nationalism and independent Libya, and with the influence of Zionism. With skill, objectivity and empathy, De Felice reveals the attitudes of rulers, movements, and ideologies toward Libyan Jewry and offers a perceptive understanding of its behavior under the stress of contradictory ideological, economic, spiritual, and personalistic forces.

In this book the author provides new information on the life of an indigenous minority in the Middle East. He shows how and why an age-old relationship dissolved, as conditions in Libya, unlike those in other North African countries, caused most of the Jews to leave before independence in 1951. The Jewish population, estimated at thirty-six thousand in the 1940s, was reduced to six thousand through mass emigration, due to intercommunal tensions and pogroms in 1945 and 1948. The majority of Jews became convinced that the Arab-Israeli conflict would make life untenable for them in independent Libya, and they were ultimately proven right. Many others, however, did not see the prospect of independence as a specific threat to themselves. The Libyan Jews' relationship to Libyan Arab culture was not a question of attraction. They were so imbued with it that they took it for granted. Those who remained in Libya after 1952 behaved toward the new state as they had always done toward their rulers: they sought and relied on King Idris' personal protection. The Europeanized Libyan Jews continued to act as cultural and economic intermediaries between Arabs and Europeans. But a gradual deterioration set in under the reign of King Idris, and almost all Jews finally had to leave in the wake of the 1967 Middle East War.

De Felice's focus on the colonial period of Libyan Jewry highlights the predicament of Jewish existence in the complicated environment of a colonized Muslim society, confirming the paradoxes of colonialism described by Jean-Paul Sartre, Frantz Fanon,[2] and Albert Memmi. The last, a Tunisian Jew, found that he was colonized three times over: as an indigenous inhabitant of a country colonized by France, as a Jew in a Muslim society, and as a member of a poor, artisan family.[3] Libyan Jews, in similarly unfavorable conditions, survived, flourished, and took pride in themselves through initiative and imagination. Some of the pictures of their life which emerge in the documents that De Felice has assembled express better than any analysis their situation. While the Jews of Libya adapted to the Italian presence and many accepted its culture, they continued to maintain traditional relationships with their Muslim indigenous milieu. But when the colony became an open field for uninhibited Fascist activities, colonial officials tried to force Jews to Italianize by abandoning some of their most cherished traditions. Thus Governor Italo Balbo, though he was a friend of Italian Jews, and delayed the extension of Italy's 1938 racial laws from the metropolis to Libya, did apply anti-Jewish measures, obliging Libyan Jews to attend school and do business on the Sabbath. As a powerless minority, beset by cultural differences between Arabized Jewish masses and Italianized elites, the Libyan Jewish community was at times unable to ward off interference in its affairs and maintain its internal autonomy. The unity of Libyan Jewry, De Felice shows, was being undermined by centrifugal forces—increasing secularism, an urge to become Italianized, indifference to community concerns. But the Jewish community did find unity and resources when necessary to deal with tensions, crises, and urgent need, and De Felice documents extensively the interplay of unifying and centrifugal forces within it. In the face of the great crises of the Second World War and the pressures of Arab nationalism, the community survived because of its unity. Though Zionism as a political movement initially met with opposition from some of the leaders of the community, its educational efforts helped in resisting assimilation and fragmentation.

Libyan Jewry emerges from De Felice's study as the object of some of the main ideologies and conflicts of the twentieth century—Fascism, colonialism, pan-Arab nationalism, and Zionism— all of which had an influence on the future of the Jews of Libya. De Felice examines soberly the issues leading to the end of Jewish life in Libya. They fit into the broader pattern of anti-Jewish hostility, described by Norman Stillman[4] as an outgrowth of European anti-Semitism which found soil in Arab nationalism and flowered with the Arab-Israeli conflict. There was also some of what Guido Fubini describes as Arab anti-Semitism in terms of a reaction of the poor against former economic intermediaries whom they identified with colonialism.[5] The end of Jewish life in Libya has meant a cultural loss for all Libyans, Jews and Arabs. They have, nevertheless, partaken of that common inner rhythm of Jewish and Arab histories, described by S. D. Goitein.[6] The two peoples have had a similar relationship to Western civilization, so that their revivals have coincided. Moreover, the Hebrew and Arabic languages and literatures have experienced their renaissance at the same time. When greater understanding between the two cultures comes about, the Jews from Arab countries will perhaps, in their accustomed role as intermediaries, have had some hand in it.

Terms and institutions which may be unfamiliar to English-speaking readers are explained as far as possible through translator's notes. Where historical documents in an English version or original are accessible, they have been quoted rather than translated. Occasional words in Hebrew or Arabic have been transcribed as far as possible according to the Library of Congress systems, except for Libyan place names and personal names. For these I have used either the form most current in scholarly English or the Defense Mapping Agency Topographic Center's *Libya: Official Standard Names Approved by the United States Board on Geographic Names*, second edition.

In addition to the National Endowment for the Humanities, I would like to express thanks to Norman Thomas di Giovanni for his review of the translation, and to the following for encouragement and help in solving problems of many sorts: Professor Renzo De Felice, Rabbi Mitchell Serels, Dr. Harvey Goldberg, Dr. David Ruderman, Mr. Raffaello Fellah, co-founder of the Jews of Libya Association, the late Dr. Lawrence Marwick and staff of the Hebraic Section of the Library of Congress, the American Jewish Committee, Dr. Dan Segre, Dr. Maurice Roumani, Mrs. Fiona Martin, and the University of Texas Press.

J.R.

Acknowledgments

Handing over my work, I feel that I must express how much I owe many people—Italians and foreigners, Jews and Arabs, scholars and colonial officials, soldiers, politicians, and ordinary citizens. With great courtesy and considerable sacrifice of time, they have helped me clarify particular aspects and events of Libyan reality and Jewish and Arab life, traditions, culture, and ideas. They have patiently discussed with me both specific and broad-ranging problems. I am greatly indebted to them all, particularly Lillo Arbib, Roberto Arbib, Raffaello Fellah, Mario Gazzini, A'be Karlikow, David Littman, Erminio Marchino, Sergio Minerbi, Janet and Dino Naim, Sion Nemni, Maurice and Jacques Roumani, and G. B. Segal. Without the help of all these people, this book could not have been written. The opinions contained in this work obviously do not commit these persons in any way, but reflect the conclusions I have freely reached on the basis of my own research and conversations.

I would particularly like to say how grateful I am for the help and contributions of my friends Ennio Bozzetti, Luigi Goglia, Mario Missori, and Augusto Segre.

R.D.F.

Abbreviations

AAEL	Archives of the Associazione Ebrei di Libia [Jews of Libya Association], Rome.
AAIU	Archives of the Alliance Israélite Universelle [Universal Jewish Alliance], Paris.
AAJC	Archives of the American Jewish Committee, Paris.
ACDEC	Archives of the Centro di Documentazione Ebraica Contemporanea [Center for Contemporary Jewish Documentation], Milan.
ACS	Archivio Centrale dello Stato [Central State Archives], Rome.
AIJA	Archives of the Institute of Jewish Affairs, London.
APM	Private Marchino archives, Rome.
ASMAE	Archivio Storico del Ministero degli Affari Esteri [Historical Archives of the Ministry of Foreign Affairs], Rome.
ASMAI	Archivio Storico del Ministero dell'Africa Italiana [Historical Archives of the Ministry of Italian Africa], Rome.
AUCII	Archivio dell'Unione delle Comunità Israelitiche Italiane [Archives of the Union of Italian Jewish Communities], Rome.
CZA	Central Zionist Archives, Jerusalem.
PRO	Public Record Office, London.

JEWS IN AN ARAB LAND

TUNISIA

Zanzur Tajura

Zuwara TRIPOLI Mesallata
Zawia Amruss al-Khums
al-Azizia Zlitin
Yafran Tarhuna Misurata
Nalut Giado Gharian
Mizda Beni Ulid Sedada
Bu'ayrat al-Hasun Syrte

Derna
Barce
BENGHAZI Tubruq
Soluq Port Bardia

Zuetina
Agedabia

Derg
Gadames T R I P O L I T A N I A

EGYPT

ALGERIA C Y R E N A I C A

F E Z Z A N

LIBYA

Introduction

The presence of Jews in Libya goes so far back into time that the historian Ismail Chemali claims that "their origins merge with those of the oldest inhabitants of the country."[1] Allusions to Libyan Jews occur in Herodotus and Strabo, and it has even been asserted that Jews established themselves in the hinterland region of Jebel Akhdar shortly after and as a result of the destruction of the First Temple in Jerusalem (597 B.C.). The first fairly reliable information attesting to the presence of Jews on the coast of Tripolitania comes down to us from Carthaginian times. Documentation from the Roman period is more extensive and exact. At that time a flourishing Jewish community, which enjoyed close relations with Rome and special privileges granted by Augustus, existed in Tripolitania. The Jewish presence in Cyrenaica can be claimed with certainty from not long after the reign of Ptolemy I in the third century B.C. It was in Cyrenaica that Jews were more numerous and active. The first settlements there, which were more or less sporadic and usually related to trading, were followed by others after the campaigns of Antiochus Epiphanes (reigned 175–163 B.C.). One of the refugees from these wars was Jason of Cyrene, an eye-witness historian of the Wars of the Maccabees. As even Josephus Flavius tells us, Cyrene became the focus of this settlement and witnessed intense Jewish artistic and cultural life. New settlements arose after the Roman conquest of Jerusalem in A.D. 70. It was not by chance, then, that Cyrene became the center from which the Jewish revolt against Trajan (then occupied fighting the Parthians in the East) began in about 115, spreading to Cyprus, Egypt, and several places in the East.[2]

This revolt, which lasted until 117, had disastrous consequences for the Jews. Roman repression reduced the flourishing community of Cyrene to insignificance and set it on the road to inevitable decline. Many of the surviving Jews abandoned the city and took refuge among the Berber tribes of Syrte. According to certain Arab historians, they founded a new coastal city, Al-Jahuda, the remains of which have not yet been discovered. Some fled into the Sahara and westward to Tripolitania, Tunisia, Algeria, and Morocco. Among some Berber tribes, these refugees set off a process of Judaization. In many respects, it was a reciprocal process. Scholars such as Simon[3] have maintained, however, that when the Arabs occupied Libya the real Jews had probably almost completely disappeared; by then there were only Christians and Judeo-Berbers.

All that we can be sure of is that after the dispersion of the Cyrene community, accounts of Jews in Libya become even more fragmentary and vague. We can only speculate that Jewish settlement must have remained modest for some centuries and that whatever happened to it was closely related to whatever was happening to Libya and its inhabitants. During the first half of the fifth century, when Gaiseric reached Libya, some recovery must slowly have been taking place. The rule of the Vandals, repressing as it did any attempt at revolt by the Roman population and therefore supporting groups of non-Roman origin, accelerated this recovery. A century later, when Belisarius brought Libya back into the Byzantine Roman empire under Justinian, the Jews paid dearly for those partial privileges. The intolerant policies of the Byzantines and the resentment of the Roman-Christian population obliged many Jews to seek refuge once again among Berber tribes of the interior. It was probably during this period, in the sixth century, that, due to necessarily closer relations between Jews and Berbers, some Berber tribes converted to Judaism. At approximately the same time, some Jews seem to have arrived in Tripolitania in flight from the Visigothic invasion of Spain. Their numbers must have been very small, for most of those exiles remained in the westernmost part of North Africa or else settled farther east than Libya. This was a trend which in later centuries would remain constant. Libya was almost totally passed over by the main currents of Jewish emigration from the Christian West; hence for their entire subsequent history the Jews of Libya were almost completely isolated from the rest of the North African and broader Mediterranean Jewish world.

For Libya and for the Jews of Libya, the Middle Ages began halfway through the seventh century. The Arab conquest, in fact, marked a decisive turn in their history, as it did in the history of North Africa as a whole. Because of the scant information available, it is almost impossible to say anything precise about this period of the history of Libyan Jews. If we are to believe Jewish and Arab traditions, the Arab conquest met initially with considerable resistance from Berbers and Jews. That may be the origin of the almost certainly legendary stories of Jewish "queens," who supposedly led the Jewish-Berber resistance. In the famous Dahya bint Tatit al Kahina, for example, Baron rightly saw "a Medieval version of Deborah, the ancient prophetess." Whatever actually took place, it is a fact that in the early centuries of Arab domination the few Jewish communities still in existence must have all but been dispersed. Their place had been taken, especially in Tripoli, by new Judeo-Berber communities, which the few written sources they left (mainly a few inscriptions on gravestones) show to have been culturally primitive.

Except at the outset and during the difficult Almohad period (a time of persecution for Jews and Christians alike), Arab domination was not particularly burdensome for the Jews. Although the so-called "Pact of 'Umar" decreed for the Jews a whole array of social discriminations and tax burdens, it also assured them status as a "protected minority." It did the same for Christians and other "peoples of the Book" vouchsafed a monotheistic vision of God, guaranteeing them the security of persons and goods and the practice of their religion. In this situation the dangers threatening Jews were ultimately the same as those of the population of Libya as a whole: general insecurity caused by frequent periods of anarchy, foreign and civil wars, epidemics, and resulting economic problems. The situation of Libyan Jews was substantially the same as that of the majority of other Jews subject to Arab rule. One can thus apply to the Jews of Libya the overall judgment expressed by Baron regarding the general situation of Jews living under Arabs:

> Insecure as life generally was in the troubled periods of Islam's decline, there was none of that feeling of personal insecurity which dominated the medieval Jewish psyche in the West. The Near Eastern, Moroccan or Spanish Jew may have legitimately feared some sudden invasion or civil war. But he knew that he would then suffer not as a Jew but together with other inhabitants of his locality, as if it had been struck by one of the recurrent earthquakes or famines. In peaceful times he was protected by law against personal assault almost on a par with the Muslim, and his average life expectancy was probably at least as high as that of his "believing" neighbor. His economic opportunities, too, as we shall see, suffered only from relatively minor restrictions. Outside of Egypt he was generally free to move from place to place. Like his Muslim confreres, he could traverse the vast expanse of the Muslim world in search of economic or intellectual benefits. The majority of Jews undoubtedly viewed all these disabilities and even the irksome humiliations as but a minor price they had to pay for their freedom of conscience and their ability to live an untrammeled Jewish life within the confines of their own community.[4]

As a matter of fact, the next period, leading up to the modern age, was more burdensome for the Jews of Libya than the Arab Middle Ages had been. This period began for them in 1510, when the Spanish took Tripoli and occupied it for about twenty years, followed by another twenty-one years (up to 1551) of occupation by the Knights of Malta. The Spanish occupation was a particularly difficult period for the Jews. When Tripoli was taken, many families (tradition speaks of eight hundred) left the city and took refuge mainly at Tajura and in the Jebel. Some of them went straight to Italy, particularly Rome. It was from Italy, as well as from Spain and Portugal, that some Jewish refugees had reached Tripoli in the years just before. Later on, some of those who had fled to the hinterland returned to Tripoli. Though some returned, the entire Spanish period (and to a lesser extent the Maltese period too) was for the Jews a time of hardship and economic decline. This was due to the almost continuous state of war between Christians and Ottomans, the restrictions and discrimination which the Spanish imposed, together with the almost complete disruption of contacts between the Tripoli community and those of Tajura and Gharian in the hinterland.

In 1551 Tripoli and Libya came under Ottoman rule, beginning a new phase in the history of the Jews of Libya, which was to last with certain interruptions up to 1911. For this period as well, accessible, precise information is somewhat sparse. Tradition and Muslim chronicles—at least those known up to now—are dim and inexact with regard to the Jews. Jewish sources are hardly more trustworthy, due to the low educational level of the Tripoli community and the fact that these sources are all late and cursory in nature. More precise but generally disjointed accounts exist only for the seventeenth and eighteenth centuries—more so for the latter—due mainly to chronicles of occasional European travelers and reports from English, French, Venetian, and Neapolitan consuls and representatives. Finally, some information is provided by the archives of the various brotherhoods and organizations, both Christian and Jewish, involved in ransoming slaves captured by Barbary pirates.[5]

Until 1711 Tripoli was under Constantinople, which ruled it through Ottoman pashas and deys. From 1711 to 1835, Tripoli was governed by its own dynasty, the Karamanlis. From 1835 until the Italian occupation, it was back under direct Ottoman rule. Of these three periods, the one in which on balance the Jews enjoyed the best conditions was probably the second.[6] This should not lead us to believe, however, that there was any substantial difference in conditions between the various periods. Except for almost imperceptible nuances, the civil and judicial status of Jews was in fact almost always the same. The governments which succeeded each other in Tripoli from the latter half of the sixteenth century until the beginning of the twentieth, conforming to Muslim principles and law, behaved substantially in the same way toward Jews. From this point of view, then, their situation was little different from that of the Arab period. What has been said regarding that period largely applies to the subsequent periods too. The differences in the three periods relate mainly to the general economic and specific political situations prevailing in Libya: whether there were more or fewer wars and uprisings, longer or shorter periods of misgovernment and anarchy, etc. As Solomon Grayzel has written, for four centuries in Tripolitania, as in North Africa as a whole, essentially the fate of the Jews depended once again on the general conditions of the country and "the whim or wisdom of the ruler[s]. . . . Every internal disorder brought persecution; every new tyrant exacted the last possible penny."[7]

Recovery had already begun in the first period. In the second half of the sixteenth century many families from Jebel Nefusa, Gharian, and Zlitin went to Tripoli and renewed contacts between the communities of the hinterland and that of the capital. Other families arrived from Spain and Leghorn. Among Italian Jewish communities, Leghorn was the one which for a long time kept up the best relations with the Tripoli community. At the same time, religious and community life revived. Both had been declining and deteriorating for a long time due to the Berberization of Libyan Jewry and in the more recent past to Spanish rule. Rabbi Shimon Labi, a Spanish refugee traveling from Fez to Palestine, seems to have played a decisive role in the revival. Arriving in Tripoli in 1549, he became aware of the extreme decline of the community. Many of its members had very cursory knowledge of religious precepts and were even ignorant of traditional rites and prayers. He decided to interrupt his trip and devote himself to bringing the Jews of Tripoli back to the Torah. According to local tradition, it was Rabbi Labi who actually restored and organized the modern community, and it was he who revived religious life in Tripoli.

In 1589 the revolt of a religious leader, the false Mahdi Yahya Ibn Yahya,* inflicted a serious blow on the Jewish community of Tripoli, which was still in a precarious condition. The community was subject, among other things, to many forced conversions, so

---

*One of numerous revolts by Arabs against the Turks. The latter used Jews to pull their cannon in battle, and when they were defeated and massacred, many of these Jews were also killed. See Ettore Rossi, *Storia di Tripoli e della Tripolitania dalla conquista araba al 1911* (Rome: Istituto per l'Oriente, 1968), pp. 162–164.—Trans.

that its recovery was slow. It did not really recover until the eighteenth century. When recovery did occur, it was due mainly to the relative peace, economic growth, and tolerant policies practiced by the Karamanlis, together with trade related to Barbary piracy, which had persisted since the seventeenth century. By the nineteenth century, a Muslim observer wrote·

> The Jews, who have three synagogues in Tripoli, are treated somewhat better than in Morocco. There are about two thousand who dress as Muslims do; only the cap and slippers must be black, and the turban usually deep blue. There are about thirty very rich families, the others being craftsmen or goldsmiths. Trade with Europe is almost entirely in their hands: they deal mainly with Marseilles, Leghorn, Venice, and Malta.[8]

The last period of Karamanli rule, when the economic recovery of Tripoli's Jews had already begun, is well described by R. Micacchi:

> Since all the region's trade had been in the hands of Jews for a long time, they were the richest group in the city. Because of their relations with Italian Jews they had acted as intermediaries in ransoming Christian prisoners. In fact, through fellow-Jews in the Jebel, the Jews had also taken over trade with the Sudan, where a major part of the spoils of piracy went. The fortunes they amassed led the Jews to lose their usual caution and flaunt their wealth. They thus aroused the resentment of the Muslims, who hated the Jews all the more since they were dependent on them in trade.
>
> Already at the beginning of the century a marabout from the Uadai incited the lowest classes of Tripoli's citizenry against the Jews, threatening the Pasha himself with God's anger if he did not require them to wear special clothing distinguishing them from the believers. Despite his tolerant views, Iusuf had to give in and order that thenceforth the Jews would have to give up rich clothing. From then on Muslim fanaticism against the Jews remained fierce, while gradually also the favorable position which Iusuf had granted them in the early years of his reign was eroded. The Jewish community was already subject to heavy taxation (head money, the provision of various supplies to the Court, such as fat, perfumes, toiletries, etc.), not to mention donations to officials on every major Muslim holiday. The community was now obliged to pay a sum of thirty-five thousand lire annually. Another of the Pasha's more serious provisions was that all property not guaranteed by written title was considered the state's. The provision was serious because, according to the Rabbinic law of *hazakah*, anyone living in a house for more than three years without the owner's contesting it, himself becomes its full owner. The provision thus held in store large-scale confiscations.[9]

It was in this same period that the Jews of Tripoli (like the rest of the population) were subject to the greatest danger, affecting both persons and property. The first occasion was Ibrahim Sherif's expedition against Tripoli from Tunisia in 1704 and 1705, and the second the occupation of the city in 1795 by Ali Burghul, an Algerian who had succeeded in having himself appointed Pasha of Tripoli by the Sultan. The dangers were so great that, in memory of the two events and the "miraculousness" of their deliverance from them, the Jews from then on celebrated two local purim on the respective anniversaries: "Purim Sherif" on the twenty-third of Teveth and "Purim Burghul" on the twenty-ninth of Teveth. The last years of the Karamanlis and those immediately afterward, in which the Turks made extensive efforts to wield effective sovereignty over the Jebel and put down several open revolts, were likewise particularly hard for the Jews of that region. Willy-nilly, the Jews of the Jebel were affected by these revolts and the suppressions of them. In the last phase of the revolts in the mid-1750s, some of the small communities either participated (or were obliged to participate) on the rebel side, to which they generally provided arms and medicine, or secretly paid taxes to the Turks in Tripoli, hoping by this expedient to avoid being punished when the revolt was put down.[10]

Zorzi Tavanelli, a Venetian captain, was taken at sea by Tripoli pirates, sold to Jewish and Muslim merchants with his companions, and then ransomed through the intercession of the consuls of France and Sweden. He states that in 1749 Tripoli had sixteen to seventeen thousand inhabitants, almost half of them Jewish. This estimate is certainly too high. Another Venetian, the merchant Mariano Doxera, was probably closer to the mark in 1783 (bearing in mind that in 1756, after some disorders, many families of Tunisian Jews came to Tripoli) when he spoke of a population of about fourteen thousand, including about three thousand Jews "who, as in the other cities of Africa, are employed in trade and wear distinctive dress."[11] We lack information for other communities.

The Jews lived all together in their quarter, the *hara*, which was overcrowded and, as all travelers agree, extremely poor and dirty. There were several synagogues in it, including the Sla El Kebira, which had been built in 1628 and bore testimony to the recovery, spiritual and economic, which occurred after 1551. Like those of Tunisia and Algeria, the community of Tripoli had a venerable leader, the *qaid* or *shaykh*, who took care of relations with the government, fixed the amount of taxes each family would pay (he could have anyone who did not pay imprisoned), and presided over the council of notables, whose duty it was to advise the administration about taxes and relations among the various groups. The council had few members (in the Ottoman period, never more than seven), and they were chosen from the well-off, who contributed money to buy wheat for distribution to the poor at Passover. Except rarely, the head of the community was not a religious figure but a person of prestige who almost always came from one of the better-off families. His authority was partially limited by that of the chief rabbi, the *hakham bashi*, whose appointment had to be approved by the government. Sometimes, as in the case of Messaud Hai Raccah, the author of the commentary on Rambam's *Mishneh Torah*, the chief rabbi was sent from Jerusalem or from some other important Eastern Jewish center. This was because of the modest and often very low cultural level of local rabbis. But recourse to foreign rabbis was quite rare; the reactionary ideas of some Libyan Jews, who were more attached to their own local traditions than to real religion, and the intrigues of local rabbis in fact made such a solution extremely difficult. It was also perhaps because of this lack of authoritative rabbis that in the Ottoman period the *hakham bashi* became a kind of community representative to the government rather than a genuine spiritual leader above the other rabbis.

The most common economic pursuits were trade and metalworking. To a large extent, Tripoli's trade was controlled by Jews. Maritime trade was conducted particularly with Leghorn, and in the eighteenth century it was continually expanding. This trade was in the hands of two or three Jewish companies, which dealt mainly in henna, wool, and cereals. There was caravan trade with the hinterland, the oases of the Fezzan, and as far as northern Nigeria (from whence woven cloth was exported for finishing in Naples). Typical commodities traded by Jews were esparto, alfa, and ostrich feathers. Jews were also moneychangers and bankers, as well as the few insurers of ships and merchandise. The working of silver and gold, which was a very old craft, and silk spinning and weaving were typically Jewish crafts. There were also many dyers.[12] The silversmiths and silkworkers all belonged to guilds, having their own charters and also apparently including Arab artisans. Despite this intensive activity in commerce and crafts, the community as a whole was quite poor, most of the wealth being owned by a few families (the Halfons, Hassans, Labis, Arbibs, Ambrons, Nahums, etc.). These families usually included those Jews to whom the government had granted some public function, such as a subcontract for customs or the contract for the mint.

1. Ottoman Rule

Tripoli's return in 1835 to direct Ottoman domination (under which Tripolitania and Cyrenaica became vilayets or provinces)[1] definitely encouraged the Jews' economic activity and their contacts with other communities of the empire. In the last decades of Karamanli rule the country had begun to decline, showing ever more serious signs of political and economic disarray. With the restoration of the Sultan's power came a measure of recovery, greater security in general, and some civil and administrative progress and modernization. Furthermore, the Ottoman government repeatedly confirmed and always respected guarantees granted to the Jews. Particularly important was the imperial decree of March 21, 1865, which sanctioned the Jewish community's autonomy by granting it power and the right for Jews to be represented independently by the chief rabbi. Hence there was a growing improvement in their condition, especially in the economic and social situation of the group of mainly foreign families which handled or otherwise controlled the community's economic life. Relations were strengthened between the major Libyan communities, especially the Tripoli community, and other smaller communities in the country. This did not prevent most of these communities from remaining substantially secluded from that of Tripoli; some cave dwelling communities in the Gharian region continued to survive,[2] while the number of small settlements on the coast and inland gradually increased. Besides living in and around the main centers of population, the Jews had settled along the country's main lines of communication, whence in the course of trade they spread outward along fixed and regular routes to other centers, particularly those where there were markets. Sometimes they attended so regularly that they were made responsible for collecting the market taxes. They also had contact with scattered Arab groups and often were the only means through which the Arabs could get supplies, barter their products, and obtain essential credit. This credit was granted in the form of either money or, more commonly, deferral

of payments in kind until harvest time. There must be significance
in the fact that Arab women admitted Jewish peddlers into their
houses, while they would not admit Muslims. As Harvey Goldberg
has illustrated,[3] between the end of the eighteenth century and the
beginning of the nineteenth, Tripolitanian Jewry underwent important changes in its geographical distribution, closely linked to
changes happening in Arab society. Small Jewish communities were
subject to a process of urbanization analogous to that affecting the
Muslim population. Since some markets were increasing in importance and new ones were springing up, settlements came into existence in places where Jews either had not lived previously, or had
been present only in very small groups: Tarhuna, Beni Ulid, Nalut,
al-Khums, Zanzur, and Zuwara. At the same time, some of the Tripolitanian hinterland communities saw an improvement in their
economy, for reasons which we will examine later. It was not reflected in any improvement in Arab-Jewish relations, which were
often actually deteriorating. A member of the Alliance Israélite Universelle, a teacher at the local Alliance school who was living in
Tripoli in 1900, described the situation in these communities in a
field report mailed to Paris:

> There are many small scattered communities in the mountainous inte-
> rior. These groups all subsist by working the land or practicing crafts.
> The women spend their time weaving wool and making very beautiful
> bornouses. Some Jews have achieved relative affluence. . . . In those
> out-of-the-way places, the Jew may not ride a horse or a donkey in
> an Arab's presence. On seeing an Arab coming, a Jew must dismount
> quickly and continue on foot, leading his mount, until the Arab disap-
> pears round a bend in the highway. If the Jew forgets this or takes too
> long to dismount, the Arab brutally reminds him of "good manners" by
> throwing him to the ground. The Jews of the Jebel (one of these regions)
> told me that over the last twenty years three Israelites had been killed
> in this way. The testimony of a Jew is not accepted and he would never
> dare to accuse anyone of robbing him. Every Jewish family is under the
> suzerainty of an Arab, termed the "Saheb." This saheb, as you have al-
> ready been informed by one of my reports, enjoys all possible rights
> over the Jew's household. When I asked several men of Tajura whether
> they suffered much from the Arabs, they answered: "Ah, we are in the
> *galut* [exile (Heb.)], one must expect to suffer." They told me that some
> time ago, Arabs had plundered their little synagogue and stolen the
> Scrolls. The next day they were dumbfounded to see an Arab riding a
> donkey with a saddle made of the Torah parchment. They claimed it
> back, but to no avail.[4]

The improved conditions during the Ottoman period manifest
themselves in several ways. Figures from the Ottoman census of

July 3, 1911, published the following year by the Italian military authorities,[5] though they relate only to Tripolitania (excluding the Fezzan), are significant. Of a population of 523,176 inhabitants registered by the census, there were 14,282 Jews (7,124 males and 7,158 females) distributed according to area as shown in Table 1. Although precise demographic data for the preceding period are lacking, and the figures we do have refer almost solely to Tripoli,[6] these figures are still of interest to scholars. Despite a terrible plague which in 1785 decimated the community and the entire region, and a further epidemic which in 1910 claimed about 500 lives among the Jews of Tripolitania, there is no doubt that the Jewish population increased sharply. One must bear in mind that in 1805, after a series of disorders in Algeria, a number of Jews moved from there to Tripoli. Nor should we forget that the census related only to Ottoman subjects. Many "foreign" Jews lived in Tripoli and Tripolitania, and were among the better-off or were in trade. For these groups too, precise data are lacking. Some information is provided in a report of 1902 by Augusto Medana, the Italian consul general. According to his report, in Tripolitania at that time there were 79 Dutch subjects, all Jews, 44 Austrian subjects, all Jews, and 100 Spanish subjects, most of whom were Jews. Then there were many Jews who were British subjects (mostly from Gibraltar) and Italian subjects (mostly from Leghorn). Some of the richest businessmen were Italian Jews: a report dated April 14, 1880, by the Italian consul specifically lists Isach di E. Levi, Angelo di M. Arbib, Meborath Arbib, Abramo di R. Arbib, Scialom Arbib, Eugenio Arbib, Elia Arbib, Iuda Hassan, Iussef Naim, Labi Nimun, D'Ancona e Medina, Giacomo Solas, and Isach Hamuna, with their respective families.[7]

Two events provide undeniable proof of the betterment in civil and cultural conditions. In 1875 a group of Jewish families, wishing their sons to receive a more modern and Western education than the *hara* or Muslim schools could provide, took the initiative of establishing a school at their own expense. Through the Jews of Leghorn, they sent for an Italian teacher, Giannetto Paggi. The school opened the following year, and three years later had 27 pupils. The figures for school attendance on the eve of the Italian occupation show the pattern of education. In Tripoli, 1,460 pupils, including about 100 Jews, attended Turkish schools. About 1,730 pupils, "largely Jewish," attended the Italian schools which had opened in the 1880s. Another 200 Jewish boys attended the Alliance Israélite Universelle schools opened in 1890. This is in addition to those who attended the seven Hebrew religious schools run by the Community and the rabbinical schools.[8] Also, purely through Jewish initiative and enterprise, the

TABLE 1. *Distribution of General and Jewish Population in Tripolitania, 1911*

	Total Population	Jews
Tripoli City	29,761	8,509
Nuahi el Arba	53,325	1,040
Jebel	17,986	818
Misurata	38,738	698
Zlitin	37,738	644
Mesellata	15,579	546
al-Khums	10,813	525
ez-Zaula	28,515	518
Gharian	30,413	454
Tajura	7,633	190
Syrte	13,920	122
Zanzur	6,088	97
Nalut	14,431	11
Fassato	17,745	10

SOURCE: Ottoman census, July 3, 1911.

first Tripoli newspaper in a Western language, the *Eco di Tripoli* [Tripoli Echo] edited by Gustavo Arbib, was founded in 1909.[9]

Since economic life was also flourishing in the Jewish communities, there appeared to be only two clouds on the horizon. First, from both the moral and the legal point of view, the Jews were subject to a certain arbitrariness, since Ottoman laws applying to them were enforced mainly on the basis of individual interpretation, varying with the feelings, resentments, and venality of local officials. Second, within several communities, especially Tripoli, there was a serious and increasing financial and social gap between rich and poor, and between foreign and indigenous Jews.

In Tripoli in 1861 a group of Jews formed a committee to restrain the arbitrary decisions of the local officials (decisions which usually came down much harder on the poor than on the rich, who in most cases had better means to defend themselves)[10] and encourage the authorities to take a more serious view of acts of contempt or violence against Jews. Its members were rich traders and Jewish leaders, most of whom were foreign citizens and members of the Alliance Israélite Universelle. The aim of the Alliance, founded [in Paris] the year before, was to alert international public opinion to the need to emancipate the Jews, to resist anti-Semitism, and to give needy Jews moral and material support. It would also request the embassies of major European powers to intercede, directly and through their diplomats and consuls, with the governments of countries in which Jews were not yet emancipated or where they suffered persecution. It provided the European powers with all the information needed to make their intercessions on behalf of Jews as timely and effective as possible.[11] Thanks to the work of the Tripoli committee and an allied committee which was soon established in Benghazi, as well as to the Alliance's own intervention, some concrete results were obtained. These, however, were limited to having some crimes and abuses against Jews punished, or rather to having any losses suffered made good. The results, as regards effectively preventing incidents of violence and abuse, were practically nothing.[12] It was even more difficult, and nearly impossible, to do anything to stem the growing economic imbalance and financial crisis engulfing some of the major communities, and in particular the Tripoli community. Steps to encourage and increase communal and individual charity and to give the poorest boys a start in life by providing them with meals and a basic religious education amounted in practice to pouring water into a sieve. A group of local benefactors (first in Tripoli, then in almost all the centers where there were Jewish communities) provided funding for impoverished schools, including the well-known Talmud Torah, of which more will be said in later chapters. Their efforts were insufficient and turned out to be counterproductive. In the first place, the schools indirectly encouraged the dependence of those who used them as a way of avoiding looking for a job. Some work, however much effort it might have taken, would have helped those people along and prevented them from sinking later into unemployment and poverty. These schools also kept the younger generation from contact with a slightly more modern culture, which might have helped the youngsters to enter the new society which was even then making tentative inroads. In the second place, these charitable efforts absorbed more and more of the community's already scarce financial resources,[13] thus forestalling other efforts which might have met the need while making better use of the community leaders' own energies and cultural abilities. By extension the charities absorbed the energies of the mass of Jews, who were already psychologically and culturally inclined to view their own lives in a mood of fatalism, in the static framework in which they had lived for centuries. The Jewish masses were content with their own condition as long as they did not have to abandon the sure anchor of tradition or risk jeopardizing their relations with surrounding Muslim society.

If the Israelite population of Tripoli had been oppressed by the harsh persecution of a tyrant or exposed to the repeated attacks of a fanatical priest, the need to cluster together, which our forebears felt strongly whenever they were cruelly and unjustly persecuted, would have been understandable. But here the Israelites have been saved from such suffering. Ought they not to take advantage of the freedom which they have to improve their own situation, and concern themselves a little with their own well-being? They can do this, and they must; only if they do will they be able to strengthen themselves physically and morally. It seems, though, that their minds are far from open to such ideas. Isolated in one of the four corners of the city (since the city walls, rising to a considerable height, partially close off the quarter) they are born, vegetate, and die in this kind of ghetto. They trust in their profound ignorance, and are nourished by prejudices which for them supersede reason. Their superstitions take the place of real religion, blind them, and make them completely resistant to progress and incapable of imagining any improvement.

Once, they suffered these restrictions out of necessity; now they are free, but they have not changed their way of life. The cause has vanished, but the effects persist.[14]

These bitter words—written by an Alliance teacher in 1901 to depict for his superiors in Paris the condition of the Jews in Tripoli—largely sum up the psychological and cultural aspects of the drama of much of Tripoli's Jewry. I would like to emphasize one particular aspect strongly right from the start, since in the Italian period as well Libyan Jewry was hamstrung by this fact, which affected in many ways both events within the community and the community's relations with the outside society. The drama of Libyan Jewish life was summed up in the contrast intensifying from decade to decade between foreign Jews (and the Europeanized Libyan Jews influenced by them) and the mass of Libyan Jews. The latter huddled in their ghettoes in the main towns, especially Tripoli, and had little relation even with Arab society. One group was dynamically oriented to the outside and the future—active, enterprising, determined to create for themselves an ever broader and surer place in society, ready to take advantage of and even anticipate social changes. The others were inward-looking and almost immobilized by tradition—psychologically and culturally incapable and fearful of confronting the new reality which was taking shape.

What actually happened was that in the late eighteenth century the economic situation of smaller Jewish communities in the hinterland and on the coast improved overall, and in Tripoli the affairs of the richer and more enterprising—as I have said, usually the foreign Jews—prospered remarkably. However, the situation of the mass of the Jews of Tripoli and of the towns closest to the capital, such as Amruss,[15] continued to worsen. Many Jews fell to a minimum level of self-support and many below, to begging. The situation was exacerbated, especially in Tripoli, by a high birth rate and a considerable population influx to the city from the hinterland. This urbanization was partly a physiological symptom of the process of change taking place in Libyan society, and partly a pathological one—in other words caused by the worsening of relations with the Muslims which was occurring at the time. The worsening was more marked in the smaller towns where Ottoman authority was less active or more independent of Constantinople. Under such conditions, life in the *hara* of Tripoli became yearly more difficult and for many reached a critical pass. Overcrowding, dirt, poverty, promiscuity, and disease increased continuously, and with them the passivity of those who should have prevented them. Many dwellings consisted of only a single room, in which four, five, or even more people lived together, often using a single "alcove" which served as "bed, sofa, buffet, and wardrobe," and everything else. A low table, a couple of stools, and a few other wretched objects often made up the rest of the furnishing. In slightly better-off dwellings there would be in addition a few chairs and a chest of drawers.[16] This is how the *hara* of Tripoli was described in 1906 in a report sent to Alliance headquarters:

> Anyone who wants to know what their poverty is really like should visit the *hara*. In winter, however, it is difficult to enter. I took advantage of a beautiful day to go and see this ghetto. Despite the good weather, I foundered in mud in those narrow and tortuous alleys. How could it be otherwise, when everything—refuse, the blood of slaughtered chickens, slop water—is thrown into the street?
>
> The dwellings of these wretched folk hardly deserve to be called houses. I visited two, and I still wonder how people can live there. They showed me to a door so low that I had to bend double in order to get through. I found myself in a small courtyard surrounded on all sides by a crumbling wall containing four doorways covered with matting. When I pushed one of the mats aside, what did I find? . . . The sight of such misery left me dumbstruck. Imagine a room with no opening other than the door . . . and what a door! In this hovel where air and light hardly penetrated, there was not even a table which could be used as a bed. There were four bare walls, a frayed mat on the floor, a few sacks which probably served as blankets in one corner, and nothing else. That was the home of a family, and a large one. Is it amazing that these wretched people are ill, and many of them anaemic? It would be amazing if they were healthy!
>
> In the next hovel sat a young woman. She was as thin as a rake and as yellow as the plague. Beside her were two little children, dirty, with

rumpled hair and tattered clothes; they were trembling with cold, and the younger one was gnawing on a piece of dry bread. I was told that the mother was consumptive. How could those little ones avoid catching the disease when they were breathing that poisoned air!

The number of people I encountered in the *hara* who were squinting, blind, or old was incredible . . . The large number of old people struck me forcibly at first. I met many women who I would have said were in their eighties or nineties. How could people who have known only deprivation and suffering live so long, I wondered. I was soon enlightened. Those wrinkles, white hair, and bent backs were not a sign of age, but of poverty. These women who, I thought, were already grandmothers or even great-grandmothers, they told me, have children thirteen or fourteen years old.

Another thing that struck me in the *hara* was the shouting that goes on on all sides. These people are incapable of talking softly.

At the end of a winding alley, I saw a crowd gathered. What was it for? A woman was throwing a pot at her husband's head, and he was trying to tear up her barracan [cloak]; beside them a five- or six-year-old child cried copiously watching its parents fight each other. It was not until a Turk came by that they were separated; the *hara*-dwellers watched the spectacle with the greatest indifference, which goes to show that they were used to it.

Is it surprising that children living in such surroundings are so deprived?[17]

In fact, these two factors were not the only dark clouds marring an otherwise fair outlook. There is no doubt that under Ottoman rule the civil, cultural, and particularly economic situation of the Libyan Jews, especially the richest, most enterprising and forward-looking, did improve significantly. However, in the latter half of the nineteenth century, a shadow until then unknown, or at least different in consistency and character, began to fall over their lives. Relations between Arabs and Jews had been fairly good on both the inter-community and personal levels during the Middle Ages and even during the early centuries of the modern age—though, as for instance under the Almohades, there had been initial difficulties and exceptional incidents. Occasional outbreaks of religious fanaticism on the part of the Arabs had occurred, usually due to the preaching of some particularly fanatical holy man or in conjunction with certain calamities. It is well known that popular thinking at its crudest level often accuses "foreigners," those who are "different," or "outsiders" in the narrow community of being responsible for such calamities. On a popular level, Jewish-Muslim relations had become something of a system working together with the traditional and religious influence of the so-called "Pact of 'Umar." On the whole, the system made the lives of Jews somewhat less insecure, difficult, and dangerous than in many Christian countries. The daily struggle to survive and the shared exposure to the continual threats of nature, war, internal upheavals, and the whims of those in power had brought the two communities together. There had grown up between them a sort of necessary symbiosis, which was not exactly fusion or integration but made for a relationship which, outside exceptional circumstances, prevented serious expressions of racial or religious intolerance. Obviously, the fact that Jews specialized in particular types of work useful to the Arabs and the fact that Libyan Jews spoke Arabic both contributed. Even the Talmud Torah curriculum was taught in Arabic dialect, and Libyan Jews used Hebrew script for writing the dialect. Though they were strongly attached to their way of life and religion (a very traditional and for a long time very elementary form),[18] Libyan Jews were also strongly Arabized in their customs. Even their clothing, though it was different from the Arabs' (largely out of respect for Islamic law), was much less different than the dress of Jews in Eastern Europe was from that of Europeans. In small Libyan towns European travelers often could not distinguish Jews from Arabs.

This symbiosis was particularly strong in the small towns (especially in Cyrenaica, where tribal society had different characteristics from that of Tripolitania), but it existed also in Tripoli. Especially strong in the coastal regions, it was less so in the interior. Here regulations, such as the one forbidding Jews to ride horses and obliging them to give way to Muslims and greet them first, were very congenial to the proud and warlike tribal spirit. Despite the symbiosis, Arabs and even Berbers (with whom relations were better)[19] believed that Jews were "different" and felt a mixture of superiority, mistrust, and hostility toward them, due to causes partly religious and partly economic. The fact is, though, that for centuries these feelings had for the most part remained latent or, if manifested, did not generally assume an acute form. The main cause of friction with and animosity against Jews had for a long time been the question of usury (in both direct and indirect forms, i.e., as payments delayed until harvest-time). Borrowing was necessary for survival, especially for poor Arabs, but it aroused in them a mixture of secret resentment and contempt.[20] There was certainly just as much need for it in the Ottoman period, so that at the Italian occupation moneylending was still flourishing. To be sure, it was not only Jews who practiced it, but also Greeks. But Jews handled most of it, especially in the interior and particularly small loans, the most burdensome for those who depended on them. Just before the end of the Ottoman period, the ordinary rate charged on pledges was 60 percent per annum, but the rate for the smallest amounts was as high as 90 percent.[21]

Toward the middle of the nineteenth century, the status quo began to crumble and changes took place. There were at least three reasons for this.

The first and most general one was the continual spread of discontent which, as I have said, had already made itself felt during the later Karamanli period. The Arab community began to chafe at increasing economic hardship[22] and at the influence of Jews in Libyan and especially Tripolitanian society. The writing of this period often revealed the causes and nature of this discontent. An episode narrated by Manfredo Camperio seems to me particularly indicative, since Camperio's comment on it—"it is very strange, but the Israelites of the Orient and Barbary states have now acquired great influence, not over the people but over the government"—obviously echoes reactions which he had sensed among the Arabs. In 1880, after a Jewish moneychanger had been killed by an Arab, a delegation of Jewish notables went to the Turkish authorities and, contrary to usual practice, succeeded in having a rabbi and two representatives of the Jewish community present at the trial.[23] An innovation that may have contributed to the new anti-Jewish attitude was the Banco di Roma's introduction, in addition to ordinary credit, of a system of loans and pledges similar to pawnbroking. (The bank opened branches in Libya in 1907.) This freed many Muslims from the need for recourse to moneylenders, while allowing unfavorable comparisons. Since the Banco di Roma did not accept pledges worth less than five francs, thus obliging the poorest to continue borrowing from moneylenders, the new service sharpened the resentment of those who could not use it.

The second basic cause of change was the crisis affecting the necessary symbiosis that, as we have said, had existed over the centuries between Arabs and Jews. As with any traditional society based on a subsistence economy, this symbiotic relationship could not help but reflect the socioeconomic changes taking place. The relationship had to bend to the modest degree of modernization which Libyan society in general and Tripoli in particular were experiencing. This was all the more true because the changes and modernization were leading the Jews inexorably to a new role in Libyan society. Whether they liked it or not, the Jews were less and less a necessary factor in the Libyan equation. The Jews were tending more and more to become merely the intermediary between the old society which was beginning to crumble and the new one which was taking shape among Arabs and Europeans.[24] This position brought the Jews definite advantages but also, in that phase of the country's modernization, uprooted them from their traditional context and made them more and more disliked. The Arabs felt even more exploited by the Jews than before and saw them more and more as foreigners at odds with the Arab economic, cultural, and spiritual universe.

The third and last cause of change was the spread to Libya of an early, elementary form of Muslim nationalism (a kind of embryonic expression of an Arab-Islamic political renaissance), which was tainted from its birth with anti-Semitic elements of European origin. Until the revolution of the Young Turks in 1908, it does not appear that the government in Constantinople favored those trends in Libya or that it particularly encouraged the spread of anti-Semitic ideas among the masses. On the contrary, partly because the Sultan's government was interested in drawing on the meager local economic resources to develop Libya's economy as a partial counterbalance to European penetration, and partly due to pressure from Western governments (whose own concern for what happened to Jews was aroused by strong organizations established in the late nineteenth century, such as the Alliance Israélite Universelle and the Anglo-Jewish Association), the government's attitude to the Jews became continually more open and better disposed. The only exception, though it is not clear whether responsibility lay with Constantinople or with the local representatives of the Turkish government, was the imposition of a special tax[25] on those not doing military service (which, moreover, was not obligatory in Libya until 1908). On a popular level these early nationalist expressions took the form, especially after the French occupied Tunisia and the British Alexandria, of riots and xenophobic demonstrations against Europeans. Other, more serious cases of nationalist zeal occurred as a result of the Russian-Turkish War of 1877–1878. In almost all cases, the Jewish presence was seen as a symptom of European influence. More seriously, from 1870 on, following the example of what was happening in Turkey due to the Greeks,* the Jews in Libya were subject to accusations of ritual murder.[26] Arab hostility to Jews took other forms as well. In the late nineteenth century, forced conversion, maltreat-

---

*Cases of blood libel (accusations of ritual murder) were rare in the Ottoman empire until the Damascus Affair of 1840. In 1864 the Jews of Izmir were accused of kidnapping Christian children before Passover. There were similar accusations in Constantinople in 1868 and 1870. Many blood libels in the Ottoman empire in the late nineteenth century originated with Greeks, due to commercial rivalry between Greeks and Jews (*Encyclopedia Judaica*).—*Trans.*

ment (even in public places), stonethrowing, and threats against Jews became more frequent in both Tripolitania and Cyrenaica.

Since Ottoman sources are either lacking or unavailable, in order to reconstruct a picture of this new state of affairs, we must turn to the richest and most accessible documentation, that of the Alliance Israélite Universelle. It offers valuable information on particular events, and also allows us to form a precise idea of how widespread the new anti-Semitism was. We can also trace the reaction which the hostility aroused among Libyan Jews and the Alliance's attempts to have outsiders intervene on the Jews' behalf.

Obviously, individual episodes cannot be described in detail here. We shall therefore limit ourselves to recording those which were most discussed and were the subjects of intervention by the Alliance. In early 1864 the synagogue of Misurata was desecrated and sacked. In 1867, incited by the qadi, a crowd of Muslims set the synagogue of Zlitin on fire. In 1870 a Jewish notable, Saul Raccah, was murdered. A report from the Italian consul, dated September 6, 1876, shows that the coronation of Abd ul-Hamid II was being celebrated on that day, and as a result the populace's fanaticism had been aroused. The Arabs of Tripoli could not hide their delight at the rumor that the new Sultan would oblige Jews to observe Muslim law to the letter. In 1897 the synagogue of the Idder quarter in Misurata was sacked.[27] In none of these cases did the Jews succeed in getting justice from the Ottoman authorities. In the case of the Zlitin synagogue, the Jews received compensation for damages and were able to build a new, much larger synagogue. In the case of Saul Raccah's murder, the Jews managed to have the murderer sentenced to fifteen years in prison, but the sentence was later annulled. The specious argument was made that the prosecutor was European, a situation not allowable under Ottoman law.

Although significant, these episodes give only a pale idea of what the situation was like at the time. The last decades of Ottoman rule were characterized less by these notorious events than by a rapid deterioration in the general atmosphere and the spread among Muslims (including Berbers) of hitherto unknown anti-Jewish feeling. There were repeated demonstrations of intolerance, impatience, and contempt, as well as violent acts from the trivial to the serious. These ranged from thefts of produce from the fields of Jews in the hinterland to the profanation of cemeteries and to murder. All this took place against the almost total indifference of local authorities. Some excerpts from the correspondence between the Alliance committee in Tripoli and the central committee in Paris will give a clearer idea of the situation and how the Jews felt about it:

July 10, 1879

During the evening of January 2 last, in Zlitin some Muslims attacked the house of a Jew. They stole all he had, and seriously injured him. During the evening of February 24 at Amruss, Muslims entered the house of another Jew, stripped him of all his possessions, struck and injured both him and his wife and killed his twenty-year-old son. On the evening of March 29 at Tajura, Muslims robbed a Jew of all his belongings, injured him, and killed a young child at its mother's knee. Finally, on the evening of June 25 at Zawia Garbia, only seven hours away from here, the Sacred Synagogue was plundered and profaned. The intruders profaned it in every way possible. After making off with three Torah Scrolls, they threw all the rest into the street and trampled on them. If the women's incessant screams had not put those wretches to flight, they would have burned the whole building down.

As soon as these facts came to the knowledge of the Very Reverend Eliau Hazan, the chief rabbi of this community, he hastened to the governor-general, His Highness Mahmud Geradden Pasha, to request the punishment of those responsible. Unfortunately, it has not yet been possible to obtain justice—this is why the Muslims, emboldened by their impunity, still threaten a people who do them no harm.

Taking into account the dangers to which the Jews in all the towns and neighboring villages are exposed due to the unsatisfactory attitude of the local authorities after the events described above, I have considered it necessary for the members of the committee to ask for protection. My colleagues representing Britain, France, Italy, and the United States of America were approached by the committee, as I myself am unable to act except in my capacity as representative of Austria-Hungary. Those gentlemen received my request with great concern. We decided unanimously to persuade the governor-general to have the guilty persons sought out and made an example of, so that such deplorable excesses would not happen again.[28]

March 9, 1880

Today I sent you the following telegram from Via di Malta:

In addition to murders, profanation Zawia Synagogue mentioned, unpunished, yesterday afternoon near city gate, Muslim killed Rahamin Eidan. Local justice deplorable. Dismayed community begs help.

I sent it to inform you that yesterday about four P.M. at the city gate a Jew by the name of Rahamin Eidan was killed by a Muslim for no cause whatsoever. The murderer was immediately apprehended by several Jews and taken to the local authorities. He denied the whole thing, saying that he had been taken for another, though there was no doubt that he was the guilty party—five people had seen him fire the shot from which, a few minutes later, Eidan died.

This new murder has made a very strong impression on our Community. It is a result of not exacting payment for the previous murders and the sacking of the Zawia Synagogue. The committee, meeting in an emergency session, has therefore decided to present itself before His Excellency the Governor-General and to demand justice. At the same time the committee has appealed to the consuls of France, Italy, Austria-Hungary, and Great Britain, imploring their help so that the crimes which have been committed against Jews for some time do not escape the punishment they deserve.[29]

February 21, 1897

The situation of the Jews in all parts of Tripolitania is very dangerous. From all the rights which, through his known goodness and generosity, His Imperial Majesty the Sultan has granted to all his subjects without distinction of race, we are unfortunately excluded. We suffer from extreme ill-treatment and persecution at the hands of the Muslims in our country, under the governorship of our present Vali [governor (Turk.)], Hamik Bey, who does not wish to aid us nor protect us from the cruel and inhuman Muslim population. Here are some examples of the misfortunes we have suffered recently.

In the town of Jebel an Arab wounded a Jew with a gun. God be thanked that he did not die from the wound, for some fellow Jews arrived in time to take care of him. The authorities put the culprit in prison for only a few days, even though he had been caught and recognized without a shadow of doubt.

In the same town thieves entered the home of a prominent man, killed him in his bed, and destroyed everything they found in the house. Even for that cruel and fearful murder, the authorities, as usual in the case of a murder of a Jew by a Muslim, remained indifferent and the culprits went unpunished.

In the Tripolitanian courts there is no judge of the Jewish faith, despite the fact that any people and any nation has the right to have a judge who is one of them in every court, to represent his nation.

We have recently been obliged to bring a chief rabbi by imperial *firman* [Ottoman decree] in the hope that this rabbi will protect us against our enemies. But the governor did not want to cooperate. The rabbi made repeated approaches to the governor to obtain their rights as citizens for the Jews. But the Vali not only has done nothing for the Jews, but has refused even to reply to the rabbi's requests. No matter what dangers threaten the Jews living in the villages of Tripolitania, the Turkish authorities do not concern themselves at all, perhaps fulfilling their religious duty to blot out all peoples who do not practise Mohammed's religion. Some months ago, the Jews of Idder, part of the village of Misurata, sent a letter to the chief rabbi, begging him to ask the governor on their behalf to order the village *qaimaqam* [lieutenant] to restore the night guards, who had some time before been removed from the Jewish quarter, where they had been stationed on imperial orders for about fifteen years. The chief rabbi told His Excellency the Vali of this request, but as usual he did not reply. Unfortunately, last Saturday, some Arabs broke the doors and windows and entered the Idder Synagogue. They stole all the valuables they found there—money, ornaments, and the crowns of the *sepharim*—[Torah scrolls]—and, what is even more dreadful, they tore up the Scrolls of the Law. On being informed of all this, the chief rabbi notified the governor of the crime, but still received no response.

A similar occurrence had taken place some time beforehand in Zlitin, where Arabs destroyed the synagogue and stole everything in it. Forty of these robbers were discovered and imprisoned by the court, but a few days later they were set free without the slightest punishment; not only that, but, unbelievably, they were not even made to return the objects stolen from the synagogue and discovered in their houses.

Last Thursday, a Jew was killed by Arabs while returning to his village and his companion was injured. This happened at some distance from the capital, and the authorities have not attempted to find the criminals.

It is quite evident that, to the Muslims, Jews are of no account, our personal safety cannot be guaranteed, and our belongings are not our own.

This is why we beseech you to have pity on your unhappy brethren languishing under the weight of all these misfortunes and come to their aid to alleviate their affliction and suffering. The consul-general of Her Britannic Majesty has already visited the chief rabbi asking for information about matters in Misurata, and the rabbi has told him of all our persecutions.[30]

November 4, 1901

Disturbances at Amruss. Last week disturbances took place at Suq al-Jum'a, a market held at Amruss, a village not far from Tripoli. To demonstrate their unhappiness at being drafted into the Turkish army, and in order to attract attention, the local Arabs could find nothing better to do than to avenge themselves on weak, defenseless creatures. In full daylight, a horde of malefactors attacked some unlucky Jews who had come to the market to sell their wares. The Jews were forced to abandon their stalls, which were destroyed; they themselves were beaten and one of their number seriously wounded. As soon as the Vali of Tripoli was informed he took energetic steps and set in motion a very thorough inquiry. He promised the Jews who had been robbed that he would compensate them for most of what they had lost. After making about twenty armed robbers return their ill-gotten gains, he put them in prison, then requested and obtained from the rich inhabitants of Amruss the remaining sums that the Jews claimed. He summoned them and, in the presence of chief rabbi Kamhi, reimbursed each one in full for the amount which he swore had been stolen from him. Happy at obtaining prompt and fair justice, the Jews gave him a spontaneous ovation. Later, they sent a message of thanks to the Vali through the chief rabbi. When he took the message the Vali said to him, "Tell your fellow Jews that they do not owe me thanks, since I have only done my duty. Am I not like a father to them, a father who should safeguard their interests?" Such actions and words are rare in these troubled times and surely ought to be brought to everyone's attention.

I think that if you put a few lines in a newspaper in Paris or Constantinople praising our Governor's behavior, he would be very flattered and would be encouraged always to follow the same policy.[31]

Undated [received March 29, 1909]
There was consternation last week among the Jews of Zawia, a village seven hours from Tripoli, at the news that the murderer who, in full daylight, had killed Fergela Schelek, the head of the community, had been freed (Mr. Slousch described that crime in his report). The judges absolved the murderer after two years in preventive detention, despite overwhelming evidence. They say that he was freed because he had liberally handed out the stolen money. The victim's sons and brothers have come to Tripoli crying for retribution and saying that if such an obvious crime remains unpunished, they feel safe in Zawia no longer. They requested me to telegraph Constantinople on their behalf and ask you to intervene at a high level. I explained to them that the Alliance does protect all oppressed Jews, no matter where they are, but that it only intervenes when steps taken locally to obtain justice have had no effect.

I added: "In your case, since a judgment has been reached, you should file an appeal in Constantinople, and if there is reason for intervention, the central committee may perhaps examine the matter." They thanked me for the advice and I think they have requested their lawyer to initiate the appeal. Will they win justice? And so, despite the constitution and the equality of all, there are judges in Tripoli who absolve a Muslim murderer because his victim was a Jew.[32]

In the face of this rapid deterioration in intercommunity relations, it is not surprising that almost all the Europeans visiting Libya at the turn of the century spoke of "racial and religious hatred" between Arabs and Jews. They may have exaggerated it and projected it back into the past, seeing it as something which had always existed. They did not realize that changes had occurred in recent decades in intercommunity relations and that this new hostility differed from the traditional kind.

In the preceding pages we have referred more than once to relations between Libyan Jews and the Alliance Israélite Universelle after 1861. In its constant search for help and protection, Libyan Jewry also set up contact during the late eighteenth and early nineteenth centuries with other international and national Jewish organizations. From the documentation currently available, however, we can find out very little. We can say for certain that none of these relations came close in importance to those with the Alliance. Only relations with the Zionist organizations of Vienna are worth specific mention. The first Jews who set up contact with such organizations at the turn of the century were some community leaders in Benghazi.[33] After a fire started by Arabs damaged about twenty Jewish shops in September 1908, the community officials sent an urgent appeal to the Jewish Territorial Organization (JTO): "We can find no remedy to these sufferings but to put ourselves in God's hands and yours, our dear brothers, entrust ourselves to your help and protection, and hope that you will respond to our petition."[34] These contacts are interesting, since they show that the Libyan Jews already had connections with the Zionist movement, if only in the form of an appeal for help. Libyan Jews lived under difficult conditions. Nevertheless, the Zionist organizations, and even Theodor Herzl himself, gave some consideration to Libya as a home for the overflow of Jews—"le trop plein de l'immigration juive"—for whom there would not be enough room in Palestine. Those were Herzl's words in January 1904 to Victor Emmanuel III. Herzl made clear his belief that soon the Jews might benefit in Libya from the "lois et institutions libérales de l'Italie."* Though the king did not respond to this suggestion,[35] in the next few years the JTO studied in detail the possibility of setting up an agricultural community in Cyrenaica for Jews from Eastern Europe.[36]

How important were these Zionist plans? Italian designs on Libya were no secret at the time, and the Jews had full equality and freedom in Italy. Although these factors obviously bore some weight, another one arose toward the end of the nineteenth century. Despite the inferior legal position in which Jews were kept by Muslims, until the beginning of the second half of the nineteenth century Libyan Jews had in their own way been good subjects of the Karamanlis and the Ottoman empire and had never taken any interest in the idea that Libya might come under the sovereignty of another state, even a European one. They never even considered it. In such an out-of-the-way place as Libya, the principles of the French Revolution had made few inroads. Even though the Jews' main commercial and family ties across the Mediterranean lay with Italy, the majority of those who were Italian subjects did not particularly desire Italian sover-

---

*Herzl reports of the meeting: "And finally I broached my Tripoli scheme —'de déverser le trop plein de l'immigration juive en Tripolitanie sous les lois et institutions libérales de l'Italie [to direct the surplus Jewish immigration into Tripolitania, under the liberal laws and institutions of Italy]'" (*The Diaries of Theodor Herzl*, trans. Marvin Lowenthal [New York: Grosset, 1956], pp. 426–427).—*Trans.*

eignty over Libya. A report dated 1861 by the Italian consul, G. B. Ansaldi, is explicit. Among the Italian subjects in Libya, very few families "could be considered really Italian." Most Jews appreciate "any nationality, merely in order to have the protection of a consulate. . . . Most of the Tuscans are of Jewish descent; lacking any feeling for Italy, like the Maltese and the Neapolitans, they are ignorant and indifferent; the word patriotism has no meaning for them."[37] If those were the feelings of the supposedly Italian elite, one can well imagine those of indigenous Jews. However, things began to change toward the end of the century. As daily life became more difficult and relations with the Muslim population grew worse, an idea began to gain ground among the better-off and more Westernized Jews. It was that only under a non-Muslim government could they have a secure position, in other words, one which would be favorable for business. The Jewish masses had such anti-Muslim feelings that they believed that anything would be better than Muslim rule. It was only a short step to looking toward Italy, a direction in which political trends were already pointing. Italy was not only the closest of the countries facing the Mediterranean, but also the one with which the Libyan community had traditionally had most contact, so that Italian was the European language most spoken. Many of the wealthier and more influential families either were Italian or had some Italian origins. It was these families who had the strongest relations with the Italian colony in Libya; in 1880 Eugenio Arbib had founded a club frequented by the best European, especially Italian, society. "Italianizers," though they were few, were not lacking among the Westernized and educated Jews. On the eve of the Italian occupation two of these, Halfalla Nahum and Mario Nunes Vais, were counselors of the Tripoli committee of the Dante Alighieri Society. Many families sent their children to local Italian schools, and young people were frequently sent off to study in Italy. For all these Jews, Italy was the most natural and obvious solution. Giuseppe Bevione, *La stampa*'s correspondent in Libya, captured the attitude of the rest when he wrote in 1911:

> The Jews, however resigned and patient, tolerate these painful conditions with suppressed anger and an unquenchable thirst for equality. The difference between their wealth and culture and the Arabs' poverty and ignorance makes the injustice even more bitter. The situation can continue only because their rulers, the Turks, are Muslims and, purely by holding power, reinforce their fellow-Muslims the Arabs and oppress the Jews, who are unbelievers. The moment Turkish domination is overturned and a non-Muslim power is set up in its place the situation will be reversed: Arab preponderance will have no more encour-

agement, and equality in conditions will be achieved and guaranteed. The Jews also, for better reasons than the Arabs, yearn for European occupation of Tripolitania, for this will signal an end to their degradation.

The European nation that the Jews would prefer for this task of redemption is evident from the fact that the most well-to-do and prominent in the community have been Italian subjects for generations.[38]

In order to appreciate the attitude of Libyan Jews toward Italian rule, it is necessary to understand this mechanism and what determined it. Otherwise, one runs the risk of misunderstanding the meaning of the indisputable favor with which the Jews viewed it. Most important, this attitude renders comprehensible Jewish history in Libya over the next half century, under Italy and after Italian rule ended. The Italian occupation was a positive event only for a particular economic and cultural elite. It was a choice for Europe and modernization (in other words against traditional Libyan society), partly the choice of a particular national allegiance, and ultimately one for assimilation. For the Jewish masses it was a fact which had only one positive aspect: they would no longer be inferior and subject to the Muslims. For the first group it meant distancing themselves from traditional Libyan society and Libya itself; for the second, it meant achieving freedom and personal dignity. Few of the second group ever felt themselves to be Italian; their real country was, despite everything, Libya. They wanted to live with the Muslims but in equality; and, like the Turks, the Italians were useful in their time but an extraneous element.[39]

2. Italian Occupation (1911–1916)

We now know that we cannot understand the Libyan Jews' real attitude to Italian occupation merely by accepting what Italian and foreign writers have to say.[1] The Jews, they tell us, welcomed the Italian troops with enthusiasm, collaborating with them and quickly establishing close, sincere, and enduring relations with the new political reality. Though all the writers agree, we must look at what the Jews' behavior implied. We must try to understand whether the unanimous view of the writers was completely correct and, if not, why so many of them subscribed to it.

First, distinctions must be made between Jews in Libya (indigenous and Italian) and Italian Jews in Italy. Both Italy and the world received their initial impression of how Libyan Jews regarded Italian occupation through the views of the press and official organizations of Italian Jewry. These views and public positions enthusiastically favored Italian occupation. Sometimes deliberately, sometimes with the best of intentions, they ignored the true nature of the problem as well as the profound differences that characterized the Libyan community.

Links already existed between Italian and Libyan Jews and, as we shall see, in 1911–1912 such links intensified enough to have a decisive influence on the subsequent life of Libyan Jews. One motive for the unanimous opinion of observers was that Italian Jews were not familiar with Libyan Jewry. Another was that partisan ideas and news were brought to Italy by Italian and Italianized Jews who had left Libya in haste when Italian-Turkish relations took an abrupt turn after the Italians presented their ultimatum.[2] There were three main additional motives for this opinion:

(1) The first lies in Italian Jewry's high level of integration, with pockets of actual assimilation. This was why a good proportion of Italian Jews, those who "counted" and controlled the Jewish press and organizations, largely shared the state of mind and nationalist

and patriotic feelings prevalent among the Italian bourgeoisie at the time, thereby viewing the Libyan enterprise with favor.

(2) The second and more Jewish motive lies in the general belief that the Libyans could not help but long for the equality of Italian rule, since the Turks kept them in an inferior position. Thus, Italian Jews had a duty to support the Libyans' "liberation" and the improved legal and social position that would come with it. Typical of this is the editorial in the October 1911 issue of *Il vessillo israelitico* [Jewish Standard]:

> Let us exult! Our banner, the symbol of freedom and justice, is flying over the picturesque *konak* [governor's palace]. Once more the lyre of Israel throbs joyfully among the banners of the Motherland. Mystically, it seems to tell our Jewish brothers of Libya, now initiated into a new life, "Lift up your hearts! In that most joyful and free of territories, these standards also saluted the courage, heroism, and genius of Israel in a whirl of light! With your heads held high, serene of heart, you may proceed along the magnificent paths of progress in the shade of these same standards. Jews of Libya, heap blessings on the holy banners of Italy!"[3]

Regarding this conviction, it is significant that in the early months of the Italian-Turkish conflict Italian Jews often reiterated their support and enthusiasm for the "liberation" of their Libyan fellows, but did not pursue very far the idea of asking the government to make concrete promises regarding Libyan Jews, however obvious a step this might seem to us. They did not do so until July 1912, when rumors were heard in Benghazi of the "persecution" of Jews, and after an unpleasant encounter between the chief rabbi of Rhodes and the Italian military authorities. Ferruccio Servi, chief editor of *Il vessillo israelitico*, wrote to Giovanni Giolitti, the prime minister. In reply, Giolitti recalled the "spirit of equality and deep respect for all religions" which the Italian parliament and government had been observing for over half a century, and he assured Servi that "the Jews of the new Italian provinces may therefore feel quite happy to live under the aegis of our free institutions."[4]

(3) The third motive for the Italian Jews' attitude toward the occupation of Libya lies in the desire of many Jewish spokesmen, particularly those closely associated with official organizations, to refute and deny certain insinuations and accusations that were being made against the Zionists and by extension the Jewish community by the most extreme nationalists—first and foremost, the movement known as "L'idea nazionale" [National Idea].[5] Such nationalists accused the Jews of being hostile to the "Italian cause" and of

being potential partisans of the Turks. Negotiations were going on at the time between the Zionist organization and the Sublime Porte [the government in Constantinople] for Jewish emigration to Palestine. An Italian victory might jeopardize the negotiations. Another reason given was that in such a situation it was "obvious" that among Jews "Jewish nationalism must" prevail over "Italian patriotism."[6] At the first warning of this campaign, *L'idea sionista* [Zionist Idea], the main Italian Zionist publication, had voluntarily stopped appearing. It was a vain effort to muzzle the nationalists and thus prevent anti-Semitism from rearing its head in Italy as it had elsewhere. This precedent makes it easy to understand why, when hostilities began, it was so important for the Jews to show their patriotism, even to the point of adopting more militant positions and tones than normal. Thus we can understand why the Italian Jews took such pains to declare for all to hear how pro-Italian the Libyan Jews were. They asked the rabbis of Tripoli and Benghazi to step up their efforts to "Italianize" their fellow Jews and, even more indicatively, praised the heroic part played by Jewish soldiers in overseas operations.

So much for the "public" attitude, directed at the outside world. In order to have a more complete idea of how Italian Jewry dealt with the new situation of finding itself actively involved in events surrounding Libyan Jewry and, whether it liked it or not, held responsible for its fate, we must look behind this façade and try to understand how Italian Jewry expected to deal with this new responsibility. The Jewish press was extremely reticent on the subject—a fact which indirectly confirms how unfamiliar Italian Jews were with the situation and problems of Libyan Jewry. The little that was said never rose above the level of generalization—the need to eliminate superstition, spread education, and so forth. Professional training was thought particularly necessary, in order to direct the masses thronging the *hara* to manual and agricultural work. It was believed important to act so that "in a not far distant future, all will speak Italian and know the history, life, and soul of the great Mother."[7] Italian Jews had a tendency to pose all problems in terms of "progress," "civilization," and Italianization, not realizing how abstract and simplistic such a program was. The Italian press failed to realize that this program would inevitably conflict on a mass level with the traditions, culture, and religious feelings of Libyan Jewry and was thus destined to multiply rather than to resolve existing divisions and misunderstandings. Organizations oriented to religious and community life did little more than reflect the same attitude as the press. After the initiation of formal contacts between the Italian

Jewish Universities Committee* and the Tripoli Community—contacts which aimed at affiliating the Libyan Communities to the committee[8]—the only notable initiative for a long time was the attempt to have an Italian appointed to the post of chief rabbi of Tripoli. Moreover, it is not clear whether this initiative came from the committee or whether it was suggested by the government.[9] All that is certain is that contacts were made with Assistant Secretary Battaglieri. The government's motive may have been to have better control over Libyan Jewry, or perhaps to solve at the source a problem that might have given the Italian authorities difficulty.[10] This would at least partly explain why the Italians did not take the same initiative in Benghazi, which did make similar suggestions, but where conditions were not susceptible to political complications, as in Tripoli. The initiative was a complete failure, though. A chief rabbi was not appointed until 1920, and even then the question had not really been resolved.

It is not easy to explain why this initiative failed. Initially, a series of disagreements and quarrels, personal and official, between the chairman and secretary of the committee, Angelo Sereni and Anselmo Colombo, and the Florentine rabbi, Samuel Zevi Margulies, certainly contributed. The latter was perhaps the greatest Jewish spiritual and cultural authority in Italy at the time. These conflicts gave rise to two opposing candidacies and to visits to Tripoli by both Margulies and Colombo in late 1912 in support of the candidacies. Later on there were also economic obstacles (probably of deliberate creation). Finally, the reluctance of the Jews of Tripoli and

---

*An official umbrella organization of Italian Jewish Communities, *università* being another term for *comunità.* Beginning in 1911, Italian Jewish Communities were gradually being brought together into a national organization, a consortium being voluntarily organized in 1914. The Community itself was an entity (whose legal basis went back to before the unification and thus varied depending on the region) run by a board or council and responsible for administering to the religious and social needs of the Jews of a particular town or city through various committees. The Libyan Jewish Communities were also cohesive entities with a legal status under Muslim law and responsible for all the social needs of their own members. Thus the Italians were able to incorporate the Libyan Communities fairly successfully into the more organized Italian structure. The word Community often refers to the legal entity as a whole and the community institutions in particular, rather than the much looser meaning of the word implied in the American term "Jewish community." For precise historical explanations of Jewish communal organization in various areas, including North Africa, see *Encyclopedia Judaica,* entry entitled "Community," and for Italy, see Renzo De Felice, *Storia degli ebrei italiani sotto il fascismo,* 3d ed. (Turin: Einaudi, 1972), pp. 123–124.—*Trans.*

of the local rabbis to have a chief rabbi imposed on them also contributed. He would be alien to their world in culture, mentality, religious expression, and language[11] (all this apparently did not escape
Margulies, who incidentally was the rabbi the Tripoli Jews would
have preferred). The chief rabbi might also have created difficulties
for the community leaders who, as we shall see, were absorbed in
disputes and power struggles.[12] Even so, one root cause was probably
the Italian Jewish leaders' cultural and psychological inability to understand the problems of their Libyan coreligionists. Another was
their wish to take the Libyan Jews under their wing, to "civilize"
them, and also to avoid misunderstandings and dissensions or, worse,
hostile encounters with the colonial authorities or with the Arabs
that might involve the committee in controversies with the government and arouse popular displeasure or political attacks of an anti-
Semitic nature in Italy.[13] Confirmation of this shortsightedness is
shown in a report drafted by Colombo on his return from Libya in
late 1912. He had gone there to set up links for the Italian Jewish
Universities Committee with the Tripoli Community, enroll the latter in the committee, and resolve the question of who would be chief
rabbi. After a stay of twenty days, the secretary merely sketched a superficial and rather rhetorical outline of the Community's main institutions, giving little information on smaller communities and not
even touching on the real problems of Libyan Jewish life. His proposals were limited to one: the need, while preserving their culture,
to Italianize Libyan Jews, above all excluding "any infiltration by
other countries"—in practice, French influence through the Alliance Israélite Universelle.[14] A similar affirmation was made in the
only statement issued by a Congress of Italian Jewish Communities
held in Rome in May 1914. It considered that efforts ought to be
made to encourage Libyan Jews to take up farming, as Jews were doing in the colonies of Palestine.[15] It is obvious that this proposal was
an entirely abstract one; to put it into practice, the committee would
have needed means which it hardly had at its disposal. It would have
required the government's active cooperation, which was entirely
out of the question. It would have meant adopting an anti-Arab policy in Libya—the exact opposite of what the government desired and
practiced (which was a cause for concern and complaint on the part
of the committee).

So much for the attitude of Italian Jewry. Before examining Libyan Jewry's point of view, we should look at the position of the Italian occupation authorities and of the government in general. This
will enable us to assess the range of attitudes within Libyan Jewry.

The Italians had a basic illusion about the Arabs' feelings. They thought the Arabs were generally hostile to the Turks and thus, if not exactly favorable, then not averse to Italy. Just before hostilities began, the Italians knew that their greatest support was from the Jews, with whom they had had contacts of various sorts for some time. Nevertheless, from the earliest phase of the operation, the Italians were aware—within the framework of Italian-Arab relations—of the political meaning that relations with the Jews were bound to assume. Thus the Italians realized that collaborating with the Jews was a matter of expediency. This awareness in many political and military officials went together with a sincere sympathy for the Jews and a wish to emancipate them from the inferior status which Muslim law imposed on them. The Italians were also aware that they had to avoid complications with the Arabs, whose good will they needed most of all. The orders which General Pollio, the army's chief of staff, gave to troops deployed in Libya are indicative in their brevity: "The Jews must be treated like the other inhabitants, and it is recommended that advantage be taken of their commercial skills. Treat them firmly but not harshly."[16] The military authorities withdrew somewhat from these guidelines when they saw how things developed. There were cases of active collaboration when the Italians disembarked. In several places, Jews were victims of Arab attacks, of which more will be said later. The wealthier and more enterprising Jews expressed their sympathy for the Italians.[17] In view of those conditions, the Italians realized that the Jews were important to them. From the point of view of language in particular, Jews were essential for making contact with the Arab population and ensuring that numerous offices formerly run by Turks continued to function.[18] During the initial weeks of the occupation the military authorities moved slightly away from the guidelines, sometimes favoring the Jews and allowing themselves expressions of sympathy and preference. Some examples are General Caneva's receiving Jewish notables right after the diplomatic corps and before the Arab leaders, and the Tripoli headquarters' authorization of a collection among the troops for the poor of the *hara* and refugees from anti-Jewish violence. These actions amounted to little in themselves. But they went with a somewhat aggressive and superior attitude which the Jews, especially those in closest contact with the Italians, adopted. They aroused immediate anger and accusations from the Arabs and later concern among the military authorities, for whom relations with the Arabs were becoming the most pressing problem. A passage from the internal staff bulletin of January 8, 1912, concerning the

situation in Libya is significant in this regard. It describes the point
of view of a pro-Italian Arab notable and shows why many Arabs did
not support Italian rule:

> The Italians should be suspicious of the Tripolitanian Jews, whose aim
> is to keep them apart from the Arabs so that they can continue to be
> the only possible intermediaries between Christians and Muslims. We
> [the Italians] must reassure the Arabs, destroy the legend of cruelty
> which the Turks spread; we should also foster relations between im-
> portant Arab families and Italian officials; we should trust what pro-
> Italian Arabs say and not give easy credence to people who denounce
> them. They are often Israelites, who have some interest in doing so,
> wishing to air old resentments or reacting as a race long oppressed and
> humiliated.[19]

By December 1911, and even more by early 1912, without really
changing their attitude, the Italians were more cautious in their relations with Jews. They were trying to avoid hurting the Arabs' feelings unnecessarily and stirring up the more fanatical Arabs, as well
as Turkish plotters. They wished to discourage those Jews who were
taking advantage of the new situation.

The Jews soon grasped this adjustment in the Italian attitude.
They lamented in public and in private,[20] often overdramatizing the
situation,[21] just as the Arabs had done. They were unaware of contingent factors motivating the Italian military authorities, not realizing that once the Italians were more familiar with the situation in
Libya, they would inevitably view the Jewish component in a different way. The Italian attitude would then be based on criteria and perspectives more appropriate for the needs of Italian colonial policy
and reflecting the prevailing legal and administrative system in Italy.

On the level of institutional planning, the Italian administration's first real political act, aimed at establishing the basis for re-
organizing all Jewish institutions, occurred on March 10, 1912. On
that day Governor Caneva issued a decree making the Jewish Community of Tripoli and the main Jewish charitable institution for the
sick subject to "the surveillance and guardianship of the governing
authorities."[22] To understand the reasons behind this, as well as subsequent developments and political perspectives on it, we must read
what Domenico Caruso, the director of the Civil Service in Tripoli,
reported in his "General Conditions of the City":

> Confidential sources had informed me that a foreign element had infil-
> trated the administrative bodies of the Jewish community. Since this
> element was more intelligent than the uncultured indigenous Jews, it
> tended toward a certain hegemony liable to create an influence any-
> thing but favorable to Italian interests. Moreover, administrative influ-

ences prevented the decree of March 10, 1912, by which the Commander-in-Chief established regular control over the administrative actions, from being fully implemented. I knew from my own experience that it would be useless to expect that this powerful community could be reorganized. It has about fifteen thousand inhabitants and its own assets, and provides public services for the Israelites through the elected officials of the Community. There are many claims on the funds it distributes. Such an important entity cannot be left to itself, nor can control of it be merely a restraining hand. And so, exercising the powers of surveillance which His Excellency the Commander-in-Chief granted me, I have called on F. Quarantelli, one of the most capable accountants in my civil service department. He is familiar with this type of work, for in Italy he was assigned to work with Israelite universities. I have entrusted him with assisting the community administration in its various functions, and with overseeing the running of the entity, for which I am responsible. The measure also applies to the Israelite charitable organization for the sick.

The officials have welcomed this step, since it facilitates their reorganization of the community. It gives closer control, while allowing the institution its autonomy, traditions, and customs. It illustrates the principle that I believe should be applied in the political administration of the colony, that local institutions should be respected as long as they do not conflict with our national interests or with civilized standards in general. At the same time we should ensure, through special inspectors, that the institutions function in an orderly fashion, in harmony with out interests.[23]

We can reach some understanding of what Italian policy in Libya was aiming at, and why—though the hopes of Italian Jews had been raised[24]—this policy was not able to make full use of Libyan Jews in intermediary functions. The studies and initiatives which the civil service administration took to reorganize and modify the school system in Tripoli when the March 10 decree was issued are important in this respect, even though they were not intended to have any direct effect on Jewish life. Prior to the Italian occupation, school attendance in Tripoli (not counting Muslim and Jewish religious schools) was as high as 3,390; there were 1,460 pupils in Turkish schools, 1,030 in Italian, 700 in Franciscan, and 200 in Alliance. When the schools reopened, the number of pupils had fallen by 1,837. In view of the exceptional circumstances—and the fact that this reduction was largely due to the departure of many Turks who, "as the dominant people" had in the past constituted "the highest and most intellectual element"—the Italian authorities were not worried by this aspect of the problem. They were concerned, though, by the great disproportion—in both absolute terms and percentages—between Jews and Arabs. Apart from the Alliance schools and of course exclusively religious Muslim and Jewish schools, there were 811 Jewish pupils and only 259 Muslims. The Italians could explain this by the special circumstances and the Jews' enterprising character and spirit of initiative,[25] but they could not commend it. As the director of the civil service wrote:

> Though the motherland has an interest in instructing and educating the new young spirits of a population as active and energetic as the Israelites, it has no less if not more interest in doing so for the indigenous Muslims who, one might say, comprise the entire population of the new Italian territories. The Muslim population, precisely because of its huge numerical advantage, is the real and greatest source of cooperation with the motherland . . . It is no overstatement to say that the school is the most forceful nonviolent means for realizing a fusion of spirits and intentions between the indigenous and Italian populations in the joint pursuit of civilization and progress. We shall thus be doing what is in our interests as well as those of the indigenous populations when we summon them to school in large numbers and make education easily accessible for them.[26]

From the point of view of policy, the real problem for the Italian administration was not whether to encourage or hold back the Jews. Its problem was quite another—one which was both simpler and more complex. Faithful to the liberal spirit of the time and the Italian tradition of a unitary state, the administration wanted to ensure that the Jews would receive full civil equality, respect for their culture and traditions, and the same autonomy they had enjoyed under the Ottoman government. But, so as not to arouse bitterness and resentment, the administration also wished to avoid favoring the Jews over the Arabs. Two difficulties beset the first course. One was how to make respect for Libyan Jewish culture and traditions coexist with the prevailing idea of "civilization"—in effect, Westernization, Europeanization, and secularization. The other was how to adapt and mold the autonomy of the Libyan Jewish Communities to the principles and imperatives of the Italian state. The Jewish Communities (especially the Tripoli Community, since it was so large) were composed of Libyan subjects, Italian citizens, and foreign citizens and subjects. This gave rise to a whole series of legal and political problems which made autonomy and complete equality among the various groups impossible, since for the Italian state their statuses differed. One should not underestimate the influence and attraction which the systemization of the Italian Jewish Communities by the Rattazzi Law of July 4, 1857,[27] had for the Italian authorities. The second policy guideline was further hindered by two obstacles. One was an objective condition: the disproportion between the Jews' civil, cultural, and economic level and that of the Arabs; the other was a practical problem: the Italian civil and military administration's need to rely on and exploit to the full the Jews' business networks and ability in enterprise, both to meet immediate needs and to develop the Libyan economy. This was in view of the almost complete absence of Arab business activities and the paucity of Italian enterprise. In practice—to the annoyance of both the Arabs and some Jews themselves—it was impossible to avoid favoring the Jews. Those annoyed were the more traditional Jews, who cared most about their own administrative autonomy, particularly when it was a question of aspects of Jewish life, such as family matters, which had religious origins or implications. After the decree of March 10, 1912, the first institution to come under the ax was the rabbinical court. In the early days of the occupation, the Muslim qadi's court and the rabbinical court had both ceased functioning. But the Muslim court was restored before the end of 1911. The rabbinical court began to function again only after its existence was recognized by General Caneva's decree.[28] The following year the new legal order in Libya (March 20, 1913) prescribed that disputes between Muslims should remain under the qadi's court (subject to the sole condition, also valid for the rabbinical court, that the laws to be applied should not be incompatible with the spirit of Italian law). However, it also prescribed that disputes between "indigenous" Jews, relating to their civil status, family law, and inheritance, could be submitted to either the rabbinical court or the Italian court, where in any case inheritance decisions had to be confirmed (if the court rejected the decision, it had to be submitted to the appeals court) and all other decisions approved. This measure was received favorably by the more modern Jews, who looked forward to greater juridical precision and the avoidance of erroneous or contradictory interpretations of Mosaic law by the rabbinical courts. The measure was considered oppressive and discriminatory by the more traditional Jews, who looked on it as favoring the Arabs. This gave rise to grumbling and protests whenever the subject arose, and echoes of this may be found in the Italian Jewish press.[29] The protests did not subside until 1916, when the regulations under which the Jewish Community of Tripoli would function were passed. Some changes were introduced in the regulations set up three years before.[30] The protests really died down only after the 1921 legal reform, which sanctioned the equal treatment of Italians, Muslims, and Jews, guaranteed the courts' autonomy, and abolished confirmation and approval.

The main problem was the legal basis for the Community of Tripoli. It was also the main problem for Libyan Jewry, because of its implications for other Libyan communities. It was obvious to all, and prescribed also by the Caneva Decree, that a new legal basis was necessary. Nevertheless, preparing it was an unusually lengthy and difficult process. The Community leaders did not pursue the legal basis with much zeal; it was not until September 9, 1913, that they approved draft statutes and submitted them to the local authorities in order to make their wishes and suggestions known. The major delays were caused by the Italians, due partly to the excessive work load on the Tripoli Civil Service, partly to the Italians' lack of clear ideas on the subject, and partly to uncertainties in Rome as to how to confront such a naturally sensitive subject. The matter was made still more sensitive and complex by unnecessary fears and worries. Not until June 1915 was an ad hoc commission set up. It consisted of the deputy, Leone Romanin-Jacur, Professor Francesco Scaduto, and Angelo Sereni, and was attached to the Ministry of Colonies. It was not until over a year later, on August 26, 1916, that the regulations were finally published. Their effectiveness was limited, this being a clear sign of the dire necessity under which they were drafted and of the perplexity which would hang over them, which meant that they had to be viewed as little more than experimental. The regulations covered only Tripoli and adjacent communities (Tajura, Zawia, and El-Sahel). The Community of Benghazi (smaller, but in a politically more sensitive area), remained for years without its own regulatons, simultaneously left to its own devices and under the direct control of the colonial authorities.[31]

The substance of the legislation was closely modeled on the Rattazzi Law. There was controversy regarding who was a member of the Community and what rights this entailed. There was also controversy over the problem of the chief rabbi and, as we have seen, over the rabbinical courts. Involved in the discussions were the Community itself, the Tripoli office of the director of the Civil Service, the Ministry of Colonies, and the Italian Jewish Universities Committee. The committee acted as mediator, using for this purpose the good offices and technical assistance of Senator Vittorio Polacco.[32]

The community leaders would have liked any Jew so desiring to be a full member of the Community.* They wished anyone twenty years and older who paid community taxes† of not less than five lire or two lire and fifty centesimi (depending on whether he lived in

---

*It is interesting to compare these suggestions with the statutes governing an Egyptian Jewish community. See Jacob M. Landau, *Jews in Nineteenth-Century Egypt* (New York, 1969).—*Trans.*

†I have used the term "taxes" rather than "dues," since they were obligatory rather than voluntary.—*Trans.*

Tripoli or another town of the region) to be entitled to vote. They wished anyone over the age of twenty-five who had been a voter for a minimum of three years to be eligible for election as an adviser. He must also be literate in one European language, Hebrew, or Arabic (it was obligatory only that the president know Italian). They wished the chief rabbi to be elected by the Community Assembly, in a choice between three candidates proposed by the Community Council. In the draft Community Statutes of 1913 the chief rabbi's citizenship was not specified. It is obvious, though, that the Tripolitanian Jewish leaders, expressing the wishes of the vast majority of the Jews, had in mind a local rabbi and Libyan subject. In any case, if the assembly was given the right to choose, the possibility of an Italian rabbi's being elected was obviously slight.

These requests turned out to be unacceptable to the Ministry of Colonies. In the ministry's view, the formal organization of the Jewish Community could not, on principle and as a policy, ignore the differences in status among Italian citizens, Italian subjects, foreign citizens, and foreign subjects, especially since the Community was not a purely religious organization. In some areas it had "real jurisdiction" over its members. Hence the need for membership to be obligatory rather than voluntary and for the chief rabbi to be Italian. Moreover, in Rome several institutions of Tripolitanian Jewry were considered "offensive to the European way of thinking," despite Rome's expressed wish to respect as far as possible the Community's autonomy and to foster Jewish culture and traditions. The ministry officials tended to argue that these institutions should be gradually eliminated and transformed. They thus distinguished between Italian citizens and Italian subjects and obviously wished to prevent foreign intervention, giving preference to the Italians in the Community administration, in order to restrict the powers of the traditionalist and religious elements.[33]

In view of the governing authorities' attitude, on the more controversial points the formal organization which the Romanin-Jacur Commission drew up turned out to be very far from what Libyan Jews sought. They were partially satisfied only regarding the problem of rabbinical courts. The Romanin-Jacur arrangement made into obligatory members of the Community "all persons belonging to the Israelite rite who have domicile or residence, or one of these alone, in that area." But only male, adult, Italian citizens and subjects registered as tax-paying Community members could vote. All voters literate in Italian, Hebrew, or Arabic were eligible for election. The chairman and secretary of the governing board had to know Italian. The chief rabbi had to be Italian. The Community leaders' attempts to allow foreigners resident in Libya for five years or more to be eligible for election or voting (with the reservation that foreigners elected could not comprise more than a sixth of the council's membership) and for the chief rabbi to be either an Italian subject or citizen were fruitless.[34]

Libyan Jews registered little reaction and not all of it negative, or so it appeared. The formal organization nevertheless ignored many of the Jewish leaders' requests and, more important, ran against the expectations and feelings of the vast majority of Jews. The motives for such otherwise incomprehensible behavior can be understood only in the light of what had occurred within Libyan Jewry during the previous five years. It is important that when the system was approved the First World War had been in progress for two years, Turkey had proclaimed a holy war, and for over a year Italian troops in Libya had been having serious difficulty with the spreading Arab revolt, which the Turks actively supported.[35] Like it or not, Libyan Jewry was practically obliged to forgo protest under those conditions. Pro-Italian Jews did not protest because of their Italian patriotism, because their destiny would thenceforth be doubly linked to that of Italy, and because some of them were afraid that holding out for better treatment and broader access to the privileges of Italian citizens might entail military duties. Traditional Jews, wanting to show how loyal they were, did not protest. That way they avoided accusations of making trouble and supporting the rebels and the risk of being enrolled in the auxiliaries as a punishment and sent off to Italy.[36] And the most religious and Zionist Jews did not protest because the war was theirs too, since the liberation of Palestine and the possibility of creating a Jewish state there depended on its outcome.[37]

When the Italian-Turkish War broke out in 1911, Jews living in Libya almost unanimously supported Italy, although their motivations and the extent of their support differed among the various groups. Italian Jews and many of the richer and more modern Libyan Jews, already Italianized and integrated into the local Italian community, were most supportive. They had ongoing relations with Italy and were well aware of the business advantages which the Italian occupation would bring.[38] Many of them had not hidden their feelings, with the result that in the days just prior to the opening of hostilities, several hundred of them had had to leave Tripoli hastily and many others had had to ask the Italian consulate and those of other European countries for protection so as to avoid the hostility of the Turks and fanatical Arabs. Jews also actively participated in the process of occupation. For example, the Italian ships which bombarded Tripoli in preparation for the landing had on board two local Jews who, with their knowledge of the city, showed the Italians the main targets. Such occurrences did not happen only in Tripoli. In Benghazi too, there were cases of active collaboration. When the Italian troops landed, the shipbuilding brothers Aron and Effraim Halfon made their floating docks, tugboats, and the hands to work them available to the Italians, and the same was done at Zuetina. One of the notables of the Benghazi community, Juseph Aboub-Bouaron, was known to have persuaded Arabs to surrender; other Jews collaborated with the landing troops, guiding them into the hinterland and contacting Arab leaders in the interior to persuade them to cease resistance and to convince them of the Italians' "civil and peaceful" intentions.[39] It is easy to understand, in view of these facts, why Turks and Arabs viewed the Jews with suspicion and hostility and why in a few places they committed acts of violence against the Jews' persons and goods. The most notable incidents happened in Zanzur and Amruss, where Jewish homes and businesses were destroyed, and their owners forced to flee to Tripoli.[40] Less serious incidents occurred in other places. The Jews who suffered most were the richest and most prominent.[41] Incidents also occurred in Tripoli, where just prior to the Italian occupation many of the homes and businesses of Jews who had taken refuge in foreign consulates were destroyed by crowds of famished and violent Arabs.

Though it is difficult to say so with certainty, it is quite probable that this violence played a large part in determining the attitude of the mass of Libyan Jews. This mass was composed mainly of traditional elements, generally withdrawn in the shell of their microcosm and indigenous society, with no particular links to Italian society and Italy. Their relations with the Arabs had been deteriorating for some time and were rife with usually small, but still psychologically wounding, episodes of intolerance and petty contempt. The strong sense of solidarity was reinforced by the arrival in the Tripoli *hara* of refugees from the hinterland whose misery and desperate condition were obvious to all. The solidarity which characterizes all minorities, especially the Jews, acted as a multiplier for these incidents. One has to conclude that these incidents of violence contributed considerably to stimulating the desire of the mass of Libyan Jews to escape from Muslim rule and thus to their regarding the Italians with sympathy and hope. Any other explanation of the sympathy with which Libyan Jews welcomed the Italian occupation is challengeable. Even the explanation which puts forward an economic motive is less convincing. For most of the more traditional Libyan Jews, for those who were simply poor and had to live off the charity of more fortunate Jews and the Community,[42] or for those whose commercial activities hardly had any market except within the Jewish community or among the lowest Arab society, the immediate benefits (long-term benefits not entering their calculation) from the Italian occupation were almost nil. The fact that "many" Jews found openings and business opportunities with the new military and civilian administration does not alter this. These cases mainly—if not exclusively—involved Jews who spoke Italian, which in itself made them part of an elite. They should not be confused with the mass of Libyan Jews. Likewise, the large- and medium-scale merchants who soon saw what opportunities and prospects the Italian occupation offered them should not be confused with the more numerous small and petty shopkeepers. For them, the Italian occupation meant little or nothing, and they were not in a position to find other openings for themselves in Libyan society. The most that we can suppose is that the attitude of the masses was affected somewhat by the hope, acquired mainly through contacts with richer and more modern Jews, that the rule of a European power would bring improvement to the economy as a whole and thus to their own situation. Further than this motivation it does not seem possible to go. The situation as a whole leads one to think that the pro-Italian attitude of most Libyan Jews resulted mainly from their wish to be free of the Muslim yoke, a desire which became more fervent in reaction to Arab violence when the occupation took place.

These differences in motivations and level of the Jews' support of the new regime are confirmed in the dynamics of events following the occupation.

The richer, more modern Italian and Italianized Jews decisively, wholeheartedly, and enthusiastically took advantage of opportunities in the new situation. They sometimes revealed an impartial ambition to take advantage of all the possibilities which the situation and their own resources—economic and cultural—could offer. There were many who found work as interpreters and office workers with the Italian military or civilian administration or with Italian enterprises that were being established or expanded in Libya. The most results and advantages were won, however, by the large- and medium-scale merchants. They were the entrepreneurs who through their enterprising spirit, their connections, and the means at their disposal succeeded in cornering the market for supplying the occupation troops, for construction and roadbuilding contracts, and for services (especially port and transportation services), and who managed to break into the new Libyan banking industry. Out of twelve discount officers employed in the Tripoli branch of the Bank of Naples in 1915, seven were Jews, including some of the most socially prominent in Tripoli: Halfalla Nahum, Moise Hassan, Ercole Nunes Vais.[43] Sometimes the enterprising spirit of certain businessmen bordered on unscrupulousness and led them to commit crimes. Some of these crimes were much talked about, and their perpetrators had to face justice.[44] But on the whole the Italian authorities—especially the military, for whom efficiency and prompt delivery of needed services was what counted most—appreciated the contribution these Jews made to the new life of the colony. The civilian authorities were slightly less satisfied, since they had other problems to deal with, and had to pay closer attention to the political aspect of Arab reactions.[45] Also, their dealings were with the mass of Jews rather than with the Italianized elite.

When one looks through the available documents, it seems that what most plagued the Italian civilian authorities was the problem of the Sabbath. The vast majority of Libyan Jews, being very religious and traditional, were extremely observant regarding the day of rest.[46] Almost nobody worked on a Saturday, either in Tripoli (the *hara* or the rest of the city) or in other places. This caused considerable difficulties for business because Jews were so important in the Libyan economy. Consequently, there were protests and ill-feeling on all sides—among Italians, Arabs, and Jews. With the hypersensitivity characteristic of minorities, the Jews saw the Italian authorities' attempts to change the Sabbath day of rest to Sunday as unacceptable on religious grounds, another form of discrimination in favor of the Arabs, and almost an expression of anti-Semitism.[47] This is without mentioning the fact that for Muslims Friday is not a holy day of rest, but merely a day for the most solemn prayers, so that for them to adapt to Sunday was not a serious problem.

The problem of the Sabbath was in fact only the most visible aspect—the tip of the iceberg—of a much deeper problem, which I have already had occasion to mention. It was how to modernize and "civilize" Libyan Jews, which the Italian administration dearly wished to do. Most Jews, while experiencing the process imperceptibly every day in their contacts with the new reality created by the Italian occupation, stubbornly rejected it. One result was that their problems and internal divisions gradually worsened. Another was that their tendency to orient themselves to the outside, directly or indirectly, also increased. The two results became a political fact, regarded as such by the Italian authorities as well as by the Italian Jewish Universities Committee.

The range of positions can be broken down into four groups. At one extreme were the modernizers who were integrated or even assimilated (mainly Italians) and at the other the extreme traditionalists. Between these two, there was almost no possibility of dialogue, since the first group considered the second little better than barbarians, while the second group was always ready to condemn any expression of Europeanization, even the most innocent and perfunctory form. In 1916 the rabbinical court of Benghazi was at the point of ostracizing two young men for playing billiards in a "European bar."[48] Two years before, also in Benghazi, there had been a great scandal. At the inauguration of a new synagogue, the golden key of the ark was symbolically given to the governor's representative and in the official speech praise was given to the Italian "motherland." The speaker described the Italian occupation as the "redemption of the people of Israel oppressed by fanaticism and intolerance" and recalled the greatness of ancient Rome.[49]

In between these two extreme positions were those whom we could roughly define as "reformers," themselves split into two groups. Very different in nature, they had begun to differentiate themselves more and more clearly—especially after the Italian occupation and as a result of its repercussions on Libyan Jewry, particularly the Jews of Tripoli. The first of these two groups included many of the most dynamic businessmen and those who had integrated best into the new Libya. Whether they realized it or not, the businessmen were much closer to the modernizers than to the traditionalists. They tended not to show it, in order to avoid creating more internal schisms and polemics. They were particularly wary of disagreements involving the rabbis, who had great authority and influence with the mass of Jews. This group had also held most Community responsibilities under the Turks. After the occupation, it had strengthened its position, particularly in Tripoli, and to a large extent represented the Community leadership. On Jewish affairs, however, it lacked a precise cultural and political outlook. The group argued about a series of contradictory demands: how to remain faithful to tradition but adapt somewhat to the new situation because they considered it objectively advantageous and in practice inevitable or because they were afraid of offending the Italian authorities through their support of the Arabs and thereby arousing Italian anti-Semitism. This group largely consisted of a few exceptional individuals[50] who struggled to keep the components together and to prevent internal dissensions from tearing local Jewish life apart. As an elite, what this group did left much to be desired, since it patently lacked any real political position. It was also affected by a paternalistic and self-serving distribution of power and a string of personal feuds and power struggles. There was paralysis in the Community leadership, made worse by the need to act under conditions of legal transition. Until the new regulations on the legal status of the Community were issued, its leaders' powers were only provisional. This was at a time when clear ideas and programs were needed in order to face up to a changing objective and psychological reality. Things came to their predictable head a few years later rather than right away, and after advance warnings, when the impact of the Italian occupation on Libyan Jewry was more tangible and serious. It was not only the extreme traditionalists who became concerned but also those—mainly young people—who were influenced by Zionism. While agreeing that some reforms were needed (such as accepting an Italian chief rabbi) and that Jews had to adapt to the new situation, the young Zionists did not want these to jeopardize the fundamental moral, cultural, and religious values of Libyan Jewish life nor its long-term survival.

Zionist activities were initially of a cultural sort: Hebrew language classes, study sessions, lectures, etc. These were followed by the founding of a cultural club. This initiative ended in failure, however, since the club lacked the Community's financial and moral support. As far as I can understand, it failed through pure insensitivity, through fear that an exclusively Jewish initiative would displease the Italian authorities, and through personal and intergenerational jealousy. Toward the middle of 1915 there was more and more heated controversy between the Community leaders and the group of young pro-Zionist people who had organized the club. Its moving spirit was Elia Nhaisi, the Tripoli correspondent of *La settimana israelitica* [Jewish Weekly] and founder the following year of the Circolo Sion [Zion Club].[51] From the specific question of the cultural club,[52] the controversy soon extended to a whole series of more general questions, ranging from the moral and material crisis which Libyan Jewry was experiencing[53] to the way the Community was run. It drew in many other Jews of Tripoli who were so unhappy with the Community management that they involved the Italian authorities.

The decisive event in the controversy was an article by Nhaisi, "Vital Questions of Libyan Jewish Life," published in *La settimana israelitica* on September 8, 1915. It began with the statement that many Jewish men and women had "fallen into bad ways" in contact with European civilization, behaving immorally and failing to respect the Sabbath, and that even more of them lacked sufficient education to enable them to grow morally and intellectually and make their way in society. The article directly attacked the leaders of the Tripoli Community and asked the Italian authorities to enact the statutes organizing the Community. Meanwhile, two petitions had been submitted to the governor of Tripoli, General Ameglio, on August 26 and 30.[54] The first one, signed by 230 Community taxpayers, asked for the Community administration to be dissolved and a committee of Community leaders to replace it. These would be "specifically charged with running the Community administration on a temporary and provisional basis, reporting to the governor on its material and moral situation, and then submitting [to the governor again] proposals aimed at attaining a timely, appropriate, and definitive legal basis for the Community." The second petition, broader in scope and more elaborate, was signed by only five people (Vittorio Arbib, Moise Cesana, Abramo Forti, James Arbib, and Federico Ortona). It amounted to an indictment of the Community leaders. They were accused of following a course which was "inappropriate to the needs of the hour," of never submitting their management of Community affairs nor their draft Community Statutes for approval by the assembly, of reducing the Community administration to a "family affair," and of pursuing private interests. Hence, the five signers of this petition, all close to the Nhaisi group, also believed that the government ought to intervene promptly:

> In the long exposition preceding [they concluded], the undersigned have tried to describe for Your Excellency the truly deplorable state of the Jewish Community of Tripoli. The size of its membership and the diverse sentiments which animate them mean that, administered intelligently, it could become a useful pillar of Italian sovereignty in Libya, and an example of civilization to other indigenous populations.
>
> The undersigned call on Your Excellency's organizing spirit to reorganize the Jewish Community of Tripoli swiftly. It in no way deserves to be neglected and left to itself, but needs a skillful hand to guide it to its best potential.
>
> The reins up to now have been held by powerful but incompetent persons. We have seen what they are capable of; the time has come for them to be replaced by others who, though not so favored by fortune, are more capable of confronting, with strong proposals and confident hope, the arduous task of a basic reorganization.

It is obvious that these accusations and the crisis underlying them were serious. Nevertheless, the most important blow that concerns us in the polemic was not the two memoranda to the governor, but Nhaisi's article. It seems doubtful that the ringleaders of the revolt against the Community administrators really thought that they could persuade the colonial authorities to intervene when the authorities had a longstanding reluctance to get involved in internal community affairs and deal with the Community leaders. But the authorities were chiefly reluctant because the Italian parliament was in recess, and they were uncertain regarding what to do about the Community, being largely occupied with Italy's entry into the war and the spread of the Arab revolt. The most that the authors of this twofold initiative could expect was that the new Community regulations would soon be issued and thus officials would be appointed in a regular fashion. It is hard to believe that they could have expected anything else; nor did things turn out any differently.

The administrators of the Tripoli Community (Meborath Hassan, Simeone Haggiag, Halfalla Nahum, Maïr Levy, Ruben Nahum, Isach Nahum, and Eugenio Nahum) submitted another petition to the governor on September 4, in which they tried, rather weakly, to rebut the accusations against them.[55] A few days later General Ameglio received the most prominent of the five opposition leaders, the lawyer Ortona, but their dialogue led to nothing. The governor probably merely gave the opposition spokesman reassurances that the regulations would be issued in the not-too-distant future.[56] He certainly did nothing to persuade the Community administrators to change course or to bow to their opponents' criticisms.[57]

When all these elements are taken into account, it is clear that for the instigators of the attack on the Community administration what really counted was not the two petitions to General Ameglio but Nhaisi's article. The petitions' purpose was to win as much support as possible, prepare the ground for the future elections, and perhaps reassure the Italian authorities regarding the nature and intentions of the initiative. The article was intended as the first step in provoking the intervention of *La settimana israelitica* in the controversy. This publication, whose moral and political support the opposition coveted, carried much weight in Italian Jewish affairs at the time and was headed by the few Italian Zionists. The weekly's intervention came at the end of September with an editorial entitled "The Moment of Decision for Libyan Jewry."[58] It praised the Tripoli "rebellion": "The mere fact of having been able to bring an act of rebellion to fruition has our consent and applause: an act of rebellion is always a sign of vitality and today, in Jewish affairs, we sorely need to show ourselves and others that we are alive." The editorial gave the rebellion a Zionist tenor, clearly showing that Zionism was the basic viewpoint which had moved the Nhaisi group, even though they had preferred to give their initiative an obscurer and less ideologically compromising appearance. No doubt they preferred vagueness because they were aware of their own numerical weakness and feared isolating themselves from the broader context of "reformist" Jews and alarming the colonial authorities, who were anything but favorable to the politicization of Libyan Jewry in a Zionist sense.

If one takes into account all these events, together with the war which was going on, one can understand why when the regulations governing the formal organization and functioning of the Jewish Community were issued the following year they aroused little negative reaction. By that time, the problem was no longer so much one of the rights which the regulations should grant or withhold. It was rather simply one of how to get the regulations, escape from the five years of deadlock in community life, and decide who, by applying the regulations, would run the Community in the immediate future.

3. Arab Revolt and Italian Reconquest (1916–1931)

The period 1915–1931 was marked in Libya by a series of differing events which can all be grouped under the common heading of the Arab revolt against Italian colonial rule. As was to be expected over such a long span of time, there was much variety in the phases, progress, intensity, and expressions (some military and some political) of the Arab revolt and Italian response to it. All these elements were affected by regions, population, general and particular conditions, the resources available to the conflicting parties, and political trends prevailing in each camp. Without going into details, we need only highlight the general trends and most important events of this period around the country, military developments (i.e., control of territory) and political events (i.e., the search for a mutually acceptable arrangement).[1]

The progress of the revolt from the military territorial standpoint and the operations aimed initially at containing and later at suppressing it can be summed up as follows. The Arab revolt began simultaneously with the outbreak of war in 1914, before Italy entered the First World War in May 1915. The revolt received support from the Turks and to some extent the Germans as well. It quickly achieved widespread success, forcing the Italian troops to evacuate the hinterland and cluster in defense of a few key positions on the coast. By mid-July 1915, the area which the Italians occupied in Tripolitania had shrunk to Tripoli, its immediate surroundings (a coastal strip of little more than a hundred kilometers), and al-Khums. In Cyrenaica the revolt centered around the Sanusis,* who were hostile both to Italy and to the Turkish plans for reassuming sovereignty over Libya, and were therefore cool to the Tripolitanian movement, which was closely linked to the Turks.[2] The territory which the Italians managed to hold on to in Cyrenaica was more extensive:

---

*The Sanusi Order, founded in the nineteenth century, was an Islamic revivalist movement which led the rebellion against the Italians in 1914–1915. —*Trans.*

a broad, deep area surrounding Benghazi, Derna, Tubruq, and a few minor regional centers. Throughout the war however, the Italian forces were in serious difficulty in Cyrenaica, being reduced to defending the coast and unable to launch any counteroffensive. This was because the supreme commander had no intention of depriving the Alpine Front of troops in order to send the reinforcements needed—if anything, he would have done the opposite. The situation did not improve until April 1917, when a *modus vivendi* was reached with the Sanusis. With several renewals and modifications, the *modus vivendi* remained in effect until 1923 and gave de facto recognition to the authority over Cyrenaica of the Sanusi leader. The agreement produced no territorial changes: hostilities were merely suspended while, more importantly, free trade was renewed between places in Italian hands and the rest of the country, which the Sanusis controlled.

In 1918 the end of the war marked a new phase in the Italian-Arab conflict. Under the new conditions now prevailing, the Arabs lacked the outside help which they had enjoyed before, while the Italian army was able to transfer seventy thousand troops to Libya. The reconquest did not however begin until three years later, in 1922. The Italian government undertook the reconquest with many doubts and only when the government was clearly unable to reach a satisfactory agreement with the leaders of the Tripolitanian movement. By late 1922 the area which had been reconquered to the west and southwest of Tripoli reached from the Tunisian frontier to Nalut, Giado, Gharian, and the coast immediately east of Suq al-Jum'a. The following year, when the Fascist government had come to power and the last doubts had cleared, the area was extended east of Tripoli, beyond Misurata on the coast and south as far as Beni Ulid. In 1924 the area which the Italians controlled reached from Gadames on the Tunisian frontier to Syrte on the sea, including Derg, Mizda, and Sedada in the hinterland. The regions further in were not occupied until 1928–1929. In Cyrenaica the Italians broke the agreement with the Sanusis in 1923 and reconquered the coastal region south of Benghazi as far as Agedabia. The area immediately inland from Benghazi was occupied the following year, and the rest between 1925 and 1930–1931, after a fierce and sometimes merciless struggle. The Italians occupied Fezzan last, in 1930.

The main political phase of events related to the Arab revolt took place between the end of the war and 1922–1923. This was when the Fascist government decided to use greater force and, more importantly, to re-establish full Italian sovereignty over all of Libya. The military effort took place mainly in Tripolitania. In Cyrenaica,

solidly under Sanusi control, negotiations were like relations between states. One cannot speak of any political entity, even embryonic, apart from the Sanusi Order. The political phase went as
follows. In November 1918 what is known as the Tripolitanian Republic* was proclaimed. Its capital was Misurata and its chief propo-
nent Ramadan al-Suwayhli, one of the most prominent post-1914
Arab leaders. This initiative aimed in the short run at reaching an
agreement with Italy similar to the one concluded with the Sanusis,
or even at establishing a kind of protectorate. The Italian government would not accept this proposal. Its reasons may have been economic and military or concerned with prestige. The Italians may
have known that the real power and cohesiveness of the Tripolitanian Republic, unlike that of the Sanusis, was extremely precarious
and beset from the outset by disagreements among leaders and tribes
and between Arabs and Berbers. In view of the military situation, the
Italians had been almost forced to conclude the agreement with the
Sanusis, based on the *modus vivendi* of April 1917. By 1919 the situation had completely changed. After lengthy discussions, an agreement was reached in May 1919 on the basis of which, a month later,
Tripolitania was granted a Basic Law. This law provided for full
equality between Italians and indigenous inhabitants and established a locally elected parliament and an autonomous administration to be controlled jointly by the Italian governor and the local parliament. The Basic Law also gave Tripolitianian citizens freedom of
the press and of association, exemption from military service, compulsory primary education in Arabic, and exemption from Treasury
tax unless approved by the local parliament. The Basic Law in fact
was never fully implemented, due to a number of problems, including the lack of instruments such as the electoral law for implementing it.[3] The law also failed to go into effect because just after it was
issued, while the majority of Italian troops were being withdrawn,
some of the Arab leaders who the year before had founded the Tripolitanian Republic now set up a Central Committee for Reform,
which had the official purpose of assisting the governor to apply and
improve the Basic Law, but which actually amounted to the unified
leadership of a genuine Libyan independence movement with pan-
Islamic leanings. This committee even had its own newspaper in
Tripoli, *el-Liua at-Trabelsi* [The Tripoli Standard], linked with both
the broader pan-Islamic movement active in other Arab countries

*Repubblica Tripolina. "Tripolitanian Republic" is usually preferred by
scholars over "Tripoli Republic," as it is a closer translation of the Arabic.
—*Trans.*

and the Socialist Party of Tripoli—minute, but important because of its ties with the Italian Socialist Party—as well as Muslim political groupings connected with the Third International. The Tripolitanian movement was represented by one of its most important spokesmen at the Revolutionary Muslim Congress in Moscow in 1921.

The Central Committee for Reform, however, found it practically impossible to carry out its program under conditions then current in Tripoli. Disagreements among tribes and leaders were too sharp (sometimes the Italians had a hand in them) for the movement really to assume a nationalist and unitary form. Because of the disagreements, the committee exhausted itself in a series of endemic and sometimes bloody internal conflicts. In August 1920 Ramadan al-Suwayhli was killed in an attempt to impose his own and the Misuratans' supremacy on the Orfella tribe by force of arms. The conflicts bred disorder, hatred, and famine among the populace. The result was that some tribes rallied to the Italians, while the movement crumbled into a series of precarious agreements among leaders. Its first National Congress held in November 1920 at Gharian demanded the

> institution of a government approved by the masses, a government empowered by and established on the basis of *shari'a* [canon law of Islam] and under the authority of a Muslim elected by the nation; this head of government cannot be removed except by an act provided for under *shari'a* and by resolution of the Chamber of Deputies. The head of government has full religious, civil, and military powers within the limits of an Organic Law to be issued by the Tripolitanian Nation through its deputies, and the government's authority extends over the entire country within the established borders.

When the leaders of the movement subsequently decided to give the Tripolitanian nation a leader, they had to look for one outside their circle and Tripolitania. Although they had no sympathy for him, they turned to the Grand Sanusi, offering him in 1922 the title of Amir of all of Libya.[4]

The Arab movement in Tripolitania really never managed to become a unifying national force. This is not to say that its leaders did not express a genuine anti-Italian sentiment, even though it was still very simple and traditional—more a tribal than a nationalist movement. There can be no doubt, however, that the movement played an important role in regional affairs by keeping them in a state of endemic agitation, punctured by occasional outbursts of hostility against the Italians (who gradually had to relinquish almost all the garrisons and army posts recovered in 1919), against tribes allied with the Italians (in late 1920 most of the Berbers were forced out of

the Jebel), and among the very tribes which the movement represented. There was therefore a general and almost continual state of
tension which had serious repercussions on the economy and gradually heightened during 1920 and 1921, until the situation as a whole
was as precarious as it was politically insoluble.

A new phase led up to the Italians' decision to become deeply
involved and to use force to impose their sovereignty. Their aim was
to implement the Basic Law without being hamstrung by the constant difficulties raised by the Central Committee for Reform. This
phase began in 1921, when Giuseppe Volpi was appointed governor
and Giovanni Amendola took over the Ministry of Colonies. After
some initial doubts, Amendola adhered to Volpi's belief that, if they
were to prevent the situation from becoming more poisoned or to
resolve it, the Italians would have to adopt a firmer and more vigorous stand than before. They reoccupied Misurata Harbor by military means, upon which the Arab revolt broke out again. General
Pietro Badoglio came to make a military inspection of the situation,
followed by Amendola himself. In mid-July 1922 Volpi imposed a
state of siege "wherever rebellious acts had been committed or there
were rebels." The reconquest of the area southwest of Tripoli began
at the same time. After the Jebel had been reoccupied and a harsh
defeat inflicted on the Arabs, a difference of opinion arose between
the government in Rome on one side and Volpi and the military field
commanders on the other, over whether it was better to pursue military action or use the current military advantage to pressure for
peace as envisaged in the Basic Law of 1919. The dilemma was solved
almost as soon as Fascism came to power. Mussolini and Luigi
Federzoni, the new minister of colonies, immediately came out for
continuing the reconquest of Tripolitania and extending operations
to Cyrenaica. Their pretext was that the Tripolitanian leaders were
maintaining contacts regarding the Amirate with the Grand Sanusi.
Thus negotiations with the Arabs and political concessions to them
effectively ended.

Events in Libyan Jewish life between 1915–1916 and 1931–
1932 must be viewed in this context. Only by seeing it against the
background of the Arab revolt and its suppression can one understand why and how this period so profoundly affected all aspects of
Jewish life, aspects ranging from the economic and social spheres to
relations with the Arabs and Italy. The Arab revolt had differing economic consequences for the Jews of Tripolitania and those of Cyrenaica. The Cyrenaican communities, especially in Benghazi, suffered relatively little damage, and that largely limited to the early
years and the worst moments of the struggle. The *modus vivendi*

which the Italians and Sanusis reached in April 1917 brought them compensating advantages. Jews benefited from the return of free trade between Italian- and Sanusi-occupied areas. Due to their enterprising spirit, linguistic abilities, and relative marginality to the Italian-Sanusi conflict, Jews were the most appropriate intermediaries between the two zones, especially in trade with the Sanusi hinterland. The Jews of Tripolitania played a similar intermediary role and probably encompassed an even broader range of functions. In view of their numbers and business activities, much larger than those of the Cyrenaican Jews, there is no doubt that the Arab revolt in Tripolitania (which was much more widespread, violent, and lasted until 1923 at least) caused greater harm to the Tripolitanian Jews that the Cyrenaican Jews. Smaller communities suffered real damage, since their links to Tripoli were repeatedly broken. On several occasions they were the victims of Arab violence, with the result that over two thousand Jews had to abandon their homes and businesses and take refuge in Tripoli or among the Berbers. This state of affairs improved somewhat in 1919, with the new climate in Italian-Arab relations preceding the Basic Law, but it was a mere parenthesis. There was another interval of improvement in late 1921. To stimulate the faltering economy of the Tripoli area and as a political gesture, Volpi reopened the markets of Tripoli and other Italian-controlled towns to all indigenous people. Thanks to this measure, the whole economy of the Italian zone received a breath of fresh air; customs receipts almost doubled and the caravan trade revived. Though there is no actual information, it is possible that the governor's decision was influenced by requests from Jewish merchants. An indirect hint can be gleaned from a telegram dated August 8, 1921, from Volpi to Giuseppe Girardini, defending Volpi's point of view. He held that it was necessary to combat the wiles of Arab intriguers, not only through force and by implementing the Basic Law "in substance and rapidly" but also by demonstrating the advantages that the Arabs would have from "participating in our economic activities." He cited the convincing example of the "most capable metropolitans* and Jews residing in Tripoli."[5]

This hint is meaningful in view of attacks which were made on Volpi almost immediately from Italy. He was accused of paying "too much attention" to "interested" pressures from "the Tripolitanian Jewish element" even in his decision to reoccupy Misurata Harbor: "because if a military operation is successful, new trade starts up as a result and they can earn more profits; if, though, the operation is

---

*The metropolis was Italy in colonial usage, and metropolitans therefore were Italians who had settled in Libya.—*Trans.*

not carried out or fails, it is not the Jewish element which suffers."[6] Definite improvement did not occur until 1922–1923, as the reconquest proceeded. The reconquest opened the hinterland and coastal region of Syrte for business for the Jews of Tripoli and allowed many who had taken refuge in the *hara* to return to their home towns and start afresh. Though the initial revolt and its later suppression had greatly impoverished the Arabs, the reconquest created particularly favorable conditions for the Jews, in both small- and large-scale businesses. As long as the pacification of the country was not completed and Italian civilians not yet a significant and accepted presence beyond the main coastal towns, the Jews' mediating role continued to be essential in colonial economic and social life. In his report on the importance of Jews in Tripolitania, delivered to the Colonial Studies Congress in Florence in 1931, Elia S. Artom stressed this aspect. He was the chief rabbi for Tripoli from 1920 to 1923 and had kept in close touch with Libyan Jews, so that he was well aware of the situation:

> The importance of Jews to the metropolitan population and hence to the colonizing power is greater than their numbers would have one believe. Metropolitans generally have more contact with Jews than with Arabs, and almost all relations between metropolitans and indigenous people take place through Jews. This is due to the Jewish nature as it has developed through living together with other peoples, not only in Tripolitania, but also in all countries where they have not been oppressed by the dominant population. Such has been the case in Arab and Turkish countries, where Jews have generally enjoyed broad freedoms. The Arab is very withdrawn, almost trying to hide from the European; the Jew does not hide, but puts himself on display; he does not refuse to collaborate with the European, but even offers to do so. Thus, while the Arab merchant deals almost exclusively in indigenous products and handmade work, the Jew provides for the needs of both his fellow-Jews and the entire local population, and even introduces European products to the indigenous population. While the Arab artisan produces only items for indigenous use, the Jewish artisan works also for metropolitan use. . . . Though the Tripolitanian Jews express their attraction to Europe and Italy in so many ways, this is not why they stand out from the dominant indigenous group. Though most of them, especially the young people, can understand Italian and express themselves in it to some extent, their habitual mode of speech is the local Arab dialect. They write it in Hebrew characters and it is all that they use in relations with each other and with Arabs. The latter, by nature withdrawn and diffident, are less suspicious and reserved toward the Jews, with whom they have lived for a long time, than toward Europeans—this is why Jews served well as intermediaries between metropolitans and indigenous people. Moreover, they speak the languages of

both groups, having had easy or at least not difficult access to them. The Jews, generally of lively intelligence and ready ingenuity, come between the two extreme population groups in culture and civilization. In the best sense, in Tripolitania Jews can fulfill the role of intermediaries and importers of not only goods but also ideas, as they did in Europe in the Middle Ages. The condition of the indigenous population in Libya could generally be described as medieval—hence the importance of the Jews, if they are used well.

While it is difficult for the metropolitan to penetrate Arab urban society, it is even more difficult, well nigh impossible, to do so (by peaceful means, of course, not a military operation) in the hinterland. There are not many Jews in the interior and if, as I suspect, conditions have not changed over the last few years, relations between Arabs and Jews in the hinterland are cooler than on the coast. The Jews nevertheless, for the reasons which I have explained, are the best and moreover the only element which can facilitate contacts between metropolitans and hinterland Arabs. I regret not being able to give precise information on this important point, but there is no doubt that most relations with the hinterland indigenous population take place through the Jews.[7]

One point in particular is important for a full appreciation of the repercussions which the Arab revolt had on the Jews of Tripoli. Business was shrinking, due to the overwhelming reduction in the Jews' links to other towns in Libya and in their own economic activities in the city. At the same time, all economic activity, especially trade with Arab-controlled zones, required a large capital investment and involved greater risks. The result was that between 1915 and 1922–1923 the gaps between income groups were widening. At one extreme there was a growing mass of the poverty-stricken, in the middle a modest number of small- and medium-scale shopkeepers and craftsmen, and at the other extreme a tiny group of large-scale merchants and entrepreneurs, whose fortunes were continually on the rise. Signs of this phenomenon are many, even though it is not easy to quantify them. Given the documentation available, the most useful data come from examining the list of members of the Tripoli Chamber of Commerce in 1923.

First, these data[8] show the various types of business in which Jews participated. There were very few Jews in farming. Only three farms were registered as belonging to Jews—one Italian Jew near Tripoli, and two Libyans near al-Khums. On the whole, Jews were not evident in industry—at least they do not seem to have been; obviously, in order to judge more precisely one should know about possible Jewish employment in companies and enterprises owned by non-Jewish Italians.[9] Jews were present to some extent in specific industries, such as distilleries (ten companies out of thirteen in Tripoli, four out of five in al-Khums, and one out of two in Zuwara), mineral water bottling (three out of eight), soap manufacturing (two out of four), and printing and engraving (three out of six).[10] In handicrafts, Jews completely monopolized silver and gold work (all twenty-one shops in Tripoli and the only one in Zuwara) and work in ivory (five out of five). The only private banker registered in the Tripoli Chamber of Commerce (Abramo Nahum, an Italian) also turns out to have been Jewish, as were one moneychanger, two builders of sailing ships, and two maritime agents. Jews were most evident, however, in trade. Not only were they active in almost every branch of commerce, but also their overall presence was out of proportion to their numbers in the total population of Tripoli. In 1922–1923 Jews constituted about 22 percent of the population of the city, while Muslims comprised about 57 percent and Europeans (mostly Italians) 21 percent. Businesses and shops registered in the Chamber of Commerce under Jewish ownership reached a total of 30 percent. If we add businesses in which Jews worked, this percentage rises still higher, to 40 percent (see Table 2).

The second element which emerges from these data is the scale of Jewish businesses. The members of the Tripoli Chamber of Commerce were classified according to the size of their businesses into thirteen classes, grouped into four categories. The first category (classes 1–3) comprised businesses paying 400–1,200 lire in Chamber of Commerce dues; there were no Jews in this category. The second category (classes 4–6) comprised businesses paying 250–350 lire; in this category there were thirty-two Jews in the fourth class, thirteen in the fifth, and thirty-five in the sixth. The third category (classes 7–9) comprised businesses paying 100–200 lire; this category included twelve Jews in the seventh class, thirty in the eighth, and forty-one in the ninth. All other businesses owned by Jews were covered by the fourth category (classes 10–13) which consisted of small shops paying 12–72 lire. In other words, two-thirds of Jewish businesses and shops were very small. The other third consisted almost equally of medium and medium-to-large businesses and shops. Though they are significant, these figures give an incomplete and largely distorted picture of the composition of the Tripoli Jews' commercial activities. In fact, the picture changes markedly when one goes further and examines not only the numbers and nature of businesses and shops, but also the distribution of their ownership. It then emerges that while the smallest shops (in the fourth category) and the majority of the medium-size shops (third category) belonged to businessmen who generally had only one shop each, the owners of medium-to-large businesses and shops (second category) almost

TABLE 2. *Enterprises Registered with Libyan Chambers of Commerce, 1922–1923*

Line of Work	Tripoli					al-Khums				
	TCC	LJ	IJ	FJ	TJ	TCC	LJ	IJ	FJ	TJ
Importers-exporters	71	14	9	7	30	2	1			1
Traders with Nigeria and Sudan	16	1	2	1	4					
Leather and wool exporters	13	5	4	1	10					
Franchise holders and commission agents	101	23	8	11	42					
Shippers	15	5			5					
Brokers	6	3			3					
Commercial travelers and auctioneers	21	1			1					
Dealers in foodstuffs	232	73	4	1	78	28	17			17
Military supply contractors	8			1	1					
Military equipment suppliers	7	1			1					
Lumber merchants						1	1			1
Dealers in oriental items	2		1		1					
Baraccan sellers						2	2			2
Livestock dealers, butchers	104	41			41	1	1			1
Shopkeepers	97	27		1	28					
Shoemakers	18	4			4	3	3			3
Stationers, booksellers	16	6			6					
Grain merchants	16	6	1	2	9					
Bric-a-brac dealers	30	26			26					
Grocers	70	32	3	3	38	1	1			1
Dealers in cotton and yarn	8	3		3	6					
Ironmongers	16	7		7	14					
Flower-, fruit-, and vegetable-vendors	30	1			1					
Food-vendors	80	6		1	7	47	19		3	22
Henna dealers	43	23	4	2	29					
Construction material suppliers	10	4	1		5					
Haberdashers and bazaar traders	25	11			11	2	1			1
Precious metal dealers	4	3	1		4					
Secondhand furniture dealers	5	2			2					

Zuwara					Remarks
TCC	LJ	IJ	FJ	TJ	
					Almost all the rest Italians
					No Muslims
					No Muslims
					No Muslims
					All the rest Muslims
70	30			30	Many of the rest Muslims
					Many of the rest Muslims
					All the rest Italians
					No Muslims

TABLE 2 *(continued)*

Line of Work	Tripoli					al-Khums				
	TCC	LJ	IJ	FJ	TJ	TCC	LJ	IJ	FJ	TJ
Fashion and dressmakers	11	1			1					
Hide and leather merchants	6	5		1	6					
Ostrich-feather sellers	7	5	1		6					
Perfume vendors, hairdressers	22	4			4	3	1			1
Tailors	12	6			6					
Silkmakers and dyers	4	4			4					
Beverage sellers	54	54			54	8	5			5
Crockery and earthenware sellers	4	1			1					
Tobacconists						7	3			3
Sellers of woven and hand-made work	65	54	4	2	60					
Wine and oil merchants	25	2			2					
Sellers of Arab kitchen utensils	14	11			11					

TCC: Total number of enterprises. IJ: Italian Jewish enterprises.
LJ: Libyan Jewish enterprises. FJ: Foreign Jewish enterprises
TJ: Total Jewish enterprises.

always owned two, three, or even four. In other words, larger enterprises were concentrated in fewer hands than appeared on first sight (the eighty businesses in the second category belonged to only thirty-three persons, thirty-two of whom owned more than one) and, moreover, were concentrated within precise and limited family groups.[11] This means that there were several business chains (often linked not only by ownership but also in the line of business) of very large dimensions. Their ownership was registered individually in the Chamber of Commerce as second-category businesses, but looked at as a whole they should have been under the first category of large-scale businesses.

This gap between large and small businesses had its origins in the history of Tripolitanian Jewry. It is clear, though, that the period of the Arab revolt fatally exacerbated the tendency to drift further apart. The opposite trend held in the Cyrenaican communities, where the gap was less and less obvious and the revolt affected the economy less. During the reconquest and the calmer times between 1931–1932 and the outbreak of the Second World War, in response

Zuwara					Remarks
TCC	LJ	IJ	FJ	TJ	

to the general improvement in the Libyan economy, the number of businesses and shops owned by Jews in Tripoli expanded (despite the large increase in Italian ownership), particularly in certain lines. These new commercial enterprises were, with few exceptions, on a medium or small scale. At the same time, large enterprises were being concentrated and increasing in numbers and strength, while the older small- and medium-scale businesses either remained the same or showed modest growth. In early 1931, Rabbi Dario Disegni summarized the condition of the Jews of Tripoli to the leaders of the Union of Italian Jewish Communities* as follows: there were one

*The Union replaced the Consortium of Italian Jewish Communities, which had been set up on a voluntary basis in 1911 to coordinate the Communities. The Union was established on an obligatory basis by a law of October 30, 1930. The law defined the prerogatives of rabbis, including authorization to perform marriages provided the relevant articles of the Italian legal code were read. It laid down that all those considered Jews by Jewish law automatically belonged to the Community unless they made a formal renunciation (*Encyclopedia Judaica*).—*Trans.*

multimillionaire, three or four millionaires, three thousand "who are comfortably off," four thousand "who are managing," and eight thousand "ragged indigents." The "insufficient and degrading charitable relief" on which the poor depended drained off almost a third of the Community budget.[12] This situation and the way it was developing can be confirmed and elaborated on by examining the Libyan population census of 1931, the industrial and commercial census of Tripolitania for 1928, and the electoral rolls of the Tripoli Community for 1930.[13]

Table 3 shows the numbers of Jews in Libya according to the 1931 population census. The single comparison which can be made with the 1911 Ottoman census is a significant one. While Tripoli Jews had increased considerably in number (from 8,509 to 15,279), the number of Jews residing in the rest of Tripolitania had remained practically unchanged (having increased from 5,773 to 5,859). This can be explained solely by political and military developments in the region, the resulting depopulation of small hinterland communities, and the transfer of refugees to Tripoli (by 1931 many had not yet returned to their former homes). The only location showing a normal increase in Jewish population (from 525 to 688) was al-Khums, which was held by the Italians all along, but which had not received any significant influx of refugees. Otherwise, the Jewish population was distributed as in Table 4. The Jews made up 3.57 percent of the total population of Libya. Of this figure, 62.3 percent of the Jews lived in Tripoli (of whose population they comprised 19.07 percent) and 11 percent in Benghazi (of whose population they comprised 6.4 percent). The rest of the Jewish population, 26.7 percent, lived scattered over the country in twenty-one localities. Precise data are lacking for these. We can, however, have some idea of the professional characteristics of the Jews of Tripoli and Benghazi. On the basis of the social position of the head of the family, their professions are as shown in Table 5.

As R. Bachi has noted,[14] these data, together with those relating to the median age at which Jews in Tripoli and Benghazi began and finished working, women's domestic work, and knowledge of Italian, show unmistakably that Benghazi Jews were superior in social standing to Tripoli Jews. This confirms what has already been said regarding the differing effects which the Arab revolt had on the two communities.

While specific data on employment are lacking for Cyrenaica, much information on the Jews of Tripolitania can be deduced from the 1928 industrial and commercial census. It gives a clear impression of relations among various groups within Tripolitanian society.

TABLE 3. *Jewish Population of Libya by Citizenship, 1931*

	Libyans	Italians	Foreigners	Total
Tripoli	15,279	319	39	15,637
Rest of Tripolitania	5,859	12	—	5,871
Benghazi	2,062	51	654	2,767
Rest of Cyrenaica	824	3	1	828
	24,024	385	694	25,103

TABLE 4. *Jewish Population of Libya by Geographical Distribution, 1931*

Tripolitania

Zuwara	621	Menzel Tegrina	256
Zawia	516	Haret el-Aggab (Tajura)	189
Zanzur	61	Qusabat	333
Amruss	1,158	al-Khums	688
Zlitin	529	Gharian	85
Misurata	702	Orfella	44
Syrte	261	Tarhuna[a]	73
Yafran	322		

Cyrenaica

Agedabia	41	Derna	293
Soluq	21	Tubruq	175
Barce	248	Port Bardia	45

[a] Classified as seminomads.

TABLE 5. *Professional Characteristics of Jews in Tripoli and Benghazi, 1931 (per Thousand)*

	Tripoli		Benghazi	
Employment	Libyan Jews	Total Population	Libyan Jews	Total Population
Agriculture	2	98	—	135
Industry and transport	463	503	251	473
Trade and banking	374	202	459	185
Public and private administration	41	94	63	93
Religious offices and professional positions	20	21	38	14
Domestic services	29	11	1	11
Nonprofessional property owning and independent wealth	71	71	188	99

SOURCE: 1931 Census of Libya.

TABLE 6. *Ownership of Enterprises, 1928*

	Jews		Italians	
	Tripoli	Other Locations	Tripoli	Other Locations
Mechanized enterprises	14	—	106	26
Nonmechanized enterprises	1,860	937	1,117	284
Subtotal	1,874	937	1,223	310
Total		2,811		1,533

SOURCE: 1928 industrial and commercial census of Libya.

Table 6 summarizes the situation for industrial and commercial enterprises. It accounts only for indigenous Jews and thus gives the impression that there are fewer Jews than there actually were.

Relating these figures to those of the general population gives the following percentages: 14.01 percent Jews, 8.65 percent foreigners, 7.64 percent Italians, 1.65 percent Muslims. The proportions speak for themselves. They are even more eloquent when one completes them with the percentages of employees in those firms: foreigners 22.28 percent, Jews 20.74 percent, Italians 20.22 percent, and Muslims 3.15 percent. The breakdown of these business activities shown in Table 7—based again on the 1928 industrial and commercial census—is particularly significant.

It is almost certain that in 1923 a number of the very small businesses were not registered with the Chamber of Commerce, and that the lists which we have used of those registered give the impression that there were fewer than was in fact the case. Still, a comparison of these data with those for 1928 clearly confirms that there was indeed an upswing in the economic activities of the Jews of Tripoli, as a result of the suppression of the Arab revolt, the re-establishing of effective Italian sovereignty over Tripolitania, and the consequent improvement in the economic situation. One way in which the improvement showed was a marked increase in the Muslim population, due partly to the return of exiles, but even more to a considerable migration to the city from the hinterland.[16] The criteria used in 1928 for entering statistics, particularly the fact that many types of work were grouped under generic names, or less specific names than those which the Chamber of Commerce used, tend to conceal another process. It is that, parallel to this increase, the businesses themselves were being extended, rationalized, and modernized.

The fact that the increase favored large enterprises in particular

Muslims		Foreigners	
Tripoli	Other Locations	Tripoli	Other Locations
7	1	12	1
2,085	4,501	294	45
2,092	4,502	306	46
	6,594		352

is confirmed by the list of voters registered in the electoral rolls of the Community of Tripoli in 1930. Because of the Community's electoral system, the list of voters also comprised the roll of Community taxpayers.

What first stands out is the limited number of taxpayers with a taxable income. Besides 4 rabbinical judges and the Community secretary, who were exempt, there were only 600 taxpayers. This was among a population of about 15,000 which (on the basis of dividing into ages or of the average composition of families)[17] included at least 3,400 men of working age. Even supposing that on average each taxpayer would meet his fiscal obligation through the work of about one-and-one-half sons of working age as well as his own, one infers that at least 1,900 men of working age must have been unemployed or underemployed. These two groups and their families must have comprised the 8,000 "ragged indigents" whom Rabbi Disegni mentioned at this time.

The second, equally important piece of information is that the taxpayers can be subdivided according to wealth (see Table 8). From this breakdown it emerges that slightly more than 3 percent of operators (19 in all) controlled a little over 18 percent of business, 29.2 percent (176 in all) controlled a little less than 47 percent, and the remaining 405, equalling 67.5 percent, shared control of the remaining 35 percent and a little more. Once again, the picture which Rabbi Disegni mapped out confirms the situation in 1923 and the trends which were developing: a large number of small businessmen and craftsmen (paying up to 100 lire in taxes) and a very small number of large businessmen (paying more than 500 lire) who comprised a sort of well-to-do industrial and commercial class. The picture does not change when one identifies who the members of this little group of the wealthiest were. Apart from one of the property-owners

TABLE 7. *Business Activities of Jews in Tripolitania, 1928*

Activity	Tripoli Enterprises	Employees
Industry		
Fishing	5	20
Lumber	67	109
Food	112	161
Leather	31	52
Paper	3	3
Printing	6	21
Machinery	174	312
Mining other than metals	8	30
Building	25	31
Textiles	22	43
Clothing	297	509
Health and sanitation	35	54
Chemicals	1	2
Transport and communications	19	39
Total:	805	1,386
Commerce		
Credit, exchange, insurance	10	9
Livestock	32	57
Wholesale food	9	15
Wholesale yarns and fabrics	6	9
Other grocery supplies	49	104
Business services	100	104
Metalworking and machinery	13	23
Retail food	348	413
Retail yarns and fabrics	194	252
Furniture and glasswork	25	35
Artwork	23	31
Chemical products	31	31
Secondhand trade and peddling	42	48
Miscellaneous trades	43	67
Hotels, restaurants, cafés	131	173
Various types of business	3	5
Total	1,059	1,376
Grand total	1,864[15]	2,755

SOURCE: 1928 industrial and commercial census of Libya.

Other Locations		Total	
Enterprises	Employees	Enterprises	Employees
—	—	5	20
24	30	91	139
18	25	130	186
40	40	71	92
—	—	3	3
—	—	6	21
82	99	256	411
1	1	9	31
3	3	28	34
—	—	22	43
86	118	383	627
11	12	46	66
—	—	1	2
4	4	23	43
269	332	1,074	1,718
—	—	10	9
1	—	33	57
1	1	10	16
—	—	6	9
7	9	56	113
6	6	106	110
2	2	15	25
502	563	850	976
13	13	207	265
2	2	27	37
5	5	28	36
—	—	31	31
54	55	96	103
16	17	59	84
58	65	189	238
1	10	4	15
668	748	1,727	2,124
937	1,080	2,801	3,842

TABLE 8. *Jewish Community Taxpayers and Amount Paid in Tripoli, 1930*

Number of Taxpayers	Amount of Tax Paid Individually (in Lire)	Number of Taxpayers	Amount of Tax Paid Individually (in Lire)
28	50	20	250
256	60	13	300
62	75	6	350
4	80	14	400
55	100	1	450
1	120	6	500
45	125	4	600
35	150	2	700
2	160	1	800
4	175	4	1,000
34	200	2	1,300
1	225		

SOURCE: List of taxpayers, Jewish Community of Tripoli, 1930.

(who in 1923 was a trader in general merchandise and livestock) they were all merchants (seventeen) and franchise-holders (one), and the same names crop up over and over again. The only difference, if it can be described as such, is that one of the family groupings, the Nahums, seems to lead the field. Five members of this family, particularly the four sons of Raffaele Nahum, in 1930 between them paid 4,800 lire in Community taxes, thus representing the most obvious wealth in the Tripoli community.[18]

The final important details which the Community electoral rolls offer complete the information provided by the industrial and commercial census of two years before. These details concern the professions and economic activities of the taxpayers themselves. Thanks to this, our knowledge of the composition of the working Jewish population of Tripoli in 1930 becomes much more precise. Apart from eighteen taxpayers whose work was not indicated, Table 9 gives a precise picture of the work which Jews did in Tripoli. One can also see that in 1930 the community must still have been largely self-sufficient. In other words, helped by the fact that the vast majority of Jews still lived in the *hara*, the community was able to provide most of the goods and services which it needed for daily life. This is in addition, of course, to goods and services which the Jews produced and delivered for the Arab population and the Italian colony.

The above covers the strictly financial aspect of Jewish life. Documentation available allows us to broaden the picture to include some social aspects. These are particularly useful in highlighting another important aspect, linked to the economic, though not reducible simply to economics. It is the differing degree of "civilization," in other words, the extent to which Jews, as compared with Muslims, were integrated into Libyan colonial society.

One very important element in their integration was skill in the Italian language. The 1931 census shows that only 4.6 percent of the indigenous population spoke Italian. This percentage was obviously higher in the cities. In Benghazi 34.5 percent of Arab males spoke Italian, and 1.6 percent of females; for Tripoli the figures were 29.2 percent and 2.6 percent. These percentages were considerably higher for Jews: there were 67.1 percent male and 40.8 percent female Italian speakers in Benghazi, and 43.8 percent and 29.7 percent in Tripoli. Since all indigenous Jews and almost all Italian and foreign Jews (except for a few recent immigrants) spoke Arabic, it is easy to see how important these skills were for functioning socially, as well as for work.

Other elements besides language are useful for assessing the living conditions of the Libyan Jews, which were clearly superior to those of the Muslim population. This was despite the fact that, especially in Tripoli and the interior, many of them lived in poor circumstances.

One of these elements is school attendance. I have already mentioned the contrast that existed in Tripoli between the numbers of Jews and Muslims attending public schools, and the Italian civilian authorities' concern at the great imbalance. This imbalance was never adjusted, despite the Italian administration's efforts. And if it diminished slightly, rather than increasing, this was not because of the Arabs' efforts but because of the Italian administration. Partly due to lack of funds and partly to restrict the imbalance, the administration did not meet the requests of the Jews, particularly the Tripoli Community, to set up new classes in public schools or give Community institutions financial help in transforming their own religious schools into modern ones, capable of giving academic as well as religious instruction. Table 10 shows clearly that between 1921–1922 and 1939–1940, though Arab school attendance increased considerably, it still remained far below Jewish attendance, in proportion to the size of each community.[19]

More can be learned from hygiene, health conditions, and use of medical services.[20] Regarding health, it should suffice to say that in Tripoli in 1939 the number of stillbirths was 101 out of 2,500 births among Muslims, and 22 out of 785 among Jews (with 36 out of 1,309 among Italians). Although precise figures for infant mortality are not

TABLE 9. *Professions of Community Taxpayers in Tripoli, 1930*

Profession	Amount of Tax Paid (in Lire)
1 architect	145
1 lawyer	100
1 teacher	60
3 other members of liberal professions	145 (average)
53 office-workers	72 (average)
1 bookseller	75
1 stationer	60
1 photographer	60
1 pharmacist	200
5 property-owners	382 (average)
6 industrialists	185 (average)
23 makers of handicrafts	115 (average)
1 entrepreneur	300
250 merchants	179 (average)
23 franchise-holders	129 (average)
3 brokers	78.3 (average)
2 moneychangers	67 (average)
4 shippers	93 (average)
1 hide merchant	300
3 distillers	120 (average)
3 printers	78.3 (average)
11 dealers	90 (average)
4 shopkeepers	86 (average)
8 druggists	95 (average)
17 butchers	74 (average)
1 fried-food seller	60
2 pastry sellers	60 (average)
14 bartenders	75 (average)
12 tavernkeepers and wine-shop keepers	74 (average)
2 milkmen	85 (average)
3 barbers	95 (average)
5 peddlers	66 (average)
17 silversmiths	90 (average)
31 goldsmiths	84 (average)
3 machinists	103 (average)
1 blacksmith	125 (average)
1 coppersmith	60
1 electrician	125
1 bicycle mechanic	75
3 marblecutters	65 (average)
11 bricklayers	83 (average)
1 stonecutter	60
1 miller	60 (average)

TABLE 9 *(continued)*

Profession	Amount of Tax Paid (in Lire)
2 weavers	60 (average)
2 saddlemakers	60 (average)
4 carpenters	60 (average)
3 cabinetmakers	110 (average)
25 tailors	77 (average)
1 charcoal seller	60 (average)
2 fishermen	92.5 (average)

SOURCE: List of taxpayers, Jewish Community of Tripoli, 1930.

available, it was still much higher among Muslims than among Jews. Statistics for services which the traveling clinic of Tripoli provided in 1931 give useful information on use of medical facilities (Table 11).

The difference between the two communities in employment rates of minors and the elderly is also significant. In a population as poor as the Jews of Tripoli were, the 1931 census shows that employment of minors (between ten and fourteen years of age) was 17.3 percent (12.8 percent in Benghazi) as opposed to 22.5 percent (21.6 percent in Benghazi) for Arabs. For the elderly (over sixty-five) the rate was 37.2 percent (18.4 percent in Benghazi) compared with 41.8 percent (40 percent in Benghazi) for Arabs.

The period of the Arab revolt and its suppression was important for the development of Libyan Jewry from another point of view besides the socioeconomic. Jewish-Arab relations were affected in three ways.

The first relates directly to what has been written in earlier pages regarding the economic and social benefits which Libyan Jews achieved during those years as well as to the change in relations between the two communities in progress for several decades and accelerated by the Italian occupation. Under the conditions prevailing in Libya at the time, the impoverishment of the Muslim masses and the Jews' simultaneous rise in socioeconomic importance could not fail to affect intercommunity relations. These phenomena made the Arabs yet more dependent on the Jews' economic activities (including moneylending) and their role as intermediaries, and there was nothing to re-establish balance in the situation. The two communities could only have been brought together in the political arena, i.e., in a common attitude toward Italy as Libyans. But in politics as well, Jews and Arabs were in fact divided.

TABLE 10. *School Attendance in Libya, 1921–1922 and 1939–1940*

	Arabs		Jews	
	21–22	39–40	21–22	39–40
Italian public schools				
Infant schools	—	4	128	—
Elementary schools	31	40	789	—
High schools	3	32	58	—
Arab public schools				
Infant schools	—	94	—	—
Elementary schools	668	6,194	53	—
High schools	—	94	—	—
Arts and trades schools	—	—	—	—
Jewish public schools				
Infant schools	—	—	—	556
Elementary and profes- sional schools	—	—	—	2,074
High schools	—	—	—	77
Private religious (Catholic) schools	25	14	70	—
Koranic schools	798	10,995	—	—
Talmud Torahs	—	—	1,266	1,235
Totals	1,525	17,467	2,364	3,942

(Header: Tripolitania)

SOURCE: See note 19.

During the war, as we have seen, Libyan Jews supported Italy, though with differing motives and to differing extents. After the war was over, there were some Jews, especially in Tripoli, who favored a political solution to the Arab-Italian conflict and were sympathetic to the Basic Law of 1919, to the extent of supporting Arab political groups active in the city,[21] in some cases from motives of human solidarity and support for emancipation, self-government, freedom, and democracy—ideals aroused by the war—and in others, for reasons of self-interest, looking forward to the end of the Arab revolt and the return of peace. Such cases, however, were in the minority and were not imitated by the masses, among whom hostility toward the Arabs was widespread (especially following the renewed violence against hinterland Jews during the early stages of the revolt). Hostility to the Arabs existed despite the feeling that the Italians were an external element and that they might even be a dangerous one due to their potentially negative influence on the moral and religious coherence of the Jewish microcosm. Later, when it was obvious that the Basic Law could not be effectively implemented and the revolt broke out

Cyrenaica				Total			
Arabs		Jews		Arabs		Jews	
21–22	39–40	21–22	39–40	21–22	39–40	21–22	39–40
—	1	31	—	—	5	159	—
18	67	278	—	49	107	1,067	—
9	16	6	—	12	48	64	—
—	—	—	—	—	94	—	—
545	2,313	—	3	1,213	8,507	53	3
6	30	—	—	6	124	—	—
65	—	—	—	65	—	—	—
—	—	—	—	—	—	—	556
—	—	—	436	—	—	—	2,510
—	—	—	—	—	—	—	77
6	9	15	—	31	23	85	—
582	1,267	—	—	1,380	12,262	—	—
—	—	218	511	—	—	1,484	1,746
1,231	3,703	548	950	2,756	21,170	2,912	4,892

again, no Jews supported the Arabs. This is not surprising when one considers the militantly Muslim and pan-Islamic nature of the Arab nationalist movement and the claims on which it based its actions. If the movement had succeeded, Libyan Jews would have faced the prospect of submitting again to Muslim religious law and all the discrimination which it implied. Libyan Jews, both the masses and those operating on a larger economic scale, were confirmed in this attitude by the economic problems which the extended Italian-Arab conflict was causing and by their desire to see an end to the conflict and freedom of trade in Libya. It was clear that free trade would not be brought about, given the respective positions of the two conflicting parties, unless the Italians used force. This explains why, throughout the revolt and reconquest, no Jews joined the Arab cause. The only two possible cases were cleared of suspicion. The first involved two brothers in Tarhuna, who were accused of spying and smuggling for the rebels. The second case involved Eugenio Nahum, a rich merchant and industrialist well known for his pro-Italian sentiments, but accused of "complicity in acts directed at revolt" by passing on

TABLE 11. *Use of Medical Facilities in Tripoli, 1931*

Medical Field	Jews	Arabs
Surgery	14,742	15,883
Medicine	3,226	1,986
Pediatrics	4,465	1,316
Ophthalmology	45,879	26,484
Venereal diseases	13,823	17,941
Total	82,135	63,610

to Jusuf Gurgi, an Arab nationalist, some letters which Abdessalam el-Busseiri, the secretary of the Gharian delegation in Rome, sent to Libya in early 1922.[22]

It should be added, in order to judge the Jewish attitude toward the Arab revolt accurately, that there were no cases of Jews taking an active part in the suppression of the revolt. Thus one can say that the attitude of the indigenous Jews was favorable to Italy during this period, but that they did not participate actively in the struggle against the rebels. The Jews wished not so much for the rebels to be "punished" and put down by force, as for them to lay down their arms and bring the fighting to an end. This explains why, despite the absence of cases of active Jewish participation in the struggle, there were cases of Jews who acted as intermediaries and mediators attempting to conclude partial accords and terms for honorable surrender, in other words contributing to restoring peace. Halfalla Nahum's facilitation of initial contacts and personal participation in negotiations between February and May 1919 at Sawani al-Biabsa are particularly important in this regard. He helped in negotiations at Khallat-az-Zaytun between General Giuseppe Tarditi and the leaders of the Tripolitanian Republic, negotiations leading to agreements from which the following June the Basic Law emerged. For his efforts, the Italian authorities gave Nahum the title of *commendatore.* Nahum used his personal ties with Abd-er-Rahman el-Azzam (subsequently secretary of the Arab League) and the Koober family. Events in Misurata in late 1919 are significant as well. Since the rebels refused to return some Italian prisoners, Governor Luigi Mercatelli had ordered trade with Zlitin, Misurata, and Syrte to be cut and the steam packet which had provided communication with them to stop calling. This caused serious problems for the local tradespeople, many of whom were Jews. That is why this class made an approach to the rebel chiefs, leading to the freeing of the Italian prisoners.[23]

Despite these nuances, there is no doubt that the Jews' attitude toward the revolt and its suppression did not cause Arab hostility to soften, nor did it elicit any gratitude. The Arab masses saw the Jews as friends of the Italians, and unworthy of the respect which force and whoever wields it command. They thus saw the Jews as enemies, or at least people profiting from the Arabs' misfortunes. Though less important than the other two, a third aspect of the problem should not be underestimated. This is the marginal but growing influence on Muslim-Jewish relations and on sections of the Arab masses at the time of a vaguely pan-Islamic attitude which could not be called anything more definite than that. At the same time, the Arabs were attentive and receptive to the growing Arab nationalist movements in other countries, particularly Palestine, where Jews and Arabs were adversaries. As we shall see, among Libyan Jews, particularly in Tripoli and Benghazi, Zionism was growing. Interest in and concern for fellow-Jews living in Muslim countries, particularly Palestine, were also growing and were often manifested in public expressions of opinion, which Italians supported in the pre-Fascist period.[24] Such pronouncements were bound to hurt the sensibilities of the more politicized and religiously extremist Arabs, or those most hostile to Jews.[25]

This latest deterioration in Muslim-Jewish relations did not cause a great stir. Its consequences, however, increased the unease, latent tension, and suspicion that were already clouding Arab-Jewish coexistence. Minor expressions of intolerance and petty spite were on the increase, especially on the side of the Arabs. These incidents generally took the form of brawls and scuffles between boys of the two communities, and adults were sometimes involved as well. In some schools in the hinterland these incidents were quite frequent "and on some occasions even took a violent turn."[26] In Tripoli and even more so in Benghazi, serious incidents took place during and after the period under discussion (for example, in June 1933). Their origins generally lay in some trivial act of provocation, which cannot be reconstructed precisely or in which it is difficult to distinguish whether the cause was latent hostility between the two communities or merely a common criminal act.[27] Sometimes the cause was oversensitivity toward the arrogant or derisive attitude of an Arab or Jew, and sometimes the unexpected spread of a marketplace brawl or one between boys. In most cases these conflicts were quelled promptly by the forces of authority, with an admonishment to the leaders of the two communities. This did not prevent them from recurring every so often. Such a point was reached in 1932 that the secretary of the Union of Italian Jewish Communities, summarizing for Felice Ravenna the news brought from Libya by a representative of Libyan Jewry, Babani Meghnagi, could express himself as follows: "Not a day passes without some scuffle with the Arabs; in fact, the situation today can be described as worse than before the Italian occupation."[28]

Here is a typical case of a fairly serious incident as it emerges from the report filed by the Tripoli correspondent of *Israel*, and published on October 10, 1927:

> On the eve of the Arab *Milud** (September 8 and 9) many groups of Arabs, no doubt organized, converged to attack the Jewish quarter from several parts of the city. They were following beacons made of barrels of tar and kerosene and were armed with sticks, clubs, and even worse weapons. The Arabs, whose purpose in coming to the Jewish quarter was to molest the Jews, soon began their provocative acts. The Jews were thus obliged to defend their lives, dignity and property in the face of a crowd of fanatics.
>
> Fortunately, the brawl did not last long, due to the effective intervention of some fascist *militi*† together with the duty officers assigned to the Jewish quarter and the prompt appearance of several patrols of metropolitan soldiers held in readiness in case the Arabs provoked any disorder.
>
> About twenty-five Arabs were arrested for disturbing the peace, about ten of them being referred to the judicial authorities. Two Jews were also arrested (perhaps because they defended themselves against the Arab aggression, as the Italians did in Tunisia when attacked in the same way). One of the Jews was referred to the judicial authorities. Several people were wounded in the fight: five Arabs, one Jew, and one policeman. The Jew, young Isacco Atton, was seriously wounded and is in the Colonial Hospital.
>
> We must wholeheartedly congratulate the Fascist *militi*, the royal

---

*The *Milud* is the birthday of the prophet Muhammad. He died on Monday, the twelfth of the First Rabi' and his birthday, the date of which is not known, has been arbitrarily placed on the same date. Generally known as *maulid* or *molid*, the festival began to be celebrated, according to Sunnite historians, in the year 1207. With the growth of Sufism in Egypt, the *maulid* took root there and spread relatively quickly to the rest of the Muslim world. It is a popular innovation which theologians were hesitant to approve, and consists of recitation of the Koran and stories of the prophet in verse (panegyrics known as *maulid* poems), processions, and feasting. For details, see G. E. von Grunebaum, *Muhammadan Festivals* (New York: Henry Schuman, 1951), pp. 73–77.—*Trans.*

†Members of the Fascist Voluntary Militia for National Security (Milizia Volontaria per la Sicurezza Nazionale), a military Fascist organization founded by a decree of March 25, 1923. Part of the *squadre d'azione* (action squads) defined as an armed sentinel of the Revolution. Its divisions had Roman names: legion, centuria, squadra. It was dissolved in 1943 by the Badoglio government after the fall of Fascism.—*Trans.*

*carabinieri** and the metropolitan troops for their effective intervention and the admirable patrol service which they have established and
maintain on a daily basis in the Jewish quarter.

Large patrols of soldiers and *militi* stand guard in the Jewish quarter
day and night, forming a real barrier, while in the streets inside there
are other, larger patrols continually inspecting the quarter, giving it the
appearance of a small town under siege.

The old customs house has been transformed into a small barracks
for changing the patrols. The public security authorities and the *carabinieri* have been inspecting the Jewish quarter continually.

As we write, the Italian soldiers are still mounting guard in the Jewish quarter for the strict and all the more necessary enforcement of law
and order.

Such serious incidents were generally quite rare. Usually their
origins lay, significantly, in the spread of news about events in Palestine or in a momentary reawakening of pan-Islamic sentiments
among the Arabs, following some event of importance to all Muslims, such as the outstanding Turkish successes against the Greeks
in Asia Minor in the autumn of 1922.

The most typical of the incidents which can be linked to the
Arab-Jewish conflict in Palestine occurred in Tripoli and Benghazi in
1920. The incidents in Tripoli were not serious, and the situation
was resolved by the guard protecting the *hara* being tripled for a few
days.[29] The incidents in Benghazi were much more serious. According to Gustavo Calò, the chief rabbi of Benghazi, who until a short
time before had been in Salonica, there was actually an attempted
pogrom; in the opinion of Elia Fargion, the president of the Community, who was better able to make a realistic judgment in view of his
longstanding familiarity with local conditions, this assessment was
exaggerated. The seriousness of the incidents is shown by the fact
that after quelling them the Italian authorities thought it necessary
to bring together the leaders of the two communities and have them
solemnly commit themselves in writing to preventing episodes of
the sort from being repeated. On May 3, commenting on this, Rabbi
Calò wrote to the Consortium† in Rome as follows:

*Derived from *carabina*—the weapon of soldiers. The Arma dei Carabinieri
was founded in 1791 in Piedmont by Vittorio Amedeo III, as a military police
force, and was refounded in 1814. In war it served either in combat (eg., Pastrengo,
1848) or as a police force. It is now responsible for enforcing laws and statutes,
for security, public order, and information, and serves in military police duties,
anti-espionage, honor guards, etc.—*Trans.*

†Consorzio delle Comunità Israelitiche Italiane [Consortium of Italian
Jewish Communities]; see note to p. 61 above.—*Trans.*

After the painful events on which I have touched, nothing else serious has happened, since the Arabs have seen that the government is willing to take serious steps and they have understood that it is not yet the right moment to defeat the authorities. The coincidence of the events here, though, with the fighting in Jerusalem* is curious and leads one to suspect that something was planned.

It is certain, though, that the agreement between Jews and Arabs is only for appearances' sake. The governor wished for a written compromise between Arabs and Jews, committing both sides to keep the peace and teach the people tolerance. Despite all this, scuffles still occur; insignificant in themselves, they indicate the degree of Arab intolerance, which perhaps is only waiting for the right moment to break out. The Arabs held a demonstration to protest the capture of Constantinople and we joined in it with them, saying that we desire respect for all religions.[30]

Since it comes from a Jew, making this connection between what happened in Benghazi and events in Palestine may seem somewhat forced and beside the point. However, there can be no doubts about what Alberto Monastero, the special government commissioner for the Community of Tripoli, wrote in the same vein nine years later. He was a conscientious Catholic official, then responsible for overseeing the Community. Referring to the current tension in Tripoli between Arabs and Jews and explaining to the president of the Consortium why he had forbidden all demonstrations and fundraising in support of the Jews of Palestine, who were involved in a bloody struggle with the Arabs, he summarized the situation as follows:

> The tragic events in Palestine had no less effect on the spirits of the Italian Jews of Tripolitania than on the Italian Jews of the Kingdom. This community, which responds as its fellow-communities in Italy do, would have liked from the beginning to express in the most solemn way its bitter sorrow, its sympathy for and solidarity with those who fell, and to demand sanctions and compensation. Personally, I would not have held the slightest difficulty in agreeing to and participating in such demonstrations myself.
>
> However, I had to consider that in Tripoli the Jews live together with a very numerous Arab population, largely ignorant and fanatical, which would have made any demonstration dangerous. Though Jewish demonstrations might not ignite here that destructive flame which we de-

---

*The causes of the Arab riots in Palestine may have been the Weismann-Faisal agreement of January 3, 1919, and the convening of the first of the Palestine Inquiry Commissions to examine the possibility of establishing a national home for the Jews, in accordance with the Balfour Declaration. In April 1920 Jewish settlements in Galilee were attacked, and in March 1921 there were anti-Jewish riots in Jerusalem (*Encyclopedia Judaica*).—*Trans.*

plore in Palestine, thanks to the Government's carefulness, they could certainly have fed a wave of hatred and resentment. Every Jew has the duty and interest to prevent this, for the sake of public order and to protect families. Here we must reinforce more than elsewhere the links between Jews and Arabs, for the sake of peaceful coexistence and joint progress under the Italian Standard.

These considerations led me to discourage those who wished to demonstrate and spontaneously began to collect funds, because it would not be possible to do these things covertly; also, references to the painful events in Eretz Israel would have incited the discontent of the Muslim population.[31]

Other incidents between Arabs and Jews will be discussed in later chapters, in connection with the effects which this state of tension and animosity had on internal Jewish relations, particularly the attitude of the Community leaders, and on relations between Jews and the Italian authorities, in both Libya and Italy. Discussing them in detail at this point would not be useful. What is important from a historical point of view is not the cataloguing of these events, one of which is like another, but what they implied on a general level. It is important to discover which elements in them were traditional and which were new, resulting from the new conditions produced by the hardening of the Italian-Arab conflict and the role that Libyan Jews were assuming in it, partly deliberately and partly involuntarily, for reasons inherent in the situation as well as the Jewish community's particular historical characteristics.

4. Life in the
Jewish Community

The previous chapter described the main repercussions which the Arab revolt and later the Italian reconquest had on Jewish life in Libya. This and the next will focus on two particular aspects of the history of Libyan Jews: first, the important internal developments within the community and, second, the relationships of the administrative organizations of the community with the Italian metropolitan and colonial authorities, as well as with leaders of Italian Jewry.[1] The time spanned by these two aspects goes beyond the period of the revolt and reconquest discussed in the last chapter. In fact, there is so much continuity between the period 1916–1931 and the years immediately following (up to 1938–1940) that any other division of time would be artificial. The period might safely be stretched to Italo Balbo's death in 1940, for as long as he was governor of Libya the condition of Libyan Jews did not undergo substantial change. However, we must also weigh what the Fascist government's adoption of racial policies in 1938 implied and how important it was to Jews in Libya. We must take into account as well the fact that the Fascists refrained from applying these policies to the Libyan Jews for a while thanks only to Balbo's political instincts and his humanitarianism. It should now be clear why I have preferred to break off discussion of the problems in this chapter and the next at 1938, at the very moment when the "racial policy" was officially being introduced in Italy.

Internal developments within Libyan Jewry and the community's external relations with the Italian authorities have a single, definite meaning when their general frame of reference is clearly sketched. The economic, social, and civil repercussions on the Libyan Jewish community of the events between 1915 and 1931 are an important component of this frame of reference. In order to appreciate them fully, they must be related to the effect of the Italian occupation on Libyan Jews. One can only understand the meaning of what was happening within the Libyan Jewish community between

1916 and 1938—and to some extent its relations with the Italian authorities—when one identifies the roots of both the internal developments and the external relations. These roots lay in the almost impalpable, slow, yet relentless sharpening of the problems, contradictions, and contrasts, particularly in the two main centers but above all in Tripoli. They were exacerbated by the new realities of the Italian occupation; specifically, the Jewish community's exposure to more and more direct confrontation with the modern Western way of life. In other words, the gulfs and divisions within the Jewish community between traditionalist and modernizing elements were deepening. Concern about the spread of centrifugal forces was also deepening, as were efforts to prevent pressures for integration and assimilation from growing. Efforts were also intensifying to preserve the spiritual and cultural integrity of Libyan Jewry without rejecting the Jews' development as citizens, their adaptation to the new conditions in Libya, and the opportunities for social progress thus opened for them.

Only when we see them from this viewpoint do all the major problems (ranging over the chief rabbinate, education, and the Sabbath) and new signs of cultural and organizational life (first and foremost, the spread of Zionism) fall into a coherent pattern. These problems and new phenomena that characterized Libyan Jewish life of the period were the subject of lively and heated discussions. They profoundly affected the existence and work of community organizations, as well as the community's relations with the colonial authorities and Italian Jewry. Similarly, only from this viewpoint can we grasp why this situation hardly changed in more than twenty years. No problem was really solved, and no response to any problem was really viable or effective. The result, especially in Tripoli, was that the one tendency which really took shape was the one which almost all the Jews deplored: a slow, yet under the circumstances irreparable splintering of the Libyan Jewish community into two camps, the traditionalists—mainly the poor and socially marginal— and the modernizers—mainly the rich and enterprising members of society. The two groups were linked on a religious and spiritual level in ways which grew more and more formal and perfunctory. The traditionalist group was destined in the long run to stagnation and isolation from the rest of Libyan society; the modernizing one was launched haphazardly along the course which the Jewish communities of Italy and central Western Europe had already taken.

Anyone today surveying with an unprejudiced eye the vicissitudes of Libyan Jewry during Italian colonization will agree that this was its path up to 1938, until the Fascist racial laws arrested these developments. In a sense, the community was subject to the same trends up to the postwar pogroms. The result of these was that the vast majority of poorer and more traditionalist Jews left for Israel. The pogroms also challenged the "Libyan identity" of many Libyan Jews—generally the younger members of the modernizing group—who had nourished the hope of being able to regard the new independent Libya as their homeland. One can also see that, rather than the Jews' desiring and consciously pursuing this tendency, outside circumstances imposed it on them. This was to some extent a result of Italian policy, but to a much greater extent the result of the forces of history itself. The tendency to emigrate was imposed by the modernization of Libyan society, and by having to choose among three possible identities: their identity as Libyan Jews, and the two main components of this, the Arab and Italian elements. These latter were both theoretically alien identities, but each in practice was accessible in a different way. Concretely, they offered two possible futures, attractive in widely differing ways.

There were a few individuals—"people ready to change their colors according to the situation"[2]—who for their own advantage attached themselves as much as they could to the Europeanized elements. Otherwise, a lively sense of tradition, reflected in both individual and community life, characterized Jewish life in Libya during the Italian period. Jewish life followed time-honored forms and was "entirely dominated in public and private by one law and one tradition." These were so tightly knit and interdependent that it was almost impossible to distinguish between the effects of Jewish law and tradition and outside influences resulting from centuries of contact with the surrounding Arab society.[3] Jewishness was "intense and shared by all"[4] and, on all levels, expressed itself in numberless ways. An intense, self-sufficient community life existed and developed independently of surrounding Arab or Italian society—hence, among other things, the extreme reluctance of the Jews of Tripoli to live outside the *hara*. In contrast with Jews in other Arab countries, Libyan Jews did not imitate outsiders, did not hide their Jewishness,[5] and had no doubt that they were an essential component of Libyan society. They believed that they had their own special characteristics and role in society, in no way inferior to the Arabs' role.[6] The Sabbath rest was strongly adhered to, as were dietary laws regarding meat and wine. Assimilation was practically nonexistent. Mixed marriages were extremely rare, and when they did occur almost always they involved Jewish women, hardly ever men. Everyone followed ritual practices. Rabbi Artom, illustrating the conditions of Jewish life in Tripoli in 1922, described religious life there as follows:

There are thirty public and private houses of prayer, which are half full even on civil holidays. The *hazanim* do not lead the services; always some member of the congregation spontaneously offers to do it. Discussions at the Community meetings are interrupted at the prescribed hours for Minhah and Arvit. These expressions of Jewish life take place in public, without the Jews feeling that they need to withdraw from the sight of outsiders. In all synagogues, prayers are conducted with the doors open onto the street; funerals wend their way through the streets to the singing of psalms and on special holy days the *sepharim* are solemnly carried in procession to the sound of Jewish melodies.[7]

Although obviously there were various ways of understanding and practicing this sense of tradition, it was shared by all, traditionalists and more modern Jews, rich and poor, the least educated and the most cultured. From this perspective, the real differences lay not within Libyan Jewry itself but between it and Italian Jews living in Libya. The contrasts and differences with regard to Italian Jews were clear. Even the richer, more cultured and "modern" Libyan Jews had much more in common with the Libyan Jewish mass than with metropolitan Jews.[8] They dressed like Europeans, adopted Italian culture, sent their children to Italian schools, lived outside the *hara*, mixed in colonial high society, and practiced a religion shorn of the originally Arab superstitions common among more traditional and unlettered Jews; despite all this, they remained *Libyans*, psychologically and morally linked to local traditions and expressions. They were substantially different from Italian Jews, who felt themselves to be Italian first and foremost and generally looked on Libyan Jews as underprivileged relatives who ought to be raised to their own level of civilization. What is more, the modernized Libyan Jews remained *Jews*, frequently combining their sense of local tradition with a thorough religious education no longer so common in Western Europe. In the twenties and thirties it was not unusual to find businessmen and rich merchants attending the *Yeshivot*, which the rabbis would hold on the Sabbath, and even inviting a few friends to their homes to study the Talmud together.[9]

Because of this conscious or unconscious cultural reality and basic moral commitment, individual attitudes toward the new situation caused by the Italian occupation subjectively differed little between traditionalists and modern Libyan Jews (except in special and untypical cases) and did so more on the formal and psychological levels than in substance. Those who were hostile to and flatly refused any form of interaction with the new situation (going as far as strongly discouraging families from sending their offspring to Italian schools) for fear that this might be to the detriment of their Jewishness and might lead Libyan Jewry down the path of integration and ultimately of assimilation, were a minority which in practice became more and more marginal. The majority did not reject interaction and, as we have seen, considered it inevitable, socially positive, and politically necessary. Divisions and differences arose principally in respect to two questions:

(a) How to overcome the problem, which was especially serious in Tripoli, of the large numbers of impoverished Jews without education or economic activity worthy of the name, living almost entirely off charity and begging, oscillating between a rigid and superstitious traditionalism and a lack of any real Jewish principles, and thus constituting a growing source of moral, economic, and political concern.

(b) How to overcome the negative consequences of interaction; in other words, how to prevent the contact with modern society and Italian culture from loosening the bonds with tradition, weakening the sense of Jewish identity, and thus launching an assimilative process, or more probably a process of spiritual and cultural hybridism, in Libya.

As we have seen, the problem had already appeared in the early years of Italian occupation. As time passed, however, the problem became more acute and obvious, as the situation in Libya emerged in the 1920s from the precariousness and uncertainty of wartime and of the immediate postwar period. Moreover, the progressive "pacification" of the country was involving the Jews of Libya to a greater and greater degree in the processes of transformation and Italianization of the colony.[10] Reduced to its essential terms, this process consisted of two aspects, the first cultural and the second political.

We shall limit discussion for the moment to the cultural aspect. Its nature is clearly expressed in a passage from Rabbi Artom's previously cited lecture of 1922 on Jewish life in Tripolitania and Libya:

> In such an atmosphere of persistent attachment to tradition, it may be said that assimilation does not exist. . . . But anyone who looks carefully beneath the surface may see that the process of decay has already begun and is making gradual headway. As long as the Jews had contact with Arabs alone, the danger practically did not exist, since the latter's lower level of culture held almost no attraction for the Jewish mind. The situation has changed since the Italian occupation, and a certain degree of imbalance, posing a threat to the very foundations of Jewish life, has been created.[11]

In order to appreciate the significance of Artom's words one must bear in mind that the problems were of two orders of magnitude. On the one hand, his words reflect certain events which had had broad repercussions in Libyan Jewish life, but which as individual cases did not seem such symptoms of crisis as to justify much alarm. A rare case of mixed marriage or prostitution, or of a butcher's selling ritually impure meat, a certain increase in the custom among impoverished women of working as servants in Christian homes, some increase in alcoholism and gambling, an occasional young man's habit of playing billiards in Italian bars and, in the worst extreme, cases of lack of respect for the Sabbath: all these could scandalize and arouse protest.[12] But viewed overall the episodes involved were so sporadic that, until the end of the twenties, these events were not in themselves enough to arouse real concern in a society being convulsed by the crisis in its ancient fabric which the Italian occupation provoked. On the other hand, there was justified cause for concern in the purely cultural conditions of Libyan Jewish life. These cultural conditions exacerbated the original problems, so that it could be assumed that if the conditions were to persist and intensify there would be a rapid increase in the number of such episodes.

Only by delving into the cultural conditions themselves can we understand the following:

(a) Why Libyan Jewry was so attached to its traditions and its Jewishness. This was despite the fact that the situation was from all accounts so serious and vulnerable to the long-term effects of the changes set in motion by the Italian occupation.

(b) Why the "threat" of which Artom spoke did not derive only from the "superiority" of the Italian culture confronting Libyan Jewish culture, but also and primarily from the fact that, on the mass level, what characterized Libyan Jewish life was less a truly Jewish culture than a sense of tradition.

Although, as has been said, the elements which a solid Jewish culture provides did in fact exist (in general, the fruit of a family education or private teaching by better-educated rabbis), among the masses the specifically Jewish cultural education of the Libyan Jews generally did not extend beyond what they had learned as children. This training, in the Talmud Torah or rabbinical schools, lasted from the age of six to the age of thirteen or occasionally to eighteen or twenty. I omit from mention those who were described as lacking practically any form of education, "Jewish or non-Jewish," and who were notable for their "unquestioning attachment to local customs and practices . . . which were completely foreign to Judaism."[13] Nor do I include the women, who, among the masses, did not receive any type of education, since by tradition and the influence of the Arab environment they were excluded from it and destined for marriage. Any parents who wanted their daughters to study had no other choice than to send them to Italian schools or, more and more seldom, to the Alliance schools.

In the Talmud Torah, as generally in the rabbinical schools, the instruction was utterly insufficient and superficial. The teachers were completely unendowed with modern culture and tied to antiquated teaching methods, while the material taught, consisting entirely of Jewish religion and learning by rote, was quite inadequate. It included no grammar, no history (not even Jewish history), and no languages, except for the Judeo-Arabic dialect and a little Hebrew. The Hebrew was hardly enough to recite the prayers and participate in public functions, and almost never sufficient to understand well what was being read. In practice the instruction amounted to spending six or seven hours a day chanting, translating the Parashah into Judeo-Arabic, and studying the Law.[14] We must bear in mind that for many this was their only form of education (those who continued their studies in the Yeshivot being a small minority) and that those who attended Italian schools[15] (simultaneously with the Talmud Torah or after attending it for a few years) encountered an entirely different and more stimulating world. It is obvious that the traditional type of education was unable to make room for an effective symbiosis of traditional Jewish culture and modern Italian culture. One may understand that, in the prevailing situation, the alternatives offered to the younger generation were almost utter ignorance, which entailed social marginality; complete cultural Italianization; or, the most common alternative, a sort of cultural hybridism. This last, from a Jewish point of view, could not fail to lead to a decline in religious devotion. Over time, all three alternatives would have inevitably rendered both the unifying value of the sense of tradition and the sense of Jewish identity itself continually weaker, more formalistic, and more superficial.

How serious this situation was emerged more and more over time, and particularly so in the mid-twenties. This was occurring just as Jewish life as a whole was taking a new turn due to the impact of the gradual pacification of the country, and as the basic outlines of Italian colonial policy were crystallizing. This policy was quite soon understood fairly clearly among more aware and responsible Jews, so that it became the focal point of the "politics" of the Jewish community in Tripoli after the First World War. It should be emphasized that all the important questions of the time—education, the question of the chief rabbi's appointment, and that of the

Sabbath—were directly or indirectly linked to this central issue of colonial policy.

The connection with the question of the Sabbath is obvious. Respect for the Sabbath rest, as well as being a religious duty of the first order, acquired due to its public nature the significance of a symbol; it was the most easily perceptible and indicative sign of how much Jews adhered to religion and tradition, and thus of their ability to resist the allurements and pressures of the outside world. This was the reason why the rabbis, the community officials, the more traditional elements, and the Zionists all wanted the Jews to respect it. In fact, until the early 1930s most Jews did respect the Sabbath. The few exceptions were almost all spontaneous lapses. Although some Italians and Arabs censured the Jews for their stubbornness in observing the Sabbath and criticized it as uneconomic and as hindering the development of normal social life (there were even some who saw it as an unwarranted form of competition with shopkeepers who did not open on Sundays), up to this time the government had made no real attempts to force the situation.[16]

The connection with the question of the chief rabbinate is also clear. This problem, in turn, was associated with several others, in particular that of the rabbinical court, and in course of time with the problem of establishing a chief rabbinate with jurisdiction over Libya as a whole. Unlike the question of Sabbath observance, however, this one was already complicated in its premises by the importance which the Italian central and colonial authorities also gave to the chief rabbi's appointment. This explains its particular significance and delicacy and why it quickly also involved the central organs of the Italian Jewish community. Italian Jewish organizations, particularly those involved in matters of civil status, had substantially refrained until the early thirties from involving themselves deeply in the internal problems of their coreligionists overseas.

Under the conditions of Libyan Jewish life, the presence of an Italian chief rabbi in Tripoli acquired particular significance. Beyond considerations of local politics, individual jealousies, and individual or group power maneuvers, which should not be underestimated, it is clear that the presence of an Italian chief rabbi, to whatever extent he might combine the qualities of both an orthodox and a political appointee, was a fact which had to have a profound impact as a force for transformation and, ultimately, "modernization." Hence the lively polemics and differences of opinion, in public and especially behind closed doors, which the question of the chief rabbi's appointment aroused over a long period, even, as we have said, involving the leaders of Italian Jewry. These leaders, for their part, were unable to adopt a really firm and coherent position on the subject, and more than once complicated it with their own schisms and political misgivings about the candidates. In the mid-thirties the question provoked a serious crisis with the Italian colonial authorities, who originally, in the Liberal-Democratic period[17] and even in the Fascist period[18], had tried to facilitate a solution to the problem.

The modernizers, more aware of how serious the situation of Libyan Jewry was and of the steps which would have to be taken in order to cope with it practically, were favorable to the appointment of an Italian chief rabbi. These elements would have liked to have a chief rabbi not only in Tripoli (where his presence was required by the 1916 statutes) but also in Benghazi. Among those favoring an Italian, the Zionists and young people influenced by them were predominant. To them the appointment of an Italian chief rabbi meant that the community would at last possess a religious and moral focal point in an individual who would be educated and aware in both the Jewish and the modern Western spheres, and who might be a force for integration and provide the encouragement needed for a true renewal and cultural modernization of Libyan Judaism along clear Jewish and Zionist lines. The previously mentioned memorandum which the Circolo Sion drafted in 1918 and sent to the Italian Jewish Universities Committee and *Israel* is significant in regard to this proposal. For the Circolo Sion, there were only two possible ways of finding a solution to the crisis in Tripolitanian Jewry: to reform the Talmud Torah and to immediately appoint "a chief rabbi who would take initiatives, someone endowed with a well-grounded and thorough Jewish and non-Jewish education, both a Zionist and scrupulously observant in Jewish life." In other words, an Italian rabbi was required, not only because the statutes of two years earlier stipulated it, but also because there was no Libyan rabbi possessing those qualities. We read in this same memorandum that even the acting chief rabbi at that time did not possess "the ability to be even an ordinary rabbi" and that "certain personages" (the reference was clearly to the notables of the community) "though fully aware of this, desired and officially tolerated" his presence because they were submissive toward him.[19]

Those who, through conviction or opportunism, opposed this view were much more numerous. Among the latter were a good proportion of the notables of the community. Some were against the appointment of an Italian because they feared opposing the local rabbis and the sentiments of many of their fellow Jews (and electors), and others because they wished to prevent any interference in their own way of running the community. The rest had many motives. The spectrum ran from the extreme traditionalists, for whom nothing should be changed and an Italian rabbi would be little else than a heretic, to those who viewed the appointment purely as a government imposition, moreover a discriminatory one, since nothing of the sort was imposed on Muslims. There were those who based their hostility on the differences in culture and tradition between Italian and Libyan Jews and the fact that an Italian would not know the local language. Finally, there were those—and they were many, especially among the masses—who still viewed the position of chief rabbi in the same terms and as having the same functions as the *hakham bashi* did in the Ottoman period—in practice, a sort of representative of the Community to the government rather than a spiritual leader. They considered the office as practically useless in the new politico-administrative situation and above all a considerable burden on the Community's budget.

The task was to find a suitable Italian rabbi who would be willing to move to the colonies, acceptable to the Italian Jewish leadership, to that of the Community of Tripoli, and to the Italian authorities.[20] It was obviously almost impossible in such a climate of opinion to find a candidate who, possessing all these qualifications, could weather all sorts of hostility, suspicion, difficulties, and power maneuvering. The impossibility is proved by the fact that after the initial contacts immediately following the Italian occupation, interrupted by the need to wait for the government regulation and then by the war, the position was not filled until mid-1920, when Elia Samuele Artom became chief rabbi.[21] However, a little over three years later when Artom felt obliged to resign, the problem arose again. The official reason for his resignation was the Community's initial hesitation and subsequent refusal to give him a contract for a reasonable period of time. The fact was that, despite his personal talents and the trust which the Zionists, Zionist sympathizers, and, at least initially, the governor[22] had in him, Artom did not succeed in gaining support. He did not manage to make inroads among the more traditional elements even though he was accused of being too conservative. He did not win respect for his position from the masses, nor was he accepted by the majority of the Community leaders.[23] In the meantime, a silent power struggle had been unleashed around him.[24] After Artom's return to Italy, the position in Tripoli remained vacant until 1930. Then the Consortium was obliged to take vigorous action under pressure from the Ministry of Colonies, at the time of yet another and more serious crisis in the community. Putting an end to the laborious search for a candidate who would be welcome to all parties, the Consortium sent the assistant rabbi of Turin, Dario Disegni, to Tripoli as visiting rabbi. He had the support of Emilio De Bono, the minister, and was sent to take responsibility for "the religious reorganization of the Tripoli Community and to study and find a solution for the most important problems."[25] Disegni was no more successful than his predecessor. He tried to reorganize certain cultural institutions and make them more effective, promote the cultural and professional education of women, and encourage the genesis of a Jewish periodical, *il messaggero israelitico* [The Jewish Messenger], which survived for less than a year.[26] Thus it cannot be said that, on his return to Italy in March 1931, the situation had changed substantially. All the outstanding problems with which the chief rabbi should have dealt remained unresolved,[27] while their harmful effects on Libyan Jewish life in general and life in Tripoli in particular became ever more apparent. A new attitude on the part of the Italian administration toward the Jews and their Community was maturing, partly out of discouragement and partly because of broader political considerations. The new attitude was harsher, less understanding of the Jews' problems, and more prone to direct intervention.

Twenty years after the beginning of the Italian occupation, the problem of the chief rabbi's appointment was therefore almost back at its starting point. The Consortium was searching vainly for the "right man" without succeeding in finding him, and in the process of displeasing almost everyone, both those who wanted to find one and those who did not. The only difference was that twenty years later the context of the problem had deteriorated considerably. The situation from then on was bound up with a series of crises which had to be weathered and whose roots lay to a large extent in matters beyond the Jews' control—the impact of modern realities and Italian colonial policy on local Jewish life. Some of their roots also lay in the community's twenty years of inability and unwillingness to face up to the situation. In March 1933, the first Congress of the Union of Italian Jewish Communities discussed the Libyan situation at length, without reaching any definite conclusion.[28] The tones of the discussion were reproachful and somewhat critical of the Consortium, on the side of the Libyan delegates. Thus the position of chief rabbi of Tripoli was still vacant when events took over, following the incidents of June 1933, which, as we shall see, occurred in an atmosphere already turbulent due to the Sabbath problem in the schools. In all haste, the "right man" was then finally found in the person of the rabbi of Padua, Gustavo Castelbolognesi. As we shall see, however, the situation had already deteriorated too far for one man, even one of such distinction as Castelbolognesi, to cope with it without displeasing almost all the parties to the problem. Finding himself almost completely devoid of supporters among the powerful Libyans and not wishing to fail those to whom he considered that he owed his first duty, the new chief rabbi eventually came into conflict with the Italian authorities as well, until he was expelled from the colony unceremoniously.

The Castelbolognesi affair did not resolve the matter of the choice of a chief rabbi. In March 1937, the Union of Italian Jewish Communities dispatched a new chief rabbi to Libya, Aldo Lattes, who remained in office until the Second World War.

The succession of appointees is indicative of the negative effects which the inability to solve the problem had on the situation as a whole. The continued presence, spiritual leadership, and actions of one chief rabbi could have provided the impulse for a real change in the cultural conditions of Jewish life in Tripoli and in Libya as a whole. He would also have been the best intermediary between Libyan Jewry and the Italian colonial authorities. The office might have served this latter purpose because the chief rabbi could have played a Jewishly committed role by harmonizing traditional and modern forces, while remaining above local factional differences. Lacking this continuous presence, the cultural problem remained in the hands of merely local initiatives, which were unable to solve it and often inherently contradictory. The problem thus remained substantially unresolved, while relations with the colonial authorities, in the absence of mutual understanding, grew worse and worse until they degenerated into an absurd confrontation over an entirely secondary issue.

We will be able to understand the internal political life of the Libyan Jewish community in all its complexity only if we are aware of its cultural conditions. This is particularly true of Jewish politics in Tripoli and how they affected relations with the Italian authorities. The problem of education is the third and last major issue linked to the cultural aspects of the situation. As is obvious, we must view it from the specifically Jewish viewpoint rather than in the general terms which were applied in the previous chapter. Obviously, from the point of view of commitment to Jewish tradition, the rise in the number of Jews attending Italian public schools during these years was not an entirely positive development.

Rather than painstakingly reconstructing particular details, it is preferable to grasp the essential outlines. The question of education arose on two different levels: that of the Jewish schools, in practice the Talmud Torah, and that of the Italian public schools.

In addition to the Jewish schools' inability to meet the needs of most of their potential pupils, the schools were afflicted, as we have seen, with two basic ills: the curriculum and the teachers. From this fact arose the need, which was broadly felt, though there was some strong opposition to it, for a radical reform of the curriculum. It had to be adequate to meet new needs, from both the Jewish religious point of view and the modern and social one. A completely new teaching body was also needed. It is obvious that before a true reform of the curriculum could be carried out, teachers capable of applying the reform had to be found. Since these were lacking and could not be found in Italy (principally because Italians did not know the language), they would have to be trained. But in order to do this, skilled professors were needed. Thus the problem was practically unsolvable, at least within a reasonable period of time. At first the Jews thought that they could solve it by bringing a few teachers from Palestine, where some young Jews knew Italian. The project was soon allowed to drop, however, both because of greater difficulties than anticipated and because the Italian authorities showed that they did not approve. In the mid-twenties, the idea arose of sending a number of young Libyans to study in the Jewish teachers' training colleges in Palestine, "so that after a while there would be a sufficient number of teachers in Tripoli capable of providing the new impetus that the times and the renewed hopes of the Jewish people asked of the Community's schools."[29] This plan as well, however, turned out to be unworkable, since the expenses entailed could not be met. And so, in the early thirties, the community finally directed its efforts, under the leadership of Disegni, toward sending the needed number of young men to Italy. In Florence they would be able to attend both teachers' training classes and courses at the rabbinical college. But even this initiative ended in failure. To meet the needs of Tripolitania alone, it would have been necessary to send twenty or thirty young men to Florence, laying a financial burden on the Community of from 2,500 to 3,000 lire per student per year. In 1931 three of the most promising young Tripolitanians were sent. The experiment was far from successful. Partly because they had difficulties in acclimatizing themselves, partly because they were not committed to learning, the three disappointed the hopes placed in them and returned to Tripoli without completing their studies. This result, together with the colonial minister's refusal to provide matching funds, marked the end of the experiment. The provision of 800,000 lire over seven years would have enabled forty-eight young men to study in Florence. The minister's refusal was motivated by the two-edged argument that a teachers' training college had been opened in

Tripoli in 1932 and that Jewish teachers should restrict themselves to religious education. The failure marked the end of attempts to form a pool of local Jewish teachers qualified not only in Italian but also in Jewish studies.[30]

Proposals for curriculum reform did not meet any better fate. The Tripoli Community had been involved in these plans since 1917–1918, immediately after electing its first council according to the 1916 regulations. It emerges in a letter dated January 18, 1918, from Halfalla Nahum to Angelo Sereni,[31] that the plan was to set up a Jewish school parallel to the Talmud Torah. It would offer the same curriculum as the Italian elementary schools and, in addition, a series of subjects such as Hebrew language, literature, and history, which would be given equivalency by the Italian authorities. Somewhat illogically, and despite requests, this solution was not to affect the Talmud Torah in the least. The official explanation is to be found in Nahum's speech of August 11, 1917, outlining the syllabus. The justification was that other concerns, including not alienating the traditionalists, who gave a fair amount of the funds, and the more directly political concern of not alienating certain groups of voters, should be taken into account in finding a solution.

Nahum's speech was delivered at the inauguration of the recently elected community council. The Talmud Torah had been born in 1893 in order to save the poorest children from begging and crime by putting them under the care of volunteers in various synagogues.[32] In a short time it had acquired such importance and widespread influence (even beyond Tripoli) that subsequently a group of rich benefactors (since deceased) had donated a suitable building. However they imposed the condition, accepted by the Community, that in the building "no subjects other than religion should ever be taught for any reason." In the face of this freely accepted condition, the Community could do nothing:

> The wishes of the deceased, whether they be right or wrong, and the conditions of those who have made gifts, are and shall remain sacred, and no leader of the community shall dare to modify them. Respect for these conditions is a duty for each and every citizen, an obligation for every moral person. The execution of their wishes is a guarantee for contributors and for society. It encourages benefactors, since it assures them that their wishes will never be contravened, and that their conditions will always be met.

The best that could be done to reconcile changing needs with respect for the donors' wishes was to improvise. In view of the growing numbers of children attending the Talmud Torah, it had been necessary to open an annex in a building other than the one which had been donated. It ought therefore to have been possible to organize shifts for studying Italian.[33] Such a solution was extremely difficult to put into practice, however; to bring into being a Jewish school which would be parallel to the state school was in fact impossible. There were no capable teachers, and the financial burden would have been onerous, while the Italian authorities would have been loath to accept the school. Anything less than radical reform of the Talmud Torah meant giving up from the start the chance of having a school to integrate Jewish culture with Italian and provide a counterbalance to the public schools—one toward which the more gifted youth and those belonging to the better-off families might have increasingly been swayed.

It is no cause for surprise that this solution had practically been abandoned by 1920. Nor is it surprising that, while discussions continued regarding possible reform of the Talmud Torah,[34] the Jews hoped to win permission from the Italian authorities to arrange afternoon classes in elementary civic education. This would combine the Talmud Torah classes and intensive experimental two-year courses (for fifty boys) reserved for the best pupils of the Talmud Torah, allowing them to obtain the *licenza elementare* [certificate of graduation from elementary school].[35]

This shift was the kernel of the Community's new education policy in the 1920s; the radical school reform programs were set aside and the emphasis was put on reaching an agreement with the Italian administration which would allow at least the elementary public schools to serve Jewish needs. This idea, supported by the publication *Israel*,[36] began to acquire shape toward the close of 1921. It is only a short step to the statements of Giovanni Amendola in the Italian Senate on the need to study a new type of school for the Arabs "in which European culture would by stages be associated with Arab culture" while taking due account of the Arabs' religious needs and traditions.[37] This type of plan must have seemed the one best able to resolve the problem of Jewish education.

Real thought began to be given to an Italian-Jewish school, within the state school system but distinct, with its own syllabus and Jewish teachers. It was roughly equivalent to Halfalla Nahum's 1918 plan, integrated into the Italian education system. A plan of this type, drafted by Isacco Sciaky, was presented in 1925 to the Office of the Superintendent of Schools for Tripolitania by the then president of the Community, Simeon Haggiag.[38] However, since the political climate had meanwhile been determined by Fascism's rise to power, the Italian administration could not accept a request of this sort. One reason was that the authorities were creating a centralized system. Another clearly emerges from a document written by the superintendent of schools for Tripoli, which not surprisingly provoked an energetic reply from *Israel*.[39] The authorities did want to raise the Libyan Jews "from the condition of spiritual disadvantage which age-long servitude has imposed on them" but "without unduly raising their pride or exciting their ambitions."[40] The authorities must have thought that the Community's request was inspired by precisely those feelings.

What the Jewish Community did achieve in 1927 was that, in state schools where Jewish pupils were most numerous, special experimental classes including Hebrew were set up. As we see, this was not a great deal to achieve, but it was sufficient for the Community in later years to request and obtain more of these special classes, basing its argument on the numbers of the children who could not attend state schools for lack of space. In 1931–1932 four classes were opened for about two hundred pupils. Although this certainly did not solve the problem, the classes did serve to give young people the basics of Hebrew language and also, indirectly, some basics of Jewish history and literature, since the Hebrew teachers were Jewish. Many of them were rabbis who also taught.[41]

This picture of the problem of education will not be complete unless we mention the Zionists' part in efforts to find a solution. Their contribution was an important one. As in the case of the Sabbath question and that of the chief rabbi's appointment, the Zionists helped to awaken public opinion and foster community organizations, i.e., they played a political as well as cultural role, since they took concrete initiatives to complement official actions.

According to present documentation, the Zionists' earliest contacts with individual Jews and the Libyan Jewish community go back to the beginning of the century. However, the first nucleus which they organized, the Circolo Sion, did not emerge in Tripoli until the spring of 1916.[42] It was brought into being by Elia Nhaisi, a young photographer and correspondent of Israel, and a group of his contemporaries. In its wake, riding on the enthusiasm aroused by the Balfour Declaration and the liberation of Palestine from Ottoman rule, the Circolo Herzl [Herzl Club] emerged in Benghazi in 1919. Its first promoters were Renato Tesciuba and Benedetto Raccah.

The birth in Tripoli of the Circolo Sion, whose major supporters, besides Nhaisi, were Raffaele Barda, Felice Nahum, Raffaele Arbib, Quintino Guetta, and Raffaele Meghnagi, had been something of a struggle. A first attempt, in February 1913, had failed before producing anything concrete. A second attempt, the following year, under the guise of a cultural club to promote a renaissance of the Hebrew language and Jewish culture, likewise after limping along for a short while failed for lack of official Community support. To launch the endeavor, Nhaisi and his friends had to take their cause onto the high seas of politics, perhaps more than many of them intended. They entered the running against the Community leaders in 1915, offering themselves as the only real alternative to those leaders.

This first sally took place not only on the level of culture and ideas, but also on the level of aggressive political action. It occurred just before a period of great tension, and political and social upheavals which were bound to have repercussions among the Jews of Libya. It is therefore important for an understanding of the vicissitudes of Tripolitanian Zionism and its reflection in the rest of Libya. On the one hand, on a general level the move into the political arena doubtless favored the proselytizing activities of the Circolo Sion. By 1919 it already had about three hundred members, compared with thirty or so in 1916. The political activity enabled it to attract into its orbit Jews whom it would otherwise have had difficulty in influencing. On the other hand, the political activities markedly affected its image, creating an atmosphere different from that generally surrounding Zionism in other countries. For several years, many Libyan Jews who judged it through the Circolo Sion saw Zionism as morally desirable in theory and corresponding to a profound Jewish need, but in practice factious, divisive, and potentially dangerous from a political and sometimes even from a social point of view. This attitude explains the resistance and sporadic hostility which Zionist activism (as distinct from Zionism as an ideal) long encountered. It explains the crisis which befell the Circolo Sion after the period of greatest political and social effervescence. It is also significant that between 1918 and 1925 first Nhaisi and then Barda, its major exponents, died. Finally, it explains the concern of many prominent figures in Libyan Jewry, once Fascism had emerged, not to show much sympathy toward Zionism This political activism explains why, being fully committed in the political struggle within the Community, the Circolo Sion was only partly successful in putting into practice its educational program. It did, however, achieve good results in other areas, from that of mutual assistance (promoting two mutual aid societies, one for bricklayers and carpenters and one for shoemakers) to the area of sports (creating the Bene Sion club). Due to the efforts of Gabriele Barda and Roberto Arbib, the Bene Sion developed into the Maccabee Club, which began to publish its own bulletin, the *Diana dei Maccabie* [Maccabee Reveille] in 1932. It was very active and successful in popularizing most of the main individual and team sports among Jewish youth. Libyan Jews participated in the second Maccabiah* in polo, swimming, running, tennis, and ping-pong. The Circolo Sion was also active both in the cultural sphere (organizing conferences, entertainments, and a library) and in the sphere of emigration to Palestine. Its success in the latter was purely organizational. The operation ended in partial failure,[43] since its main target had been the unemployed in whom the desire to find immediate full-time employment was often stronger than the Zionist ideal. In practice all the Circolo Sion managed to do on an educational level was to organize a few evening classes in Hebrew in late 1919.

The real contribution which the Zionists made to solving the problem of education came later than the experience of the Circolo Sion. It disbanded in 1924 following a crisis lasting more than two years which put it in serious political and organizational difficulties. In attempting to overcome this crisis, the leaders of the Circolo Sion were obliged in 1923 to accept the viewpoint of Chief Rabbi Artom and of Abraham Elmaleh, the Jewish National Fund's envoy from Jerusalem. The Circolo submitted to their pressure to make peace with its opponent which had emerged a year earlier, Associazione Concordia e Progresso [Peace and Progress Association]. This expedient served only to stem the crisis, however. In early 1924 the Circolo was obliged to accept the fusing of the two organizations[44] under the auspices of Rabbi David Prato. He had been sent from Italy to make peace and bring order to Libyan Zionist ranks, which were now almost running amuck. The rebirth of Tripolitanian and Libyan Zionism and the constitution of the Zionist Organization of Tripolitania (OST) were a result of this fusion. They also resulted from a series of actions by the World Zionist Federation and the Italian Zionist movement, most importantly the campaigns for "Zionist reawakening and reconstruction" undertaken in 1925 and 1926 by Isacco Sciaky and in 1928 by Umberto Nahon. The Tripolitanian organization was closely linked to the Italian one. The latter was apolitical, oriented toward culture, youth, and sports activities, aid and collecting contributions for the Jewish National Fund, Keren Hayesod,† and other initiatives supporting settlement in Palestine.[45] It took more than five years to revive Zionism in Tripolitania. As well as practical aspects of organization, it was necessary during this time to solve old and new internal disagreements,[46] dispel the suspicions and fears of those outside, and find a *modus vivendi* with ex-

*Games held in Palestine for Jews from all countries.—*Trans.*

†Organization founded in London in 1920 to collect and distribute funds to encourage settlement.—*Trans.*

isting community organizations. An important success in dispelling fear was achieved in 1928 when the Union of Jewish Associations of Tripoli was established and, although not officially Zionist in nature, was put under the aegis of the OST.

It is hardly surprising that in this state of affairs the OST, which in fact had its own fairly active cultural arm in the Ben Yehuda, could until the late twenties make only marginal inroads on the problems of education. It discussed these problems and urged the community not to overlook them, but could not make any positive contribution of its own to solving them. The OST could not devote itself to education until it had consolidated itself. It entrusted the Ben Yehuda group with organizing and managing its own evening school (HaTikva School) in which ethics (religion), Hebrew language and history, civil education, and physical training were taught. It turned to the few available teachers, particularly the better-educated young people of the Ben Yehuda group itself, who would be capable of giving modern instruction, and gave them training in culture and teaching methods. The initiative soon achieved great success. In the first two years of somewhat experimental activities, 1931–1932 and 1932–1933, directed by Ammisciaddai Guetta, school attendance stood at 512 (134 boys and 378 girls) and 573 (221 boys and 352 girls) respectively. The pupils were divided into eight classes, three for boys and five for girls.[47] In the next few years, the number of students and thus of classes increased until in 1935–1936 there were 867 pupils registered (396 boys and 498 girls). The range of activities also broadened: in 1933–1934 two kindergarten classes, and the following year three, were added; in 1935–1936 evening classes for those attending the Italian schools; and in 1937–1938 a course in Italian culture.[48] Extension classes were set up in al-Khums and Zlitin, and the Ben Yehuda group set up similar classes in Benghazi. Nor should the activities of the Women's Workshop be forgotten. Although it was not a direct branch of the OST, largely because of the organization's interest and support the workshop, which had repeatedly failed to get off the ground in the previous twenty years, finally began to function successfully in 1934. Approximately 150 women, including many girls, attended its courses in tailoring, sewing, embroidery, and knitting.

The story of the Zionist contribution to dealing with the problem of education requires a few more general comments, which may serve to introduce the discussion of actual Jewish community politics in Tripoli and Libya as a whole. One should never forget that whatever happened in Tripoli was also happening in Benghazi and the other smaller Libyan towns. In Tripoli, however, all the expressions of these same events, problems, differences, and so forth, were more strident and attention-catching. They had greater repercussions and left behind fuller documentation, since all the problems underlying them were more acute. This was due to the much greater number of individuals involved, the greater economic and social weight of Jews in Tripoli, and the fact that the Tripoli community was the heart of Libyan Jewry. Its major religious, economic, and political figures resided in Tripoli, while in Tripoli also the most cohesive nucleus of modern Jewish intellectual life was coming into being (this group of intellectuals, moreover, was a magnet to other individuals, most of them from Benghazi, and induced them sooner or later to move to Tripoli). The only Jewish newspapers in the colony were published in Tripoli, and it was from there that the major, earliest, and often the only important direct contacts with Italian Jewry, Jewish international organizations, and those of other countries were made. In Tripoli, finally, there developed the true relations, those which really counted, with the Italian colonial authorities, and through them with Rome.

These developments express a fundamental difference between the situation at the end of the First World War and the situation at the beginning of the thirties. It would be simplistic to attribute this difference only or essentially to the internal vicissitudes of the Zionist movement. The OST achieved positive results, in education as in all the fields in which it was active, despite an active membership of around fifty at the most. The movement's success cannot be explained only through its maturing or the members' activism, cultural preparation, clear ideas, and spirit of sacrifice. Nor should one give excessive importance to the constant attention and political, moral, and technical support which the OST received from the Italian and Palestinian Zionist organizations. This support gave Libyans the tangible feeling of participating in a broad and active movement—something which could not be said about the always ambiguous, paternalistic, and erratic attitude to the Libyan communities of the Consortium and its successor, the Union of Italian Jewish Communities. All of this counted a lot. The basic reason for the difference between the two situations can be found, however, in the change in the general climate which characterized Jewish political and community life in Libya, particularly in Tripoli, in these two periods. The change could be seen in all expressions of Jewish life, not least in the Zionist movement. If this latter was indeed able to make an important contribution to Libyan Jewry, it was due to the changed general climate. As in all communities, Libyan Jews disagreed over many things. However, the fact is that their differences reached an exceptionally high level in the period immediately following the end of the First World War, a period unique in the number of disputes affecting and paralyzing the whole of community public life. In the thirties, though there were differences, community public life was characterized mainly by a coordinated effort to face problems and difficulties together, each one using the tools available to him, and his own possibilities for action.

During the earlier period, roughly from 1915–1916 to 1923–1924, the general climate was one of overall uncertainty and unease, both conscious and unconscious, with regard to almost all the issues. Anxiety extended from the problem of the future of Libya itself and thus of the position of Libyan Jews, to socioeconomic difficulties, and even more generally to the moral and cultural prospects of the community and the individuals composing it. To this state of uncertainty and anxiety were added the longer-range but no less clear signals penetrating from the world situation. They bore with them the suggestions, hopes, and passions let loose in Europe by the war and the subsequent sociopolitical crisis. One can therefore understand how powerful the tensions racking public life in the Tripoli community—and other communities as well—at that time were. One realizes that it was these very tensions and the proliferation of ensuing causes for dispute which to a large extent determined the semiparalysis of community organizations. These tensions were therefore the cause of the souring of the most serious current problems, at the very moment when it was most necessary to think clearly and seek solutions together.

We have seen that there were some cases after the war of Libyan Jews who initially favored a political solution to the Arab-Italian conflict and accepted as a first step the prospects which the Basic Law of 1919 envisaged. These cases were few, though, and almost all changed their minds. It became obvious later that the agreement could not be implemented and the policy of the Arab nationalist movement revealed itself to be a basically Muslim and pan-Islamic one. Cases of Jews taking an active part in the conflicts and political groupings characterizing Tripolitania and to a lesser extent Cyrenaica were at the time even rarer and have no significance except on an individual level. The exception was Benghazi, since Elia Fargion, the president of its Jewish Community, became a member of the Cyrenaican Parliament in 1921, and the majority of local Jewish leaders publicly supported the Italian Liberal-Democratic parties. Fargion was one of the figures closest to Italy. For many years from 1899 on he had headed the Benghazi agency of the Compagnia di Navigazione Florio-Rubattino [Florio-Rubattino Shipping Company]; later he became one of the founders of the local branch of the Dante Society, and then discount manager of the Bank of Italy. Elsewhere, cases of Libyan Jews (other than Italians) supporting Italian political groupings were few and of little significance.

It is easy to understand why Libyan Jews had little reaction to general political developments. The masses had two main motives:

(1) The alienation of the Libyan Jew from conflicts which, because of his long-time marginality and particularism, he believed did not involve him directly. Instinctively mistrusting such conflicts, he avoided identifying with either the Italians or the Arabs.

(2) The strong influence of traditional culture among the masses and the opinions which the rabbis expressed, leading the Jews to view the ideologies underlying the political parties as a threat to the coherence of their own Jewish world.

Among the elite—especially the young—these motives bore less weight. Other reasons produced the same attitude.

(1) One was traditional acceptance of and deference to authority, heightened by the elite's new conviction that an Arab state would imply a step backward in the Jews' civil rights. This traditional attitude was also bolstered by the fear that to take a stand regarding the differences among Italian parties might disturb the Jews' relations with Italian officialdom and expose them to possible persecution or revenge. Above all, this stand might jeopardize what they valued most: their administrative autonomy and the Community's right to govern itself. One sign of this way of thinking was that, unlike the Arabs, the Libyan Jews—though they could have done so—never established relations with politicians or parties in Italy with a view to involving the Italians and soliciting their help in Libyan Jewish problems.

(2) The other reason was the first priority which the Jewish elite felt it had to give to the problems of its own people over "external" problems. One cannot say whether this was done from conviction or calculation—the two were so closely linked as to form a single cultural element, fed by both the oldest traditions and the latest Zionist ideals.

Though they stayed outside Libyan politics, the Jews did have their own political life in the 1920s and 1930s. Such political life was lively everywhere, but particularly frenzied in Tripoli.

Community power—who was to control the agencies running the Community, which had been formally set up in 1916—was the issue. But behind this immediate objective, there lay differing—if unclear—concepts of the power and the prospects of Libyan Jewry.

The notables of the Jewish community of Tripoli (and Libyan

Jewish notables in general) saw power in a traditional, almost paternalistic way. The elections held on December 15, 1918, were the
first to have competing lists of candidates. Significantly, the notables chose a biblical verse (Deuteronomy 1:13) as their political
slogan: "Take you wise men, and understanding, and known among
your tribes, and I will make them rulers over you." Political power
was a duty and right which fell to the wisest (hence the eldest or
most mature) and the richest. In a way, power was seen as a form of
recognition given to those who possessed these attributes, since
they had connections with the authorities and so were best able to
represent the community. They wielded the influence and ability
(and usually the culture) to guide the community. When necessary
they underwrote the Community's finances from their own pockets,
"knowing that the Community could give them no material guarantee."[49] It was also the notables who, above all, assumed the burden of
public charity and set up legacies for religious activities and services. Power in this sense revolved about a few families. Inevitably,
the struggle for power became a bitter interpersonal struggle whose
aim was to affirm the preeminence of one family (and those linked
to it) over another. In the 1920s and 1930s, the feuding families were
those of Halfalla Nahum and Simeone Haggiag. Again, this is not to
imply that the consensus of views grouped around each family name
failed to reflect more political and particularly sociological and cultural motivations. In this case, the circle focusing on Nahum represented the old leadership of Tripoli, closely linked to local traditions,
though combined with a good, solid Jewish and modern culture. The
group focusing on Haggiag was the new leadership. Many of its
members had settled in Tripoli only decades before. Not only were
they more modern in their culture but they also showed a degree of
open-mindedness that the others failed to understand. From a political viewpoint, Nahum—certainly the most outstanding figure in
contemporary Libyan Jewish life—cared deeply about his followers
and took seriously his responsibilities as a leader, just as he did his
own prestige and dignity. At one stage, when he felt that the fight
was becoming too "low" and mean for his taste, he chose to distance
himself from it. Nahum had a more cautious and traditional view of
community problems than Haggiag, and a less open-minded and
original one. He was less favorable to political Zionism, which Haggiag—the more flexible politician—was not above exploiting. Nahum thought that Zionism might disturb Jewish relations with the
Italian authorities. He paid more attention than Haggiag to Jewish-
Arab relations, and in general had a more realistic idea of the actual
needs and underlying problems of Libyan Jewish life. One expression

of this was Nahum's opposition to building a great synagogue to exalt "the strength of Israel," and another his belief that Jews ought to take up farming.[50] These clusters of agreements on various issues did not lead to the formation of anything resembling parties, as we understand them now. Though they fought among themselves, the leaders of the time never organized themselves into opposing slates. The idea of a slate of candidates was in fact introduced by the Zionists in the Circolo Sion.

The Zionists saw political power in a different way. It was a modern idea in content as well as in the way they fought to win it. They conducted a real election campaign, with rallies, their own list of candidates, alignments with other slates (in 1921), and their own party newspaper, *Deghel Sion* [Standard of Zion]. It was published biweekly and then weekly between June 1920 and October 1924 under the editorship, among others, of Raffaele Barda and Raffaele Meghnagi. The biblical verse they chose as their slogan (Exodus 18:21) is as significant as the one which the notables chose: "Moreover thou shalt provide out of all the people able men, such as fear God, men of truth, hating covetousness . . ." The words epitomize the basic characteristics of Zionist activity in Tripoli at the time. The Zionists believed that power should be an expression of the will of the people and a recognition of individual ability, together with personal disinterestedness (that is, an absence of conflict of interest between the public and private realms) and loyalty to the Jewish religion. Another expression of the basic traits of this Zionism is the tone, which tinged the polemic against the leadership and contains a good measure of youthful high spirits and rivalry between the generations. The leaders were attacked for their obsolete way of thinking and their culture, their lack of policies and their wealth,[51] which inevitably made them "too much like the Westerners who are assimilating us."[52] All these basic traits existed in a framework of the most uncompromising support for the religious, moral, and cultural values of Zionism and the need, in order for them to be realized, to free the Community from its mistaken "administrative" leadership and put it on the way toward a "political" Zionist type of leadership.

The first Community elections were held on August 5, 1917. The Circolo Sion was fully mobilized; it had the support of many rabbis, and some of its criticisms of the notables and the way they had been running the Community were well founded. However, the election results ran against it. Nhaisi himself had substantial support (of thirty seats, he came in tenth, taking 519 out of 937 votes cast with 1,222 eligible voters). But the new Council was well and truly in Nahum's hands. However, a few months afterward, without any adequate explanation, Nahum together with the Executive Board resigned. Over a year later, in a letter to Angelo Sereni, Nahum vaguely attributed the resignations to "differences in views" (between his camp and Haggiag's) and an equally obscure "scarcely benevolent attitude to the Jews on the part of the municipality and governing authorities at the time."[53] Mario Nunes Vais, a member of the Nahum camp, was called on to run the Community as a commissioner until the next elections, which were not held until December 15. Twice they had to be postponed pending revision of the electoral rolls. These delays, together with the serious discord which the unexpected and largely unmotivated resignations caused, greatly benefited Zionist activities.

The resignations came at a time when, as Nhaisi and his group had been quick to point out,[54] it was vital for the Jews of Tripoli to have an active, fully functioning Community. Nunes Vais had assumed a slightly more conciliatory attitude toward the Zionists than Nahum had. More important, the war was now over and the Arab nationalists had proclaimed the Tripolitanian Republic. These two events, which led to the radicalizing of the whole spectrum of political life in Tripoli, were bound to affect the Jews as well. The final defeat of the Ottoman empire had given the Balfour Declaration a new meaning, and there were renewed hopes that there would soon be a national home for Jews in Palestine. This of course indirectly bolstered the prestige and credibility of the local Zionists.

In this new atmosphere, the elections were carried once again by the Community leaders. The Haggiag group won the largest number of seats, though they came in fifth to Nahum's first. Nevertheless eleven Circolo Sion candidates were elected.[55] The Zionists gained strength from this success and had their way smoothed by the disagreements which soon broke out among the leadership. Haggiag was appointed president, though because he was a foreigner this was legally impossible. Nahum and three other newly elected council members resigned in protest, but later withdrew their resignation, when Haggiag's appointment failed to win the approval of the Italian authorities. Finally, in July 1919, Nahum was re-elected president. For a while, it seemed that the Zionists were riding a wave of support and would soon be swept into power. In the by-elections held on November 8, 1921, nine of the sixteen seats were filled by Circolo Sion candidates, three by candidates on a list aligned with it, and only three by the notables' candidates.[56] But this second, clearer victory turned out to be the Circolo Sion's swansong.

Though undoubtedly correct on many issues, the Zionists made the mistake of politicizing the contest to the point of exasperating both sides. They did this by assuming demagogic and socialistic tones alien to the Jews of Tripoli, and by accusing almost everyone of anti-Zionism. This was at a time when Zionist ideals were becoming clearer and clearer. They generally had a less militant, more cautious expression, aimed at calming the reactions and suspicions of those around them and the Italian officials. Because of the Zionists' militantly ideological stance, an ambiguous state of mind took root among the Jews of Tripoli. On the one hand they were tired of the poisoned atmosphere which the Circolo Sion had created; on the other they wanted to rebuild the unity of Jewish life once and for all. Leaving aside controversies and extremism, they wanted to deal as harmoniously as possible with the ever more serious and dramatic problems that threatened them. The poor voter turnout on November 8 (685 voters out of about 1,300) was already a symptom of this disaffection. But the decisive event, the founding of the aforementioned Associazione Concordia e Progresso, led by Fortunato Haddad, happened soon after the elections. Between 1922 and 1924 the association published its own newspaper, *Hit 'orerut* [The Reawakening], in opposition to *Deghel Sion*. The Circolo Sion soon accused the association of being anti-Zionist. In fact it was moderately Zionist, criticizing almost all the factions in the struggle, though its main target eventually became the Circolo Sion. The association's aim was the promotion of peace and unity among individual Jews in the Tripoli community, the elevation and progress of the Jewish masses, and improvement of the community institutions.

The situation was bound to be affected by the Fascist seizure of power a few months later. As we shall see in the next chapter, the Fascist government, wanting to avoid friction between Arabs and Jews, did not approve of "excessive" Zionist activity in Libya. In such a tense situation, the founding of the Associazione Concordia e Progresso brought the Circolo Sion to an end in just over a year. The Circolo Sion was first obliged to make peace with the new organization in April 1923 and then to merge with it in February 1924. A few days before the merger, there were new by-elections for the Community council. "Under the circumstances" the Circolo Sion did not compete officially. Men from all the groupings won seats. Some of them, such as Nahum, Haggiag, Nunes Vais, and Barda, were traditional personalities in the Community administration and political life, or had recently become so; others were new faces, including the only two Jewish lawyers in Tripoli, Ernesto Gutierrez and Federico Ortona. None of them ran for office under a political label, however, and while the election campaign was lively, it was devoid of heated, politicized polemic. The Italian periodical *Israel* had previously supported the Circolo Sion, and when the Associazione Concordia e Progresso appeared, *Israel* attacked it bitterly. Only later did it change this attitude, saying:

> Having been conducted in an orderly and disciplined way, the elections had good results, bringing some new, active energies to power. . . . The new Council seems a genuinely strong one, since it represents all the tendencies and parties in the Community. If the thorny question of who should be president and how to share out the board's responsibilities is solved, we shall finally see an end to the painful crisis which has recently poisoned Community life.[57]

The 1924 elections led to the formation of a heterogeneous Executive Board under the chairmanship of Haggiag, who had meanwhile become a Libyan citizen. The elections confirmed and accentuated the change in political climate that was taking shape between 1921 and early 1923, toning down differences and opening the way to a more or less tacit agreement. As a result, the OST was able to pursue its ethical and cultural endeavors, as well as its many social, leisure, and sports activities, as long as official Community organizations did not have to be involved. Despite all this, the 1924 elections had provided only a superficial solution to the crisis. It was still smoldering under the ashes and was worsening, until in 1929 it exploded resoundingly. The depoliticization of community life and return to administration pure and simple had results which were hardly positive. Some were direct and others indirect. The change initially started the process of elimination from the Community administration of the active Zionists, many of the best trained and most aware in the community. The second direct result was a reduction in the Community's activities to almost exclusive day-to-day administration, which, because of budgetary problems, amounted mainly to dispensing charity. This left unsolved the greatest and thorniest problems on the agenda and, in relations with the Italian authorities, emphasized the trend toward adopting an attitude that was so cautious as to seem self-effacing. This was a more passive and timid attitude than that of the Arab leaders, who in their determination insisted on requesting and obtaining help and benefits for those they administered. Two other indirect results can be added. First was the increasing alienation of the Jewish masses from Community affairs, intertwined with a strong vein of criticism of the leaders and the way they ran the Community. Second, within the Italian colonial administration there was a growing feeling of disillusion, mistrust, and irritation at the way Community affairs were going. For the time being, this feeling was reflected only in a decline in the special consideration previously shown the Jews. Later it took more severe forms, becoming a major element leading to the decision to treat Libyan Jews exactly like all the other indigenous inhabitants. A letter dated February 5, 1932, from Vittorio Levi to Felice Ravenna, echoes this situation:

> The self-effacing quality of those who until now controlled the fate of this Community means that many urgent steps needed to improve the lot of the masses were not taken, unlike the case of the Arabs. If anyone hindered colonial penetration here it was the Arabs. The Jews can be reproached with nothing of the sort. Even the official attitude in ceremonies, preference, and so forth, clearly reflects the complete lack of special consideration which Jews receive from governing circles.

In view of this state of affairs, it was only thanks to outside circumstances that the crisis in the Tripoli Community was held in check until the summer of 1929. Once the nucleus of council leaders elected in 1924 had disintegrated, only Haggiag's influence prevented the crisis from occurring then. He could count on the support of many of the vaguely pro-Zionist moderates, who were often former members or sympathizers of the Associazione Concordia e Progresso. Not only many Tripoli Jews but also the Consortium leaders in Rome and the Italian colonial authorities in Tripoli were of the opinion that he was the only man ready and able to run the Community. But later on, when the right moment had passed, the situation deteriorated and hopes dissolved that, given time, Haggiag might solve some of the worst problems. He resigned as president in the summer of 1926[58] because of disagreements with other members of the Executive Board. They accused him of not preparing electoral rolls and "irregular use of his position." Though he had even lost the confidence of the colonial authorities,[59] he turned out to be so hard to replace that finally, in December, he was appointed government commissioner for three months. Both the governor and the Italian administration believed that the only way to put the Community in order and bring it into line with Fascist political and administrative principles was to reform the 1916 statutes. In the meantime, Haggiag's appointment went on being renewed for two years at a time—after all, he had run on the strength of his demand for reform of the Community statutes.[60] It was thus extended until, as we shall see in the next chapter, new elections were called in the summer of 1929. That was when the crisis really exploded.

The first signs of how important the elections were going to be happened when the electoral rolls were being drawn up. The rolls provoked a series of protests and arguments, which echoed beyond

Jewish circles and even appeared in *L'avvenire di Tripoli* [The Future of Tripoli]. The election campaign, as *Israel* wrote, was "a very close and lively one." There were four slates in the running: Haggiag's, two small slates, one of which included Nahum, and the Comitato Giovanile di Rinnovamento [Young Revival Committee] led by Maurizio Forti. The last was largely composed of Zionists and pro-Zionists, who were determined to put an end to the reign of Haggiag. This determination explains why the election campaign was so lively and why there were incidents when the votes were being counted. Elections were held on June 30. After the polls closed, the tallying began in Tripoli, where 422 had voted out of the 544 who were eligible. According to what *Israel* reported,[61] the count indicated that Haggiag's slate had lost resoundingly. The Comitato Giovanile di Rinnovamento had won ten of the first thirteen seats, representing all eligible voters in Tripolitania as a whole. On an individual basis, Nahum had the most votes, and Haggiag, with a little over 120 votes, was not even among the first thirteen. However, votes from Misurata, Zlitin, al-Khums, Zawia, and Syrte still had to come in. They were assumed to be more favorable to Haggiag, and though they would not reverse the results, they certainly could add a new dimension to those from Tripoli. That explains the tension with which the second phase of counting was awaited. It also explains why incidents occurred during the second phase, as soon as doubts were raised about the regularity of the voting procedure outside Tripoli, first among the election overseers and then among the supporters of the two lists most directly involved. The available documentation does not reveal whether the incidents were spontaneous or planned in advance, or who provoked them. It does show that, in view of their seriousness and his wish to prevent tensions from increasing, Governor Pietro Badoglio decided to annul the results "for the sake of public order."[62]

Badoglio followed this action with the obvious next step, the appointing of a new government commissioner to run the Community of Tripoli. Initially, Badoglio once again confirmed Haggiag. It is not clear whether he intended him to remain in office or whether—as is more likely—the appointment was temporary. However, the decision quickly provoked a petition, signed by hundreds of Tripoli Jews, for the appointment of some other person.[63] Then, on July 31, the most significant event in the entire crisis occurred, one without precedent in the entire twenty-year period of Community-Italian relations, proving unequivocally how these relations had deteriorated, and how the governing authorities had lost all hope that the Community of Tripoli would sort out its own affairs. It was the appointment as special commissioner not of a Jewish notable (as had always happened when the Community had been shaken by some crisis or other) but of an Italian official from the governing administration, Dr. Alberto Monastero, who, to make matters worse, was not Jewish.

From a brief indication in a report on the affair which Badoglio sent to Rome a few days later, it appears that before taking this decision he had approached "the best and most balanced figure" among the Jews of Tripoli. Did he mean Nahum? Only after this person had refused, and had suggested that a government official be appointed, did Badoglio choose Monastero.[64] We must take account of the fact that Badoglio's attitude to the Jews of Tripoli was anything but favorable, as will emerge in the next chapter. Moreover, the reference is vague, and government circles by 1926 were already considering drawing a special commissioner from the ranks of the colonial bureaucracy rather than from the Jewish community. In view of all this, it seems doubtful that Badoglio really offered the position to anyone. We must also consider that Badoglio might have made this reference to forestall possible criticism, since he was well aware that the Ministry of Colonies would have preferred a Jew to be appointed. This is shown by the fact that in the first communication regarding the appointment he had made, he protected himself by emphasizing that he had chosen "a Christian because there was no Jew to hand."[65] In my opinion, Badoglio never once considered appointing a Jew. At the same time, he carried out something which for years had been a definite aim of the colonial administration. Unlike the central government, it did not have to deal with the reactions that the appointment of a non-Jewish commissioner would potentially arouse among Italian Jewry.[66] My opinion is confirmed by the fact that hardly had Monastero taken office than he hastened to name an advisory committee (Halfalla Nahum, Vittorio Nahum, Halfalla Hassan, Clemente Arbib, Felice Hassan, and Mario Nunes Vais) responsible for assisting him in managing the Community. Though this had been requested by Rome (together with a rapid solution to the problem of the chief rabbi's appointment) it was also the expedient which the colonial administration desired in order to make the appointment of a Christian at the head of the Community less distasteful to the Jews of Tripoli and Libya at large.

Monastero's appointment as special commissioner was very important for the Community of Tripoli and by extension the other Libyan Communities as well.[67] It was somewhat of a watershed in the history of Libyan Jewish life during the Italian period.

Its first result was to signal an end to the short period of democracy which the Community had been enjoying until then. This democracy had not extended to the way the Community was actually run. Except for brief periods, the administration had always been either the prerogative of closed groups of notables who consistently ran it "more or less as a family affair" and frequently in a personalistic way, leaving little or no room for minority viewpoints, or power had been delegated to government commissioners.[68] The measure of democracy which the Community had enjoyed amounted to the opportunity for voters and taxpayers to express their opinion in principle regarding the groups and persons who took turns controlling the Community administration.

The Italian authorities, especially in Italy, saw the special commissioner's appointment as a temporary solution. There is nothing to indicate that Rome wished to deprive Libyan Jews of the right to elect their leaders and run their own affairs. The Italians were concerned about the tension among Libyan Jews because of the events surrounding the election, and considered it inopportune to impose a solution to the Community crisis by confirming the victory of one of the parties to the conflict. Apart from these concerns, the appointment was intended to allow the Community's bureaucracy to be reorganized and modernized to solve some of the most serious and urgent problems affecting Jewish life in Tripoli which the Jews on their own had not been able to solve, and to give the central authorities time to draw up new legislation for the Libyan Communities. The legislation which had modified the 1916 statutes a year before was already considered unsatisfactory. Allowing the Communities too much autonomy, it did not stop the trend for them to become, in the words of Monastero, a form of "religious municipality within the larger official one, thereby increasing the tendency among the Jews of Tripoli to follow their traditional modes and avoid observing the law." The modification to the 1916 statutes also needed to be brought into line with the new legal basis being prepared in Rome for the Italian Jewish Communities. Monastero relinquished his position on June 4, 1931. The new legislation, published in the Official Gazette the following August 19, did not abolish the electoral system.

Nevertheless, no more elections were held in Tripoli. The interim administrative commission which the governor had appointed consisted initially of the members of the special commission, now headed by Monastero: Mario Nunes Vais, Ruben Hassan, Angiolino Arbib, Alberto Fresco, and Umberto Di Segni. In order to hold elections, it would have been necessary, once the new legislation was in effect, for the interim commission to formulate, within a year after being set up, the legal regulations needed to implement the new leg-

islation, and for the governor to confirm them. But when this procedure was formulated, the situation in the Community of Tripoli was
tense. As in other communities to a lesser extent, serious incidents
between Muslims and Jews had been occurring, and Badoglio had
been taking harsh measures to stop them.[69] Before long the Sabbath
question came up, followed by the encounter between Balbo and
Castelbolognesi leading to the unceremonious expulsion of the
chief rabbi from the colony. Crisis followed crisis until 1938, when
Fascist racial legislation came into effect. Thus, through waiting for
the right moment, the commission never called elections, to the
great satisfaction of the government bureaucracy—and, as long as he
was governor, of Badoglio (Balbo's attitude is more difficult to assess). The bureaucrats had remained opposed to the continuation of
the electoral system and had not hidden this from Rome. They opposed it either because they thought it impractical, or because they
profoundly believed that it was a "strange relic" (having been abolished in Italy), "inappropriate" and "inapplicable" due to "the local Jewish population's lack of preparation" and because by politicizing Jewish life, it was "by nature a source of agitation and dissension
inadmissible in the Colony."[70]

Though it was serious and negative, this first consequence of
Monastero's appointment as special commissioner was not the most
important one. This is especially true if one looks at the problem in
view of the broader effects on Jewish life in Tripoli and Libya of the
events occurring in the summer of 1929 and Monastero's running of
the Community, and if one considers how the problem was developing and what internal ramifications it had.

Jewish life in Tripoli was traditionalist, jealous of its own autonomy, and fearful of the consequences that the new and strange might
have on its own homogeneity, on the religious values and way of life
underlying it. In such an atmosphere, Monastero's dynamic way of
running the Community, his readiness to appoint rabbis and dismiss
judges, and his unconcealed aim of modernizing Community life
and even of modifying some basic aspects of social reality and of the
Jews' way of life, aroused bewilderment, concern, and protest. These
came not only from the traditionalists, the masses, and those who
were directly affected in some way, but also from more progressive
circles. Some of these elements thought that Monastero's directions
were "more likely to lead to our spiritual ruin than a renaissance."[71]
Monastero's actions (sometimes unnecessarily) offended the Jews'
sensitivities and interests. They stirred up the still waters of Jewish
life in Tripoli, often with the approval of the more outward-looking
and progressive Jews and even of Dario Disegni, the visiting rabbi on

the commission. Monastero's actions did have two essential results: he managed to carry out or at least impose some reforms and initiatives that the traditionalism, apathy, insensitivity, hypercritical attitude, external conditions, and internal differences of previous administrations had prevented, and even excluded from consideration. Moreover, he managed to dispel as he did so part of the colonial administration's recently grown mistrust, intolerance, and occasional hostility toward Jewish issues. Monastero thus made the authorities more amenable to some of the Jews' requests, though only until 1933, when things changed for the worse again.

Monastero's achievements included paving the way for modernizing the Community's technical and administrative structure and the institutions dependent on it (the rabbinical court, the Talmud Torah, and so forth), straightening out the Community budget,[72] and meeting some of the most pressing social needs. He set up the Community registry office, opened a position for a Community secretary, and drew up three sets of regulations on how the Community was to be administered. He introduced procedures for collecting and distributing funds for charity and running the synagogues, and established a ward for Jews (who often objected strongly to being treated with the Arabs) in the new Vittorio Emanuele III Hospital. Monastero also organized the building of two medical clinics, one of them general and the other for trachoma patients. He arranged for a sea colony at the Tripoli Lido to host two hundred Talmud Torah students in two groups for twenty-five days each year, and made agreements with the school authorities to increase the teaching of Hebrew in some classes of government schools.[73]

Besides these initiatives, Monastero took two more. They were much more ambitious, and either had little result or were never completed. They are interesting because they show that he (and hence the colonial administration) wished to bring about a transformation of Jewish life in Tripoli. One project aimed at relieving overcrowding in the *hara* and gradually integrating the Jews into other neighborhoods. It was taken up again in 1937–1938 by Aldo Lattes, the chief rabbi, under Balbo's auspices. The plan was to build popular housing for poor Jews, initially acquiring for this purpose (thanks to private donations and government assistance) about three thousand square meters in Via Manzoni from the Alliance Israélite Universelle. The other project was even more important, since it aimed at directing young Jewish workers into agriculture. This plan was to purchase at a price of about 100,000 lire a concession of farmland which, since the event coincided with the wedding of the heir to the throne, was named the "Prince of Piedmont."

Farming was not a new idea. Halfalla Nahum had nursed it in 1917, and it was he whom Monastero asked to manage the concession. Nahum had argued that it was the only alternative to unemployment and underemployment, or emigration. The project had later been taken up by the Circolo Sion, which expressly talked about "going back to the land." It had also been aired less explicitly by Isacco Sciaky.[74] When Monastero announced it, *Israel* applauded with enthusiasm:

> Cavalieri Monastero's happy idea needs no comment—"urging Tripolitanian Jews into agriculture, their forefathers' first occupation." From whatever point of view one considers it, the return of any fragment of the Jewish people, in any part of the world, to working the land can only be greeted with supreme joy: it means physical and moral health, the retempering of energies. It means that Jews can aim once more at higher, broader, and more serene ideals, having rediscovered their faith in their forefathers' earliest occupation. It is fitting and right that all this can be expressed in synthesis with the Libyan Jews' faith in Italy as her subjects, in the august name of the young Prince.[75]

Twenty-five families were given work on the concession. Its initial results were encouraging (especially in tobacco-growing, which yielded 5,500 kilos from a little over a hectare and a half of cultivation). Several efforts were made to build on this. In 1932, for example, twenty thousand olives were preserved, and livestock-rearing was increased. But as a whole the concession never became viable. Except for a few young Zionists who went to work there "with the intention of completing their *hakhsharah*" [preparations for emigration to Palestine],[76] it had absolutely no effect on professional trends among the Jews of Tripoli, nor did it impel any others to take such initiatives, on either a collective or a private basis.[77] In 1938, partly in order to reduce its deficit and partly in order to obtain funds for housing construction to relieve overcrowding in the *hara*, the Community decided to sell the concession.

As we can see, in less than two years of running the Community, Monastero did a remarkable number of things. Though they did not solve the Community's problems—and even less those of Jewish life in Tripoli—his achievements did hold back the crisis, and, more particularly, gave the Community some more modern and efficient structures. However, the most important consequence of the Monastero era from a historical point of view, whatever one's general assessment, was quite a different one.

As we have seen, at the beginning of his mandate Monastero collected around himself a group synthesizing the "old" community leadership, the genuine "notables" (first and foremost, Nahum),

and central figures of community life during the Haggiag period—
Clemente Arbib, in the outgoing administration, had been responsible for matters of civil status and the Talmud Torah, while Vittorio
Nahum led the opposition. But a far-reaching change in the nucleus
of community leadership took place under Monastero. The "old"
leaders were replaced almost entirely by new ones. When Monastero
left his position of special commissioner, the new leaders took over
the running of the Community. Especially in the initial years and at
moments of heightened tension (such as when the Sabbath crisis
came up), these figures were often subject to harsh criticism. In particular, they were accused of being assimilationist, too subservient
to the colonial authorities, and largely alienated from the problems
of the Jewish masses in Tripoli.[78] Babani Meghnagi, writing in July
1932 to the secretary of the Union of Italian Jewish Communities,
indicates as much: "The present members of the Special Commission are wealthy Jews who have lived far from the environment of
the common, wretched folk. Today, though, because of their responsibilities they are approaching the people and trying to understand
its needs."[79]

A year later, Felice Ravenna, the president of the Union, gave a
harsher opinion. He had just returned from a trip to Libya after serious incidents had occurred between Arabs and Jews and the governing authorities had acted:

> I wish to record confidentially that the Government of the Colony
> made a mistake when it made up a special commission to administer
> the Community. It put on the commission honest and upright people
> who are enthusiastically devoting themselves to running the Commu-
> nity. However, they are drawn from the most Europeanized group,
> hence those farthest from the majority of Jews in a spiritual sense. It
> would have been much more prudent and appropriate to include on the
> commission some more orthodox representatives who are closer to
> the people and its soul.[80]

From a Jewish point of view, these criticisms were certainly well-
founded, though Ravenna's argument was somewhat naïve. It is obvious that Monastero's choice (and later on, Badoglio's) was not a
mistake but exactly what he intended. It was aimed at putting an
end to the more traditional way of running the Community. It was
intended to foster a more modern type of administration, which
would also be more consonant with the needs of Italian colonial policy than the previous administration. It has to be admitted that, despite all the limitations of this policy, its consequences for the Jews
of Tripoli and of Libya as a whole were not all negative. When one

considers the problem from a concrete historical point of view, one has to allow that, looking beyond specific incidents, the policy eventually gave rise to a new system of intra- and extracommunal relations, which on the whole was positive. It also gave rise to a new class of leaders technically more responsive to the realities and needs of the Jews of Tripoli. The majority of its members turned out to be capable administrators, both in the period under discussion and during the war and postwar years. From the political point of view, however, the consequences were largely negative. As will emerge in later chapters, this new leadership, which had been formed in the climate of the Fascist colonial system, during the war years and immediately after, showed itself to be inferior to the earlier leadership. This holds true of choices and independent decisions requiring not merely administrative abilities but also political skills.

From a historical point of view, the Italian colonial administration, due to its Fascist principles and the imperatives of colonial policy, not very different from those of other colonial powers at the time, was bound to favor the "normalizing" of Jewish life. It would thus conduct a policy either of modernization, thus tending to assimilationism (as it did until the racial legislation was introduced), or one of marginalization, thereby putting the Arabs before the Jews (as at least a part of the colonial administration desired). Despite these imperatives, the new system taking shape in the early 1930s did allow the most genuine and dynamic energies among Libyan Jews, led by the Zionists, to carry on their activities freely, outside the sphere of official Community institutions. The dynamic elements thus assumed the specifically Jewish functions which the Community could not fulfill and in the past had been unable to resolve. This was despite the extreme secularization of the Community, for with the arrival of Rabbi Lattes a sort of *modus vivendi* and cooperation developed between lay leaders and the chief rabbi.[81] Moreover, the new system gave the Community functions which were essentially administrative and social. It is true that they met the requirements of the Italian colonial administration, but they also responded to many of the objective needs of the Jews of Tripoli. Without this help, Jewish life would have become more and more embroiled in an insolvable crisis and increasingly divided into two separate camps. One has to conclude that, despite all its limitations, the system taking shape was objectively the best under the circumstances. It harmonized the needs of the colonial administration with those of the most modern Zionist and non-Zionist elements among local Jewry. In this way, the new arrangement kept at bay the danger to Jewish life of isolating and marginalizing the Jewish masses. This danger involving the poorer, more traditional and hidebound Jews was one of an increasingly sharp and irreparable break between the masses and the richer, more modern elements, who were aware of the issues facing Jewish life.

Obviously, this does not mean that the basic trends toward such a break had been curtailed. Nor does it mean that the differences connected with it within Jewish life in Tripoli and Libya as a whole diminished. On the contrary, subsequent chapters will deal further with the persistence of the same trends and differences. Without anticipating, one can state at this point that by the early 1930s these trends and differences were changing in character. In particular, in this new framework, Community institutions were losing much of their value as a focal point. When all forms, whether apparent or substantial, of democracy in the Jewish Community had ceased, "political" discourse as such became clearer and broader for Libyan Jews. This discourse was transferred from the false arena of Community insitutions and how they should be run to the more compelling and immediate one of Jewish relations with the Italian administration and their consequences for the Jews.

Thus, for present purposes, this is a good time to interrupt the study of developments within Libyan Jewish life, and take up a more specific and detailed discussion of Italian policy toward the Jews than has been needed so far.

Presentation of *Jews in an Arab Land* in Italy (Renzo De Felice is third from left).

An inscription from the Jewish revolt against the Romans in Cyrenaica, A.D. 115–117.

Photographs courtesy of Raffaello Fellah.

The synagogue of Tigrinna in the Tripolitanian Jebel, an area of ancient Jewish settlement before the Arab conquest.

Aerial view of the old city of Tripoli, in which the Jewish community lived side by side with Arabs, Maltese, and Greeks (late Turkish period).

Interior of the house of the Nahum family, well-known Tripoli merchants (1892).

A typical Tripoli artisan shop belonging to Jews, here shown in their everyday apparel.

The First Committee of the Jewish National Fund in Tripoli, established 1914.

Bottom left and above: two portraits of Libyan Jews in Jewish dress showing Turkish influence (1920–1930).

Chief Rabbi Aldo Lattes (of Tripoli) and Governor Italo Balbo welcoming Mussolini to the Jewish Quarter during his 1937 visit to Libya.

The entrance to a labor camp for Jews in Libya during the Second World War.

Mussolini carrying the Sword of Islam presented to him as "Protector of the Faith" by Libyan Arab leaders (1937).

January 23, 1943: the liberation of Libya by the Eighth Army of the Allied Forces.

Troops of the Palestinian Brigade of the Eighth Army leading the parade in Tripoli celebrating the Allied liberation of Libya (1943).

DICTORU is to the just
honour and glory to you MONTGOMERU

Fabr. Rsiucci - Barbino Tripoli

A golden sword given by Elia Journo to Field Marshal Montgomery for liberating the Jewish community of Libya.

The entrance to the Jewish quarter of Tripoli decorated in honor of the British.

The first British military governor, Brigadier Lush, with officers of the Jewish Palestinian Brigade, receiving a blessing in the main synagogue of Tripoli.

Forty-five unmarked graves of unidentifiable Jews killed in the 1945 pogrom.

A meeting of the British, Arab, and Jewish Reconciliation Committee following the 1945 pogroms.

Some Libyan Jews who survived the Nazi extermination camps in Germany, on their way home to Libya via Italy (1946).

A reception in honor of the Libyan Liberation Committee, on its return from Cairo (February 1948). Those present include Reshir Saadawi and Zachino Habib.

A meeting of the U.N. Advisory Council for Libya.

Spokesmen of the Jewish Community being received by King-designate
Idris on the eve of the proclamation of independence (1951).

Prime Minister Muntasser receiving the representatives of the Jewish
Community and the Jewish Agency representative Baruch Duvdevani
(1951).

ANNO III. N. 7   PREZZO M.A.L. 10

HAIENU

ORGANO BENÉ AKIVA E BACHAD DELLA LIBIA · VIA ARBAA ARSAAT 29 · P.O.B. 310 TRIPOLI

A tutti gli Ebrei di Libia

BERACHA' VESHALOM

Masthead of the last Jewish newspaper published in Libya (1951).

The founding of the Jews of Libya Association (Rome, 1970).

Muammar Qadhdhafi at the Paris Symposium in November 1973.

The destroyed Jewish cemetery of Tripoli in the Qadhdhafi period, when it was razed by bulldozers and transformed first into a port depot and later into a building site for hotels.

A memorial set up by the Libyan Jewish community in Rome honoring the
deceased buried in Libya.

5. Relations with the Italian Authorities

Relations between the Italian authorities and Libyan Jewry have been mentioned several times in the preceding chapters. However, I have referred mainly to aspects immediately relevant to ideas being developed. This chapter goes deeper into those relations during the first twenty-odd years of Italian occupation. More important, it goes forward in time, up to the point where racial laws were introduced, while examining more systematically some particular events through which the confrontation crystallized during the 1930s. During the first twenty years, though Jewish relations with the authorities were significant, they had relatively little effect on Jewish life in Libya. During the 1930s, in contrast, they became so important that one might say that much of the history of Libyan Jews revolves around them. Hence it is necessary to make these relations the pivot of our discussion of the period.

One point has to be made first in summarizing the significance of relations with the colonial authorities during the first twenty or so years. Contrary to what one might have thought, the effects on Libyan Jews of Fascist rule in Italy were indirect rather than direct. This was particularly true regarding the consequences which the reconquest and suppresion of the Arab revolt had for the Jews. Obviously, the Fascists' rise to power was felt by Libyan Jews too. But until the early 1930s they experienced relatively few of its consequences, except in particular instances, some of which were serious, but which on the whole were marginal events. There were thus even some Libyan Jews (generally only the very rich and Italianized) who sympathized with Fascism and supported the regime. It is difficult to describe even the Jewish masses as hostile to Fascism: they were merely uninvolved. The young, particularly those attending Italian schools, were more interested.[1] Fascism did not confront Libyan Jewry fairly and squarely as a problem until the "pacification" of Libya was over. The Jews appeared to be only one marginal issue among other problems: Fascist colonial, foreign, and domestic policies. The Fascist government regarded the issue of Libyan Jewry as an aspect of foreign policy toward Zionism and toward the potential usefulness to Italy of Eastern Mediterranean Jewish communities possessing more Italian or Italianized Jews, primarily Alexandria.[2] The issue of Libyan Jewry was also viewed as an aspect of domestic policy, because of the reactions which it provoked among Italian Jews. In early 1933, Felice Ravenna requested a meeting with Mussolini to apprise him of the main problems concerning metropolitan Jews and those in the colonies. When the discussion turned to the Jews of Tripoli, Mussolini remarked that one could not really speak of twenty years of Italian occupation; it had been in force in Tripolitania for only six years, and this had to be borne in mind in any assessment of what had been achieved.[3] This statement by the Duce certainly contained a large measure of political strategy. He wanted to justify himself before Ravenna, the president of the Union, so that Ravenna would moderate his demands. One cannot deny that there was also a basis of truth in his statement, however. There is no doubt that until the "pacification" was completed, Libyan Jewry was an entirely secondary problem for Italy. It was dealt with as a function of the reconquest and repression, Italian-Arab relations, and the colony's economic needs. In view of the events that had taken place in Libya prior to Fascism's rise to power, one can hardly say that this attitude was substantially different from the one which the Italian authorities (especially the military) had held, as we have seen, in the Liberal-Democratic period.

Bearing in mind that this attitude lasted throughout almost the entire initial twenty years of occupation, one should likewise not forget that, though Tripoli was "pacified" by the 1920s, Cyrenaica was not until the early thirties. This fact affected the way the problem was confronted even in already "pacified" areas. One can thus understand why there was no substantial change in attitude between the Liberal-Democratic period and the early years of Fascism. This was true not only on a practical level, but also on what might be called a theoretical one—how the problem was grasped.

Practically, in both periods the Italian authorities had to deal with certain issues—the chief rabbi's appointment, schools (and in connection with this, the Sabbath), the legal basis of the Community, etc. These interventions on the part of the authorities were almost always half-hearted. Underlying them was a lack of real interest in the problem on its own merits, leading the authorities to treat particular aspects with a mixture of boredom and lack of commitment. Having little patience with the issues themselves, the authorities concentrated on their implications and broader, more remote consequences. This explains why, when the overall context had altered and the problems worsened, it was easy in the 1930s for the authorities to switch from a moderate, condescending attitude to a less understanding, harsher one, which was more inclined toward direct and severe intervention. In the past, such intervention had been infrequent and limited to what was strictly necessary. Even after the rise of Fascism, the authorities had preferred not to become embroiled in issues that to the modern European mind were obscure as well as thorny and secondary. The Italians therefore saw fit to limit themselves to intervening in the "necessary" cases, doing so only in order to allow the Communities to function normally during crises; if the crises occurred often, the Italians would amend the regulations in order to forestall problems. Typical of this policy is an encounter in 1921 between Governor Mercatelli and the Community of Tripoli. A year earlier, the fifteen-year-old Italian daughter of Mario Nunes Vais had become engaged to a non-Jewish Italian official. Her father, an influential member of the Jewish community, at first had given his consent; then, in the face of the indignation which included protests and demonstrations by his fellow-Jews, he withdrew it. His daughter appealed to the Italian court, which in 1921 accepted her appeal and approved the marriage. The Jews of Tripoli, Chief Rabbi Artom, and the Community council continued to protest and object vigorously. The council sent a petition to the governor, the president of the Libyan Court of Appeal, the ministers of Justice and the Colonies, the Rabbinical Federation, and the Consortium, invoking the principle of freedom of conscience and of a father's right to educate his children according to his own principles. The governor reacted sharply. In a letter to the Community dated July 8, he rejected the petition and without mincing words accused the Community leaders of promoting a segregationist policy and the Jews of Tripoli of despising the laws of the country whose guests they were:

> I have read with utter amazement the petition presented to me on behalf of the Jewish Community opposing an irreversible decision of the Tripoli Court of Appeal, the highest arm of Italian justice in this country.
> I was born and raised in a land freed from oppression and am the official of a state which bases its public law on the broadest freedom of thought and conscience. I can only deplore a protest which offends our Laws and juridical bodies, and attempts to deprive a young Italian metropolitan citizen in Tripoli of prerogatives which everyone in Italy, including Jews, would acknowledge as her right.
> It is in fact amazing that the protest comes from the leadership of a

people which we lifted only yesterday from the semi-slavery in which it was languishing. It almost seems to wish to reassume those chains that we have broken in the name of humanity, and segregate itself again from the living world, derogating the laws of the country whose guests the Jews are, and disdaining this country's historical, age-old traditions.

It is even more amazing that this people should invoke the powers of the state in defense of its misguided attitude.

We are no longer in a time when it is acceptable to invoke the secular arm to violate consciences and restrict moral and civil aspirations. We are certainly not in a time when the secular arm should lend itself to anything other than guaranteeing respect for the Laws of the Fatherland and decisions of the Magistrates.

If by some wretched chance there were officials disposed to support it in its claims, the Jewish Community would soon be obliged by public opinion to confess that it had erred and sinned against itself.[4]

Governor Mercatelli's letter serves as a good introduction to the second part of my discussion—the theoretical side of the Italian authorities' way of dealing with the problem of Libyan Jewry during the first twenty years of occupation. Though one cannot challenge the legal points which the letter makes, its general tone and entire extralegal argument are highly indicative of the basic contradiction underlying the theoretical aspect. Libyan Jews formally enjoyed full civil rights and respect for their culture and traditions, as well as broad administrative autonomy on the Community level. This was true not only of the Liberal-Democratic period but also of the Fascist period. During the later era the ministries did not interfere with the Jews' civil rights, culture and traditions, or administration, though the local colonial administration in the late 1920s tried to reduce and control the Community's administrative autonomy as much as it could. This principle was seriously undermined in both periods, though. It was grafted onto an idea of civilization and progress which made any officials who had to apply it intellectually and psychologically unable to understand Libyan Jewish traditions. Italian officials supposed that Libyan Jews would integrate and assimilate just like the Jews of Central and Western Europe. Some benevolent officials, such as Mercatelli, did not even consider the Jews to be real Libyans. This is confirmed by the fact that, in mid-1927, when the colonial authorities' benign attitude was fading, the nationalist Federzoni was still advocating the "rapid assimilation of the Libyan Jews."[5] This basic contradiction also explained the change in attitude which took place in the 1930s. The change was due not only to practical causes, but also to the change in the Italian attitude toward Libyan Jewry. The idea that Libyan Jews were less fortunate brothers who should be quickly raised to the level of Italians gave way to a belief that they were neither more nor less than Libyans. Only a few of them being in a position to escape from their condition, they should thus be treated like other indigenous groups. The Italians came to believe that in the new colonial situation there was less need of Jews; continuing to consider them as non-indigenous simply created difficulties with both Jews and Arabs.

The Fascist seizure of power emboldened the local Fascists, particularly in Tripoli, and swelled their meager ranks.[6] Fascism gave more space and vigor to nationalist Italians, both civil and military. Before, this element had been champing at the bit under the "weak" policy of "capitulation" which the Liberal-Democratic governments conducted toward the Arabs. The nationalists had criticized the colonial authorities' "laxity" and "lack of firmness" in dealing with indigenous groups and their claims of equality with the Italians and Europeans in general. In this context, some animosity against Jews, especially Libyan Jews, was expressed.[7] There were many motives behind this animosity. In a minority it was a question of actual anti-Semitism; in others it was the colonialist mentality associating Libyan Jews with Arabs as indigenous people.[8] The majority had mixed motives. In some the motive was economic jealousy, in others the belief, whose echoes had already been noted in late 1921 in *La vita italiana*, that a close network of Jewish interests had established itself around Governor Volpi. Still others, who must have been the strongest force, believed that the Jews of Tripoli did not feel part of the Italian "cause," opposed it, and were harming it by provoking the Arabs. The motives most ascribed to Libyan Jews were insensitivity and desire for personal gain. The cases of the two brothers of Tarhuna arrested and accused of spying and smuggling for the Arab rebels, and of Eugenio Nahum, arrested for "complicity in acts directed at revolt," were used as proof. Nor, finally, should the subtle but widespread actions of pro-Italian Arab notables in provoking this hostility to Jews be underestimated. Under this climate of opinion, in August 1923 some serious incidents happened in Tripoli.

The first signs came at the end of May. The reconsideration of the first-degree sentence for treason against Eugenio Nahum (and his Arab "accomplice" Jusuf Gurgi) and his acquittal provoked loud Italian protests, particularly among the local Fascists. There was almost violence. On June 1, Major Giuseppe Pièche, commander of the *carabinieri* in Tripoli, reported to the governor as follows:

The news of Eugenio Nahum's unexpected acquittal by the Supreme Military and Naval Tribunal for lack of evidence of complicity produced very serious and unfavorable effects in the city. There were parties, jubilation, and celebration in the homes of the Jews who, being ignorant of the subtleties of the legal code, do not realize that despite his acquittal some doubt still lingers over their coreligionist. They realize only that he is free. There is profound indignation among the metropolitans who, though aware of the requirements of colonial policy, cannot explain this acquittal to themselves. Though they do not doubt that from a legal point of view it was a just decision, from a humane viewpoint they think it unjust. By the same legal procedure, others are deemed guilty, and have been denied their right to life.

The Arabs register surprise and scorn, seeing only that the rich supporters of the rebellion are let free. Public opinion is so disturbed that, encouraged by what the Jews themselves have been boasting, it makes malicious accusations against the Supreme Military and Naval Tribunal, and even holds that the Jewish plutocracy paid a sum of 280,000 lire to obtain absolution. My headquarters will respond to these insults to the dignity of Justice, since they affect and severely damage our prestige. In this land, since gold in the past has ruled, bringing shame and injustice, people think that money can do anything.

The Fascists, who attended the trial in Zawia in large numbers, believed that the prosecution had a case since the accused confessed. They have rebelled as one man and are threatening to take Fascist action against Nahum and his family, unless they leave the colony. Thus an abnormal situation reigns, and is damaging to our prestige. It encourages the Jews, who here form a party rather than a religion. Since the situation threatens to disturb public order, it could cause the colony serious and tangible harm.

Only one step would remedy this chaos: that Eugenio Nahum be immediately expelled from the colony. In this way only will those who live here and those who know the colony's needs realize that even when the high impartiality of a court of last instance does not find sufficient grounds for proceeding against an offender of the State, a person who may have committed treason cannot remain here while the interests of the Fatherland are at stake.

The Fascia [Fascist organization] of Tripoli made the situation even more dramatic by sending Mussolini a telegram of protest, signed by its directors:

> The acquittal of Eugenio Nahum who has been accused of and has confessed offences for which Arab leaders justly are hanged, while public opinion is disturbed and the bases of present political action shaken, arouses deep indignation in all Italians who see the principles of justice assailed by an insolent Jewish plutocracy. This Fascio feels deep moral unease as it develops its action here where, due to the impunity of traitors, dark forces which for so many years conspired against Italy, preventing the concrete affirmation of its sovereignty, rise again and assemble.

Federzone was used as an official channel for this telegram. His co-operation did not prevent an attack on Nahum by a member of the MVSN.* Tension remained and did not subside even when on the advice of the commander of the *carabinieri*, the authorities expelled Nahum from the colony and sent him to Sfax on the Tunisian coast.[9]

These were the events preceding the August incidents. The first episode happened on the nineteenth. A Fascist *milite* overturned the table of a Jewish vendor, whether by chance or deliberately it is impossible to tell. On this trivial provocation, a scuffle began in the *hara* between Jews, Italian soldiers, Fascists, and "European passers-by." The *carabinieri* had to intervene and fire into the air in an attempt to restore order.

The next evening there was a Fascist "punitive expedition," followed over the next few days by other minor incidents and fights, with Arabs also joining in. In the course of these incidents an Italian solider was stabbed to death, twenty-five Jews being arrested and later tried for their involvement in this incident. The incidents, portrayed by the local Fascists as something approaching a Jewish revolt, had considerable publicity in Italy as well as in the colony. They provoked serious repercussions and schisms within the Jewish community of Tripoli. Despite Rabbi Artom's attempt to soothe tempers by writing to the *Corriere di Tripoli*, to show the episode in perspective and demonstrate the absurdity of putting the blame for the incidents solely and squarely on the Jews,[10] the agitation continued for a long time. Lesser incidents also took place over the following two months, so that even among the Italians of Tripoli, due to a fear of growing anti-Semitism, alarm was growing at the Fascists' provocations and excesses. The *Corriere di Tripoli* of those months reveals traces of that alarm. The most significant proof of it lies in the fact that in early November the Fascio of Tripoli—probably also on instructions from Rome[11]—was obliged to make an announcement declaring that the incidents were not very serious and denying that they had any anti-Semitic motivations.[12] There were no more incidents after this. Obviously, the bitterness and fear accumulated over the months were not completely forgotten. There is no doubt that they contributed to the distrust of Zionism on the part of many of the Jewish notables. They probably reinforced the tendency, which many of the notables had already shown in the Liberal-Democratic period, to avoid involving the Community with Zionism and keep the Zionists out of its institutions.

*Milizia Volontaria per la Sicurezza Nazionale; see note on p. 76 above. —*Trans.*

Without doubt, the 1923 incidents constituted an important page in the history of Jews in Tripoli and made a lasting impression on those directly involved. However, they did not affect the attitude of the Italian colonial and central authorities toward the Libyan Jews, nor could they be seen as indicating any change in the Italian attitude. It is more accurate to place them not in the context of Jewish relations with the governing authorities or the government, but in that of the crisis which Fascism's rise to power provoked in the colony. The 1923 incidents should also be seen in the context of the illusion (and efforts it led to) of the more turbulent and extreme Fascists that they were above and beyond government authority, which they considered out of line with the "new times." As far as the attitude of the governing authorities and the government is concerned, the Fascist rise to power did not entail substantial changes for the Jews.

Even with regard to the authorities' attitude to Zionism, one cannot speak of a real change under Fascism. The government was no longer making openly pro-Zionist declarations (as Amendola had in July 1922). The local authorities, however, even before the Fascists took over, had been concerned that heated Zionist propaganda might give them difficulties with the Arabs. They thus set limits on it, prohibiting for example the screening of a film on the life of Herzl in the summer of 1921. The central authorities simply took these realities into account after October 1922, without using coercive measures, and limiting themselves to indirect actions through the Consortium, the Italian Zionists, and some Jewish leaders in Tripoli. What happened in October 1926 shows that they went no further than that, not even confidentially and in general terms. When the Zionists of Tripoli asked permission to issue their own newspaper, the governor, Emilio De Bono, an influential leader in the Fascist hierarchy, felt that he had to put the question to Rome, not only because of the newspaper itself, but ("as a guideline for his political action") to find out the government's attitude to Zionism. It was as a response to De Bono's request that the ministry confronted the problem of Libyan Zionism for the first time. Two very interesting decisions were made. They show the different ways in which Zionism was seen from the point of view of general policy and that of local policy. In the view of Dino Grandi, the undersecretary for foreign affairs, the government saw no reason to "follow a definitely pro-Zionist policy and markedly favor this religious and political movement." However, since the Mediterranean colonies possessed "numerous and influential Jewish elements" showing a "praiseworthy loyalty" to the Italian government and "staunch feel-

ings of Italian identity," it was not appropriate to slight them or oppose their aspirations "when these are not in opposition to Italian
interests." Moreover, Grandi continued, Zionism was a movement
"which we can neither avoid nor refrain from watching as closely as
the need to protect and develop our interests requires." It would thus
be useful if among the Zionist ranks there were "elements whose
loyalty to Italy can be counted on, so that the movement does not
take on a particular character on behalf of other powers whose interests in the Mediterranean conflict with ours. . . . Hence, without
openly favoring it, we should not oppose it when there are no special
reasons for doing so and we should thus make sure that Italian interests are strongly represented in the Zionist movement." In view of
these general considerations, the Ministry of Foreign Affairs saw
nothing to prevent publication of the newspaper which the Zionists
of Tripoli wanted to issue. But the Ministry of Colonies was not of
the same opinion. The minister, Pietro Di Scalea, viewed the problem in the same way as Grandi and was certainly not an anti-Zionist,
being so far from it that he shortly afterward became chairman of the
Italy-Palestine Committee. He thought that the publication of the
newspaper would damage Italian policy in Libya by causing problems with the Arabs, and thus refused to give authorization.[13]

Beyond the specific problem of Zionism, the episode, though a
modest one, is important because it confirms the Italian authorities'
attitude. Due partly to the authorities' pragmatic policy, partly to
their inability to understand the real nature of Libyan Jewry, and
partly to the urge to complete the reconquest of the country, the incident shows how Italian policy was almost always conditioned by
the belief that the problem of Libyan Jews had to be dealt with not
on its own terms but as an aspect of Italian military and civil policy
toward the Arabs.

Looking at the events of this period from this point of view we
can understand that even the restrictive measures which the governor of Cyrenaica took in 1923–1924 against the Jews of Benghazi did
not signify anti-Semitic discrimination. Some of these measures
were the result of bureaucratic zealousness and the governing bureaucracy's typically colonialist mentality. The bureaucracy tended
to make a clear-cut distinction between metropolitans and indigenous people, without distinguishing further within this second category. Other restrictive measures, such as the one adopted in June
1924, obliging the Jews to apply for a permit when leaving Benghazi,
were obviously mere precautions relating to the military situation in
surrounding areas. When the situation improved, the restrictions
were quickly lifted. Even when they were in effect, Jews who ap-

plied were granted a three-month exit permit which they could renew without difficulty. Arabs were subject to considerably more severe restrictions.[14] Though obviously it should be viewed not in the
preceding context but from a political and social perspective, the
same is true for another measure taken in 1929. It initially aroused
some alarm in the Jews, and *Il gazzettino* of Venice, in the aforementioned article of November 17, 1929, unjustifiably presented it
as directed specifically against the Jews. I am referring to the setting
up of a disciplinary court for usurers. The task of the court was certainly to combat usury, which was very widespread and largely practiced by Jews. Nevertheless, one member of the court was a Jew (a
brother of Halfalla Nahum). The judgments which it passed, besides
being on the bland side—a few imprisonments, all transmuted
shortly thereafter into warnings, so that those concerned were able
to return home—affected not only Jews but also Maltese and even
Italians.[15]

During the twenty years of occupation, in only one set of circumstances did the central authorities deviate from viewing the
treatment of Libyan Jewry as an aspect of Italian policy toward the
Arabs. Such circumstances arose twice, in 1928 and 1931, when the
1916 legislation covering how the Community of Tripoli should
function was initially renewed and extended to the whole of Libya
and then revised. Under these circumstances domestic and foreign
policy concerns prevailed over those of colonial policy. Both times,
as far as policy goes, the moderate and liberal trend in Rome prevailed over the uncompromising extreme followed by the current
governors, De Bono and especially Badoglio. It aimed at not arousing
alarm and negative reactions among Italian Jews and Jews of other,
especially Mediterranean, countries.

The governing authorities in Tripoli made their first explicit request to amend the 1916 law right after the "Haggiag crisis" in the
summer of 1926. On September 7, Ernesto Queirolo, the acting governor of Tripolitania, telegraphed the Ministry of Colonies:

> The Jewish community leaves much to be desired since as a group it is
> based on outmoded concepts. One might say that universal suffrage has
> done harm and given rise to disadvantages within the system. If one
> sought a commissioner today one would certainly come up against the
> representative of one of the personality-based movements which divide
> the Jewish camp, determining in advance that any victory would be
> completely useless for the community to function effectively. First we
> must make an institutional reform and then we can proceed in a nor-
> mal way to form a new administration, which I believe should be
> nominated by the governor rather than elected. There are no local

people capable of drafting new regulations even when the guidelines
are given them, so the task must be done by the government offices . . .
All things considered, I would not be against suggesting to H. E. the
Governor, on his return, that an office of special commissioner be set
up and filled by a government official, even a Christian if a Jew cannot
be found . . . Under his temporary administration a Community reform would be encouraged.[16]

After De Bono returned to his office, on September 25 Minister Di
Scalea accepted the proposal, authorizing the governor's staff to begin drafting the reform. However, he refused to approve the appointment of a special commissioner who was not Jewish. The governor's
office approved the preliminary draft regulations for the Jewish
Community of Tripoli on March 22, 1927. As the report attached to
the draft stated, it was based on three cornerstones:

(1) abolition of the electoral system and replacement of it with
an administrative commission appointed by the governor and wield-
ing the powers which the 1916 law granted to the council and the
executive board;

(2) the introduction of more effective control of the Community's accounting system, exercised by means of the "executive powers" which the governing authorities possessed over the major actions of the administrative commission; and

(3) consolidation of the small Communities in Tripolitania into
the Community of Tripoli.

Regarding this initial draft the Ministry of Colonies raised some fundamental issues on May 4. It questioned whether the principle on
the basis of which the draft justified abolishing the electoral system
was a correct one, implying that the model should be not the new
Italian municipal legislation but rather the legislation governing
Italian Jewish Communities. The ministry agreed that the new legislation should ensure that "the obviously indispensable strong government vigilance over policy" be exercised, but held that the proposed legislation showed "a tendency to regulate matters in an
overly detailed way" and stated that "vigilance does not necessarily
mean control" and "too heavy and demanding a bureaucratic hand
would certainly not help relations between the government and representatives of the Jewish Community." Finally, the ministry emphasized the need to extend the new legislation to cover Libya as a
whole, and thus fulfill the requests to this effect which the Community of Benghazi had been making since 1914, and especially since
1924. Since the views of Rome and Tripoli were so different, the
next step was to submit the whole affair to an ad hoc committee.

The minister of colonies set it up on June 14, 1927, with Adolfo Berio as chairman, Alberto Monastero as secretary, and Riccardo Astuto, Angelo Sereni, and Emilio Moretti as members. The committee was confronted with a new plan prepared by Tripoli which, apart from accepting the principle of a single piece of legislation for all of Libya, confirmed all the most decisive points of the first draft. The committee was strengthened by the support that Federzoni, the new minister of colonies, gave it. At his first ministerial meeting he had made it clear that the government wanted the new legislation to give the governing authorities greater powers of supervision and intervention, but it wished to do this in the context of helping Libyan Jewry to develop to the level of Italian Jews.[17] The committee eventually drew up a text which recognized some of the requests of the Tripolitanian administration, while ignoring others. Specifically, it passed over the request to abolish the electoral system, arguing that the Community, "though it also served the public interest," mainly carried out "private matters, such as religious rites and practices." The committee sent this text to the minister on March 5, 1928, and on April 24 it was submitted to the Supreme Council of the Colonies. After a few small changes it became the Royal Decree on Working Regulations for the Jewish Communities of Tripolitania and Cyrenaica, June 28, 1928, No. 1673.[18] Apart from the electoral principle, the main clauses of the new legislation were the following:

(1) The right to vote. In theory this was granted only to Libyan and Italian male Jews over twenty-one years of age, who were able to read and write Italian and who paid a tax of at least 50 lire in the larger Communities (with a population of 5,000 or more) and 25 lire in smaller Communities, or who were graduates of rabbinical schools or of higher intermediate schools or the equivalent. In practice, the provisional regulations extended this right also to individuals over thirty-five who did not know Italian and, though only for five years (in order to encourage the spread of Italian), to individuals under thirty-five as well as foreigners who, on the date of the decree, had been members of the Libyan Communities for at least five years.

(2) The right to be represented. This was granted to all voters, including foreigners covered by the provisional regulations.

(3) The number of electors serving on the councils—one for every 1,500 members of the Community, with a minimum of seven.

(4) The powers of the governor. At any time, for reasons of public order, subject to the prior approval of the minister of colonies and with a justifying warrant, he could cancel the appointment of one or more elected members of the council. It was his duty to appoint the

chairman and vice-chairman, choosing them from a list of two nominees that the council would submit. He had supervisory powers over the Community and could execute any obligatory acts which the Community might omit to perform. He approved balance sheets, new taxes, list of taxpayers, and large transfers of funds. Finally, "for reasons of public order or the interests of the Community" he could dissolve the council and appoint a commissioner to serve for a period not exceeding six months.

As we see, the new legislation largely met the governing authorities' requests, and gave them broad powers of intervention in the political leadership and running of the Communities. However, the text, the ministerial committee's report, and the opinion of the Supreme Council of the Colonies all sanctioned two principles antithetical to those which the governing authorities would have liked to see affirmed. One of them recognized the Libyan Jews' right to choose their own Community leaders. This was particularly dear to the Jews, and also, because of the implications which it had for domestic and foreign policy, important to the government. The other did not have the approval of most Libyan Jews, but received consent with varying degrees of qualification from the central authorities, the Consortium of Italian Jewish Communities, and the richest and most Europeanized Libyan Jews. It affirmed the trend toward assimilation and full Italianization. That is why, on the whole, though Libyan Jews were not fully satisfied with it, they did not seriously oppose the new legislation; it is also why the Italian Jewish leadership considered it better than what they had initially feared would be imposed. In the last analysis, those most disappointed were the colonial authorities in Libya, since they considered the spirit of the law unrealistic and the powers which it gave them inadequate.

The strength of their disappointment showed during the crisis occasioned by the Community elections in Tripoli in 1929. Badoglio, the new governor, was psychologically and politically less sensitive than De Bono to broad concerns, seeing everything from the perspective of protecting "public order" and Italian-Arab relations. He used his powers to annul the election results and appoint a special non-Jewish commissioner. Badoglio then took advantage of the situation quickly and decisively. He proposed a drastic reorganization of Community affairs and eventually managed to have the electoral system abolished and the very principle shaping the law revised. Badoglio's position emerges from his correspondence with Rome as early as the week after the elections were canceled and Monastero appointed special commissioner. It becomes clear in a long letter which Badoglio sent to the Ministry of Colonies the following year, on July 22, 1930. Justifying itself with the need to make the 1928 law conform to the new legislation for the Italian Jewish communities, the government had begun to think about amending it. Sending the ministry his staff's own draft for the new law, Badoglio wrote:

> In order to have a real idea of the new regulations contained in the at-tached draft, we must begin by examining the social, moral, and intel-lectual situation of Libyan Jews. We need a precisely aimed policy with regard to them—one based not on sentimentalism or ideology but on secure and definite convictions and a firm program of action. . . .
>
> It would be useless to put the Jews of Tripoli on the level of Italian Jews and mold their institutions and administrative procedures on those of the latter.
>
> Italian Jews form a minute minority within Italy. Nevertheless, they are not only Italian citizens, but perfectly assimilated individuals molding their social, intellectual, and moral life on those of the Ital-ians. Thus the government is able to grant their communities liberal forms of constitution and administration and to be indifferent to their activities. The communities limit these activities to meeting internal needs which accord with those of the surrounding majority, and never come into contact, much less conflict, with society.
>
> The vast majority of the Jews of Tripoli (except for a few hundred of them) are genuinely indigenous Libyans. As an ethnic group they are politically, socially, intellectually, and morally inferior to Italian Jews, with whom they have no similarity and no common ground except in their prayers. The Libyan Jews have grown very similar to the Libyan Arabs but are below them and should be raised to that level before we contemplate raising them to the level of Italians.
>
> Despite their claimed religious orthodoxy, which they set up against any other Jewish community, the Jews of Tripoli practice only the forms; on an individual level, selfishness, indifference, and material and intellectual laziness are the norm.
>
> The knowledge of this could lead to a negative program, in other words, one of indifference to the Jews of Tripoli and their organiza-tions. We would grant some apparent freedoms thanks to our political and social conscience but then give them no more thought. We would be doing this in the hope that progress would slowly affect them and one day raise them to that level of civilization and resemblance to our-selves which we desire.
>
> The government, however, having a moral responsibility for all its subjects, cannot abandon such people to their own fate; it is obliged to help them develop, which can only be done by supervising them as much as possible and obliging them to pass swiftly through the phases of human and social progress which other peoples have experienced slowly.

In view of these remarks, it is not surprising that the draft law attached to them largely confirmed the terms of the 1927 draft. It specifically excluded any form of election, concentrating all authority in the hands of an administrative commission consisting of a few members appointed "at the sole choice" of the governor. What is surprising is that a man as circumspect as Badoglio should take such a clear and extreme position without making sure that he had the complete support of the Ministry of Colonies and with the probable knowledge that Rome did not agree with him. The new ministerial commission to review the 1928 law—partly composed of the same members as the first (Adolfo Berio as chairman, Pio Jannuzi as secretary, and Angelo Sereni, Luigi Mischi, and Luigi Del Giudice)— again reached conclusions in sharp contrast to the governing authorities' requests.

The Supreme Council of the Colonies approved the main innovations introduced by the commission on May 18, 1931 [19] and they were made law in royal decree no. 957 of June 18, 1931. [20] Some of these innovations were intended to make the law conform to the criteria of the law for Italian Jewish Communities, some to make the Community administrative structures more efficient. Some of them brought together the administrative authority into a single body, the administrative committee, replacing the council and the board and consisting of twelve or nine members depending on the number of Community members. Some new provisions increased the chairman's powers. Some restricted the size of the electorate (by raising the minimum voting age to twenty-five) and the presence of foreigners in the institutions running the Community (by establishing that they could not occupy more than one-third of the seats). Two innovations were the most important from a political point of view: the one increasing from six months to a year the time for which a commissioner could hold office, and, even more important, the innovation contained in Article 37 (of the transitional provisions):

> In the case of special reasons and contingencies, and upon prior authorization of the Minister of Colonies, the Governor may suspend the application of the provisions in these regulations relating to the election of the Administrative Committee. In such case the members of the Committee shall be appointed by the Governor from among the Community members.

This article amounted to a considerable impairment of the principle of the Community's autonomy and self-government. The provision was actually only a sop to the colonial authorities and Badoglio, concealing the latest and most serious defeat they had suffered. This is shown by a whole series of facts. First, in its final report dated April 30, the ministerial commission unanimously confirmed that "the process of assimilation of Libyan Jewry into Italian Jewry, which has already clearly begun, cannot be stopped, since it reflects the adaptability and lively intelligence marking the Jewish race." Second, the principle of election for offices was once more affirmed. Third, though the governor was empowered to suspend the franchise in exceptional circumstances and himself appoint the members of the administrative committee, the new law (a) made this suspension subject to the minister's approval, and (b) stipulated that the commissioner should be a member of the Community (this being an obvious criticism of Badoglio for appointing Monastero). In the course of its work (specifically at its fourth meeting on February 3), the ministerial commission affirmed, again unanimously, "that the principle of election should be upheld," that "the system of appointment by the governor should be considered an absolutely exceptional and temporary procedure," and "that these principles should be brought to the attention of the colonial authorities so that they may use the exceptional provisions provided for as seldom as possible, with a view to ensuring a speedy return to the usual regulations covering elections." Last of all, it must be added that the new law allowed the governor to annul the election of one or more members of the administrative commission only when the members took office (rather than at any time, as under the 1928 law). He lost the right to choose the president and vice-president of the Community from a list of two nominees each, since under the new law both these appointments were made by the committee itself from among its own members. In view of all this, it is fair to say that the local colonial authorities and Badoglio had suffered a defeat.

The backstage maneuvers leading up to the passage of the new legislation reveal the Libyan colonial authorities' real attitude toward the Jews in the early 1930s. They lead one to think that the authorities must have come through it all deeply disappointed, but determined to take advantage of all the powers which they did receive, and probably, deep down, yearning to strike back and show Rome how wrong its choice had been. Before we look at how this attitude evolved in later years, we should stop a moment and try to clarify its causes. These can be related to the situation both within Libyan Jewry, particularly among the Jews of Tripoli, and in Libya as a whole. That is the only way really to grasp the causes and implications of the new phase then beginning in relations between colonial authorities in Libya and local Jews. It is also the only way to understand the repercussions which these relations were having in Italy in the ministry and especially among Italian Jews.

One interesting issue is the role which Badoglio played in this new phase. There were "objective" motivations for it beyond the governor himself dating back to De Bono's time. Their roots lay in the growing disillusion and concern of ever broader sectors of the governing authorities at Libyan Jewry's "unruliness" and "inability to be civilized." There is no doubt, though, that without Badoglio's approval and support the shift would have happened more slowly and less traumatically. Several additional facts testify to this. In December 1933, when it was a question of whether to find some compromise on the Sabbath issue or follow the path of intransigence, Badoglio chose the latter. The Ministry of Colonies let him decide as he thought fit.[21] Significantly, Badoglio was about to resign. It is therefore likely that this intransigence was his specific wish, since the simplest and most appropriate solution would have been (as it seems the ministry expected)[22] to leave the decision to his successor. Badoglio's attitude is shown by a sentence which he uttered to Arabs at a meeting of notables of the two communities after the serious incidents between Jews and Arabs had broken out in Tripoli in June 1933: "If I were not speaking in the name of Italy, a civilized country, I would say to you, "Take revenge!"[23] It is therefore necessary to understand the reasons for Badoglio's position. Though one can speak of his narrow-mindedness and complete inability to understand the psychology and identity problems of "indigenous people,"[24] there is nothing to indicate that his attitude toward Libyan Jews was based on anti-Semitism. Badoglio did make some specific arguments in connection with the drafting of the new legislation for the Libyan Jewish Communities, arguments which already formed the basic position of a large part of his civil administration. My opinion is that Badoglio's attitude was based, as well as on these arguments, on another conviction of his. He believed that the local population should be encouraged to submit. The Arab rebels had suffered a series of crushing defeats from which they would never be able to recover, especially if they lacked the support of the local people. Thus, the best attitude was to show the Arabs tolerance, refrain from raising the specter of the Sanusis, and conduct "a policy of improving the lot of the indigenous population." On June 24, 1929, Badoglio wrote to Mussolini, "At the outset the rebellion in Cyrenaica was due to political causes, but very soon economic causes took over. *Very often the troops, in the course of plundering, made no distinction between those who had submitted and the rebels.* In its resentment against this, the entire population fueled the rebellion. The rebels' *dor** were constantly receiving new supplies of recruits, arms, and food from those who had already submitted."[25]

Badoglio initially, in 1929, succeeding in winning over Mussolini and De Bono to this policy, though it cost him much effort and he never really managed to convince them that it was the right one. On the first signs of the rebels' recovery, a few months later, the Duce ordered Badoglio to "break off all contact and show no tolerance to the rebels, attack them and give no quarter."[26] Badoglio had to obey, but he remained true to his own mind and tried to continue winning over the Arab population. His attitude toward the Jews ought to be seen in this context. An attitude of "favoritism" to the Jews, whether real or apparent, would not have pleased the Arabs. For centuries the Arab masses had been used to seeing Jews as inferior, and they would not tolerate the idea of the Italians' raising the Jews to their level. Already they felt subordinated to the Jews and vulnerable to their "arrogance" and economic "exploitation." An attitude favorable to the Jews would also displease Arab groups which were more alert to events in the rest of the Arab world, particularly Palestine. These groups expressed their views from time to time in unexpected tensions and small but significant incidents with Jews. Hence Badoglio's belief that it was politically expedient to meet the Arabs' desires in this respect, by showing them that the Italians had no preference for the Jews and in fact were being particularly firm with them. This was all the easier since some of the Jews themselves were showing their feeling of superiority to Arabs and their emotional identification with what was happening in Palestine.

A second and more important issue is how Libyan Jewish life, particularly in Tripoli, changed around this time. Earlier chapters have dwelt on the consequences and trends set in motion in Jewish life by the impact of modernization. The most significant of these consequences were the following: (a) the growing gap between the rich and very rich and the poor and very poor; (b) the slow but irreparable schism into two camps, the traditionalists (composed mainly of the poor and socially marginal) and the modernizers (largely composed of the wealthy and upwardly mobile), linked on the religious and spiritual levels by ever more perfunctory bonds; (c) the formation of an embryonic new leadership, larger than the previous one and oriented in two different directions—a slow and almost uncon-

---

*Organized armed unit, described by E. E. Evans-Pritchard, *The Sanusi of Cyrenaica* (Oxford: Clarendon, 1949; rpt. 1963), p. 137.—*Trans.*

scious, but no less real, trend to integration and assimilation, and the largely coherent trend to Zionism—both of which were expressions of modernization. During the first ten years of Italian occupation these consequences had largely remained latent, barely achieving the level of trends. Only those most aware of Jewish issues saw the imbalances which the impact with modern society was causing and the cultural drama threatening Libyan Jewish life in its very foundations. In the second decade, as "pacification" proceeded, these trends became more and more clear. Mixed marriages became more numerous; a few people left the community or converted; prostitution, alcoholism, and gambling increased. The Sabbath was still respected very broadly (in Tripoli in 1932 only one shopkeeper, a Tunisian, opened on that day). However, the few government employees who were Jewish no longer observed the Sabbath. In other areas of Jewish society the day of rest had no serious challenge from the outside, and so non-observance was rare. The vast majority of Jews still lived and worked with their own people, as separate as possible from the rest of Libyan society.[27] Serious as all this was from the point of view of Jewish culture, even more ominous was the widening social chasm. It was becoming a real cultural schism, with all the inevitable consequences for intracommunity relations. The most obvious sign of this crisis was the growing numbers of the poor, the destitute, and beggars. In Tripoli the "ragged indigents" (as Disegni had called them) in the early 1930s were the most obvious characteristic of the *hara*, whence on Fridays they poured out into neighboring quarters to beg.[28] The Community was practically powerless in the face of this tragic situation and could do no more than hand out charity: "A few lire, poorly distributed through a chaotic and rudimentary organization, to people who ought to be saved from poverty rather than allowed to become heirs to beggary."[29] The Zionists' efforts in education, though vigorous and well organized, failed to make any mark on such a situation. They could slow the process down, but not stop it. They could save a few individuals, especially young people, but they could not prevent the rest from floundering in deeper or extracting themselves by the only means which seemed within reach—integration and assimilation. Another path beckoned, even more dehumanizing and humiliating: that of spiritual and cultural hybridism.

When we look at this situation, we understand why the Italian colonial authorities were concerned. Directly and indirectly, the situation was causing unrest and internal disagreements. Particularly in Tripoli, it was liable to have repercussions on the tissue connecting Jewry with the broader society and—a fact which from the Fascist viewpoint could not be ignored—on the very character of the Libyan capital. That helps us to understand why the community leaders themselves, some eagerly and some reluctantly, shared the same concerns as the authorities. This is particularly true of the Tripoli Jews belonging to the new leadership which had emerged in the late 1920s and which Monastero had mobilized. Some did not want to be involved because they wanted to avoid further difficulties with the Italian authorities and felt, if not exactly abandoned, then hardly assisted by Italian Jewry in their difficult task.[30] Some did want to be involved with the Italians because they largely expressed the new reality of Libyan Jewry and, as such, consciously or unconsciously favored integration. While seeing the necessity of stopping the obvious decline in Libyan Jewish life, they were particularly aware that the means at their disposal, even combined with those of the Zionists, were inadequate. The Jews were thus obliged to take advantage of the Italian colonial authorities' "recovery" program. This program presented many difficulties and involved solutions and methods distasteful to the majority of Jews and even the integrationists themselves. Significantly, the administrative committee of Tripoli suggested to the governing authorities on at least two occasions, in January 1932 and June 1935, that it would be useful for Libyan Jews to do military service. It hoped that young Jews would thus be brought out of their backwater and confronted with modern ideas and civilization.[31]

It is in this overall context that we should view the serious events which took place between late 1932 and late 1933 in Tripoli. Similar events occurred later on in Benghazi. All Monastero's improvements in relations between the local colonial authorities and Libyan Jews were then brought to a halt.

The origin of the crisis lay in the issue of Sabbath observance in the public schools. Jewish students had been excused from attendance on the Sabbath since Turkish times. The Italian occupation had introduced the Sunday holiday. There had been no problems during the first few years; since the majority of pupils were Jews and Italians were scarce, the solution had been to take off Saturday and Sunday. Later, when the numbers of Italians increased, since they were clustered in particular neighborhoods, the Office of the Superintendent of Schools solved the problem by closing the schools in Old Tripoli on Saturdays and Sundays, and those in the new European neighborhoods, where Jews were very few, on Thursdays and Sundays. Jews from the European neighborhoods who wished to do so, unlike non-Jews, were allowed to attend schools far from their homes. With the increase in school attendance and Jewish families living outside the *hara*, this solution became less and less practical. This was particularly so in the intermediate schools, which were less numerous than elementary schools and so more mixed. Until the 1930–1931 school year, the superintendent's office had allowed Jewish pupils in intermediate schools to take Saturdays off.[32] The following year permission was not given officially, but the leave was taken in practice. In the 1932–1933 school year, however, while the old provisions remained in effect in the elementary schools, where education was compulsory, attendance was required in intermediate schools on Saturdays, under penalty of expulsion. This provision was supposed to encourage the integration of young Jews. Three strong arguments lay behind this decision: that Jews attended school on Saturdays as a matter of course in Italy; that the previous exemption had been a serious obstacle to both teaching and learning; and that quite a few Jewish boys already attended school on Saturdays.

News of the measure aroused among the Jews of Tripoli a great clamor and diverse reactions. The most traditional Jews began to agitate. Protests were staged, and some boys demonstrated against their companions who went to school on Saturdays. Pressure was brought to bear on the families. Some parents, who until then had felt no conflict in sending their children to school on Saturdays, withdrew them from school. Other families, being unfamiliar with how things were in Italy, and refusing to believe what they were told, considered sending their offspring to study in Italy.[33] More seriously, the traditionalists persuaded the rabbinical court to protest to the governor's office, without the approval of the Community authorities, and threaten not to consider as Jews those who went along with the new measures.[34] The administrative committee took a different stance. Though it knew the serious effect that the provision had on the sensibilities and religion of many Jews, it quickly saw how inopportune from a political point of view and useless from a practical one this trial of strength was. It preferred to calm tempers down and persuade families to conform to the new measures, while trying to reach a compromise. It asked the Italian authorities at least not to oblige Jewish pupils to write on the Sabbath and to set up for the following school year schools or sections in intermediate schools for Jewish pupils where the Sabbath would be respected. At the same time, the committee contacted the Union and the Rabbi of Rome, Angelo Sacerdoti, for support and help. It wished to know what regulations the French authorities imposed on the Tunisian and

Algerian communities.[35] After the rabbinical court took its stand, Angelo J. Arbib wrote in the committee's name on December 19, 1932, to Rabbi Sacerdoti:

> . . . faced with such a serious consequence as that of preventing many young people from pursuing their education, the rabbinical court should have considered whether the circumstances did not require it to exert persuasion over the majority. It could have pointed out that, though attending school on the Sabbath (even without writing) is a "sin," this is still preferable to the more serious one the parents would be committing of making these young Jews of Tripoli abandon their studies. Moreover, it must be realized that it is absolutely essential for this important Jewish Community to create soon a nucleus of educated individuals. It is far from reassuring to see that among the sixteen thousand Jews in Tripoli, there is not a single lawyer, engineer, professor, nor teacher.[36]

As we may well imagine, this attitude on the part of the leaders of the Community aroused conflicting reactions in Tripoli. A number of boys began or continued attending school on Saturdays; about seventy others began absenting themselves every Saturday. Some adults approved the administrative committee's prudence, while others violently censured it and organized a protest demonstration against it. The reaction of the Italian Jewish leaders, particularly some rabbis, was less expected.

Though Jewish pupils in Italy had been going to school on Saturdays for over seventy years, the Italian rabbis took a stand against the Tripoli committee: some, such as the Rabbi of Rome, condemned its action in absolute terms:

> Attending school on the Sabbath is a sin. In Italy we are painfully experiencing the harmful effects of assimilation . . . Jewish Tripoli is still one of the realms where loyalty to the Torah is felt and practiced: it is still a burning beacon from which divine light can spread to other places and other countries. Don't snuff out this beacon of truth! Show that you are children worthy of your fathers who, to avoid betraying God, faced persecution and martyrdom.[37]

It was probably just after the Italian rabbis had expressed this position and due also to pressures which the more uncompromising Zionists were exerting in Tripoli, that, on January 12, 1933, the most serious episode of the whole affair took place. It transformed the affair into a political event, bringing it to the knowledge of a broader public outside Libya. *Israel* published on that date a long article entitled "For the Sabbath of Intermediate School Pupils in Tripoli." The article directly attacked the administrative committee, indirectly the governing authorities, and by implication the government itself. The journal accused the government of conducting a policy of discrimination against Jews and in favor of Arabs, working for the assimilation of Jews while protecting the religious rights of Muslims. In indictment of the committee, *Israel* published a "balance sheet" of the events which had reached it from Tripoli and which began as follows:

> For over two months the current Administrative Committee of the Community has been carrying on a vigorous and determined campaign among Jewish students in the Government Intermediate Schools. It has been trying to oblige them, particularly the indigent whom it helps with fees and books, to attend school on the Sabbath. It has been trying to persuade their parents to send them by holding that "it is high time that we abandoned the *foolish, outmoded religious* customs preventing the development and progress of local Jews within the new Italian civilization in this country, and that we put ourselves on a level with the Jews of Italy and the whole civilized world who, no longer placing such importance on it, all send their children to school on the Sabbath" and making other similarly repellent arguments. All the committee's efforts, though, have come up against the no less determined resistance of the pupils and their parents, backed by the entire Jewish population.

The governing authorities themselves were roundly accused of allowing themselves to be taken in by a few assimilationist Jews with bad intentions:

> From our point of view there can be no doubt that though the Government of the Colony has now laid down the provision which has aroused so much legitimate concern among all the healthy Jewish elements in the Community, this was only because poorly intentioned Jewish elements have succeeded in convincing it that some of their private opinions and desires are generally held by all Jews, or that they deserve preference over the views of the rest.

The government itself, though not explicitly mentioned, was also in fact being accused. No journal as aware of the differences between Rome and Tripoli regarding assimilation of Jews as *Israel* was could publish statements like the following, without intending them to be directed at the government. Nor could such a journal attribute to Badoglio a wish to encourage assimilation and in general, favor Jews over Arabs.

> At the same time that Jewish pupils are being obliged to break the Sabbath, another Order of the Governor has been posted on street corners all around the city. It requires scrupulous observance of the Muslim

Ramadan and provides for severe penalties for anyone contravening or causing the contravention of any of the precepts relating to it.

The different attitude toward Judaism provokes effusive gratitude on the part of the Special Commission toward the Authorities who are granting to the Jews alone the right to "evolution and civil progress," while other groups, including the Catholics, are left to sink ever further into "religious obscurantism." This different treatment does not reassure the "backward" majority of local Jews. Using their uncultured but uncorrupted intuition, this majority cannot fail to discern the all too obvious danger to preserving and cultivating the spiritual heritage which we have received from our ancestors, by means of how many and what sacrifices God only knows.[38]

The best proof of the validity of my interpretation regarding the objects of this attack lies in the fact that the issue of *Israel* carrying this article was promptly withdrawn from circulation by government order.[39] Besides causing a harsh argument between the Community of Tripoli, the Union, and Rabbi Sacerdoti, *Israel*'s attack must have immediately caused the colonial authorities in Tripoli to stiffen their position. Though initially they had been amenable to the possibility of setting up special sections for Jews, after *Israel*'s attack they became more intransigent. A meeting between Ravenna, the president of the Union, and Badoglio in Italy on February 8 led to nothing concrete. The governor merely invited Ravenna to visit Tripoli and see for himself the situation of the local Jews and the conditions in which he had to operate. He made the vague statement that then they would be able to look at the problem again together.[40] The Union found that the Ministry of Colonies was less inflexible, though all it did was to say that the governor himself had the responsibility to make all decisions.

That was how things stood in June, when the situation in Tripoli was jolted by new events which pushed the issue of the Sabbath into the background and eventually obscured it altogether.

Since May, there had been signs that tensions between Arabs and Jews were growing again. Small incidents, annoyances, and fights had been disturbing the *hara*. The governing authorities had intervened by reinforcing the usual security measures, but the animosity did not stop. In fact, the Arabs became more and more aggressive, taking advantage, perhaps, of the Jews' problems with the colonial administration. The Arabs' aggressiveness may also have been due to echoes reaching them of increasing tension in Palestine, which had led to two large demonstrations in Jerusalem and Haifa and a series of riots against rising Jewish immigration. Foreign Jews in Tripoli asked their consulates for help. The Community protested to the authorities, who took no further steps and merely exhorted anyone who had suffered injury or damage to sue his attackers.

The majority had reacted to this situation with fear: Jewish peddlars and handymen mostly stopped going to the Muslim quarters, while many shops closed early. A minority, who were already embittered about the Sabbath issue and annoyed at the favor which they said Arabs were enjoying as a result of Badoglio's recent measures concerning religious holidays, took a stronger stand. They did not trust the authorities' commitment to protecting public order, especially since it was often delegated to Muslim *carabinieri*. The Jews regarded them with suspicion and believed that they favored the Arabs. In this atmosphere, more serious incidents took place in late May and early June, with several wounded on both sides. Badoglio reacted to these quite differently from his usual practice, which was to send those responsible to the courts and reprimand the leaders of both communities. At the first repetition of the incidents, he informed the Jewish Community that it was being fined a thousand lire. The second time, a more serious recurrence, he took a step which for Jews was unprecedented under Italian rule: he had the main protagonists of the incidents, both Arabs and Jews, publicly flogged in the marketplace.

This exceptional step, as is easy to imagine, made a deep impression on the Jews of Tripoli. The Community's administrative committee (which had already protested over the fine) resigned on June 12, without even consulting the Union in advance. Badoglio rejected the resignation and stated that the committee did not have any right to express an opinion "regarding actions carried out by the Government [of Tripolitania] in such delicate matters which are not subject to control or appeal."

> The policing measures taken recently by the Government [he replied on June 14] have been of an exceptional nature, as was the new situation. Since neither appeals through the notables, nor advice, nor threats, nor normal sanctions were enough to quell the spreading disorderly behavior, there was no alternative but to inflict the more exemplary and serious punishment under the present regulations. Otherwise, the impression would have been created that the Government was unable to restore order.

Confronted with such an intransigent attitude, and unable to risk a complete break, the administrative committee had no alternative but to withdraw its resignation and pass the initiative to the Union of Jewish Communities.[41]

Having learned its lesson from what had happened over the Sabbath issue, the Union moved quickly, but with extreme caution. It requested *Israel* to give an account of the events "in the most cautious and neutral terms, so as not to exacerbate the situation." Though the news was reported briefly and under the terse headline "Unpleasant Incidents," it did not prevent that issue of the journal also from being promptly withdrawn.[42] Having rejected the idea of bringing up the problem with the Ministry of Colonies in Rome, the Union decided to send Ravenna, its president, and Castelbolognesi, the rabbi of Padua (one of the candidates for the position in Tripoli) to talk to Badoglio in Libya.

Their mission to Tripoli (July 19–25, 1933) was a complete failure. Badoglio reproached the Union for leaving Libyan Jewry to its own devices, and for not resolving the problem of the chief rabbi's appointment. He showed his unhappiness "with the wayward behavior of some [Jews] from the lowest class" with whom, he implied, responsibility for the previous month's incidents lay. To Ravenna, who had expressed his "deep regret" at the measures taken in that connection, he replied "frankly" that, while he himself also regretted having had to use "coercive and forceful methods," he was not dissatisfied with what he had done, "since the punishments meted out had succeeded in restoring calm." He was equally intransigent with regard to the Sabbath issue. While not entirely abandoning the proposal to introduce a section for Jews, he refused to rescind the measure. The only concrete result of the trip was to allow Ravenna and Castelbolognesi to see for themselves how serious the situation in Tripoli was and to recognize the necessity of sending a chief rabbi as soon as possible. Only a rabbi would be able to wield effective moral and religious authority over Libyan Jewry, heal internal differences, deal with the Italian administration as the Jews' legitimate leader, and constitute a channel to the Union.[43] The Union's subsequent efforts to achieve some softening in the position of Badoglio and the Ministry of Colonies had no better result. It attempted to soften the requirement to attend school on the Sabbath in post-elementary schools, if not in principle, then at least in practice. With regard to setting up one or two sections for Jews in the intermediate, vocational, and normal schools, Badoglio eventually declared himself not responsible. He passed the decision on to De Bono, who, in the end, gave a negative answer. While awaiting his answer, since the governor's measure remained in force, the Union also tried to persuade the superintendent's office to allow headmasters to excuse Jewish children on Saturdays from time to time. As I have already indicated, the Ministry of Colonies seemed favorably disposed to this solution for a week or so, especially since

Badoglio was about to leave his post as governor and could very well have left the decision to his successor. Contrary to the Union's hopes, he preferred instead to reconfirm all provisions issued the previous year for the new school year. For the Union to press the point any further would have been ridiculous. Though in Benghazi the provision did not take effect until early 1935, the school authorities in Tripoli were now beginning to expel from school any pupils absent on Saturdays.[44] The one remaining remedy was to try to set up Community intermediate schools (which would be difficult in view of the Community's severe economic situation and the lack of suitable teachers), and to hope that the new governor would be better disposed.

The new governor of Libya, appointed to replace Badoglio, was Italo Balbo. One of the most outstanding Fascist figures,* he was dynamic and efficient. By sending him to Libya, Mussolini hoped to reduce Balbo's prestige and political ambitions. This was in the wake of his trans-Atlantic flights and his role in Dino Grandi's† dismissal from the Ministry of Foreign Affairs.[45] Libyan and Italian Jews warmly welcomed Balbo's appointment. They saw him as a new kind of governor, who was not just a soldier but a politician and modern man, better able than Badoglio to understand their problems. In view of Balbo's excellent relations with the Jews of his own town, Ferrara, and with Ravenna himself, they considered him pro-Jewish and thus open and understanding. His arrival in January 1934 was marked by expressions of sympathy and enthusiasm on the part of the Jews of Tripoli, the Community leaders, Chief Rabbi Castelbolognesi (who had arrived a few weeks before), and coverage of the event in *Israel*.[46]

It would be an exaggeration to call Balbo pro-Jewish. The new governor, who had many Italian Jewish friends, was certainly not an anti-Semite. In 1921–1922 several Jews had supported him in Ferrara, giving financial help to the local Fascist organization and even joining its "squads"; such an active and achievement-oriented man had a natural affinity for anyone with the same talents. Among

*Balbo founded the Fascist movement in Ferrara, was a leader of the March on Rome, and organized aviation in Italy as Minister of Aviation (1929–1933). He led flights across the Mediterranean and the Atlantic in 1930, 1931, and 1933. He died in 1940 when his plane was mistakenly shot down over Tubruq by Italian anti-aircraft fire.—*Trans.*

†A moderate Fascist leader who tried to restrain Mussolini and criticized his party's domestic policies, Grandi was minister of foreign affairs, 1929–1932, then ambassador to London, 1932–1939. Condemned to death by a neo-Fascist tribunal in 1944, he was again sentenced after the liberation, then received amnesty.—*Trans.*

the Jews of his acquaintance these qualities were widely possessed, causing Balbo to believe that all Jews were basically similar to those he knew or had heard about. His reputation for being pro-Jewish was also based on his deep opposition to Nazism. He expressed it freely, and his newspaper, the *Corriere padano* [Paduan Courier] had several times attacked the Nazis and their sympathizers in Italy for their racism and anti-Semitism.[47] The most important element in Balbo's attitude toward Libyan Jews was, however, the state of mind and program he adopted on assuming the position of governor. However important the post was, for Balbo it meant being kicked upstairs. As such, it aroused mixed feelings in him. On the one hand, he was bitter about Mussolini's ingratitude and jealousy; on the other hand, he wanted to show the Duce, the Italian people, and the world what he could do, even in this new position. Even when his beloved flying had been taken away from him, and he had been sent off to the edge of the desert, he would show everyone his abilities as a leader. A galvanizer of energies, and an organizer, he would transform Libya into a modern country and develop its society and economy. Fascist colonization would prepare the ground for Italian initiative and hard work and give land and work to those who lacked them in Italy. After having been reconquered and "pacified," Libya now had to be developed economically, provided with a modern infrastructure, and made ready to receive mass immigration.[48]

Within this policy, in all likelihood Balbo foresaw an important role for Libyan Jews. Their abilities and enterprise in business and the resources available to them would give him a guarantee, a point of reference which he could not afford to overlook. This is particularly probable since during the pacification and especially after it had been completed, the Jews had given ample proof of their tendency to branch out, geographically and in terms of size and specialization, and respond to modern economic and technological needs. They had expanded their business to new markets.[49] The main changes in their work patterns were a small but significant increase in agriculture, in which Jews had been reluctant to work before,[50] and an enormous increase in office work. Otherwise, there had not been substantial changes. As regards distribution according to sectors,[51] Balbo must have seen as significant the changes going on within the two traditional sectors of Jewish activity, that of trade and that of industry and crafts. There were some ominous signs, in particular the undue fragmentation of businesses, which meant that many of them were only just surviving. Another bad sign was a persistent crisis in some crafts, due to overcrowding and problems in selling the products. Nevertheless, both of the main sectors were experiencing growth in varying degrees depending on the market and, in the economically more secure branches, technological and economic modernization of the businesses themselves. Tables 12 and 13 reflect fairly clearly the growth in trade and in industry and crafts. They list the main economic activities of Jews in Libya at the beginning of the Second World War and of taxpaying members of the Community of Tripoli in 1930 and 1937.[52] The process of modernization is shown by the considerable number of joint-stock companies and limited partnerships, under both individual and joint ownership, which were established during the 1930s.[53]

In the overall picture of the situation in Libya and how it was developing, these positive factors were balanced out by others which were not only negative from an economic and social point of view, but also worrying from a political standpoint. First there was the persistent and worsening crisis within some communities, particularly Tripoli. The Tripoli Community had to cope with the serious problem of thousands of Jews almost completely out of work and living in extreme poverty, a problem constantly exacerbated by the high birth rate (the net birth rate among the Jews of Tripoli reached 22 percent, the highest in all of North Africa, compared with 10 percent in Benghazi).[54] The problem was also exacerbated by the creeping impoverishment of the poorer groups in the community. All this should be seen in the context of a city whose population was expanding rapidly, due mainly to the strong immigration from the rest of the country and from Italy.[55] The second negative factor derived from the very low level of education among Libyan Jews. We need only note that in 1939–1941 there were only fourteen Jewish professionals and two Jewish artists in the whole of Libya: in Tripolitania there were four lawyers and notaries public, two engineers and architects, two economists, one accountant, one painter, and one piano teacher; in Cyrenaica there were three accountants and business consultants, one economist, and one doctor.[56]

In view of the above situation, here is how Balbo must have seen the problem of Libyan Jews, and in particular those of Tripoli.

In the short run, it was a question of stopping unemployment by strengthening crafts. Those with most appeal for tourism and export and typically Jewish crafts could be fostered without threatening similar Arab activities, and would absorb at least some of the unemployed or underemployed workforce (peddlars, shoeshiners, and so forth). It was characteristic of him that Balbo soon committed himself to reviving crafts such as silver-working (which employed about two hundred people in Tripoli, but had previously employed up to four hundred, and was monopolized by Jews) and work in ivory (in

TABLE 12. *Occupations of Libyan Jews, 1940*

Occupation	Tripoli	Misurata	Benghazi	Derna
Building, road, and port construction	7		1	
Asphalt- and tar-laying	1			
Painting and decorating	1			
Cement-making	1			
Marble-working	4			
Olive oil manufacture	3			
Milling	3			
Wine producing	2			
Mineral water bottling	2		1	2
Buha (arak) distilling	22		4	3
Liqueur and syrup producing	3			
Brewing				1
Coppersmithing and kettle-making	3		1	
Tin-plating	1		14	
Bicycle construction and repair	4		2	
Typewriter and office-machine repair	1			
Cabinetmaking and carpentry	12		21	1
Mechanical sawmill operation	1			
Upholstery and mattress-making	5			
Saddlemaking	1			
Keg-, stove-, and barrel-making	2		4	
Printing	3		1	
Photography	1			
Bookbinding and stationery	4			
Trucking	3	1		
Forwarding agencies	3			
Garages	2			
Car rental	1			
Men's tailoring	13	3	31	1
Hat-making	1			
Linen-making	1			
Tanning	1			
Shoemaking	2			

Occupation	Tripoli	Misurata	Benghazi	Derna
Carpet-weaving	1	1		
Passementerie manufacturing	5			
Electrical installation	3			
Radio	2			
Electromechanics	1			
Tubes	1			
Vegetable horsehair*	3			
Detergents	1			
Soap manufacture	3			
Silversmithing	71		9	1
Watchmaking	1		2	
Ivory work	7			
Men's hairdressing	11			
Grain and fodder (wholesale)	26		6	
Pastry shops	2		7	
Dates	5			
Bitter orange peel export	2			
Plant nurseries	1			
Henna export	5			
Fruits and vegetables (import-export)			5	
Commercial franchise-holding	76		40	3
Middlemen			3	
Business agencies	1			
Tobacco	5			
Olive and vegetable oils	6			
Wine and liquor	6		4	
Livestock (trade)	5		9	7
Eggs and chickens	6	1	2	
Meat and poultry	13	1	3	
Raw hide (export)	4	1	15	
Hides and leather	5		7	
Bone and horn	2			
Wool (export)	10		8	6
Grocery (wholesale)	24	1		5
Coffee (wholesale)	11			

*A kind of dried grass for household use (used for scouring).—*Trans.*

TABLE 12 *(continued)*

Occupation	Tripoli	Misurata	Benghazi	Derna
Coffee roasting	1			
Grocery (retail)	2		12	
Foodstuffs (wholesale)	7		26	
Pizza-making	2			
Foodstuffs (retail)		1	18	
Ointments	4			
Haberdashery	48	2	11	
Men's clothing	5		30	1
Women's clothing	1			
Men's hats	2		1	1
Shoes	8		1	3
Libyan shoes	1		10	
Shoemaker's supplies, hides	4		5	1
Saddles	2			
Fabrics	57		68	2
Cotton and wool yarn	2			
Raw silk (import)	7			
Silk thread	8			
Silk barracans	5			
Wool barracans	4			
Rags	4			
Horsehair	6			
Bags	3			
Bookshops	3		1	
Stamp shops	2			
Stationers	8		1	2
Typing agency			1	
Jewelers and goldsmiths	13		3	
Silversmiths (sales)			14	
Precious metals	9		4	
Watchmakers (sales)			2	
Housewares	10		12	2
Picture-framing	10		4	
Glassware			1	
Earthenware	2			
Oriental handiwork	19	2	5	

Occupation	Tripoli	Misurata	Benghazi	Derna
Cutlery			3	
Uncut ivory (importing)	5			
Toys	1			
Leather artwork			2	
Bric-a-brac	25		30	
Ironmongery	19		1	2
Scrap metal export	5			
Calculators and office machines	1			
Sewing machines	3			
Radios and phonographs	7			
Cars	2			
Motorcycles	1			
Bicycles	1		2	
Bicycle rental	6			
Car and motorcycle accessories and spare parts	8	1		
Kerosene, gasoline, diesel oil	6	1		
Mineral oils and lubricants	15			
Tires	4			
Perfumeries	2		8	
Pharmacies	2			
Paints	3	2	3	
Construction materials	5		1	
Sanitation, hygiene, and plumbing materials	3		1	
Wallpapering	1			
Shipping agencies	14		7	
Maritime agencies	1			
Average commission agencies	5			
Restaurants	3		2	
Peddling			40	

SOURCE: See note 52.

TABLE 13. *Occupations of Jews of Tripoli in the 1930s*

Occupation	1930	1937
Architects	1	1
Engineers	.	1
Doctors		1
Lawyers	1	
Members of liberal professions	3	3
Teachers	1	2
Interpreters		1
Office workers	53	120
Booksellers	1	2
Stationers	1	1
Photographers	1	
Pharmacists	1	2
Property owners	5	8
Industrialists	6	4
Makers of handicrafts	23	10
Entrepreneurs	1	
Lumber producers		1
Soap producers		1
Transporters		1
Merchants	250	260
Hide merchants	1	10
Cloth merchants		43
Furniture merchants		5
Franchise-holders	23	44
Brokers and middlemen	3	4
Money changers	2	3
Insurance agents		1
Collectors		1
Shippers	4	19
Distillers	3	8
Printers	3	5
Engravers		1
Weighers		1
Dealers, shopkeepers, and haberdashers	11	82
Ironmongers		8
Druggists	8	18
Butchers	17	33
Fried-food sellers	1	2
Pastry sellers	2	4
Fruit venders		4

Occupation	1930	1937
Fishmongers		3
Baker		1
Bartenders	14	7
Tavern and wineshop keepers	12	52
Milkmen	2	19
Goldsmiths and silversmiths	48	75
Machinists	3	4
Blacksmiths	1	16
Coppersmiths		1
Electricians	1	5
Mechanics		1
Bicycle mechanics	1	1
Marblecutters	3	4
Bricklayers	11	29
Stonecutters	1	1
Millers	1	1
Weavers	2	8
Saddlemakers	2	11
Carpenters	4	18
Cabinetmakers	3	3
Tailors	25	59
Charcoal sellers	1	1
Conciliators		3
Glaziers		8
Plumbers		1
Shoemenders		11
Coopers		2
Upholsterers		5
Cement-layers		1
Dyers		1
Bookbinders		1
Decorators		2
Barbers	3	12
Oil venders		2
Peddlars	5	4
Goatherds		1
Fishermen	1	

SOURCE: Jewish Community of Tripoli tax rolls, 1930 and 1937, Auc II, fasc. "Tripoli 1931–38."

which only fifteen people were employed, but which had a long tradition among Jews). He also quickly acted to foster similar initiatives in other branches (embroiderers in silver, tailors of Arab waist-
coats, hairdressers, house-painters, cab drivers, and so forth). These
initiatives were approved and supported, like the others, by the
Community leaders and the chief rabbi.[57]

In the medium rather than long run, Balbo wanted to make
much more far-reaching and permanent changes in the situation. He
was aiming at the complete Italianization of Libyan Jews, making
them into metropolitan citizens. He probably also intended to tackle
the problem of Arab-Jewish relations and solve it once and for all.
The Italian colonial authorities had always had to deal with the
problem, but when Balbo arrived in Libya, Arab-Jewish relations
were about to be changed by a new Fascist policy of *rapprochement*
with the Arab world.[58] Governor Balbo made no secret of what he
wanted, and in December 1934 made a deliberate reference to it to
Rabbi Castelbolognesi: "Bit by bit, we'll reach Italian citizenship."[59]
Balbo soon became aware that some thorough efforts were needed
before this goal could be reached. Being used to the yardstick of assimilated and "civilized" Italian Jews, particularly those of Ferrara,
he was psychologically and culturally removed from the problems of
Libyan Jews. For some time he probably held the illusion, however,
that the chief rabbi, the leaders of Libyan Jewry, and all the more
modern elements agreed with him that the resistance to his policies
was merely reactionary foolishness and obstinacy. He probably believed that they were willing to help him carry out these policies.
A letter written to the Ministry of Colonies early in 1935 shows that
he still expected such help, especially if he had the support of the
Union in Rome:

> It must be recognized that the Jews here need special help so that they
> can reach the level of progress achieved by the Jews in Italy; but the
> Jews of Libya can only be started on the way to the progress which
> everyone hopes for when the most capable leaders of the community
> persuade themselves to spread among their fellows progressive ideas
> more suitable to the requirements of civilization, and abandon cus-
> toms and prejudices which survive here, and nowhere else.[60]

A few months later, it was already clear that Castelbolognesi
would not help Balbo and had, in fact, taken sides with the most traditional Jews, thereby inhibiting those who might have been disposed to collaborate with Balbo, whether willingly or reluctantly.
Then Balbo's attitude, in form if not in substance, shifted radically.
His ultimate goal, and his conviction regarding how best to carry

out fundamental transformations, remained unchanged. He believed that education should be modernized, the Jewish masses should be helped in their economic and social development, and the largest clusters of Jewish population, particularly the *hara* of Tripoli, should be cleared and rebuilt. Unchanged also were Balbo's concern and sympathy for more modern and dynamic Jews and his clear hostility toward any form of anti-Semitism. What changed was his style and general presentation of this policy: no longer understanding and concessions, but instead a heavy hand. Anyone disobeying the governor's measures would pay dearly and, since he did not wish to become modern and Italianized, he would pay like other indigenous inhabitants, with a flogging. If the rebel was an Italian, he would not be allowed to stay in the colony. Thus, since Balbo had failed to persuade the Jews of what he thought was their own good, all he could do was to use coercion. One thing remained clear to him. Whether they liked it or not, the Jews had to adapt to modern society and become an active element: they had to give up their antiquated "prejudices" which did not accord with present-day "progress" and modern society, nor with life among people of various origins, cultures, and religions.

As we know, the Jews greeted Balbo's appointment as governor of Libya with great enthusiasm and hope. Even before he had taken up his duties, Ravenna, Balbo's friend from Ferrara, met with him to ask him to find some favorable settlement for the Sabbath question. Balbo merely replied that he could promise nothing; he would study the problem and do whatever could be done.[61] He had hardly reached Tripoli when Castelbolognesi, who had arrived two months before, in November, approached him and brought up the question again. The chief rabbi was not really the right person to deal with the new governor. In his first public speech after taking office, Castelbolognesi had taken a hardline position which was certainly not appropriate for smoothing the road to an agreement. Without mincing words, he declared that "Tripoli will be held up as an example of the Jews' loyalty to the Sabbath, and of how they guard it and honor it."[62] Later he and the headmaster of the Talmud Torah issued a report on guidelines for reforming teaching and the Jewish schools. From a technical point of view it was valuable, but it clearly revealed his concern regarding the effects which public school education was having on the young and his preference for an entirely Jewish school.[63] The meeting between Castelbolognesi and Balbo, which took place on February 19, 1934, was nevertheless cordial. Balbo was evasive, however, regarding the Sabbath question. He chose to procrastinate and changed the subject to silversmiths and his desire to encourage this

craft. He took the occasion to warn the chief rabbi of his firm intention to "de-ghettoize" and "de-Nahumize" the Jewish community.
These were harsh words, but they did clearly indicate his policy. In
general, it consisted of integrating the Jews better into Libyan society and in particular, of putting the spiritual and political influence of the traditional leadership in a new perspective.[64] In the succeeding months, the governing authorities often showed themselves
disposed to meet the requests of Castelbolognesi and the administrative committee of Tripoli. They were interested in helping the
Community to solve its deficit, in finding a site for a new kindergarten, in authorizing the school superintendent's office to allow
school premises to be used for Hebrew classes, and generally in finding the right solution for several small practical problems. The Italian authorities raised no difficulties to filling a vacant position on
the administrative committee with a candidate, Raffaello Nemni,
personally chosen by Castelbolognesi. They were even favorable
to the possible creation of a chief rabbinate. On one point alone
were Balbo and the authorities immovable: the Sabbath issue. When
Castelbolognesi brought the question up again in November, Balbo
was explicit: "With regard to this topic, my reply is an out-and-out
no and no discussions." His refusal was accompanied however by
the explicit promise to set up a section for Jewish pupils: "We will
set up the special section for Jews in secondary schools, without
classes on Saturdays, I promise you." The superintendent also made
the same promise, though he made it subject to there being enough
pupils to justify it, and in the meantime was accepting the subter-
fuge of the parents' sending an excuse every week for their children's
absence.[65] Mussolini himself said more or less the same thing about
two months later to Angelo Sacerdoti, the rabbi of Rome, who had
gone to him to request a solution to the problem. Ravenna soon
wrote to Castelbolognesi that the *duce* had told Sacerdoti "that he
would take steps so that Jewish students would be allowed to refrain
from writing on the Sabbath and Holy Days, and so that the school
problem in Tripoli would be viewed with special benevolence and
sympathy."[66]

But the Sabbath issue did not involve the schools alone. That
was only the first episode, the first step. From the point of view of
the Italian authorities, both those officials who saw the issue as one
of order and bureaucratic uniformity, and those who considered the
abolition of the Sabbath rest as an important step on the road to
"de-ghettoization" and integration, the issue was much broader and
had to be tackled at its roots.

In late December 1934 the Sabbath issue came to a head in a crisis involving Jewish shipping firms. If the shippers did not work on the Sabbath, they lost their clients or had to cover storage expenses. A makeshift solution had been found, through an agreement among all the shippers and an ordinance from the governor raising the time allowed for free storage from three days to five. But that did not solve the problem. The newspapers *Ha'arets* [The Land] of Tel Aviv and *Aurore* [Dawn] of Cairo represented this solution as a change of policy and approval of Sabbath rest on the part of the Italian authorities. The furious Balbo gave Castelbolognesi a harsh dressing-down, despite the trouble he had gone to in reaching the agreement. Balbo openly accused Castelbolognesi of not working for assimilation and not trying to get the Libyan Jews to open their shops on Saturdays. The chief rabbi replied tersely that his duty was to defend and encourage the sound religious traditions of the Jews. For the time being, the incident led to no further developments.[67] Balbo's reaction was indicative, however, of what was in store. The extent of the disillusion and growing discontent among officials at Castelbolognesi's attitude and the negative consequences which the authorities with reason believed it would have among the most traditional elements in Libyan Jewry are shown by an incident in Misurata. A few weeks earlier, the authorities had harshly punished some Jews who had put on a demonstration to protest the elopement of a Jewish girl with an Italian official. The head of the Community had been forced to resign, and three of the most troublesome demonstrators were punished by flogging.[68] Despite this episode, it is probable that a genuine crisis could have been avoided if completely unanticipated circumstances had not occurred.

The crisis was provoked by an incident which was unforeseeable, and trivial in itself. However, it unleashed opposing attitudes of intransigence which had not had occasion to show themselves before. The event was a crossed love affair between two young Jewish people, Gino Hassan, who was thirty-five, and Raffaello Nemni's daughter, who was only fifteen. It led to an unexpected *kiddushin* wedding.* Between March and May of 1935 the event set the whole community of Tripoli talking. The rabbinical court was charged with deciding whether the marriage was valid or not. The issue soon also involved the chief rabbi, the administrative committee, and the

---

*Kiddushin, the title of a Talmudic tractate, was less than a formal wedding and more than an engagement. Though the *huppah* ceremony of a wedding was omitted, the *kiddushin* could be dissolved only by divorce.—*Trans.*

Italian authorities. Balbo informed Castelbolognesi that the marriage would have to be annulled. He was partly taking into account
the girl's young age and her father's insistence, and partly annoyed
at the practice of an obsolete marriage ceremony. In Egypt in 1901
the rabbinate had taken steps to control this practice and make it
difficult to apply. It was open to abuse and in Balbo's eyes one more
aspect of the Jewish past hindering the modernization and Italianization of Libyan Jewry. At the same time, the administrative
committee was in crisis. It was already in difficulties because it had
increased the Community taxes and from several quarters was being
charged with opposing religion. Officially, the crisis had nothing to
do with whether the marriage should be annulled or not. The question played a decisive role, though, because of the political significance of the governor's intervention, the disagreements between
committee members and the chief rabbi on how to confront Balbo's
assimilationist policy, the importance of the families involved, and a
second questionable wedding in mid-May which could be viewed
moreover as a case of bigamy. In this awkward situation, while the
internal contradictions and divisions undermining the Jewish community were revealed for all to see, Castelbolognesi took a position
of complete intransigence. He cared only that the decision of the
rabbinical court should be reached in accordance with Jewish law
exclusively, and saw the more open-minded position of the Community leaders as just another proof of their support of the governor and
hostility to Castelbolognesi's antiassimilationist policy. This lack of
willingness to compromise incensed Balbo even more. He did not
miss a chance to throw in the chief rabbi's teeth that "the commission, not you, follows government instructions." Castelbolognesi's
reply was simply to hand in his resignation to the Union. Ravenna,
its president, very worried at this turn of events, quickly asked him to
withdraw his resignation. He pointed out that the situation was already too serious to exacerbate it with "political" resignations; that
perhaps Castelbolognesi had been "excessively harsh" toward the
Community leaders and that it would be better if he would try to
solve the problem between himself and Balbo on his own. Castelbolognesi should try to convince Balbo that he had acted only out of
"arch-Italian feelings" and that it was not appropriate to offend the
Jews' loyalty to traditional and orthodox religion. Balbo would create
the risk that the nucleus of traditionalists in Tripoli would become
"a group of rebels, though this group has always been a symbol of
religious loyalty." However, events were taking over: the rabbinical
court had issued its decision recognizing the validity of the marriage

in the face of strong pressures by those supporting annulment. The next day, May 31, Catelbolognesi received an order from Balbo to leave Libya immediately.[69] The governor telegraphed the order to the Ministry of Colonies and immediately afterward sent Mussolini, in his capacity as head of the government and Minister of Colonies, a detailed report on the whole affair, which follows in its entirety:

> Today, as provided for under Article 14 RD of December 17, 1928, No. 3278, I have decided to send back to Italy Professor Gustavo Castelbolognesi, the Rabbi of Tripoli, a resident of the colony since November 24, 1933.
>
> This government brought Castelbolognesi to the colony. It trusted that he would improve the general conditions of the Jewish population in Tripoli, still attached to old customs which do not harmonize with modern civilization. Castelbolognesi, though highly cultured and the product of a modern education, was taken over by his surroundings here. Instead of trying to convince the Jews of Tripoli to follow the way of life of metropolitan Jews, he was carried away by local religious feelings, practices, and customs, which have not changed in two thousand years. He lost the courage to support progress and became almost mesmerized by the Libyan Jews' attachment to their ancient customs. Instead of an improvement, the time that he has been in office shows backsliding. When he arrived in the Colony, the governor had approved compulsory attendance on Saturdays for secondary school pupils, since our school regulations only allow holidays for Jewish pupils on Saturdays and Sundays in the elementary schools. Though reluctantly, the Jews had adapted to this educational requirement. Castelbolognesi took up arms again, suggesting that the Jews insist that Jewish pupils be given leave on Saturdays. He led the way by withdrawing his son from the *liceo* [public secondary school] and enrolling him in Italy— where previously, without such scruples, he had sent him to school on Saturdays. Naturally, I have kept fully in force my predecessor's order regarding compulsory attendance on Saturdays. Castelbolognesi has also recently forbidden Jewish boys to play football on Saturdays, which they had always been able to do with their families' full approval. He has allowed Jews to leave their beards uncut for a month after Passover as a sign of mourning, setting an example himself. At the death of the lamented bishop, Monsignor Tonizza, Castelbolognesi, carried away by sectarianism, failed to attend the funeral. He thus aroused unfavorable criticism even among Jews, especially since the Muslim religious authorities were all present. The latest event leading me to take disciplinary action took place yesterday. Gino Hassan, a Jew in his forties, had for some time been assiduously courting Linda Nemni, who is fifteen, against the firm opposition of her parents. Last March he persuaded her to go out with him in his car; he took her a short way to a street in

Tripoli where two other Jews were waiting. A few sentences were spoken in Hebrew in their presence, after which the girl was given a ring. Hassan believed that he had thereby contracted a marriage according to the old Jewish practice of *Kiddushin.* When the ceremony was over, the girl was driven back in the same car to her grandmother's.

The girl's father quickly asked the rabbinical court not to recognize the marriage, arguing that the practice of *kiddushin* had been out of use for decades, particularly in Tripoli, where a regulation called *takanah* which is more than a century old, and was issued by the rabbinical court, forbade the practice for reasons of public order, under pain of excommunication. The girl's father himself said that she was not aware of the nature and implication of the ceremony, and thus insisted that the marriage was not valid. He was thinking of asking for a passport for his daughter, since he wished to take her away from Tripoli, but Hassan went to Police Headquarters asserting that he himself as the legitimate husband had to give written approval, and that he was opposed to the issuing of a passport. In the face of this and other provocations Nemni sent me two petitions, asking me as governor to intervene in the matter, which reflected on public order. I thus summoned Nemni and his daughter to my office. Since the girl explicitly declared that she had not understood at all that she was assenting to marriage on that occasion, I sent for Castelbolognesi and advised him to persuade the rabbinical court to reach a prompt, logical, and just decision on the case. Castelbolognesi indicated that he had scruples about it, because of the respect which he owed to the old customs of his race. Instead of resolving the question promptly, he put it off until yesterday. In the meantime, another similar event has occurred, also in Tripoli, but a more serious one. The present court's tendency to favor recognition of the practice of *kiddushin* soon became known in the closed circles of the city. It encouraged another Jew, a certain Ghebri Fitusi fu Baruh, a shoemaker, to abandon his lawful wife, Gamila Haggiag, since she has been bedridden for some time with progressive paralysis, and contract another marriage with a certain Gerbi Meri according to the *kiddushin* ceremony.

The second marriage would not have been possible if normal practices had been followed.

As I indicated above, after many discussions in the presence of Rabbi Castelbolognesi, the rabbinical court yesterday issued the decision approving the *kiddushin* practice. The court of a hundred years ago was more intelligent than the one of today, holding office in the twentieth century and under a Fascist regime!

In the face of this senseless decision, which has been reached in complete opposition to the instructions which I had given in the interest of public morality, and which shows, as the President of the Court of Appeals said to me, a really pharisaical attitude, I have had to take the step of sending Castelbolognesi back to Italy. Tomorrow I wish to present a proposal to replace the whole of the present rabbinical court. The decision regarding the Nemni case will not receive the approval of our judicial authorities. As an example to the citizenry, the shoemaker Ghebri will be publicly flogged.[70]

Obviously, this step made a deep impression on the Jews of Tripoli. It aroused lively protest, many shopkeepers closing for two days as a sign of their support of Castelbolognesi. Everyone was aware, though, of how serious a moment it was, and there were no provocative acts. The administrative committee withdrew its own resignation. The only public after-effects of the affair were the publication a few days later of a printed announcement to "correct" "inaccurate" opinions which many foreign newspapers had expressed on Balbo's measure, particularly their assertion that Castelbolognesi had been deported,[71] and, in August, the replacement of the Rabbi for the Tripoli Community, Josef Jona, who had tried to block the revision under appeal of the rabbinical court's decision.[72] The Castelbolognesi affair marked the turning-point in Balbo's policy toward the Jews, the moment when he decided to use force.

Felice Ravenna and Dante Lattes, who went to Tripoli on June 28 to try to patch up the situation with some sort of compromise, had to come to terms with that. Balbo was intractable with them too. He first harshly attacked Castelbolognesi's actions and accused him of portraying Balbo himself as an anti-Semite. Balbo said that he had great friends among the Jews, from Rothschild down to the mayor of Ferrara, and that he had arrested and sent back home several Nazi emissaries on their way to Libya. He said that "he would have expected some effort from the chief rabbi to improve the cultural and social conditions of the Jews of Tripoli and bring them closer to Italian civilization. Such an effort would have persuaded them to abandon some of their customs which, when viewed in the context of Western Jewish life and the fast pace of modern civilization, appear somewhat antiquated." Instead, the chief rabbi had been an obstacle to these efforts. Balbo held that the specific incident of the marriage leading to the expulsion order was "harmful for the moral education of the Jewish population." He was afraid that, if it was repeated, it would lead to moral decline and the breaking up of the family. To no avail Ravenna and Lattes tried to explain that the rabbinical court had reached its decision in full accordance with Jewish law. After two hours of discussions, the following statement was issued:

H. E. the Governor of Libya has had a long and cordial conversation with the President of the Union of Italian Jewish Communities, Mr. Felice Ravenna, and has examined with him the situation of the Jews of Libya. The Governor expressed to Mr. Ravenna his strong fellow-

feeling for the hard-working, disciplined, and moral Jewish population,
an active participant in Mussolini's new Italy Overseas.[73]

The statement was obviously only for external consumption; it dealt
with none of the basic questions. It gave no reason for thinking that
the governor had renounced his intention of obtaining by force what
he had not been able to win by persuasion.

There were no further attempts by the Italian authorities to integrate the Jews, nor any incidents, for about a year and a half after
the expulsion of Castelbolognesi. The Italians probably wanted this
pause, in order to give time for the hostility to die down and for the
Community leaders to get a grip on the situation again. The Italians
also probably did not wish to provoke incidents and protests at such
a politically delicate time. In 1935–1936, the eyes of the world were
on Italy over the war in Ethiopia. Mussolini had no intention of giving his adversaries yet another argument against him. He did not
want to risk incurring the opposition of world Jewry, which already
mistrusted him because of his ambiguous policy toward Nazi Germany but was still somewhat grateful and sympathetic to Mussolini
because of his previous rejection of Nazi anti-Semitism and the help
and hospitality which he had given so many Jewish refugees from
Germany.[74] One event shows that this was only a pause, not a change,
in Balbo's policy toward Libyan Jews. Though the event was small
and did not involve the Jews directly, those who were most alert considered it a harbinger of far more drastic measures. On November 27,
1935, an ordinance of the governor established that in New Tripoli
without distinction all shops must close on Sundays.

A year later, on November 14, 1936, when the war in Ethiopia
had ended in victory, another ordinance made into law what had
been implied in the earlier order. From December 1, without distinction, "all shops selling to the public, beyond the walls of the old city
of Tripoli, including those in Corso Vittorio Emanuele III between
Piazza Castello and Piazza dell'Orologio, must remain open for business every day of the week, except Sundays." Offenders would be
punished under the law—that is by having their business licences
revoked. The order appeared on November 5, in the official Fascist
organ of Tripoli, *L'avvenire di Tripoli*. The order was accompanied
by a commentary which is worth quoting in its entirety. Its harsh
and intransigent tone, no doubt inspired by the governor's offices,
shows better than I can the state of mind behind the measure and
enables us to appreciate fully Balbo's subsequent position:

> The commission's ordinance is putting an end to an anachronism.
> Modern Tripoli, "European" Tripoli, was entirely built by the Italians,

for a pace of life no different from that of the most advanced cities in Italy. The Jewish shopkeepers came out from behind the ancient walls and took over the new high streets. They took over the best locations in the area and set up new shops and outlets for businesses in the souk [old market]. This is all very well. Anything which stimulates local trade can only be welcome. But the anachronism was that the new, modern, Italian city on certain days of the week took on the appearance of a Jewish city, such as, let us say, Tel Aviv. That was what Corso Vittorio Emanuele—the former Via Azizia—looked like on Saturdays. Many of the shops were tightly bolted, ignoring the needs of the population. On November 27, 1935, the Governor-General had issued an ordinance to eliminate the absurd competition by which the shops would open on Sundays. That is the day when shops run by Italians, in respect for the law regarding holidays, must be closed.

The present ordinance is the logical consequence of the earlier one, and was taken as the final step to complete it, as is the constant procedure of the Government of the Colonies. Those Jews who are intelligent must have understood already that the first ordinance would eventually lead to the second. In the cities of Italy no public business, no meeting-place or shop, even those run or owned by Jews, can stay closed on Saturdays. There is no reason that the same should not hold in New Tripoli. Is it inappropriate to expect more open-mindedness from the local Jewish community, which is not so different from the Jewish community in Italy? If this progress is not feasible in certain strata, never mind; there is a place for everyone. The refractory ones can stay inside the old walls, from which they have emerged before acquiring the flexibility necessary to follow the new rhythm. The old city and souks preserve the old, traditional, local habits in trade. Yesterday His Excellency the Governor-General received the leaders of the Jewish Community to inform them of the Ordinance. He emphasized that the basic Caneva Decree regarding traditional customs and religious practices of the indigenous populations is still in force, and shall remain so. Even the most inflexible old people have a right to exist. But the old city is there precisely for them. They can certainly not presume to make their mark on the Tripoli which the Italians have built from scratch. Through sacrifice and determination, and the completely new neighborhoods which they have brought into being, New Tripoli must live to the full. It must follow our own rhythm. The new Tripoli, a doubly Italian city, must remain purely Italian. Tripoli is not Tel Aviv.

Among many Tripoli Jews, the new ordinance aroused annoyance and protests. Many Jewish newspapers, especially in Palestine, came out against it vigorously. The chief rabbi of Erez Israel sent to the acting chief rabbi, Hai Gabizon, two telegrams expressing his solidarity and suggesting resistance.[75] On November 26 the community leaders tried to persuade Balbo to modify the measure or at least delay putting it into effect. Three days earlier Ravenna had approached the minister of colonies for the same purpose.[76] The governor was adamant.[77] In the next few days there was some disorder. A "few dozen" shopkeepers, almost all of whom had shops in Via Gue and the surrounding area, and a French and a Libyan Jew in Corso Vittorio Emanuele, did not open their shops. Rioting occurred on a small scale, described by *L'avvenire di Tripoli* as an actual "attempt at rebellion." Twelve of the offenders had their business licences revoked. Two others (Sion Barda and Saul Nhaisi, a shopkeeper and a glazier respectively), who were accused of being the instigators, were condemned to ten strokes of the *kurbash,* which were dealt them two days later in the square in front of the tobacco factory. A certain Benedetto Meghidesc was also accused of leading the revolt but, since his health would not allow him to bear the flogging, was sentenced to prison for three months.[78]

As one might expect, there were vigorous responses and protests at these measures from Jews in other countries. The press and individuals raised their protest, including the chief rabbi of Alexandria, David Prato,[79] and the chief rabbi of Jerusalem. Despite these protests, the ordinance was enforced very severely. The few who on subsequent Saturdays refused to open their shops had their licences revoked, and the most obstinate received a flogging. As Rabbi Hai Gabizon acknowledged in a letter to *L'avvenire di Tripoli,* on December 23, 1936, those punished were very few, not the 214 that Reuter and *Tunis-Soir* had maintained. No steps were taken against Rabbi Gabizon, who had done nothing to convince his fellow-Jews to obey the governor's ordinance. Balbo had initially considered replacing him as acting chief rabbi,[80] but then decided not to do anything. Perhaps he did not want to provoke more negative reactions from abroad, or perhaps it was because the news of the rabbi's impending dismissal had been published in *Tunis-Soir* and spread around the world by Reuter. The chance to show that the anti-Fascist press was false was certainly worth the price of not dismissing him. It is also possible that Balbo refrained from turning the screws even tighter because Rome may not have entirely supported his policy or may not have considered it very appropriate at the time. This is suggested by the defensive tone of Balbo's dispatch to the minister of colonies on December 15, 1936, in which he minimized the situation after the ordinance had been in effect for two Saturdays and his intention to enforce it in Benghazi also.[81] The hypothesis is borne out by the fact that in late 1936 Mussolini certainly had no interest in giving a hand to his enemies accusing him of anti-

Semitism and of adopting the Nazi position.* Balbo was not an anti-Semite, but he was making it easy to view him as one. It is thus probable that Mussolini would consider Balbo's initiative politically inopportune.[82]

After the dramatic events of 1935–1936, life went back to normal for Libyan Jews for a couple of years. The Castelbolognesi affair and even more the Sabbath issue were not events that could be easily forgotten, however, and resentment and bitterness lingered. These blows were less painful in the rest of the country than in Tripoli, the center of the two affairs. Only echoes reached the small towns, where Balbo's measures remained dead letters or were enforced with much flexibility. Even in major towns, reactions differed. In Tripoli, the process of modernization and assimilation was already such a reality among the Jews, with or without Balbo's attempts to accelerate it, that it could not fail to affect the reactions of those participating. Reactions were stronger among the more traditional and less assimilated Jews and weaker or different, being affected by other considerations, among the more modernized and Italianizing group, which was also more prominent socially. In the long run, this group influenced the traditionalists, since they lacked strong leaders with spiritual authority. Moreover, due to the war in Ethiopia, Italy and Fascism itself had some prestige among Libyan Jews for a few years. Libyan Jews also drew material benefit from the economic development which Balbo was carrying out in the colony. The Italian authorities made a point of favoring the most Italianized Jews and the few Jewish Fascists.[83] These policies made certain sectors of Libyan Jewry less sensitive about a tradition that seemed more and more outdated. In March 1937 Mussolini visited Libya[84] and told Chief Rabbi Lattes, in Balbo's presence, that "the Jews of Tripoli can rest assured that the Fascist government which issued the law on Jewish Communities will always respect their traditions."[85] When this became known, many Jews thought that the worst was over. They thought that they should accept or endure the "logic of the times" (which was not even a sacrifice for many of them) as their fellow-Jews overseas had done. They saw nothing to fear by this, and much to gain.

*In September 1936 a German-Italian front began to form in Spain, and Farinacci began a campaign against Jews. Fascist anti-Semitism was still strictly unofficial, though. On October 23, a secret Italo-German protocol was signed, forming the Axis. It was then judged expedient to relax the anti-Jewish campaign in Italy. See Meir Michaelis, *Mussolini and the Jewish Question in Italy, 1922–1945* (Oxford: Clarendon, 1978), pp. 134–135.—*Trans.*

The appointment of Aldo Lattes contributed greatly to normalizing the situation. He became chief rabbi and president of the rabbinical court, arriving in Tripoli in March 1937.[86] He did not have the personal stature or the Jewish learning of Artom or Castelbolognesi, but in comparison with them he had the great advantage of being a man of action who pursued his goal with determination. His unusual practical sense made him clearly grasp what was most important and pressing, what he could ask of Balbo and what was the best way of dealing with the situation from the point of view of Jewish identity, while alienating neither the traditionalists nor the Italian authorities.

Thanks to Lattes, relations with Balbo immediately improved. An arrangement was found which was of vital importance for Libyan Jewry in later years. The governor and chief rabbi began to work together fully from their first contacts. Balbo immediately granted Lattes' request that sentences passed in connection with the Sabbath be annulled. Thanks to Lattes again, there was some normalization also in relations (which in 1936 and early 1937 had been very bad) between the Community of Tripoli and the Union of Italian Jewish Communities.[87]

Within a few months Lattes won the confidence of the governor, of the administrative committee, and, what counted most, of the majority of Jews in Tripoli. He wrote to the Union on April 26, 1938, to report on his first year in Tripoli.[88] He had quickly realized, he wrote, that there was no end to the problems and he could not solve them all at once. He also realized that that could not be an excuse for doing nothing at all. He had to begin with "problems which were of first priority" and give them all the time they needed. But he could not ignore other issues: "If we don't make a start, we shall find ourselves in the same situation as now in fifty years' time. These conditions are the same as, if not worse than, those of twenty-five years ago, when the Italian army brought its victorious banners here to the fourth shore." His chief efforts were in the struggle against laxity of morals and in education. The first problem had existed for years, particularly in regard to alcoholism and gambling. To reduce alcoholism he convinced the Italian authorities to shorten the opening hours for taverns; to combat gambling he wanted indigenous people to be denied entrance to the Casino, but did not succeed. Other blights were older, but had worsened in recent years. Lattes wrote to the Union on June 8, 1937, "Unfortunately, the Jewish family feeling has been largely lost: there is an infinite number of suits regarding abuse and desertion between husbands and wives, many between parents and children, and divorce suits are frequent. In this very month two divorce suits have been filed on the day after the wedding." The new rabbi soon took up arms against this, initiating a broad campaign of persuasion and education. He made the rabbinical court take a strong stand, and personally intervened to prevent marriages which he thought were destined for failure and forbade the marriage of persons under twenty-five unless they could prove themselves "able to provide, even modestly, for the needs of a family." His efforts in education were directed mainly at the reorganization and full development of the school system and associated problems (after-school activities, kindergartens, medical services, meals, clothing, and above all shoes for those who did not attend school because they lacked them). He sponsored a new ordinance on education which went into effect on June 1, 1938. He replaced eleven teachers who were "completely inept," partly by retiring them and partly by procuring business licences for them from the Italian authorities so that they would have alternative work. He began to grapple with what he called "the thousand forms of superstition, on which a whole book could be written, a very funny one," superstitions which had nothing to do with Judaism. Within a year he also succeeded in practically abolishing begging. He also had some results in another area very important to Balbo: convincing his fellow-Jews to dress like Europeans, "abandoning that grimy costume of theirs which consists of a single shirt (clean only on the Sabbath) over a pair of trousers."

Obviously, a lot of money was needed to accomplish all this. The Community was in serious straits, which were partly endemic and partly due to the steep rise in the cost of living (increasing the demand for charity). The 8 percent increase in salaries which the government had decided on and the decrease in Community income due to a government decree prohibiting slaughtering on Tuesdays and Wednesdays also exacerbated the situation. The tax on meat had declined from about 420,000 lire annually to a little over 300,000. In order to deal with this situation, Lattes raised Community taxes (in the face of bitter protests)[89] from 160,000 lire to 215,000 lire and asked for contributions all around, from the governing authorities, the Union (which ignored his numerous requests through all channels), Italian Jewish Communities, the ADEI* and a few rich Italian

---

*An organization under the Italian Zionist Federation devoted to cultural and educational activities in association with the Women's International Zionist Organization.—*Trans.*

Jews (in a year succeeding in collecting about 22,000 lire from the last three categories), and especially from the Jews of Tripoli, obtaining, mainly before the tax increase, a good response.[90]

Another very serious and urgent problem was housing and overcrowding in the *hara*. It affected health conditions and with the increase in Jewish population in Tripoli was becoming more pressing year by year. It had been discussed before, and efforts to deal with it had been made before Lattes arrived in Libya. It had been extremely difficult to convince the inhabitants to leave the *hara*. The problem was so great that the Community would never have been able to solve it alone. Since Balbo was also very concerned, the chief rabbi decided to take advantage of Balbo's help. Lattes devoted all his energies to it and in less than five months from his arrival completed and had approved an overall plan to improve housing in the *hara*. On July 27, 1937, he set forth the reasons for and content of the plan to the Union:

> There is one basic problem which I have only referred to fleetingly in my earlier reports, because I was afraid to face up to it. It is the need to free the Jewish quarter from its appalling overcrowding. The sun never enters the houses, because the streets are so narrow. The vast majority of Jews live there in promiscuity and filth. There are many houses of three or four cramped rooms, in which there live the same number of families of six, seven, or eight people each. In a single room sleep sons and daughters of all ages up to eighteen or twenty as well as their parents. If tuberculosis claims many victims and morals leave much to be desired, the main cause is the environment in which people are living. All the steps taken or envisaged to improve the lot of the Jews of Tripoli can give no immediate tangible results unless we succeed in solving this problem. I must add that the *hara* is becoming more cramped every day, since its population is constantly growing.
>
> H. E. the Governor has been aware of the problem for some time. Every time I talked to him, he emphasized that it was necessary to construct, not too near to and not too far from the *hara*, a new Jewish quarter with its own synagogue and school. It should not be too far, because heads of families need access to work, and not too near, because distancing the Jews from the *hara* will distance them from the quarter's sad way of life.
>
> The quarter would consist of modest, popular, one-story houses, each with a vegetable garden to help the family's budget. His Excellency promised on behalf of the Government that he would provide all possible assistance.
>
> The administrative committee had already discussed the problem repeatedly but had balked at the financial commitment needed. Finally convinced of the urgent need to solve the problem, it studied it in detail at last week's meeting. Yesterday, in a long and cordial meeting with

His Excellency, who gave useful suggestions and made promises, the following conclusions were reached:

(1) The Community is authorized by the Government to sell the farming concession which had been purchased when Monastero was Commissioner. Its unfulfilled purpose was to direct Jews into agriculture. The ownership of this concession costs the Community 20,000 lire annually. With the elimination of this expense and the expected income of 100,000 lire from the sale, the Community's financial situation will be eased considerably. This sum will be earmarked for the fund for the new quarter of Jewish popular housing.

(2) The Community is authorized to sell its only piece of real estate—a piece of land which was to be expropriated by the Government for the construction of government schools. This sale will bring in about 200,000 lire which can be earmarked for the same purpose.

(3) The establishment of a Jewish company for the construction of popular housing, with shares of 100, 500, and 1,000 lire. Jews will be invited to purchase these shares which, though they will not bring an adequate return in the first year, will subsequently constitute a modest capital investment. I say a modest one, because obviously the houses will not bring a rent of more than seventy or eighty lire a month.

(4) I invite the Jews of Tripoli who own some capital to invest it in purchasing a cottage, the estimate cost of which, with government discounts, will amount to 25,000 lire.

A cluster of fifty houses will be built initially. It is not possible to begin on a smaller scale because moving only ten or twenty families would not achieve our goal, and it would be very difficult to find anyone who would leave the *hara* and live in isolation. When a Jewish community has been started up in the new quarter, though, it will be very easy to meet our goal.

And so, in just over a year and a half, Lattes managed to achieve for the Jews of Tripoli much more than any of his predecessors. This led many Jews to believe that a new era was dawning for them. The only real setback, foreshadowing the storm which was about to break over them, was the issue of citizenship. Many Libyan Jews wanted to have Italian citizenship.[91] Lattes himself was in favor of it, believing that citizenship would help to dispel possible prejudice regarding the loyalty of Libyan Jews to Italy, would forestall the Arabs' attempts to portray themselves as the most loyal subjects,[92] and, through military service, would "discipline" the youth. Thus he pressed Balbo to have Italian citizenship granted to any Jews wishing to take it. His moves in this direction were of no avail, however. In theory no obstacle was raised, but in practice the Ministry of the Interior raised all sorts of bureaucratic problems, so that Italian citizenship continued to be granted to Libyan Jews only grudgingly.

6. Fascist Racial Legislation and the War (1938–1943)

As it was for Italian Jews, the year 1938 was decisive for Libyan Jews as well. It was a year of tragedy but also a year of recovery.

News of events in Italy usually reached the colonies in toned-down, summarized, and simplified form. In any case, Libyan Jewry's contacts with Italian Jewry soon dwindled to almost nothing.[1] The increasingly violent campaign launched by the press and Fascist propaganda to prepare Italians for the adoption of racial legislation[2] did make an unusual impact in Libya. In mid-July the notorious "Racial Manifesto" was issued. In early September, the first law was passed, prohibiting foreign Jews from living in Italy, Libya, or the Aegean islands,[3] and banning Jews from public school (special sections were set up in elementary schools, and Jewish Communities were authorized to provide for intermediate-level education themselves).* The Grand Council of Fascism met on October 6 and prepared the groundwork for subsequent anti-Semitic legislation.[4] Each of these events was received in Libya by Italian, Libyan, and foreign Jews as a dismal sign of the opening of a new period of persecution. Many Jews viewed the events as the crumbling of an illusion, sometimes of a model way of life: the illusion of Italian "civilization" and the model for living which the Italian way of life had represented for many Libyan Jews. From a psychological point of view, Fascist racial measures had no less impact on Libyan Jews than they did on Italian Jews. Some Libyan Jews, in fact, were even more shaken by them. Because of the particular narrow-mindedness and fanatical Fascism of colonial society, the Jews did not have the support from the surrounding Catholic society that they enjoyed in Italy. Italians in Libya

---

*For the detailed events of this period, see Meir Michaelis, *Mussolini and the Jewish Question in Italy, 1922–1945* (Oxford: Clarendon, 1978), esp. pp. 183–191. Michaelis argues that Mussolini himself was the main force behind the anti-Semitic measures, and that he was bowing to pressure neither from Italian anti-Semites nor from Hitler.—*Trans.*

saw the Jews as inferior not only to themselves but also to the Muslims, who at nearly the same time were being given a new citizenship status.[5] Concretely, though, the racial measures affected Libyan Jews only through minor events and often belatedly. The measures did immediately affect Italian Jews resident in Libya. Forty-six Italian-Jewish officials in state or semiofficial institutions and state-owned enterprises[6] were suspended or retired. Fascist anti-Semitism for some time affected Libyan and foreign Jews only slightly. The results were harsh in education, which was subject to the same measures as in Italy. Besides the Italian Jews, however, it was mainly the Europeanized and Italianized Jews who experienced these results.[7] Other Jews hardly suffered. They had always wanted special classes or their own community schools, so that, paradoxically, they were almost happy with the Fascist measures. On an economic level, the results of the legislation were slight, but certainly more serious from a social point of view, though even there the effects depended on the Jews' social position and degree of integration.

Two factors affected the repercussions of the Fascist racial policies in Libya. The first was the fact that Balbo was governor and the second was the Jews' economic role in the colony. Though these two factors initially converged, they were different in nature and of differing importance. Balbo's death on June 28, 1940, did not in itself bring about any change in the situation. Nevertheless, it was in fact Balbo's influence which enabled the Jews to play an economic role. Especially in a totalitarian or highly authoritarian state, choices are often made according to ideological and political considerations rather than economic ones, and according to where people stand in the hierarchy and their conformism rather than their abilities. If it had not been for Balbo's particular position, personality, and political influence, no one would have taken into account the economic role which the Jews played in Libya. Despite the fact that the measures had been hastily drafted in view of conditions in Italy alone,[8] were it not for Balbo they would have been applied with only a few adjustments in Libya without distinction to all Jews.

Balbo was not an anti-Semite. The introduction of the racial policy was for him a double misfortune. It was a new and decisive step along the road of Italy's alignment with German policy, and so of Italy's involvement along with Germany in the eventuality of war. In Balbo's opinion the new racial laws did irreparable damage to the domestic and foreign prestige of the Fascist regime, isolating it more and more. At the first outbreaks of anti-Semitism in Italy in late 1937, he had expressed his opinion frankly and had tried to assuage the old and new burning anti-Semitism of much of Libyan Fascism. He raised the issue at an assembly of Tripoli Fascists to assess the Fascist year. Roberto Arbib reports on the episode as follows in his memoirs:

> At the October 1937 meeting to close the Fascist year, held in the Miramare Theater, 2,000 Black Shirts were assembled to hear comments and possible criticisms regarding the regime's activities over the past year. Italo Balbo, the governor, reviewed the performance of each Section, sometimes praising and sometimes criticizing the leader responsible. Finally, Balbo said: "Now let us pass to the Jewish question." On this, hostile shouting came from the floor: "Death to the Jews!" "Jews out of our country!"
>
> Balbo raised his arms and in a loud voice angrily ordered complete silence. Eight of us Jews had witnessed the unpleasant scene and were about to leave the theater, when the floor fell silent. When calm reigned again, Balbo spoke as follows:
>
> "Once again, as regards the Jews, I shall testify to their untiring labor, discipline and loyalty to the regime, and I would like to explain the measure in force against them obliging them to open their shops in the New City on the Sabbath. I believed that I was acting in the interest of tourism and of the Jews as well. Many tourists in fact arrive in Tripoli from the motherland on Saturday mornings and return on Sunday evenings. Landing on Saturdays, they would find that 80 percent of the shops were closed because they are run by Jews. I thus required them to open on Saturdays which was in their own interest and would increase the business in commerce and crafts, in which Jews predominate.
>
> "The hostile exclamations of this assembly have offended me a great deal because I make no distinction between Catholic and Jewish Italians. We are all Italians, and I would like to add that from my youth until today I have only had three real friends. Would you like to know who these friends are? They are Jews, all three of them."
>
> A cold shower extinguished the frenzy of the gathering. There were six of us Jews sitting in a row in the audience and wearing black shirts like everyone else who was present. Italo Balbo called out: "Mr. Di Segni, the architect, please stand up. Raise you arm." And he did so. "Raise the other one," Balbo said. Di Segni replied: "Your Excellency, I don't have the other one." "Look, comrades: this Jew gave an arm in the Great War, fighting as a good Italian . . ."

Similarly, at the Grand Council meeting of October 6, 1938, Balbo had been the most critical of the regime's switch to racism and had done his best to mitigate it.[9] Later, as governor of Libya, he was well aware that the measures covering Italian Jews, extended to the Jews of Libya, would provoke a far-reaching crisis in the economy of the colony and would largely cancel out his achievement in economic development. It appears that in this respect Balbo's concern was not very different from that of the major entrepreneurs operating in Libya. A police report dated Milan, September 4, 1938, gave an exact account of the business community's first reactions to the adoption of the anti-Semitic legislation:

> The Bianchi agent for Libya has informed me that among manufacturers and merchants in Libya the measures against Jews have aroused serious concern. This is not because they do not accept the measures, but because they affect the elements on which non-Jewish manufacturers and merchants have to rely for commercial credit and prompt availability of cash.
>
> According to the Bianchi agent, the Jews have a very strong financial position in Libya and, especially with regard to discounting, are very prompt, in contrast with the slowness and reluctance of Italian banks.
>
> He has informed me that this uneasiness is more apparent in Libya than in Italy. The commercial system of Italian firms applies the same arrangement to sales in the colonies as it does to sales overseas. Payments for merchandise must be in ready cash or against documents. This obliges merchants in the colony to buy with cash and sell for deferred payment as in Italy.
>
> Under these conditions merchants and manufacturers in Libya must have large amounts of liquid funds. If they do not, they must apply for the bank discount, which is very limited in banks, while it can be obtained very quickly and on favorable terms from Jews.[10]

At the same time, Balbo moved to forestall those in Rome and Tripoli who wanted the Italian racial laws to be applied fully in Libya. He did it by introducing a series of considerations based on economics and local politics. They were difficult to refute and in themselves did not question the basic motives of Mussolini's new policy. Balbo was well aware that if he had questioned them his own efforts would have failed miserably. The latter part of the telegram in which Mussolini accepted Balbo's views is significant. The Duce did not pass up an occasion to argue with the governor regarding the one point in his argument that was not purely technical and factual, but of somewhat political and ideological nature. After a series of preliminary contacts to prepare the ground with Mussolini on January 19, 1939, Balbo sent this long, clever letter:

> My Leader, the laws for the defense of the race are being applied in Libya. We have made arrangements to dismiss from government service officials who are of the Jewish race, and Jewish pupils have been expelled from secondary schools. Changes have been made in banks' discount committees and in the managing boards of official and semi-official bodies and municipal councils for the purpose of implementing the provisions of the law.

I have diligently examined the local Jewish problem as a whole. Certain situations and aspects have emerged which deserve much consideration and to which I feel it my duty to call your exalted attention.

In this region the Jewish population has special characteristics both in quality and numbers. It is an important ethnic element, since *about one-fifth of the total population of Tripoli is Jewish.* The presence in Libya of strong groups of Jews dates back to time immemorial: in the time of Augustus they were enjoying the protection of the Romans. Even before the Italian occupation the Jews received protection from Italy, set up schools, and spread the Italian language. Most of them live in very backward social conditions, and do not take the slightest part in political activities. They are mostly peaceful and timid, craftsmen and peddlars keeping to their modest little workshops and stalls, intent only on making a living from their occupation.

In contrast with this vast majority, a few dozen wealthy Jews run almost all local industry and trade, are the banks' main clients, and provide the funds for most of the Muslim business enterprises.

If the Jews suddenly stopped participating in the economy before they could be replaced by a group of Catholic merchants and industrialists, *there would be economic imbalances in Libya.* Looking at the local situation on a less general level, I can point out several special cases that could not be readily solved:

(*a*) Hospitals in Libya treat numerous in-patients of the Jewish race, cared for by Jewish employees. This is essential because they obviously cannot be cared for by Muslims. Medical care for Muslim women giving birth is also provided by Jewish women, since Muslim nurses are lacking. Replacing this staff with metropolitans is both unacceptable and impossible, since it is clearly forbidden under the Decree of November 17, 1938 XVII [Fascist era]. Hence, strict application of the measures would mean that Jews would be deprived of hospital services.

(*b*) Monopoly industries whose main factories are in Tripoli* largely use trained Jewish female workers, especially for the manufacture of cigars and cigarettes. These workers may no longer be employed by the governing authorities. It is not possible to find in Libya Italian nationals who are both skilled and willing to accept the same modest wages.

(*c*) The Government and municipalities employ Jewish clerks whose conduct is irreproachable. They have been working for a long time as Arabic and Hebrew interpreters; if they were dismissed, they would have to be replaced. Though in time this would be easy for Arabic, it would be impossible for Hebrew, since only those who profess the Jewish religion know it.

I have already described all these difficulties officially to the Ministry and asked for instructions, but I have not yet received any reply. Nor

---

*The Fascist economy had been reorganized on a war footing and depended on cheap labor. Libya was part of this economy.—*Trans.*

have I received a precise reply to this inquiry: whether the regulations applying to Jews having full Italian citizenship should definitely apply to Jews with Libyan citizenship. In a country like this one, which has always had the virtue, compared with neighboring countries, of allowing Jews and Arabs to live together in full harmony, it would in my opinion be advisable to avoid making the struggle for the defense of the race a harsh one. The Jews are already a dead people; there is no need to oppress them cruelly, especially since the Arabs, the traditional enemies of the Jews, now show signs of feeling sorry for them.

No one can suspect me of weakness, since—as everyone remembers—two years ago I did not hesitate to order the public flogging of Jews, even those of high social standing, who were guilty of adopting an attitude of passive indifference to certain official measures. But I have a duty to portray the situation frankly and as it really is.

Accordingly, may I venture to advise you to give the Government of Libya authorization to apply the racial laws "to the extent desirable in view of the very special local situation."

With my sincere respect,

Your faithful servant.

Mussolini replied in the form of a short but subtly polemical telegram dated January 23, in which he approved what Balbo desired:

> Reply to your letter regarding Libyan Jews. No change should be made regarding the situations listed under your headings (a), (b), and (c). Non-indigenous Jews, that is those with metropolitan citizenship, should be given the treatment they receive in Italy under the recent laws. I therefore authorize you to apply the racial laws as above, remembering that though the Jews may seem to be dead, they never really are.[11]

A month and a half later there was another initiative, this time by the Ministry of Foreign Affairs. Wishing to avoid souring relations with Britain, it decided to suspend the measure expelling foreign Jews, "in particular British Jews" who had made a request for special treatment "or who had requested that they be allowed to remain on Italian soil."[12] As a result, on June 10, 1940, when Italy declared war against France and Britain, many foreign Jews were still in Libya. Few of them had left of their own free will. According to the measures adopted in Rome, all foreign Jews were to be put in concentration camps by September 1940. As with other enemy subjects and protected persons, only a few Jews were actually interned, first at Tajura and later at Bu'ayrat al-Hasun in Syrtica.[13] According to a letter from the Ministry of Italian Africa to the Ministry of the Interior dated September 19, 1941,[14] only a few hundred foreigners, including both Jews and non-Jews, were actually rounded up, and these were considered the most dangerous or suspect. Not having the means to organize enough camps, the Italians left most foreigners free. The Ministry of Colonies decided in late 1941 to send away all of the 7,000 or so foreigners still resident in Libya, including the 1,600 Jewish French subjects and protected persons and the 870 Jewish British subjects. The letter proves that it made the decision not because the foreigners were "treacherous" but because of the "food problems" which their presence in the colony caused. The decision was also part of a broader plan to send home all the Italians, about 10,000 of them, who were not contributing to the war and economic effort in Libya. Agreements were made on January 28 and March 6, 1942, with the French government, to facilitate this exodus and the transfer of French subjects and protected persons to Tunisia. The 2,000 British subjects, including about 300 Jews, were sent by sea to Italy between January and April 1942. After April no more groups were sent, only a few individuals.[15] Once they reached Italy, the Jews were interned in various places, most of them at Civitella del Tronto and Bagno, near Ripoli. Most of them were taken to Civitella, where they found German and Polish Jews. They were put in an old people's home (seven or eight to a room) and were allowed to go out between ten o'clock and eight (and, with a special permit, were allowed to visit the nearby town of Teramo). The Italian government gave heads of families eight lire a day, and others four. Through the Swiss legation, the British government gave them another four hundred lire a month; finally the International Red Cross sent them a parcel of five kilos of food and about eighty cigarettes once a week.[16] These interned people did not have a very difficult life until September 8, 1943. After the armistice, those in Civitella were requisitioned by the Germans for military labor along the Sangro front. Later, those who had not escaped were transported first to the Fossoli Camp (Modena) and then, in May 1944, to Bergen Belsen (from which a few were later transferred to Biberach, near Munich). Despite these dramatic wanderings, hardships, hunger, and German brutality, most of them managed to survive and were freed by the Allied troops.[17]

On the whole, the years 1939 and 1940 were not particularly hard for Libyan Jews. Even after Balbo died, their situation did not change significantly. The economic considerations which he had presented to Mussolini as reasons for not applying the racial legislation in Libya conditioned the civil and military authorities' attitude to the Jews until 1941. Two reports are significant in this respect. The first dates from late October 1940 and is from the acting federal secretary of the Fascist Party in Tripoli, Angelo Rognoni. The other was issued a year later, probably in September, and is from Renato Trevisani, the general commissioner of Acorguerra (the General Commissariat for War Supplies and Economic Coordination). The first report discusses the problem of Jews in the broader context of the situation in Tripolitania: nevertheless, the picture that emerges is an important one:

> The Muslim masses, devoid of economic resources, are under control; it is the Jews who are difficult to handle and economically are very strong. About 70 percent of the commerce is in their hands; though politically they have been done away with, financially they still dominate trade.
>
> In Tripoli alone there are about a hundred Jewish millionaires. The problem should not be approached from the same point of view as in Italy, nor can it be dealt with at present, when we need to take advantage of all the energy and resources we have. I believe that, for now, action should be limited to political and economic control, by preventing speculation and monopoly. . . .
>
> Jewish wholesalers give a provincial tone to trade, but the majority of Italian firms doing business here are not presently capable of replacing the Jews' widespread network.
>
> Apart from few exceptions, Italian firms at present have little banking credit available, compared with Jews, since Italians own little property, which is the real guarantee for money now that foreign currency has lost some of its value due to trade imbalances.[18]

The second report is devoted entirely to the influence of Jews on the Libyan economy. It is a valuable testimony to the moment of transition from the soft to the hard line toward Jews. The Italian government switched when the events in Benghazi during the second British occupation of Cyrenaica showed that in their hearts many Libyan Jews supported Italy's enemies. It is worthwhile quoting:

> The Jewish population of Libya amounts to roughly fifty or sixty thousand. It consists of a minority which, having considerable capital available, wields a major influence, and a mass of Jews with very limited means.
>
> Jews form a good proportion of the total Libyan population. Their situation is quite different from that of Jewish communities in Italy and other European countries, since Jews can be viewed as one of the elements composing the population here, almost a local race.
>
> Very little land is owned by Jews: they own more buildings, but most of their capital is invested in commercial and, to a lesser extent, industrial enterprises. Their business as franchise-holders for Italian and foreign firms is especially important. Until a month or so ago most im-

ports from Italy and abroad were ordered through Jews. This business has shrunk because of the smaller volume of imports due to the war. Still, almost all the requests for import licences come from Jews.

The poor masses engage in petty trade and dominate the widespread distribution network, in which even Arabs take part, despite their traditional racial hatred.

Since the Jews control so much business activity, it is obvious that it is they who most frequently speculate and corner markets. Previously, until strict controls were introduced for military purchasing on the market, the strange phenomenon existed of the German Expeditionary Force largely using the Jewish network for major purchases of all sorts of provisions in Libya.

Moreover, some Libyan Jews have subsidiaries in Tunisia and even Egypt and thus tend to transfer their funds—which are generally liquid or easily encashable—from Libya to Tunisia or vice versa. This occurred particularly during the British offensives, when these Jews withdrew their deposits from banks and either hoarded cash or tried to smuggle their lire to Tunisia. This may be one of the main sources feeding the clandestine currency trade between Tunisia and Libya.

Apart from the general regulations to suppress speculation and monopolies, which all branches of the police are enforcing strictly, the government has adopted various sorts of measures to suppress the Jews' activities.

The General Commissioner for War Supplies and Economic Coordination, together with the Party, has decided to exclude Jews from the wholesale trade in rationed goods; higher authorities wish to apply this criterion gradually rather than totally. Thus the Jews' participation in the wholesale business has been reduced considerably.

The Commissioner for Supplies has also promised two measures, which are presently under study by the appropriate agencies. One of them aims at regulating all business transfers, and the other will prohibit Jews from owning real property. Recently there has been a tendency among Jews to buy land. . . .

All the measures adopted can only be partial solutions to the problem. Effective results can only be achieved by radical steps—such as putting the Jews into concentration camps—since excluding Jews from particular activities will only exacerbate the situation and make control more difficult (Jews officially excluded from commerce might practice it under other names). One should remember that the distribution network is composed almost entirely of Jews and thus eliminating them would cause a disruption of the market.

It would be advisable, though, to exclude Jews from the activities of importing, franchise-holding and commercial representation, since these are easier to control.

It can be stated, in conclusion, that the Jewish problem in Libya is being viewed and dealt with as a political issue. The economic aspect is merely a consequence and can only be resolved within the framework of a decisive racial policy.[19]

In late 1938, 1939, and early 1940, until Italy entered the war, in many of its aspects the life of Libyan Jews went along almost undisturbed. The real leader of the Jews of Tripoli and, as far as it was possible of Libyan Jews, was Aldo Lattes. He led them until the British occupation of Tripoli and even afterward, until he died in October 1944. Trying to assure the Italian authorities of the Jews' loyalty and patriotism was one of the most pressing problems with which Lattes and the Community leaders had to deal.[20] The other was education: how to organize the schools needed for educating youth. The intermediate schools were solely the Community's responsibility, while the elementary schools had become more necessary than ever as means of keeping the Jews united and giving them secure moral and cultural prospects for the future. Considerable effort was made toward this end. In the school year 1938–1939 the first technical school had opened in Tripoli with four classes attended by more than sixty students, and other technical schools were opened soon after in Tripoli and Benghazi. The collective enthusiasm for these projects was remarkable. During the first two days of collecting funds in Tripoli for the schools, 50,000 lire were contributed. No one objected to Lattes' decision to establish a sliding rate of school fees depending on the pupils' family situation (200, 130, or 60 lire per month.)[21] One thing must be strongly emphasized: the fellow-feeling that quickly inspired all Libyan Jews and enabled even the least prepared psychologically to confront and overcome the trials they had to undergo in those years. These trials restored to Libyan Jewry the unity which it had been losing and a deeper feeling for Libyan Jewish identity. It is no figure of speech to affirm that it was precisely the dramatic years between 1938 and 1943 that led to the recovery of Libyan Jewish life. This recovery enabled the Jews to weather the equally dramatic trials of 1945–1948 and to pass through these as well spiritually unscathed.

The situation worsened when Italy entered the war. The French and particularly British bombardment caused serious damage and many deaths in the *hara* and obliged many of its inhabitants to seek refuge outside Tripoli. Again, the spirit of initiative and collective solidarity were decisive in coping with the situation. The Community did not have any means for dealing with the new needs. Sion Nemni organized a special committee to help the poor. It appealed to all the Jews of Tripoli to give help and money. In the first three days it collected 600,000 lire and with the funds rented houses outside the city for the homeless, put in some basic furniture so that they could live there, and, immediately after, built a large underground air-raid shelter, two hundred meters by six, on the edge of the *hara*, so that those left behind could continue working at their businesses in the city, secure in the knowledge that they could find refuge when there were bomb attacks.[22] Apart from the bombings, 1940 was not a particularly difficult year. There were some peripheral events, such as the sentencing in Tripoli of one Iusef Naman to thirty days in prison "for failing to stand and salute during the lowering of the flag."[23] Such events resulted more from bureaucratic and patriotic zeal than actual anti-Semitism. A change began in 1941, due to many causes. Nervousness was spreading among Italians at the Italian army's uneven and on the whole far from brilliant showing in the war. There was concern about the high cost of living and food scarcities. It was also undeniable that from the purely economic point of view the Jews, especially the rich, were prospering, while Italians were falling upon increasingly hard times. Thus some bitterness was growing against the Jews, and accusations against them spread. These accusations went from the more general one of being "the worst profiteers" and indulging in illicit speculation and cornering of markets, to more specific accusations such as causing "spiraling" prices in real estate by "scooping up" houses as investments for their profits. More serious from a political point of view were the accusations of setting beacons to guide the British bombers to their targets and planning to "lord it over us" when the time was ripe.[24] The resentment and accusations explain some of the measures which the Italian authorities took in 1941. As the Acorguerra report indicates, for example, steps were taken to deprive Libyan Jews of their monopoly on the wholesale trade, and the Maccabee sports association was accused of subversive activities and disbanded.[25] The main cause for the change in Italian public opinion toward the Jews, for violent incidents in Tripoli and elsewhere provoked by civilians and soldiers,[26] and for the policy of the Italian authorities in Libya and Italy was the behavior of the Jews of Cyrenaica, particularly Benghazi, during the first British occupation between February and April 1941, and the news that spread of their conduct.

The British occupation of Cyrenaica provoked differing reactions among the Jews living in the region. The majority naturally saw it as a sort of liberation, specifically, the end of a period of moral inferiority and fear for the future. Thus the Jews were generally sympathetic to the occupiers and, when they arrived, even jubilant. Most did not go any further than this. There were some cases, though, of outright collaboration with the occupiers (especially by British and

French Jews) and even some incidents of vandalism and violence against Italian persons and property. When Benghazi was reconquered on April 3 and 4 by the Italians and Germans, reprisals and bloodshed broke out against the Jewish collaborators known to the Italian population.[27] The news of the behavior of the Jews of Benghazi spread throughout Libya, arousing much hard feeling and some calculated reprisals. The police soon began to search for the Jewish culprits responsible in Benghazi. Most of them had followed the British withdrawal, though a few were arrested. Three of them were brought before the special tribunal on May 7 and sentenced on September 19. Abramo Abib, a forty-year-old shoemaker, was condemned to death. He was not executed, since he petitioned for mercy and during the delay the British occupied Benghazi again and freed him. He was found guilty of aiding the enemy, of defeatism, of insulting the honor of the Head of State, and of calumny. Angelino Gabso was sentenced to twenty-three years' imprisonment for defeatism, for contempt for the Italian nation, and for insulting the honor of the Head of State. Jacob Mimun received three years' imprisonment for insulting the honor of the Head of State.[28] Fifteen other Jews (nine French, two British, three Libyan, and one Italian) who, together with thirteen Muslims, had collaborated with or shown "sympathy to the British" were identified from a photograph published by the Greek newspaper *Estia* on March 10. Three of them who had not followed the British withdrawal like the others were arrested,[29] but nothing is known of their fate.[30]

Further incidents of the same sort, more serious and numerous, occurred when the British occupied Benghazi and Cyrenaica for the second time in December 1941 and January 1942. This time, the Italian reconquest was followed by a much harsher repression. Two Jews were even arrested for running a bar reserved for the occupation troops.[31] One Dadusc Mohai, who had acted as barber and interpreter for the British commander of the port of Benghazi, was sentenced to twelve years' imprisonment.[32] More serious punishments were inflicted on twelve Jews who had been arrested and ten who had left with the British, and were accused of vandalism and theft of Italian property. Three of them, Abramo Bedusa and the brothers Iona and Scialom Berrabbi, were sentenced to death and shot on June 12, 1942. Three others, Elia Barda, Scialom Frig, and Isacco Zard received twenty-three years' imprisonment. Five were found innocent and absolved.[33] But the most serious aspect of the repression was Mussolini's order to send all the Jews of Cyrenaica to a concentration camp.[34]

The "clearing out," as it was officially called, of the Jews of

Cyrenaica initially went very fast. The British subjects have already been discussed. French subjects and protected persons were extradited to Tunisia. By late July, 591 Jews had been "cleared" and only 33 were left in Cyrenaica, waiting to leave. An internment camp was set up for Libyan and Italian Jews at Giado, 235 kilometers from Tripoli. At the end of June, the process was halted. Giado lacked adequate facilities and provisions, so that some Jews were sent to another camp for foreigners at Gharian. There were some transportation problems and resistance on the Jews' part. Many requested exemption. By late June, 2,584 people (2,537 Libyans and 47 Italians) had been removed and 380 remained, in addition to 172 receiving special treatment. Living conditions in the Giado camp were hard, but not terrible. In December 1942 there were some confirmed and suspected cases of typhus. General Ettore Bastico, the commander, concerned that an epidemic might break out, freed many of the internees in Tripolitania.[35]

The drastic steps taken against the Jews of Cyrenaica were only one part of the measures adopted in 1942 to deal with the Jews of Libya. It is impossible to say whether or to what extent the others may have been a direct reaction to what had happened in Benghazi and Cyrenaica during the British occupation. They may simply have been a result of the gradual expression of already prevailing trends (such as excluding Jews from the wholesale trade), of polarization in the Libyan situation (related to the ever-growing German presence and influence in the colony), and of the military's growing shortage of manpower. There is little doubt, though, that the events in Cyrenaica had some weight. In Rome as well as in Tripoli, the views of extremists were reinforced, while those who had tried to balance them or had seen the problem from the point of view of economic opportunity and thus tried to avoid disturbing the economic structure in Libya became more cautious. Confronted with the events in Cyrenaica, they probably preferred to avoid exposing themselves to accusations of being pro-Jewish and being held responsible for any disorder committed by the Jews of Tripolitania.

The first of these measures was the governor's decree no. 105 of May 30, which became effective on June 2, 1942.[36] It was officially dictated by the "obvious need to protect the Libyan economy from speculation which, especially at present, can be most harmful and elusive of general discipline," and intended to "regulate the Jews' manufacturing activities, business and the practice of certain professions."[37] It forbade Jews to sell, purchase, or lease property or farms to or from Aryan Italians or Muslims. The measure did not cover gifts to charities and charitable institutions, as long as they were ap-

proved by the governing authorities. Authorization was also necessary for transferring commercial and manufacturing concerns for
any purpose, for setting up companies and for practicing the professions of broker, commercial traveler, commission agent, and franchise holder. In addition, the measure established that:

> The practice of industrial and commercial activities on the part of
> companies and other entities in which the interests of metropolitan
> Italian or Libyan citizens of the Jewish race are represented, or on the
> part of persons belonging to the said race, except as provided for under
> the limitations and conditions imposed by laws and provisions apply-
> ing to Libya, shall be subject to the control of the Government, to be
> exercised, until new provisions are passed, through the General Com-
> missariat for Wartime Supplies and Economic Coordination.
>
> Enterprises and citizens indicated in the first clause are forbidden to
> practice import and export of merchandise from or to Italy and abroad,
> the wholesale trade, and trade related to the military defense of Libya.
> However, for reasons of public interest, the Governor-General may, on
> a temporary basis, grant individual approvals to continue practicing the
> said commercial activities, provided that they do not contravene policy
> interests and legal precedents, and that those concerned in practicing
> their business obey discipline and the duties required by the present
> situation, particularly as regards rationing policy and supplies for Libya.

On June 28, less than a month later, another measure was adopted,
and it went into effect on July 11. As had been done in Italy,[38] the
measure established that all male Italian and Libyan Jews between
the ages of eighteen and forty-five were liable for civil mobilization
and could be called up for labor according to their physical capability
and professional skills. All Jews had to declare their personal data,
residence, and profession to Acorguerra, on penalty of being sent for
labor immediately.[39] In August a camp was set up at Sidi-Azaz, about
150 kilometers east of Tripoli. A thousand Jews were sent there from
Tripoli to work as laborers behind the front and along the communication lines with Egypt (the Italian and German troops had joined at
El Alamein at the time).[40] In fact only relatively few Jews were set to
work. The largest group, of about 350, was employed near Tubruq,
where it found itself in serious difficulties during the last British offensive. When the Axis forces withdrew, the group was abandoned in
the desert and had to make an exhausting march across Cyrenaica,
Syrtica, and Tripolitania to reach Tripoli.[41]

Law no. 1420 of October 9, 1942, published in the *Official Gazette* on December 17, extended to Libya the racial laws in force in
Italy since 1938. The report with which it was presented to the Cabinet[42] states that the law was intended to rectify the difference in

conditions between Italian Jews and Libyan and foreign Jews (whom the law linked to the Libyans). The difference had been in favor of the latter. The new law regulated everything relating to the circumstances "which require that firmer restrictions be imposed" and covered relations not only with the "Aryan race" but also with Muslims. The new law integrated the measures taken by the governing authorities into those previously applied to Italian Jews, and made them harsher. It sanctioned the moral and legal inferiority of Jews,[43] with regard to Muslims too,[44] and imposed new restrictions on them. In addition to the restrictions established by the governing authorities' decree of May 30, the new law forbade benefiting from land, agricultural, forestry, and mining concessions; owning or managing credit, insurance, navigation, transport, and shipping agencies; participating in companies; and publishing anything not strictly related to religion. The law changed the legal basis of the Community by establishing a special Community for Italian Jews in Tripoli, severing Libyan Communities from the Union of Italian Jewish Communities, and depriving them of all public functions previously entrusted to them. Finally, the discrimination provided for under Italian law was extended to Libyan Jews as well. In addition to the special treatment under Italian law, Libyan Jews were liable for any which might arise "during the present state of war."

The law took effect on December 17, 1942. In practice, it was not widely enforced. It was already clear who was going to win the fight for Libya. On November 8, when the Italian and German troops retreating from Egypt were almost at Sidi-Barrani, the British and Americans had landed in Morocco and Algeria. Marshal Rommel, because of this new event, immediately became convinced that it was necessary to abandon Libya and concentrate on defending Tunisia. Mussolini and Hitler were not of this opinion: they believed that Libya should be defended inch by inch. It became obvious that this was impossible and that Rommel was right when he argued that the choice was between losing Tripoli a few days later together with the whole Italian and German army, or losing Tripoli a few days earlier and saving the army in Tunisia. Abandoning Libya and Tripoli itself thus became inevitable and urgent: on January 23, 1943, while the bulk of the Axis forces was forming a bridgehead in Tunisia, the civilian authorities of Tripoli handed the city over to General Montgomery. He had arrived from the east, only three days before a French column reached the city from the south.

The last racial measures were not actually implemented, and the life of the Jews of Tripolitania was not disrupted by such dramatic events as those which the Jews in Cyrenaica experienced during the last year of war in Libya. Nevertheless, their existence did become more and more difficult. After April 1941, serious anti-Semitic incidents and violence did not reoccur. Some animosity still lingered among Italians, aroused by echoes of the events in Cyrenaica and occasional accusations of amassing profit, cornering markets, and indifference, even outright hostility, to the Italian cause. The Arabs' attitude was not very different. Many Arabs had been concerned at the measures taken against the Jews; their concern was mainly due to a fear that the racial policy might sooner or later be applied to them. Otherwise, apart from old hostilities, the Arabs also put a large part of the blame for the difficult economic situation on the Jews. Their attitude was hardened because many Arabs still thought that the Jews were closer to the Italians than to themselves. Those most politicized already projected this judgment into the future and were worried at how the Jews would "lord it over them" if the British took over. A small episode which occurred in the area of Misurata confirms this. To escape the bombardments, a number of Misurata Jews had moved to Zawiet el-Mahjub, about twelve kilometers from the city. Initially relations with the local population were normal. However, when the refugees wanted to build a small synagogue, relations quickly deteriorated, so that the Jews ended up by going back to Misurata.[45]

The situation of most Jews was made more difficult by the overall gradual worsening of conditions in Libya in 1942. The economy was in disorder, prices spiraled, food and all products usually imported were scarce, and there was black market dealing and crimes against property. Refugees from Cyrenaica and agricultural villages further west were a problem. The Arabs had an ambiguous attitude to the Jews. Tripolitanian Arabs were more cautious than those in Cyrenaica, but they were alert to and affected by the ebb and flow of the war and sensitive to British propaganda to the effect that if they were victorious the British would give "the land to the native people." Acts of sabotage spread alarm among the Jews. Last but not least, there was the continual threat, to all the inhabitants of the colony, of bombing and machine-gun fire from British planes.[46] The mass of poor Jews living in the *hara* of Tripoli suffered more from these conditions because of their isolation and the hostility around them. The hostility expressed itself in discrimination: just before the British occupation, when food supplies were lowest, the Jews in Tripoli received fewer rations than the Italians and Arabs. The *hara*-dwellers suffered especially from uncertainty about the future and the fear that the ever-growing German influence and presence would lead to much more dramatic turns for them. The Community organization was in a desperate state and had to limit its activities almost exclusively to helping the poor.[47] Several thousand Jews abandoned their homes in locations most exposed to air attacks and sought refuge in Gharian, Tarhuna, and Zuwara, which were less exposed. In December 1942 they were evicted from Zuwara to make room for military offices and had to return to Tripoli. These groups had to adapt to extremely precarious living conditions. For those who stayed behind, the last months were the worst. In December the city was attacked eighteen times, by day and by night. Food shortages got worse, and Jewish shops often received their supplies last. The Jews were more and more isolated. At the very end, just before the British troops came in, German soldiers sacked the shops in Suq al-Turq.[48]

It was only natural that the Jews felt liberated by the British troops' arrival in Tripoli and greeted them with expressions of enthusiasm. It is understandable that, after years of humiliation, fear, and violence, some of them said that the Italians had treated them more inhumanly than the Germans would have.[49] It is significant though that, once the fear was over and they had to deal with the realities of occupation, the women of the *hara*, whenever some group of drunken British soldiers tried to break into their houses, would shout "Long live Italy!" as they fled to the rooftops.[50] That cry, though the Jewish women were probably not aware of it, showed that four years of wretched Fascist anti-Semitism had not completely obliterated in them the awareness of what the Italian presence in Libya for over a quarter of a century, despite all its limitations and mistakes, had meant for Libyan Jewry.

7. British Occupation
(1943–1951)

British occupation lasted from 1943 until December 24, 1951, when the British handed over authority to the new Kingdom of Libya. For the history of the Jews, this period should be divided at early November 1945 into two very different subperiods. For the Jews, the pogroms of November 1945 affected every aspect of the situation, marking the most decisive turning point—or, rather, break with the past—in two thousand years.

Libyan Jews experienced in 1943 a year of euphoria. Though in the first few months the Italians and Germans bombed Tripoli a few times, for the Jews, as for the Arabs, the British occupation really meant the end of the war in their country. It also meant an end to moral and juridical inferiority and to the violence and repression they had suffered under Fascist racial policy. The Jews of Cyrenaica and all those put to forced labor, interned, or evacuated for reasons of war, had a chance to get back home and down to work again.[1] The Libyan economy had been almost paralyzed by a serious crisis, particularly in 1942. It clearly benefited from the first year of occupation. An immediate and in some sectors strong recovery began. It aroused expectations, stimulated initiative, and induced many to try their hand at making easy money and the dubious and illegal activities typical of such conditions.[2] In this situation Jewish businesses very soon recovered. Within the communities, people worked to rebuild what had been destroyed by the war. Outward-oriented activities, such as joint ventures with Arab businessmen, also prospered, inspired by a shared hope in a better future for Libya. Mohammed Idris es-Sanusi, the head of the Sanusi Order, had returned to Cyrenaica after the British had occupied it. In return for the help which his guerrilla fighters had given the British troops, he hoped to win recognition of his sovereignty over Cyrenaica and if possible over all of Libya. His hopes were bolstered by Anthony Eden's statement to the Commons in January 1942 that the British government opposed the reimposition of Italian sovereignty over the Sanusis in

Cyrenaica.[3] In Tripolitania the Arab nationalist movement was still very weak and lacked leaders. In both regions during those early days Arab-Jewish relations (especially in the small towns and among elites) seemed to be settling down and were characterized by a sincere desire on both sides to live and work together peacefully. The desire was reinforced by their common trust in the British, who were soon expected to grant the country independence or more probably a protectorate which they would administer. The good results from the initial forms of cooperation in the Tripoli Municipal Council, the courts, and the police, into which Jews had quickly been readmitted by the British, also promised well.[4]

Though there were some problems with the occupation authorities and some internal differences, social and cultural activities also started up again quickly and vigorously. This recovery was made easier by the Jewish awakening which had taken place during the years of Fascist persecution and the encouraging presence in Libya of the members of the Palestinian Jewish Brigade. Having taken an active part in the operations of the British Eighth Army, they symbolized the new type of Jew created by Zionism and the colonization of Palestine. A few minor events were significant: the first wedding in Tripoli after the British occupied was a Jewish one, and the first football match was played between two Jewish teams. The best proof of the recovery is the speed with which the Maccabee Club (in March) and the Ben Yehuda Association (in July) resumed their sports, leisure, and cultural activities.[5] These older associations were soon joined by others, all of which had Zionist leanings and were aimed largely at the young: The British promoted the Jewish Boy Scouts (Zofim) as well as a similar association for Arabs, which did not materialize. The soldiers of the Palestinian Brigade founded the Noar organization. There were also the youth organization of Hechalutz (of which more will be said later) and subsequently, between 1944 and 1945, the Hamaccabee Hatzair group and the Tripoli Social Committee. Since there was no purely Zionist organization, this committee had to fill that role, overseeing and coordinating the various youth organizations.[6] At the same time, an effort was being made to reopen the Talmud Torah and community schools, which had been closed for two years because of the continuous bombing and because many pupils had been evacuated. All these activities were taking place in an atmosphere of great enthusiasm and, especially among the young, of intense religious and Zionist fervor.

The *Annual Report* for 1945 of the British Military Administration in Tripolitania contains important information concerning the spread of Zionist ideals. The report repeatedly attests to how far these ideals were spreading. It rightly states, regarding the young Jews of Tripoli, that "their political consciousness found vent in Zionism."[7] It insinuates, though, that this Zionist commitment was one of the causes of the pogroms in November 1945. Without discussing the merits of this insinuation for the moment, this is how the document most clearly describes the spread of Zionism:

> Though aloof from politics in the territory, the Jews have been more active and outspoken in their profession of Zionist ideas. Jewish Clubs and youth organisations, all of Zionist bias, flourished; Zionist literature was imported from Palestine and emigrants to Palestine were selected and trained in agriculture. The presence of Palestinian troops in the territory has been an added stimulus as well as a source of propaganda. The self-assertiveness of the nationalistically-minded Jew, and the very growth of this new nationalism, have alienated Arab friendship and tolerance.[8]

The council of the Jewish Community of Tripoli had been given a new start right after the British had arrived. Halfalla Nahum, since he was still the most representative, respected, and powerful figure in Libyan Jewish life, had been asked to preside over it again. Despite this choice, and despite the pressing and grave tasks facing the new council, Community institutions soon became embroiled in difficulties. These increased the following year, when the death of Chief Rabbi Lattes deprived the Community of its linchpin. Very soon the position of president was abolished in practice and its responsibilities were rotated among the vice presidents. This expedient only solved the problems on the surface and did not eliminate the more or less explicit differences lying beneath. These were largely the same as those which had wracked the Community before the racial legislation. They were made worse by the fact that several of the twelve council members were more concerned with their personal affairs than with those of the Community. They were thus neither very committed to Community interests nor willing to jeopardize for them their own relations with the British authorities and the Arab elite. There were intergenerational conflicts and latent disagreements between Italian elements and indigenous Jews (concerning how Italian domination should be judged as a whole and Libya's future prospects). Otherwise, the main differences were those between traditionalists and integrationists, and the closely connected disagreements about how to deal with Zionism, the enthusiasm which it was generating among Libyan Jews, and the occupation authorities' obvious hostility to it. No one was actually against

Zionism. There were many viewpoints, however, on how Zionism should be understood and what attitude the Community should take to it. For some, Zionism was the answer to everything: it meant the future, the national identity of the Jews, and as such had to be turned into an official fact and given every encouragement. For others, Zionism represented a way of protecting, conserving, and activating Jewish religion and tradition in the modern world, but it was not to jeopardize relations with the occupation authorities, on whom largely depended the future of Libya and thus that of the Jews. Nor was it to jeopardize relations with the Arabs, with whom the Jews had to live as best they could. For this second faction, the first priority was for the Jews to integrate completely into the new Libya which was coming into being. It was no less a priority than preserving their own religious and cultural character. In the new Libyan society which would emerge after the war, it would be necessary to come to terms not with an attractive "higher" civil and social culture (as for Jews the Italian had been) but rather with Arab civilization which, they argued, could constitute neither a cultural nor an economic threat. In fact, it took less than three years to show the weakness of this position; at the time, though, many genuinely saw it as the most balanced and realistic one. The view was reinforced when it grew clear that the British had no intention of allowing any active Zionist presence in Libya. The British Military Administration forbade the reinstitution of the Libyan Zionist organization and entry to teachers or anyone from Palestine who might carry on Zionist activities. It even refused financial help to Hebrew schools (though it helped Arabic and Italian schools), using the specious argument that Hebrew was not an official language in Libya, and invited the Jews to send their children to Arabic schools. Despite the Jews' sincere belief in the need to work together with the Arabs, the vast majority certainly could not accept this suggestion. The Arabic schools were finely tuned to Islam; the Jews traditionally preferred either their own or the Italian schools; and, rightly or wrongly, most Jews considered Arab culture inferior to theirs and if anything felt closer to European culture. And so the result of the British decision was to channel the vast majority of Jews, who could not find a place in the Community schools or were not happy with the education given in the Talmud Torah or Alliance Israélite Universelle school, to the Italian schools.[9]

Despite these initial disappointments, and though much of the earlier euphoria had dissipated by 1944, making way for deeper and deeper concern, until November 1945 the Libyan Jews remained strongly pro-British.[10] Faith in Britain survived until the 1945 pogroms. Even the most convinced Zionists, those of Ben Yehuda, saw the British position as a temporary result of practical political imperatives related not only to Libya and its future but also to the difficult situation in Palestine. Two facts give indirect proof of this and show that even the Zionists thought that the restrictions on them would soon be lifted. These facts are that at the time there were almost no cases of clandestine emigration to Palestine[11] and that the special Hechalutz organization was set up in 1943 under the auspices of the Ben Yehuda Association (thanks to the efforts of Yosef Maimon and Sion Nemni) to give training in agriculture to young pioneers expecting to move to Palestine.[12]

In 1944 and the first ten months of 1945 there were other worries. Most were related to the economic situation.[13] The recovery which had occurred immediately after the British occupation very soon turned out to have no real economic base, since it resulted almost entirely from the sudden increase in money supply and the opportunity for easy profits due to the presence of the occupation forces. When the first phase of the occupation was over and large numbers of troops had left for Italy in 1944, a vague economic malaise became more and more tangible. It was caused by the slump in trade and production, the scarcity of jobs, and the crisis in agriculture, particularly the most productive branches, which the Italians had run. They had been forced by the war, Arab violence, the constant insecurity, and lack of resources to abandon their agricultural villages and lands or reduce production to subsistence farming. One should also weigh the consequences of the fact that the Libyan economy had received considerable investments from Italy, while the British made almost none. Even the Arab and particularly Jewish capital which was present found few investment opportunities, and its owners were loath to risk it. There was thus a general economic slump, affecting everyone, Arabs particularly, who suffered most from unemployment, though the mass of Jews was not spared. The situation in Tripoli and its immediate surroundings was particularly serious. Tripoli swarmed with demobilized soldiers, freed prisoners, and unemployed Arabs who had flocked to the capital from the interior in the vain hope of finding work. The situation became even more critical in the autumn of 1945 just before the pogroms in November, when Wadi al-Majanin flooded, thrusting thousands more into destitution, while bad weather made the lives of this mass of homeless people even more difficult.

The economic problems were exacerbated by those deriving from the gradual deterioration in Jewish-Arab relations. These had been excellent in 1943 and had led people to think that it would be possible to live and work together peacefully. These relations also began to change in 1944. The change in the main did not involve the traditional elites. The Arab notables, the secular and religious leaders, rich merchants, and entrepreneurs in this period never fell short of their attitude of tolerance and sincere desire to work together with the Jews. The Arabic newspaper of Tripoli, *Tarabulus el Gharb*, repeatedly wrote that "Arabs and Jews are compatriots" and that "religion belongs to God and the country to everyone" and supported stronger cultural, economic, and social relations between the two communities, under the aegis of the democratic British government.[14] One month before the pogroms, relations with this elite were still so good that when Suleimen Karamanli died many of the Jews of Tripoli attended his funeral and the Community donated a considerable sum to the Muslim relief committee. Jewish-Arab relations were equally good in the towns of the interior, on the coast, and in Cyrenaica, where Idris would even show them off.

The situation was different, though, among the masses and what could be defined as the new Arab elite. The change in the attitude of the masses undoubtedly originated in the worsening economic situation. It is significant that such accusations as that the Jews were "starving the people," growing rich on the people's backs, hoarding goods, and practicing cruel usury began to break out again and become more insistent as economic hardship increased. Small but repeated incidents, brawls, and stone-throwing by Arab boys and young men against Jews also began to break out again at the time, especially in Tripoli and particularly on Sunday evenings in the New City. The Community repeatedly informed the authorities and advised Jews to refrain not only from provoking incidents but also from reacting in any way and merely report them to the police. On the whole, until far into 1945 there was not much concern about the situation. It seemed on the one hand almost a traditional condition and on the other a passing phenomenon which would disappear when the economic situation improved and the Arab masses gained more civil rights. Arab notables were of the same opinion, belittling the problem and, more crucially, not being influenced by it. Some alarm was aroused in July by fanatically anti-Jewish sermons which the local qadi gave in the mosque of al-Khums and in October by the spread of an accusation in Tripoli that Jews had killed an Arab girl by throwing her into a well. In each case alarm soon died down. The qadi of al-Khums immediately received an official reprimand, and it was ascertained that the girl had been thrown into the well by an Arab woman of the neighborhood.

The real state of Arab-Jewish relations cannot be appreciated fully by looking at either the attitude of the traditional elites or the kind of reaction, likewise traditional, which economic difficulties provoked from the masses. One can understand why someone approaching the problem from this dual viewpoint could be unaware of how far these relations had deteriorated in less than two years and could overlook the new element rendering the situation explosive. The view of the president of the Tripoli Community, Zachino Habib, was typical. Only three weeks before the pogroms of November 1945 he told an American that no serious problems were likely to arise between Arabs and Jews.

The new element, which substantially escaped observers, was the fact that during 1944 and 1945 the traditional Arab elite in Libya, particularly Tripolitania, was being joined by a new, pan-Islamic, and fanatically nationalist elite. This phenomenon hardly existed in Cyrenaica, where Idris and the Sanusis held the situation under tighter control. The new Tripolitanian elite was still weak and unable to act openly, but it was well aware of the situation and resolved with all means available to make its presence known. For this elite, because of the Palestine situation, the Jews were both the main enemies and the easiest target. By directing old and new popular resentments against them, the elite could build itself a base among the politically aware and manipulable masses. This would allow the new elite to begin undermining the old elite's prestige and to turn the masses against the British and toward full independence for Libya. The indigenous nucleus of this elite consisted of the minor urban Arab intellectuals and some small new groups of petty shopkeepers and small-scale entrepreneurs. These groups wanted to make their mark in regard to both their Jewish commercial competitors and more established Arabs closer to the Italians and British. Significantly, when the November pogroms took place, the only region of Tripolitania where they occurred on a small scale was the central interior where, unlike the coastal areas and Tripoli, this nucleus was almost nonexistent. The movement's cadres were drawn largely from members of the el-Hizb al-Watani nationalist party, linked to Egyptian nationalist groups and the Arab League (founded on March 22, 1945). Many were exiles of the Italian period who had returned to Libya after the British occupation, and some were "imported Arab personnel," the red fezzes. These were Syrians, Palestinians, and especially Egyptians who followed the occupation troops and frequently staffed the auxiliary services and police forces. A typical case was that of 'Awn Ben Suf, who returned to Libya a month before the pogroms. He was the Cairo head of the Tripoli Defense Committee, and his name appeared in a list of leaders of the el-Hizb al-

Watani party that was found on the second day of the pogroms in an Arab cultural club in Tripoli, the Wadi al-Adabi. Practically nonexistent in 1943, these groups began to form the following year and in 1945—due to their skills in organizing and at exploiting discontent with the economic situation, religious feelings, and embryonic pan-Islamic trends—though still small became an important factor in Tripolitanian urban politics. The 1945 *Annual Report* makes this significant statement:

> This return of Arabs [exiles] is not without political repercussions . . . the exiles from Egypt often arrive in this territory imbued with nationalist ideas and pan-Arab sentiments. . . . If one particular problem could be singled out as "problem of the year" it would be this growth of nationalist consciousness and agitation among the Arabs.[15]

In only a few months these groups had in fact set the stage for a new situation extending beyond the Arab masses' view of Jews to the broader problem of the future of Libya. In changing that attitude, they skilfully exploited news from the Middle East and reports in *Tarabulus el Gharb* on positions taken in the press of countries belonging to the Arab League.[16] Again, the best evidence of this is in the 1945 *Annual Report*:

> If a plebiscite on the future government of the country could have been taken in the middle of the year, there would have been a predominant vote for a British protectorate. This is still true of the tribal areas. But among the urban population nationalist ambitions were gaining ground, and hopes for the future became focussed upon complete independence or close affiliation with the Arab League.[17]

This is the economic, emotional, and political context in which the pogroms broke out. From November 4 to 7, 1945, they ravaged Tripoli and the surrounding area from Zawia to Jebel a Qusabat (Mesallata), with the sole exceptions of Yafran (significantly, a Berber area) and, partially, the central hinterland area of Gharian, where only a few cases of plundering occurred. The pogroms stained Jewish life with blood and threw it into disorder.

The pogroms began in Tripoli and gradually spread to the areas indicated in a crescendo of unheard-of violence and cruelty. If it had not been for the British troops' intervention, even belated, the violence probably would have spread even further. Among other actions, the troops evacuated the Jews from Beni Ulid, surrounded the Jewish quarters of several other towns to prevent possible attacks, and attempted to calm the hostility aroused by news from Tripoli among Arabs in yet other places. The Tripoli Community's sum-

mary of the pogroms included in the official report by the president,
Zachino Habib,[18] gives a terse picture of those tragic days:

In the later afternoon of Sunday, 4th November, the President of the
Jewish community received news of the first serious attacks, which occurred simultaneously, as if by a pre-arranged signal, in different parts
of Tripoli. He rushed to police headquarters to report the attacks and
urged that immediate measures be taken to prevent further trouble.

No police officer, however, was to be found at headquarters, and it
was also impossible to trace them elsewhere. Noncommissioned police officers who were at the station confined themselves to assuring
the President that all the police were on duty. It seemed that order
would be promptly re-established. Though the reports on 4th November had been numerous and simultaneous, they did not last so long, nor
were they so extensive as to give reason for the belief that they would
increase with greater severity on the two successive days.

On Monday morning the riots broke out afresh. (The rioters in the
town were joined meanwhile by several thousand Arab villagers.) The
heads of the Jewish community proceeded early in the morning to report to Headquarters of the Senior Civil Affairs Officer of the Province,
Lieutenant-Colonel Oulton. This officer, who had been out of Tripoli,
returned to Headquarters at about 9 that morning. He was immediately
informed of the gravity of the situation and urged to take steps at once
to quell the disorders with the aid of British troops, since the civil police had revealed their inability to keep the situation under control:
Lieutenant-Colonel Oulton promised that he would give his immediate attention to the matter. Unfortunately, however, the British Forces
were not actually called upon to intervene until more than forty-eight
hours after the outbreak of the riots, despite the fact that on the same
day, Monday, both the Chief of the Tripolitania Police and Colonel Mer-
cer, Chief Secretary to the British Military Administration (since the
Chief Administrator, Brigadier Blackley, had been out of town for some
days), were also informed by Jews and Arabs of the increasing severity of
the riots and exhorted to take energetic and proper measures against
them. Indeed notwithstanding the curfew imposed on the Monday that
same evening, and on the following Tuesday, 6th November, large-scale,
renewed attacks, plundering and firing of Jewish homes occurred. On
Monday evening the few troops that began to appear on the streets took
no action against the mob or used their arms to repress the rioting.

Only on Tuesday evening (6th November) and on Wednesday (7th
November), did the Military Commander finally take action. At first
he prohibited the assembly of crowds and the carrying of sticks and
other offensive articles, and later he proclaimed a State of Emergency.
British patrols began to patrol the streets and to search passers-by and
Arab houses.

In Tripoli this firm stand on the part of the authorities was sufficient
to diminish the disorders considerably, without resort to arms, as from

Tuesday night. The arrest of Arabs guilty of acts of plundering and aggression did not, however, take place until the Wednesday. The Jewish quarter of Hara had been previously attacked by bands of Arabs at different external points, but they did not succeed in penetrating the quarter, owing to active defence measures taken by the Jewish inhabitants. Meanwhile thousands of Jews swarmed from the more exposed places to take refuge there.

In other places, at Zanzur and Zavia for instance, the mass slaughter of Jews occurred on Tuesday night.

In Tripoli, the most serious attacks occurred in the streets of the old city, where there was a mixed population, and in the busy parts of the new town, where the Jews lived in isolated houses and were therefore unable to resist the attackers to any appreciable extent. And indeed the rioters could make no mistake, since some mysterious band [sic] had previously marked the doors of houses and shops of non-Jews with suitable signs. During the riots only one Arab was killed, presumably by one of those attacked in self-defence.

On Wednesday, 7th November, and Thursday, 8th November, it was possible to provide for the burial of the victims of Tripoli and Zanzur. The funeral, directed by the President of the community, aided by the personnel of the Burial Society, took place at the beginning of the curfew, following a route largely patrolled by armed troops but, as a sign of protest, unaccompanied by relatives or coreligionists. Administrative and military authorities, however, were represented at the funeral. The other communities arranged the burial of their dead on the spot. British officials inspected and photographed some bodies, especially those on which signs of the attackers' cruelty were more evident. With the exception of two (Rabbi Saul Dabuse and Rabbi Abraham Tesciuba), the victims were buried in only one section of the Jewish Cemetery of Tripoli (Kever Ahim).*

The number of dead, including those slaughtered—some with unimaginable cruelty and some even burned alive[19]—and those who later succumbed to their injuries, amounted to 130. There were 5 Arab victims. Of the dead, 35 were from Tripoli, 38 from Amruss, 7 from Tajura, 3 from Qusabat, 34 from Zanzur, and 13 from Zawia.[20] The victims left 30 widows and 92 orphans.[21] In some cases whole families were wiped out. There were also many wounded. In Tripoli alone, 159 Jews were sent to hospital and 106 treated at first-aid posts. In Qusabat many women and girls were raped, and many men and women, in order to save their lives, were compelled to abjure their faith and embrace Islam.

Direct and indirect material damage was enormous. Besides

*"Anti-Jewish Riots in Tripolitania," CZA, S/25/6457, pp. 1–3.—*Trans.*

nine synagogues profaned, plundered, and burned (five in Tripoli, two in Amruss, one in Tajura, and another in Zanzur), hundreds of homes, shops, and stores were plundered, destroyed, or damaged. Those who suffered most were the small merchants, shopkeepers, and artisans, many of whom were reduced to penury.[22] The Community of Tripoli calculated that direct damages amounted to about 300 million Military Authority Lire. The figure does not seem excessive when one considers that the claims lodged amounted alone to over 268 million[23] and that property damage in Tripoli, Amruss, and Tajura alone (since there was no information for other towns) was estimated at more than 10,000 pounds sterling (the official rate being 480 Military Authority Lire to the pound) and damage resulting from loss of assets and from idleness at 150 times this figure. Those made homeless and those who fled their homes in the Arab quarters of Tripoli and smaller centers numbered over 4,000. About half of them found refuge in the refugee camps which the British Military Administration (BMA) set up and in the Talmud Torah schools and Italian schools for Jews; the rest were taken in by relatives and friends living in the *hara*. Besides these homeless, approximately another 4,200 were reduced to poverty because their houses and shops had been plundered.[24] Perhaps the most significant fact in appreciating this aspect of the tragedy is that 10,000–12,000 Jews were being fed every day by the BMA during the first week after the pogrom.

About six hundred Arabs were arrested in connection with the pogroms. According to reports in the press,[25] proceedings were brought against 289 of these. Eighty-five of them were acquitted or absolved. Two hundred and four received sentences, two of them death sentences (one for homicide and one for possession of hand grenades), one of fifteen years (for assaulting a British official), one of ten years for crowd incitement. Most of the rest received various sentences up to a maximum of eight years for plunder, illegal possession of objects, disturbance of public order, and acts of violence. Six received suspended sentences. Four Jews were also sentenced for "provoking disorder," and one for assaulting a police officer, to terms ranging from three to four years.

After the British troops had restored order, sometimes even by using firearms, *Tarabulus el Gharb* roundly condemned the pogroms and criticized those who had participated in them, pointing out the potential harm to the cause of self-government and Libyan independence. On November 8, in an editorial entitled "We Must Maintain the Dignity of the Libyan People," the Tripoli Arabic daily wrote:

Yesterday we visited Suq al-Turq and some parts of the Old City. We observed signs of destruction and violence, showing the seriousness of the disorders caused by groups of troublemakers who were devoid of all conscience and oblivious to the disastrous moral and material results that such actions would bring to the Arab people of Libya. These are blameworthy actions which we condemn and cannot tolerate.

These plunderers and aggressors have caused harm to the people of Libya with their behavior toward a minority which has lived with us for centuries in peace and tranquillity. The people of Libya today finds itself on the eve of the decision regarding its future. It is held accountable for its every action, which unavoidably affects how its future is decided.

The unfortunate acts of bloodshed and violence have aroused profound reactions in the hearts of all sensible Libyan patriots, jealous for their people's honor and human feelings.

These events are deplorable and out of character with a people which holds itself worthy of assuming the responsibility of self-government.

We bitterly regret that our intellectuals and leaders were not able to prevent such acts.

It is the pressing duty of us all to confront this tragedy which will tarnish the history of our country and leave a black stain on it. We must act with all means at our disposal to bring this wave of vandalism to a halt. Not only this, but we must also, with all means at our disposal, make any sacrifice to allay its serious consequences.

Then we shall show the world that we are worthy of what we aspire to. First and foremost, we must show that we are human and a people with a high sense of honor. Otherwise, we will cause a part of the world to condemn us as barbarians, and we will emerge morally and materially defeated.

The next day, in an article entitled "The Wise Man Considers in Time the Results of His Actions," the newspaper labeled as "irresponsible" those who had taken part in the massacres and violence. It stated that "sensible people" and "patriots" had surely not been involved, blamed the passivity of the "most influential leaders" who did not act in time to prevent it, and emphasized the need for Arabs and Jews to work together again in peace and tranquillity:

We fully believe that sensible people and real patriots were not involved in these events in any way, and that the rash persons who committed acts of brutal violence in the last two days were led by desire for plunder.

However, we deplore the lack of intervention on the part of our most influential leaders, who might have prevented these actions from developing. If they had intervened, much bloodshed and material damage would have been spared. . . .

The Jews of Tripolitania should know that the Arabs are ready to come to terms with them by all possible means and at the right moment. Though it may be difficult at present, they must believe that the majority of the Arab people is completely indignant at the recent events which have taken place between Arabs and Jews.

We believe that it will be possible to reach understanding with the Jews in the future, as existed in the past, on condition that the atmosphere of understanding be free from subversive elements on either side.

We must thus track down these elements, destroying them by all means in our power and striking them mercilessly. Only in this way can we attain true peace and tranquillity between the two communities, which have lived in perfect harmony for centuries.

On the same day, in the mosques of Tripoli and Suq al-Jum'a, the grand qadi and the mufti of Libya also condemned the "unpleasant event" and exhorted their fellow-Muslims to heed "the duty to revive feelings of friendship" between Jews and Muslims and work together "for a return to peace and prosperity" between the two communities.[26] Two days later *Tarabulus el Gharb* reported that a collection committee for Jewish victims of Arab violence had been formed in Zawia under the chairmanship of the qadi. Arab notables in Tripoli and elsewhere made similar declarations.

After the way had been thus smoothed for reconciliation, the notables of the two communities had their first official meeting after the pogroms on November 27, at the initiative of the British, and resolved to set up an Arab-Jewish Committee for Cooperation and Reconstruction, under the chairmanship of Qadi Sheikh Mahmud Burchis and Halfalla Nahum. The official account of the meeting was published in *Corriere di Tripoli* and *Tarabulus el Gharb* on December 1. Here is the text:

On the afternoon of Tuesday, November 27, 1945, an initial meeting took place in the British Military Administration Hall between notables of the Arab and Jewish communities, with the participation of Brigadier Blackley, the Chief Administrator.

The purpose of the meeting was to remove possible misunderstanding between the two communities and to study and implement—with the Authorities' assistance—all steps necessary for a return to friendly coexistence between Jews and Arabs in Tripolitania and a recovery of mutual trust for the good of the country.

Present on behalf of the Arab community were Qadi el Cudat, Sheikh Mahmud Burchis; the Mufti of Libya, Sheikh Mohammed Abulsaad; the notable Salem bey Muntasser; Sheikh Senussi Ftes, Justice of the Superior Shari'a Court; the notable Ali bey Karamanli; Mahmud bey Muntasser, Mudir of the Waqf of Tripoli; Hag Mustafa Mizran, Director of the Arts and Crafts School; Professor Kamel el Hemmali, School

Inspector; Commendatore Bekir Treso, Government Adviser; Taher bey el Emreied, a notable of Tarhuna; Bescir Zeghellai, a businessman; Taher Bekir, Municipal Councillor; the Jewish community was represented by the following: Commendatore Halfalla Nahum, former President of the Community; Zachino Habib, President of the Community; Rabbi Hai Gabizon, President of the Rabbinical Court; Scialom Nahum, Vice President of the Community; Ruben Hassan, Member of the Jewish Advisory Committee; Raffaello Nemni; Musci Hahum di Ididia, Joseph Barda, a businessman; Messaud Hassan, a businessman; Zachi Haggiag Liluf, a businessman, and Mr. Lillo Arbib, accountant.

At 5:10 P.M. Brigadier Blackley entered the hall and was received by S.C.A.O. [Senior Civil Affairs Officer] Col. Oulton and C.A.O. [Civil Affairs Officer] Tripoli City Major Arkin.

Brigadier Blackley opened the meeting with the following remarks:

"I came to greet you and tell you how happy I am that you have sought this occasion to meet each other. This is the first day since the disorders began that I have glimpsed a ray of brightness through the clouds. I am glad to see you meeting around this table. I hope that you will do everything in your power to combat the bitter arguments and rumors being spread around by men of ill-will and that formal and informal contacts between you will give some guidance for those of a lower intellectual range than yours.

"I hope that by consulting each other in a neighborly way you will be able to induce others to participate in meetings more broadly representative of both communities.

"Friendly relations have existed between you in Tripolitania for over a thousand years. I hope that, with God's help and your wisdom, these can be achieved again to the benefit of everyone living in the Territory. Never hesitate to ask for all the attention that I and my officers can give you."*

After his speech, H. E. the Brigadier took leave of those present and delegated Colonel Oulton to represent him in carrying out the work of the Commission.

The Qadi el Cudat, Sheikh Mahmud Burchis, next addressed the meeting as follows:

"Gentlemen, H. E. our esteemed Governor has invited us here to dispel misunderstandings between the two communities and renew the cordial and friendly relations which have joined us for centuries. For this purpose, we must first forget all those painful events which have had no precedent in the history of Tripolitania, events which we view as common crimes, committed by minors and persons unaware of the seriousness of their crimes. All wise and sensible people on both sides condemn such acts in the most absolute terms and desire only tranquillity and peace.

---

*Brigadier Blackley's speech has been translated.—*Trans.*

"I should like to close by invoking the Omnipresent to consolidate the ties between us and guide us along the straight road to peace."

Commendatore Halfalla Nahum replied on behalf of the Jewish Community. He said that the joint committee's task was not to express recrimination or investigate the past, inasmuch as what happened in the past had now been entrusted to the judicial process which will take its course without any need for us to influence it. He stated that the committee has the responsibility of rebuilding mutual trust between the Arab and Jewish communities, and strengthening the foundations for living together in peace and respect, in the interests of the two communities and the country itself.

On behalf of the Jewish Community, Commendatore Nahum thanked all members of Libyan communities—Arabs, Italians, Maltese, and Greeks—who during the sad days of the disturbances gave help and hospitality to many Jewish families, and thanked His Eminence the Qadi and His Beatitude the Mufti for all that they had done and written during this time.

Colonel Oulton spoke next. Referring to the speeches of H. Em. the Qadi and Commendatore Nahum, and evoking the longstanding friendship uniting the two communities, he declared his faith that the Committee would be able to build the basis for peaceful coexistence between the two communities. Colonel Oulton ended by expressing the prayer that the Committee's work would be crowned with success in its efforts for good and harmony.

Colonel Oulton, followed by Major Arkin, then left the room and the Committee began its discussions.

His Beatitude the Mufti, Sheikh Abulsaad, and Salem bey Muntasser, on the Arab side, and Rabbi Hai Gabizon and Zachino Habib on the Jewish side, took part in the exchange of ideas which followed.

His Beatitude the Mufti confirmed again the moral and material need for an understanding between Arabs and Jews, who have never had and should never have disagreements even regarding material interests, inasmuch as their activities complement each other, one side devoting itself mainly to commerce and the other to general agricultural work.

Mr. Zachino Habib, the President of the Community, took the occasion, since he had not been able to do so earlier through the press, to express to the Qadi and the Mufti the feelings of gratitude of the entire Jewish Community. He also thanked the Muslims and members of other communities who had given proof of their noble, humanitarian sentiments by granting hospitality and protection to Jewish families which took refuge with them. He concluded by saying that in order to maintain a lasting peace, everyone must agree on how the two parties might continue consolidating their ties of friendship, and must examine the various problems as clearly and objectively as possible.

People must spread the spirit of mutual understanding and work for mutual trust in order to live together in an atmosphere of brotherhood and harmony.

The meeting closed at 6:15 P.M. in an atmosphere of great cordiality and friendship.

The Commission will convene again in the next few days in order to pursue its efforts.

One can doubt neither the uninvolvement in the pogroms of the religious and civil leaders and Arab notables, nor the sincerity of their wish for reconciliation when the pogroms were over. They had too big a stake in good relations with the Jews not to desire harmony between the two communities. Moreover, it is clear that the pogroms were a strong blow to their prestige, creating a political space for the new nationalist elite. The pogroms materially discredited the notables' demands for Libyan independence and self-government, offering the British the pretext to reject them or whittle them down with a handy proof of the country's immaturity and its leaders' inability to govern it. Nevertheless, it is still a fact that when the pogroms occurred the attitude of a good portion of the Arab leaders and notables was ambiguous and uncertain. The criticism directed by *Tarabulus el Gharb* against "the most influential leaders" for failing to act in time to prevent the pogroms was not altogether unfounded. The Tripoli daily had its own share of responsibility, though, since on November 4, the day when the pogroms started, it once again gave extensive coverage to news of disorders and violence against Jews in the preceding two days in Cairo and Alexandria,[27] thereby contributing considerably to inflaming the masses. Whether it did this deliberately or not is hard to say, since there is no information on whether nationalist elements had infiltrated among its editors.

In some smaller places, especially in the east of the province, as the *Annual Report* has it, "the notables were on the side of law and order; it was largely due to their influence . . . that the disturbances spread no further."[28] In other places, and in Tripoli in particular, the notables' attitude was less decisive, to the extent of being ambiguous. In Tripoli during the morning of November 5, some Arab and Jewish notables went together to the British civil authorities to ask for measures to be taken to put a stop to the rioting. The situation grew worse, and by the afternoon the British had not taken any steps, despite their assurances of the morning. Several Arab leaders then went to the military authorities and asked for tanks and motorized units to bar the city from the troublemakers flocking from the country and troops to protect the *hara*. The Arab leaders and notables did nothing else besides helping and giving refuge to a few

Jews fleeing from danger. The bewilderment and uncertainty aroused by the ambiguity and weakness of the British authorities must have played a large part in this passivity. This does not seem sufficient, though, to explain the absence of subsequent appeals to the British and any attempt to calm the riotous and unruly mobs. To explain it one must assume that there was, if not serious doubt regarding the real intentions of the British,[29] then a lively fear—both physical and political—at the idea of going against such a broad and brutal mass action. The following passages from the *Annual Report* confirm this clearly:

> The moderate Arab elements and all responsible leaders of the community at once dissociated themselves from the riots. Yet frightened by this expression of mass hatred they hesitated before identifying themselves openly with the Government's efforts to suppress and punish, and to assist the victims. They have done so now, and are giving their full support and active help. Jews and Arabs have formed a committee for the revival of the racial friendship. Yet a century-old bond so suddenly broken and so unpredictably ignored can be re-knit but slowly. . . .
>
> Leading Arab personalities severely censured this shameful aggression. But no general, deep-felt sense of guilt seems to animate the Arab community at large: nor has it been too active in offering help to the victims.[30]

However significant it is, the problem of the behavior of the traditional Arab elite is not the most important one for a proper understanding of the pogroms, together with their causes and consequences for the subsequent psychological and political attitude of Libyan Jewry. In order to understand the pogroms, issues involved in the attitude of the British occupation authorities are even more important.

The BMA *Annual Report* for 1945 tends to speak of a multiplicity of concomitant causes, emphasizing the lack of positive elements which might have led it to foresee the pogroms or even merely fear that they might happen, and to exclude the existence of any organization behind the pogroms. One cause mentioned with the others was the "self-assertiveness" of Libyan Zionists. As for the Arab nationalists, the BMA report mentioned that the Arab moderates blamed them for "having inflamed the minds of the masses" by their "propaganda of intransigeance." However, the report stated that—despite all the information gathered and numerous arrests of its members—"the anti-Jewish riots could not be traced back to any concrete machinations of the Nationalist Party." The party had certainly contributed to the inflamed atmosphere in which the pogroms took place, and had just as certainly emerged discredited by them.

The BMA thought that the most correct way of understanding the events of early November was the following:

> The growth of Zionism must be considered one of the motives behind the anti-Jewish riots which broke out in November. The others were— Arab envy of the more prosperous Jews; jealousy of a minority which, once downtrodden, succeeded in attaining positions of importance, especially during the British occupation; and fear, nourished from Arab sources in Egypt and Palestine, of Jewish supremacy.
>
> This racial antagonism had manifested itself before: there was much talk about Jewish arrogance and money-making; an anti-Jewish sermon was preached in a provincial mosque; and Sunday-night brawls between Jewish and Arab youth in Tripoli had become a common occurrence.
>
> Yet beside the century old friendship between Jews and Arabs in Tripolitania these symptoms of racial feeling appeared insignificant. Nor can the riots be interpreted merely as an expression of racial hatred, suddenly grown to terrifying proportions. The dormant antagonism flared up owing to many factors: the uncertainty of the country's future had fostered an unhealthy political atmosphere; intensified Arab nationalist agitation added excitement and tension; so did the news of anti-Jewish demonstrations in Egypt and of Jewish violence in Palestine. The economic distress among the poorer classes and the prospect of easy loot proved powerful incentives; while the wholly unprecedented nature of the outbreak and the uncertain loyalty of the Arab police prevented quick and decisive action on the part of the Government. The criminal elements of the City, prostitutes, workshy, and the disorderly youth were soon involved. Thus a common Sunday night brawl was carried on by its own momentum, rapidly growing into mob violence, wholesale murder, incendiarism and widespread looting.
>
> If it was thought that Arab extremists, whose propaganda had in the past threatened violence and the use of force, had organised or guided the disorders, this assumption could not be proved. A number of Arab politicians of extremist views was detained and questioned; but neither their interrogation nor police investigations and the trials of the rioters provided any evidence of an organising agency behind the disorders.[31]

As a general indication, this analysis is no doubt correct and largely acceptable, at least as far as it serves to explain the widespread nature of the riots and violence. In order to agree with it entirely as a historical judgment, though, two corrections must be made. The first concerns the "growth of Zionism." Though it cannot be excluded that this might have given rise among some Jews, especially the young, to the "self-assertiveness" of which the *Annual Re-*

port speaks[32] and that Zionism together with this attitude could in turn have increased the hostility of Arab nationalists toward Libyan Jews, there is no basis for maintaining that the same reaction occurred among the Arab masses. Among the masses, Zionism was practically unknown or was assumed to be part of Jewish identity, while the BMA's assertion is contradicted by the fact that during the pogroms no one ever heard any shouts against Zionism.

The second and much more important correction concerns the role of Arab nationalists. In this respect, the *Annual Report* deliberately alters reality, just as it does when it implies that nothing could have led anyone to foresee the possibility of anti-Jewish disorders.

Against the second statement one may cite the information collected by the author (probably a soldier in the Palestinian Brigade) of the report entitled "The Arab Anti-Jewish Riots in Tripolitania, 4–7 November, 1945," preserved in the Central Zionist Archives in Jerusalem. According to this report, the British security officer for Tripolitania had been warned since the morning of November 4 that an anti-Jewish demonstration supporting the rights of Palestinian Arabs was being planned for the ninth. Though this information does not exclude some surprise on the part of the British at the unexpected hastening of events (probably due to emotion aroused in the Arabs by news published that very day of anti-Jewish disturbances in Syria, Lebanon, and Egypt), it does discredit the affirmation that nothing could have led them to predict that disorders would also break out in Libya. The first and more important affirmation, that there was no evidence to prove the accusations leveled at the Arab nationalists from several directions of organizing and directing the pogroms, can also be discredited, and even more surely. Obviously, saying that the nationalists played an important role is not the same thing as saying that they were the sole cause of the pogroms, but rather that without their intervention the events almost certainly would have turned out otherwise, and been less violent, lengthy, and widespread. The affirmation is contradicted by a coded telegram sent on November 8 by the British commander in chief for the Middle East to the War Office and transmitted by the latter on November 20 to the Foreign Office.[33] It states that the violence in Tripolitania was initially thought to be a spontaneous consequence of the similar disorders which had taken place in Egypt and an expression of fanaticism aroused by the situation in Palestine. Later on, however—probably following the arrest of twenty-eight nationalist leaders and the numerous searches carried out by the army—"evidence points to local political instigation on part of Arab extremists." What this evidence was is not known. Even without such concrete evidence, numerous elements point to the conclusion that Libyan nationalists played a leading role in the pogroms. Probably one would need actual proof to attribute the false rumors exciting the mobs to nationalist agitators. The rumors were that the Jews had murdered the mufti and the qadi and set fire to the Shari'a Court. It is well known that such rumors can arise and spread among the masses under certain conditions. The disorders began almost simultaneously in various parts of the city—very differently from the isolated Sunday incidents between Arabs and Jews which the BMA cited to show that initially it was another incident of the same sort which suddenly deteriorated. Large numbers of troublemakers promptly flocked to Tripoli from the surrounding areas and, at the same time, the movement spread to other towns. All these facts, together with the pattern of events and numerous specific episodes, leave little room for doubt regarding an organization behind the masses. The facts confirm the conclusions reached by the Community of Tripoli: "It was in fact a *real treacherous* [sic], *planned, and simultaneous attack perpetrated against the Jews.*" Moreover, the author of the Zionist report was of the same opinion, writing less laconically:

> Immediately after the first incidents early Sunday evening outside the electric plant, the riots took on the character of an organised affair. Outbreaks flared up simultaneously in various parts of Tripoli city. Only Jews and Jewish shops were attacked. Well dressed Arabs were seen chalking the doors of homes and shops with the words "Jew," "Italian," "Arab" in Arabic and the shop of one of the leading Arab merchants of Tripoli, Ahmad Krewi, was observed as being used as one of the headquarters of the rioters. To this shop, one block from BMA Headquarters, and to another Arab shop nearby, gangs of hoodlums were seen coming to pick up bludgeons, clubs and other weapons which Krewi and other well dressed Arabs, some of whom BMA authorities say were members of the Hizb al-Watani, distributed to them from inside the shops. One very reliable report indicates that certain Jews were singled out for attack. The attacks in the communities outside of Tripoli were also led affairs. In Suk Al-Juma, the tossing of a hand grenade into the synagogue was the signal for the Arabs to attack and in Zanzur, where nearly forty out of the total Jewish population of 120 were killed, the mob gathered in front of the police station and kept the police imprisoned in it while the attack was going on against the Jews. The extent to which this "unruly mob" . . . was controlled can be gathered from an eye-witness account who saw Arab gangs stop passers-by, demand their identity card, and if the bearer was Italian or Arab he would be allowed to proceed, but if he were Jewish, he was beaten. The same source also saw well-dressed Italian women passing unharmed through excited Arab mobs bent on killing and destruction.

The report concludes by agreeing with those who maintained that "the entire affair was organized from beginning to end," and it repeated a current explanation:

> Several British officers and Jewish leaders have suggested that the riots in Tripolitania were incited by the Nationalists who sought to express their solidarity with other Arab countries by having their own local anti-Jewish demonstrations and who at the same time wanted to make a show of strength to gain support for their claim for recognition from the British Military Administration.[34]

One reason for the BMA's alteration of the facts in the *Annual Report* may lie in its desire to avoid appearing too favorable to Jews in the eyes of the Arabs, and in the pro-Arab leaning of many British officials, a number of whom had previously served in Palestine and were embittered by Jewish terrorism.[35] Another reason may be the administration's need to justify however it could its behavior during the pogroms. There lies the heart of the problem. Suffice it to say that even today many of the Jews of Tripoli are convinced that the 1945 pogroms were organized or at least instigated by the British. They argue that the British had already practically lost their bases in Palestine and Egypt and wanted to replace them by a lasting presence in Libya. The British, they say, thus saw the pogroms as a chance to give the world—which at that time was particularly sensitive to what was happening to Jews because of the Nazi persecutions[36]—proof that Tripolitania was completely unable to govern itself and therefore aspire to independence. Additional proof for those who believe this was provided by what was happening at the same time in Cyrenaica. There too a situation existed similar to the one in Tripolitania, hence seething with anti-Semitism; there too news from Egypt and the Middle East aroused deep emotions and anti-Jewish demonstrations; but in Cyrenaica there were no acts of violence or plunder because the Grand Sanusi made sure to prevent them in order to protect his credibility as a future monarch. The only Jewish casualties during those days, one dead and three wounded, could not be clearly defined as victims of political rather than common crime. Even those who had been there themselves and were reluctant to accuse the British of instigating the pogroms did criticize the BMA's inefficiency, whole behavior, and subsequent failure to publish the inquiries. Their clearly negative appraisal is such as to lead one to conclude that the BMA, with its hesitant and tardy intervention to restore order, in practice made itself responsible for the exceptionally high rate of murders, injuries, and damages.

It is difficult now to get a clear idea of how broadly based—especially among the Jews—this accusation of BMA complicity was. I shall cite only the most significant accusations,[37] starting with the position which the Community of Tripoli adopted, since it was the Community which raised the issue. A clear expression of its attitude and the criticism which the Jews of Tripolitania immediately leveled at the BMA can be found in the official Community report on the pogroms between November 4 and 7 quoted earlier. Even more expressive is the report's second conclusion: "the British Military Administration did not anticipate the disorders, and despite the desperate appeals of the leaders of the Jewish and Arab Communities did not adopt timely and adequate measures to suppress it." This is mild, compared with the letter and spirit of several telegrams which the Community sent after the pogroms to the British prime minister, Attlee, Rabbi Stephen Wise in New York, the Board of Deputies of British Jews, the World Jewish Congress, the American Joint Distribution Committee, the South African Jewish War Appeal, and the Alliance Israélite Universelle. The Community did not merely denounce what had happened, request moral and material assistance, and protest the inefficiency of the BMA, but made two requests which leave no doubt as to what judgment lay behind them: that an "impartial" commission of inquiry be sent to shed light on the events and that steps be taken "to ensure the security of the population with British and *European* troops to prevent riots from reoccurring and punish all persons guilty of murder, plundering, and *inefficiency*." The practical effect of these telegrams was almost nothing. It was an easy matter for the government in London to close the issue by responding vaguely to questions in the Commons and delaying the whole controversy until the official BMA *Report* came out. There were broad echoes in world Jewry, however. The World Jewish Congress asked the Foreign Office for explanations and approached the State Department,[38] and the Jewish press gave the events much coverage. Jewish correspondents went to Tripoli to try to shed light on how the pogroms really came about, and largely confirmed the accusations of inefficiency and ambiguity.[39] Thus, though demands for international intervention in Tripolitania and the question of British responsibility came to nothing, the doubts and suspicions regarding the BMA's behavior remained. This was to carry decisive weight in the subsequent attitude of Libyan Jews toward Britain and the issue of their future in Libya.

From a historian's perspective, the deep and decisive significance of the 1945 pogroms is that a radical change took place not only in Arab-Jewish relations, but in the relation of the Jews to Libya itself, their homeland for two thousand years. From this point of view the issue of British responsibility, however important it may be, obviously becomes a secondary one. Despite that, British responsibility should not be viewed only through its consequences, in other words without trying to understand the causes of the inefficiency and ambiguity in the behavior of the BMA and hence how far it was responsible.

After clearing away the misleading problems, three things can be stated with certainty. First, despite what a large proportion of Libyan Jews, some Arab notables,[40] and Italians believed, there is no concrete evidence supporting the contention that the British organized or instigated the pogroms. No one who has approached the issue objectively has found such evidence. The well-informed Zionist report which I have used several times to reconstruct aspects of the pogroms refers neither directly nor indirectly to such responsibility. Another important report written after the 1948 pogroms by Ben Segal, an important figure who had been sent to Tripoli on a mission for the Central British Fund, the Anglo-Jewish Association, and the Board of Deputies of British Jews, also considered the accusation groundless and opted for the theory that the 1945 pogroms were stirred up from abroad through the local Arab nationalists and elements from other Arab countries.[41] Second, the accusations of inefficiency and ambiguity leveled against the BMA by Libyan Jews were, on the other hand, well founded. Everyone more or less explicitly agrees with this. Third, the only real argument which the BMA made to justify the slowness and ineffectiveness of its interventions—the insufficient numbers of native civilian police and especially the disloyalty of some of them and lack of British personnel to lead the Libyan ranks[42]—is no real justification: even reliable forces were not used decisively and lacked arms and protective shields. If native police were indeed unreliable, the army should have been called in right away. One Sudanese contingent was sent to patrol the New City of Tripoli at about eleven o'clock on Monday morning, with orders not to fire. The army was not brought in until Wednesday the seventh, when General Bertram Temple, the military commander of Tripolitania, proclaimed a state of emergency and assumed powers to enforce "the restoration and preservation of peace and public order throughout the territory."[43] The next day order was restored and the military court began its proceedings against those arrested.

Having established these three certainties, the available documentation allows us to affirm that as long as the civil administration was in control, it underestimated the seriousness of the situation,[44] and then attempted to deal with it with inadequate means, even when the disloyalty of the native police was not a factor. At a time of the year when darkness fell early, the curfew was introduced in a limited way on the fifth between the hours of 9 P.M. and 5 A.M., so that it was ineffective, and the following day had to be extended from 5 P.M. to 6 A.M. The measure banning meetings of five or more persons and carrying sticks or other offensive weapons and announcing that plunder was a crime punishable by death was taken not by the BMA but by General Temple.[45] The best confirmation of the BMA's inefficiency lies in the fact that, after order had been restored, the army continued to hold all powers until December 17.[46] The commander in chief of British forces in the Middle East, General Barnard Paget, in his message to the people of Tripolitania, used terms such as "acts of barbarism," "instigators"—very different from those used by the BMA.[47]

When we are confronted with such printed facts and such fatal consequences, we have to ask whether or not the behavior of the BMA could be explained only by the inefficiency of its leaders and the disloyalty of Arab police under it. It seems impossible to say that it could; even if we agree that these two factors led the British first to underestimate the seriousness of the situation and then to lose control over it, there is always the fact that the BMA did not call out the army even when it was already obvious that only the army could put an end to the pogroms. This is without raising the thorny and controversial issue of whether the BMA asked for the army to intervene or whether (as the Zionist report affirms and as many tend to believe) General Temple decided on it independently. In other words, one can only think that the BMA's conduct was strongly affected by a *political* concern not to adopt too harsh a position and not to annoy the Arab masses or alienate them, thereby playing into the hands of the nationalists whose goal was clearly independence. By then, Libyan nationalists could rely not only on the general support that the major nationalist, pan-Arab and pan-Islamic movements and the Arab League were giving all the Muslim independence movements in Asia and Africa, but also on their special relationship with the powerful secretary-general of the Arab League, the Egyptian Abd-er-Rahman el Azzam Pasha, who for thirty years had been involved in Libyan affairs and had had close contacts with the Libyan nationalist movement. During the First World War he had been an agent for the Germans and Turks, in 1917 for the Sanusis, in 1918–1924 adviser to the leaders of the Tripolitanian Republic and later of the anti-Italian revolt, and later an important spokesman and minister of the Egyptian Wafd Party and protector of the Defense Committee of Tripoli. This political concern is indirectly confirmed by the fact that, even though the British military authorities did not have large forces available and had to bring the whole region under control, they were careful not to deploy the soldiers of the Palestinian Brigade in restoring order, keeping them closely consigned to barracks. The British obviously wanted to avoid being accused of using Jews against Arabs and permitting Jewish vendettas. There still remains another thorny issue: that of the pro-Arab orientation of some of the British civil and military officials and whether any of them suggested using the situation which developed in Tripolitania to influence British policy in Palestine in some way.

"An unprecedented blow has been dealt to the Jews' sense of security and any illusions they had for taking initiatives: there is terror, poverty, disease, and suffering, without a glimmer of hope to brighten the dark future. Should they go away? If so, how? And where?" These words, written about a year later by Haim Abravanel, the director of the Alliance Israélite schools in Tripoli,[48] summarize, without exaggeration or flourish, the whole drama of the Libyan Jews brought about by the 1945 pogroms. They show what the Jews were going through in human, social, and political terms up to February 1949, when Britain, having recognized Israel, finally authorized emigration. One point has to be brought out, because only if it is quite clear can we understand community relations between Arabs and Jews and within Libyan Jewry after the pogroms. Though some tension lingered for a while,[49] after the British army restored order intercommunity relations were on a good footing for a couple of years. Nevertheless, for the vast majority of Libyan Jews—not only in places where there had been pogroms, but throughout the country, including Cyrenaica—the real problem was now a different one. It was no longer that of healing the deep wounds in the community fabric nor the more general one of relations with the Arabs, nor the even broader one of the political future of Libya. All these obviously were present, but as secondary and temporary problems. The real problem was how to leave Libya and find a secure refuge elsewhere, since the future looked bleak, trust in Britain had given way to mistrust and hatred, and no longer did any Jew feel safe in Libya. For the masses (whether Zionists or not) this refuge could only be Palestine. Until February 1949, since the British were refusing the necessary exit visas, this refuge was unreachable. Only very few, the bravest or most desperate, were willing to emigrate clandestinely. There could be no other solutions, on either the subjective or objective level, for the mass of Jews. It is important to note that this was their thinking right from the 1945 pogroms, and that the 1948 pogrom merely confirmed their state of mind and added more energy to their already active resolve. To the Jews' fear and desperation about their own future in Libya was added confidence in Palestine as a refuge once Israel had become a reality. This is shown, to give only one example, in a report dated June 7, 1948 (before the second pogrom), by Max Gottschalk of the American Joint Distribution Committee (AJDC), on a meeting which he had had two days earlier with Zachino Habib and the AJDC representative in Tripoli. The report[50] contains this explicit statement: "The entire Jewish community is ready to move to Palestine." Only a tiny minority, consisting mainly of the wealthiest Jews, those with large interests in Libya, and some who were foreign citizens, mainly Italian and British, could consider other objectives, whether they were primary or secondary. They saw their future as either in Libya or in Europe or America. This is the central point which must be absolutely clear, since it gives the only frame of reference for understanding the collective drama of Libyan Jewry. Involved in this drama, either actively or marginally, were many events and initiatives which occurred after 1945. These doubtless had their own significance and importance, but should not be overemphasized and, in particular, do not apply to the vast majority of Libyan Jews, but rather to a small minority.

There is little left to say about the economic and social situation of Libyan Jewry between late 1945 and mid-1948. That was when it was shaken by the second pogrom, apparently a much less dramatic one than that of 1945, since it was restricted to Tripoli and was much smaller in terms of victims and material damage, but actually almost as devastating. The panic that it provoked swept the whole country. It fused with fears aroused by the progress of international negotiations on the future of the former Italian colonies and by the political situation in Cyrenaica, which was clearly evolving toward independence under Idris, and leading many Cyrenaican Jews to move to Tripoli. It caused many Jews still living outside Tripoli to close their businesses and flock to the city in search of a haven. Especially among the masses, recovery during these two and a half years was slow and limited. It was made more difficult by the fact that many refugees (including the whole Zanzur community) were reluctant to return to their places of origin. A general crisis was looming in the Libyan economy,[51] and in 1947 a serious drought particularly affected the rural population of Tripolitania (part of which emigrated to Cyrenaica) and, directly or indirectly, Jews as well. Those who suffered most were proportionally the small- and medium-scale artisans, who lost everything in the pogroms, even the tools of their trade. Making rigid distinctions among categories could be distorting. An assistance fund was set up for the artisans. Almost six million BMAL were collected, and many were set up in business again.[52] Other categories got no special help and, despite the Community's repeated requests, the British administration gave no compensation and few loans. By the end of 1948 only 12 of the 240 requests made by the Jews of Tripolitania who had suffered losses in the pogroms had been accepted.[53] The number of Jews paying Community taxes is indicative: 2,700 in 1943, and only 600 in 1947.[54] Thousands of Jews must have been receiving total or partial assistance at this time. A minimal part of it came from the Community, which was practically unable to help. The rest came from several international Jewish organizations, particularly the American Joint Distribution Committee, the contribution of which eventually became stabilized at about ten thousand dollars a month.[55] This is how Umberto Nahon described the situation in Tripoli in a letter of March 1948 to Raffaele Cantoni, the president of the Union of Italian Jewish Communities:

> The general economic situation in Tripoli is one of great depression. A large-scale shopkeeper told me that business is down to zero. Apart from a few exceptions, the Jews are either craftsmen, shopkeepers, or businessmen trading with other countries. Craftsmen are suffering from the general depression resulting from reduced purchasing power and a concealed boycott on the part of the Arabs. Shopkeepers are also in a difficult situation: the British do not spend a penny outside the NAAFI,* and tourism has completely stopped; there has been a drought for two years, causing poverty among the Arabs of the interior who no longer are able to buy. Walking around Suq al-Turq, Corso Vittorio Emanuele, and Corso Italo Balbo, you see empty shops and little activity. Ninety percent or more of these shops are Jewish. On Saturdays, in both the Old City and the New, all Jewish shops without exception are closed and only one or two non-Jewish shops happen to be open. The merchants trading overseas, mainly with Italy, now have little to do; the BMA now applies quotas to everything and follows such a restrictive policy that nothing gets done. They are "just passing through." Considering that urban development between 1928 and 1939 was one of the main factors in economic growth, you can understand what a bad situation the majority of Jews are in. Measuring growth from 1928, since that was the year when I last visited Tripoli, without exaggerating it has become a different city since that date: the seaside promenade was hardly begun and now has become one of the most beautiful of its kind. Public buildings, large hotels, like the Uaddan and the Mehari, where I stayed, have gone up in large numbers; broad and spacious streets lined with arcades have replaced the low buildings which twenty years ago dotted the surroundings of the city. The cathedral, which was under construction in 1928 and was at the edge of the inhabited area, is now right in the center. Considering that all the new

*Navy, Army, and Air Force Institutes (responsible for clubs, canteen, and provision of some items for messing of British armed forces).—*Trans.*

buildings had grown up in ten years, since obviously everything stopped in 1939, I was constantly filled with admiration.[56]

The panorama of political life looked more stormy. One must remember that participation in political life involved only a minority, while the figures representing it, often reluctantly, held positions of responsibility in the Community or constituted the elite of Libyan Jewry. Whether they liked it or not, they were the Jews most involved in Libyan life and were not able, as the Jewish masses were, to shut themselves off in the inevitability of their condition and wait until it would be possible to leave the country. The Zionists (especially from a linguistic and cultural point of view) were preparing future emigrants to Palestine and meanwhile organizing clandestine emigration for those who were most resolved. The Haganah, a self-defense organization, was being organized to meet by force of arms possible and predictable repetitions of Arab violence. This armed organization was initially the work of a few bold men who, it seems, had been greatly influenced by the rebukes and exhortations of a military rabbi among the British occupation forces. He had reminded them of the words with which the poet Bialik had asked Russian Jews to react to pogroms with force: "Instead of laying your neck on the altar of the Goyim and saying 'Shema Israel,' kill your murderers and let them say 'Shema Israel!'" In May 1946 this organization was taken over by "Uncle," an expert who had come secretly from Palestine. Under his guidance, the Haganah soon became quite an effective, secret, military group. Its members were organized into small units unknown to each other and underwent regular training in deserted places around Tripoli. They acquired arms on the black market and through the Arab underworld, without the British knowing anything about it.[57]

These activities, rather than being a real political life with its own vision of Libyan reality and its own development over time, were clearly related to a state of necessity. The political attitude of the Jewish elite was otherwise largely determined by external conditions over which the Jews had no influence and which were determined by events in the Arab world. The conditions related to the Palestine question and process of nationalist and pan-Arab mobilization going on among the various parties, and what was taking place among the great powers with regard to the future of Libya, the former Italian colony.

For the Libyan Arab leaders, whether moderates or nationalists, the two issues were closely connected. Since they were aiming at independence, the specific problem for them as regards the Jews was how to find some sort of *modus vivendi* (more or less provisional and "liberal," depending on their position). Such an arrangement would deprive Britain or any other country of one of the arguments most wielded against the Libyans' readiness for self-government. It should also portray the Jews as agreeing with and joining in the cause of Libyan independence. By 1946—as Arab political forces became better defined and organized and the Libyan United National Front was being formed* while the British position grew more ambiguous—this dual tendency became more explicit. It was clear on a political level, among the Arab members of the Arab-Jewish Committee for Cooperation and Reconstruction set up after the pogroms the year before. It was also made clear in personal relations between Arab and Jewish notables, and especially through open pressure and intimidation. At the beginning of May, for example, the Arabs launched a massive psychological campaign. The Jews feared renewed Arab violence due to the report of the Anglo-American Palestine Commission of Inquiry (held to be too favorable to Zionism) and the Arab League's reaction. In particular, the news spread that Abd er-Rahman el Azzam Pasha had had a dream in which Arabs were warned not to persecute the Jews. Concrete pressure was also put on the Community and the most prominent Jewish figures to persuade Jewish organizations and individuals to join the United National Front.

On May 2 a sudden rumor spread that the next day the Arabs would stage a huge protest strike. Panic gripped the Jews of Tripoli. Many fled from their shops in Suq al-Turq. Many Jews residing in the new city took refuge in the *hara*. The strike did not take place the next day, but—despite a request for calm and trust in the "Arab brothers" which the Community posted in all the synagogues—the fear persisted, especially when further wild rumors said that the strike would take place on the following Friday, the tenth. In this mood of tension, operation "Join the United National Front" was launched. This is how an anonymous contemporary account, which appeared in Italy, describes and comments on the campaign:

> The threats and blandishments have been simultaneous and have had a single aim, that of tying the Jews hand and foot to the Arab cause. Pressure has been put on several prominent Jews and the president of the Community. Fear made this monstrous thing, union with the November murderers, and joining a movement which heads the Arab League and opposes the realization of our national ideals, acceptable or even desirable to some. Unfortunately, many Jews saw only the anomalous

*Like the Labor Party, founded in September 1947, this party wanted a united Libya under Sanusi leadership. See Lorna Hahn, *Historical Dictionary of Libya* (Metuchen, N.J.: Scarecrow, 1981), p. 57.—*Trans.*

feature about this movement, that it would constitute a talisman against possible Arab attack. The Jews who have joined were made responsible for making propaganda among the ignorant masses. In vain did someone wisely suggest that the Jews had an excellent pretext for not following this path in the still recent bloodshed of November and that the new party and future independence offered the Jewish population no effective guarantees. Individual Jews continued to go or were taken by Arab friends to the nationalist party headquarters, where they were obliged to join. Meanwhile, the net was tightening ever closer around the terrorized Jewish masses and their leaders who were afraid of being responsible for more bloodshed. As the fatal Friday came closer, on Wednesday the president of the Maccabee club was summoned by the Arab Circle demanding that the Maccabee and Ben Yehuda Clubs join a program honoring the secretary of Ibn Saud, a rebel condemned to death by Italy, who was coming to visit and should be received with all possible honor.

While the illustrious guest did not arrive, Friday did, but without any strike; people began to breathe again. The Italian newspaper, *Corriere di Tripoli*, published by the British propaganda office in Libya, ran an article entitled "Making Things Clear," affirming Arab-Jewish brotherhood and the distinction Arabs make between Jews and Zionists. The short article is officially inspired, probably by the usual ringleader. Zionist circles in Tripoli are very concerned at the turn of events, but can have no effect on the situation. What is all this leading to? Why this sudden need of Arab-Jewish brotherhood? On Saturday the answer to this question came. It was already implicit in everything that had happened during the last few months, beginning with the November pogroms. When the first news came out about the turn being taken regarding Italian colonies at the Paris Conference, during the daytime on Saturday, May 11, 1946, the Arab, Italian, and Jewish notables were assembled. Among the Jewish notables only the president of the Community attended. The fruit of the previous months of careful preparation was gathered. The head of the Jewish Community, a non-elected British citizen, appointed by the British government, made common cause with the Arab citizens and on behalf of thirty thousand Jews declared that he opposed any solution excluding independence for the territory and, in their names, signed a telegram full of lying opinions about the thirty years of Italian rule. On Sunday, May 12, the president of the Community, having acted without consulting the Council, was nowhere to be found. People claiming to have seen him, attempting to calm those who were indignant at his taking such a position, affirmed that his words had been distorted and that he acted under psychological pressure. But this was later denied by the president himself, who took full responsibility for his words and actions. However, he is mesmerized by the threat of another pogrom. He can make no corrections or retractions, but considers it necessary for the Jews of Tripoli to back him. These threats, and the fear of taking any responsibility toward the

defenseless masses, paralyzed all reaction. Sunday went by without incident. It seemed that the Arabs intended to abandon themselves in a
xenophobic demonstration, but the moderate elements, together with
the president of the Jewish Community, succeeded in delaying the
demonstration until Wednesday and turning it into a mere protest. A
strike was organized for Wednesday, May 15; almost all the shops, including those of metropolitans, stayed closed. There were no incidents.
The army and police were confined to barracks. Arab and Jewish civilians (the latter in the Old City) maintained order. The president of the
Community and some members of the Jewish section of the Arab-
Jewish Peace Committee (formed after the November pogroms at the
wish of the British administration) continued exerting strong pressure
on the Ben Yehuda and Maccabee clubs for them to take a stand regarding the Libyan United National Front. In vain did the presidents of the
associations repeatedly point out in several meetings their associations'
apolitical nature. In vain did members of the associations' councils resist taking a positive stand. After a week of beating about the bush on
the associations' side, the president of the Community asked the clubs
to define their attitude to the Libyan United National Front. Put in a
corner and subjected to veiled blackmail on the part of powerful members of the Jewish Section of the Arab-Jewish Peace Committee who
warned of the danger of another pogrom, the clubs have finally made a
general declaration of sympathy for the independence movement led
by the United Front. One has the impression that this is only a beginning, one fears that all Jewish activities will be stifled, and that attempts will be made to compromise the Jewish community more and
more in the eyes of the Italians, and draw it away from active participation in the Zionist movement.

This system of blackmail, threats, and moral violence, worse than
the Fascist one, determines how things go in a country which aspires to
self-government, under the auspices of a supposedly democratic one.

Despite what the president of the Community said, despite developments which followed and are to follow, what can be said is that on
Saturday, May 12, as soon as the news spread that the Italian administration would probably be returning to Tripoli, there was a real
sense of relief among all Jews, from the highest to the most humble, a
sense of relief which changed to deep depression after the careful
maneuver which the Arabs made together with the president of the
Community. Despite anti-Italian propaganda, which consciously ex-
ploits the misdeeds of the Fascists (the racial legislation, the pogrom in
Benghazi on April 3, 1941, the Giado concentration camp, and forced
labor), all the Jews of Tripoli know that Italy has brought to the colony
civilization, culture, order, hygiene, work, and security for all citizens.
The Jews know that Italy would be able to guide the country toward
independence. They see Italy as the nation that in the name of a democratic and humanitarian ideal would give them full liberty to develop
their national characteristics and allow them to join in the rebirth of

the Jewish Homeland in Palestine (it should be noted that the British Administration in Tripolitania, despite numerous requests, has not yet allowed the Zionist Organization, which even functioned during the Fascist period, to be re-established).[58]

This document is important. It gives an overall picture, and clearly shows three characteristic aspects of the situation at that time: (1) the forced and opportunistic nature of much of the support for the United National Front (on the council of which there was even a Jewish representative); (2) the effect on political developments in Libya of the issue of the Italian Peace Treaty and what it proposed for the Italian colonies; (3) the profoundly different positions to which these facts gave rise in the Libyan Jewish elite, ranging from pro-Libyan (whether sincere or opportunistic) to pro-Italian and Zionist stances. A Jewish Agency attempt, two years later, to heal the schisms by sending Umberto Nahon to Tripoli to launch a coordinating committee for all Jewish and Zionist organizations, ended in failure.[59]

Until the Israeli government took a stand in favor of independence for Libya,[60] in the fall of 1949, the Zionists stayed apart or tried to avoid as far as possible being involved in the Arab maneuver, while striking a middle course between pro-Italian and pro-Arab tendencies. The gulf between the two was clear and deep from the beginning. There was conflict of ideas on policies and principles regarding how the Jews should behave toward Arab nationalism and how to view the consequences which the future independence of Libya would have for Jews. The immediate issue was the support, political and moral, that the Jews were peremptorily being asked to give to the demand for independence. The conflict brought out the difference, latent since 1943, between Italian and Italianized Jews on the one hand and indigenous Jews on the other. The situation of citizens of other countries was more complex, since, until the 1945 pogroms, they had generally been close to indigenous Jews, whereas now, apart from British Jews and those closely connected to the British administration, most of them either supported the Italians or stayed out of the dispute. The document quoted shows clearly the issue at hand and the state of mind of each side. The pro-Libyans wanted to avoid irritating the Arabs, giving the more xenophobic Arabs a pretext for more violence, and letting already precarious British-Jewish relations deteriorate even more. Hardly any Jew trusted the British any more. Many still held them responsible for the 1945 pogroms. However unreliable they were, the British were the only force able to prevent further massacres. A minority saw this problem as basic and wanted to build up good relations with the Arabs. The vast majority saw it as ancillary, a result of chance, or, if one prefers, necessity. They wanted time to pass in the most painless way possible until, when the national and international framework had settled down, they could emigrate. Some of the pro-Italians did not want to emigrate or, if they had to, did not want to go to Palestine. The pro-Italians were playing their Italian card, since Libya's future had not yet been decided by the victorious great powers and many still hoped that Italy would somehow come back to Libya.[61]

It should also be noted in this connection that initially—when Italy's chances still looked minimal—pro-Italians did not express themselves and even privately did not support the return of Italy, but rather the U.S. declaration of September 20, 1945, backing a U.N. trusteeship—that is, an international administration with a neutral governor.[62] Later on, the Libyan political situation worsened and there were pressures to marshal the Jews into the United National Front. Moreover, after the Paris conference of foreign ministers of the four great powers, it looked more likely that Italy might get the trusteeship of Libya, or at least of Tripolitania. At the same time, the danger was emerging (expressed in the request by Egypt and Iraq to the next Paris Conference of Twenty-One) of the trusteeship being granted to an Arab state. The pro-Italian position then emerged more clearly, even though, in order not to jeopardize relations with the Arabs, it was not publicized. It was expressed in clear statements to the Union of Italian Jewish Communities and through the Italian government and aimed at counterbalancing pro-Libyan statements. The statements probably began to undermine the position of Habib, the president of the Community, and led to his resignation a year later, followed by the appointment of a government commissioner in the person of Scialom Nahum.[63] The pro-Italians also clarified their own position by declaring themselves favorable not only to an international administration, but also and especially to an Italian one. A secret memorandum sent to Rome between late 1946 and early 1947[64] gives definite testimony to this. It also leads one to think that this attitude lay behind an article by Raffaele Cantoni, the president of the Union, published a month or so later in *Italia socialista* [Socialist Italy], pointing out the agreement between the Jewish and Italian points of view concerning whether the United Nations should grant trusteeship of Libya to Italy.[65] The article shows how the pro-Italian position had crystallized in those few months and how its advocates now staunchly defended the positive meaning of the Italian colonial administration for the Jews. They now minimized as much as they could all its negative aspects, including those of the later Fascist period, previously singled out for attack. Since this text is of interest, I reproduce it in full:

The Jewish community of Tripoli has always had many links with Italy. Even before the Italian occupation in 1911, it was largely Jewish students who attended the Italian technical and commercial school, directed by Giannetto Paggi. After the occupation Jews welcomed with joy the new government, which brought the colony civilization, culture, order, hygiene, jobs, and, above all, security for all citizens.

Even after 1922, under the Fascist regime, the Jewish community as a whole did not suffer from discriminatory laws; though the policy of Badoglio and Balbo showed little understanding of its spiritual needs, issuing laws imbued with the Fascist spirit and irritating part of the population (compulsory school attendance on Saturdays for Jewish intermediate school pupils, the forced repatriation of the Chief Rabbi because he refused to carry out a governor's order contrary to the spirit of Jewish law, and the compulsory opening of shops in the New City on Saturdays).

Government officials and especially Governor Italo Balbo did their best to diminish the consequences in the colony of the new Italian racial laws. Nevertheless, employees were dismissed and Jews were no longer invited to official ceremonies. Jewish pupils were excluded from intermediate schools, though Jewish elementary schools continued to function at government expense.

The later racial laws, more serious than the earlier ones, were not applied, since they were decreed in early January 1943. Great unease nevertheless developed among the Jews, increased, and became serious anxiety during the war and especially after the arrival of large contingents of Rommel's Afrika Corps. The Jews of Tripoli attributed the fact that even then real persecution did not occur in Tripolitania to the moderating efforts of government officials. The pogrom of April 3, 1941, in Benghazi (carried out by Fascist elements in the lapse between the first withdrawal of the British and the return of Italian troops), the Giado concentration camp and forced labor, and constant humiliation and degradation of Jews had promised the worst.

Before it left the country in January 1943, the Italian government set up a civil guard which, though small, was still able to keep the peace and prevent attacks on citizens and the plundering of their goods. The Jews welcomed with relief the British troops liberating them from the Nazi-Fascist yoke. That did not mean that they hated Italy; when the Community could not get the British Military Administration to agree to provide funds for a Jewish school as it had for the Italian and Arab schools, the Community decided, as the Administration had proposed, that the children of the Jewish Quarter should attend the Italian school as well as the Arabic school.

From the liberation until the pogrom of November 1945, the Jewish community devoted itself to rebuilding its institutions, since when the racial laws were promulgated its educational activities had almost entirely stopped. It now directed its efforts at the education and improvement of youth, orienting itself mainly toward the Jewish national ideals. Nevertheless, the occupying government did not allow the Federation of Zionist Organizations to be reestablished, nor teachers and emissaries to be sent from Palestine. It encouraged an anti-Zionist campaign in the local Arabic newspaper (run by the PIO, the British information office) which intensified in the days immediately preceding the pogroms of November 5, 6, and 7.

Despite this, accounts and reports in the local press during and immediately after the pogroms (which can be compared only to Nazi atrocities) clearly show that the rabble directed at plundering and murder was incited by false rumors of a purely local nature (the murder of the qadi, burning of mosques by Jews, etc.) without any political expression whatsoever.

The Arabs attacked Jews in obedience to mysterious orders. Their outburst of bestial violence has no plausible motive. For fifty hours they hunted men down, attacked houses and shops, killed men, women, old and young, horribly tortured and dismembered Jews isolated in the interior—all of this with the proven complicity of the local Arab police and the most absolute inertia on the part of the administration and armed forces of the occupying power responsible for protecting order.

The details of those terrible days are too well known (the article from the American newspaper *P.M.* in *Israel* reflects the absolute truth) for me to dwell any longer on the description of the slaughter. The great majority of Italians, the technicians, doctors, and hospital staff on that occasion gave proof of their humanitarianism. But on the other side there were some Italians who spread the aforementioned false rumors, whipping up the anger of the Arab masses.

The Jews asked for a Commission of Inquiry to examine the events and give compensation for losses suffered. It was in vain. Many of those arrested for participating in the pogroms have been released. Only four sentences were passed and one of them carried out. Moreover, the Jews who acted in self-defense have received sentences.

The Jews have emerged from this crisis completely demoralized and mistrustful, since something which never happened under the Ottoman government, the Fascist government, or Nazi control happened under the British Military Administration. Fearful, unacquainted with blood and violence, powerless to react, the Jews found themselves defenseless and at the mercy of savages, without anyone to defend them. It is thus natural that the majority of Jews, expecting any amount of pressure, has lived since then in a constant fever of anxiety and in terror that the tragic events will repeat themselves.

The response of the Palestine Inquiry Commission sharpened these fears. The strikes and anti-Jewish demonstrations that wild rumors had repeatedly predicted did not take place. But precisely at the moment when the tension was at its height, the more educated Arabs began to put strong pressure on the Jews to join a newly-formed Arab nationalist party aiming at independence for Libya.

It was clear that threats and blandishments were inducing the Jews to support *what was presented as the Arab cause* and, despite their memory of November, join with a movement which heads the Arab League, which is clearly opposed to the realization of Jewish national ideals.

Jews who joined this movement saw it as a way to save their defenseless, threatened lives.

This explains why, on Saturday May 11, 1946, as soon as the news spread of the change at the Paris Conference regarding the fate of the Italian colonies, the president of the Jewish Community summoned to the Administration together with Arab notables, joined the latter's protests and, on behalf of thirty thousand Libyan Jews, declared that he opposed any solution not bringing independence and signed a telegram full of lying opinions about the thirty years of Italian administration. It should be noted that the president of the Community, who is a British subject appointed by the administration rather than elected, with exclusively consultative and administrative functions, was taken by surprise and acted without even consulting the Community Council.

A feeling of discontent and rebellion immediately spread among the Jews, but since another pogrom was threatened, a fear of being responsible for any harm to the defenseless masses paralyzed any attempt to react.

Most Jews believed that the president could not have acted in any other way. The Council of the Community, assembled over a week later to approve the president's action, had no choice but to do so. The president declared, against the protests of some council members, that if he did not get a unanimous vote of confidence he would resign and immediately tell the United Front why he had done so. Some Jews approached Commendatore Valenzi and the Bishop, who were almost the sole representatives of the Italian community, to tell them how the council really felt.

Subsequently, strong pressure was put on Jewish clubs to join the Libyan United Front. Under duress, the clubs issued a declaration through their presidents declaring their apolitical nature but expressing general sympathy for the United Front's hopes for independence.

The Zionists are quite concerned at this situation, which could have other, unexpected developments. They fear that all Zionist activity will be stifled and that there will be attempts to compromise the Jewish community even more in the eyes of the Italians.

Given this situation, whatever statements individuals or organizations may make under duress, the true aspiration of the Jewish community is that the country should have a strong government, capable of making itself and the aspirations of the subject peoples respected, keeping the peace and encouraging peaceful coexistence among the various sectors of the population, as the pre-Fascist Italian government did.

While we respect the legitimacy of the Arab people's claims to independence, like the claims of any other people, we believe that it can be said that the Jews of Tripoli believe that democratic Italy, alone or together with other powers in a joint trusteeship, Italy which has done so much for this country and has so many interests to protect here, would be able to guide it toward the political maturity needed for it to win true independence.

Under such a government, the Jews are sure that they would be able to develop their national characteristics, work for the good of the country, and cooperate actively in the rebirth of the Jewish Homeland in Palestine.

While these clarifications and strengthening of the pro-Italian position aroused concern and discussion, there were fortunately no traumatic consequences and unhealable ruptures within the leadership and Jewish elite of Tripoli. The rapid changes in the Palestine situation in 1947, the U.N. vote on November 29 in favor of partition of the country between Arabs and Jews, the decision which the Arab states took two weeks later in Cairo to organize a struggle to prevent it, and the subsequent collapse toward open warfare, all these contributed to the substantial (though undeclared for fear of the Arab reaction) erosion of the pro-Libyan position. The war preparations were echoed in Libya by a telegram which local leaders sent to the Arab League stating that 2,500 armed Libyans were "ready and eager" to join in the "liberation" of Palestine. The British responded in Cyrenaica with a policy more obviously favoring independence under Idris and, in Tripolitania, with a less neutral attitude, even on a formal basis favoring Arabs over Jews.[66] The erosion of pro-Libyanism occurred a few weeks before the arrival in Libya of the Four Power Commission of Investigation. As provided for under the Peace Treaty with Italy of February 10, 1947,[67] the commission's task was to determine what opinions the inhabitants of Libya held about their future, so that the four great powers would be able to put the question of the former Italian colonies before the United Nations General Assembly and a solution could be reached.[68] Under these conditions the two points of view became much closer to each other than they had been (or had appeared to be) a few months before, particularly in private and on an unofficial basis, and favored the Italian position more and more. Umberto Nahon, who as we have said was in Tripoli on behalf of the Jewish Agency at the time, was able to see this process directly and evaluate its actual progress

while the Four Power Commission was on the spot making its inves-
tigations. Nahon wrote to Raffaele Cantoni on April 2, 1948, as
follows:[69]

> You may be interested to hear about the attitude of the Jews to the Four
> Power Commission, which was in Tripoli during my visit. The Com-
> mission heard two different tunes from the Jews: the official one from
> the Community representatives, and the unofficial one from individu-
> als whom it questioned among the Jewish masses and individuals who
> approached the Commission themselves. Though the two tunes seemed
> to sound completely different, in substance they both echoed what
> could be called the unanimous hope of Tripoli Jews: the return of Italy.
> The dissonance is due to the fact that after the events of November
> 1945 the Community has sought a rapprochement with the Arab lead-
> ers. Since the community is not protected by the occupiers, one can
> understand the tendency to establish relations with the Arab nation-
> alist leaders to win security. The most developed among the Jews of
> Tripoli are well aware of the dangers which a future Arab administra-
> tion would pose; for the mass of Jews, the specter is downright terrify-
> ing. Still, the official Community leaders, by supporting the Libyan
> United Front, maintain that they have ensured a relaxation of ani-
> mosity and prevented further incidents. One must remember that
> nothing like what occurred in November 1945 has occurred in Tripoli
> for decades, and the impression it made was thus all the more acute
> and deep; people talk to you about the pogroms as if they happened yes-
> terday, over two and a half years later. Thus the Community—or rather
> the Community Council—has unanimously decided to present a mem-
> orandum supporting aspirations "for the independence and unity of
> Libya." When the Commission invited the Community to send a three-
> man delegation to present the memorandum, the degree of enthusiasm
> and spontaneous support for the memorandum showed themselves in
> the fact that no one wanted to go. Eventually they chose by lot the two
> who were to accompany the poor president, Dr. Maurizio Forti, an Ital-
> ian Jew who seems like a fish out of water. There has also been much
> recent talk about a reception to be given for Arabs who have come from
> outside to express their desire for independence. They have discussed
> whether to give a tea or a picnic lunch on the concession of one of the
> members of the Community Council. After lengthy debate, they de-
> cided to give the lunch, "so that no one would have to speak," while at
> the tea they would have had to give speeches, but at the last minute the
> owner of the concession where the lunch was to take place backed out,
> saying that there was no reason why he should be the only one to "stick
> his neck out." He held that the tea should be given in a public meeting
> place and not on the property of a private individual who would be ex-
> posing himself more than others, and that if it was a question of cost,
> as long as he did not have the lunch *chez soi* he was willing to pay the
> difference, and so forth. I am telling you this so that you will have some

idea of how spontaneous the whole thing was. When I left, neither the lunch nor the tea had taken place. There was a tendency to think that just talking about it was enough, and the reception would be given . . . after the visitors had left. Now for the other tune: during the tour of the *hara* the Commission interviewed many people and, as I understand, they were unanimous in saying that the Jews want Italy to come back. They told me some of the reasons and I will give them to you for what they are worth: "we were all right" (this reply is certainly true, because I heard it from everyone); "we felt safe" (same again); "we got white bread and what we earned was enough to live on"; "we are afraid of the Arabs"; "we don't want the British"; "Italy used to spend a lot of money here"; "the Italians were good to the Jews"; "the Italians will let us go to Palestine"; "the Italians used to encourage business"; and so forth. I heard in the city that some individuals were considering approaching the Commission as an opposition to the Council, but did not make up their minds, since they were discouraged by the fact that the Italians, or a group of them at least, headed by a certain attorney Cibelli, had also approached the Commission declaring support for Libyan independence and unity. It was said that others had written, but these were rumors, and it is understandable that everyone was keeping quiet. I know for sure that one person went to the Commission, and since he will soon be in Italy he will come and give you more details.[70]

This was in February 1948. On May 14 came the proclamation of the State of Israel, and the next day the first Arab-Israeli war officially broke out, though it had really been going on since December. In Tripoli and all of Libya the repercussions were immediate. The situation soon became tense for the Jews, especially when a few days later there began to flow in from Tunisia first dozens, then hundreds, and ultimately thousands of Arabs from French North Africa on their way east to join the Arab armies. Day by day, their presence stirred up the local Arabs more and more, particularly nationalists and their sympathizers. Fearing further violence, the Community leaders approached the British asking that security measures be taken. The French consul, concerned about the many Jews who were French subjects or protected persons, also approached them. General Blackley, the governor, gave assurances that order would be maintained at all cost. The only actual initiative which the British took seems to have been setting up a bus service between Tripoli and Capuzzo to facilitate and hasten the passage to Egypt of the Arabs coming from Tunisia. In this situation of growing tension, as threatening rumors against the Jews spread more and more every day, June 12 arrived. The first incidents took place in the afternoon. In the Tripoli Arab quarter of Bab el-Horria, a sort of Casbah where the poorest Arabs lived and which was considered the haunt of the worst common criminals, so that even in normal times Italians and Jews avoided it, several thousand ruffians banded together. They were armed with sticks with razor blades stuck in them, iron crowbars, and knives. The unruly mass surged out into the mixed quarter of Sidi Omran, where the initial brawls began, then pressed on toward the Jewish quarter. At its gates the Arabs met strong resistance. Young men, girls, even children, organized by the Haganah and ready for anything, resisted them with stones, bombs, and Molotov cocktails. The rioters retreated, leaving many dead and wounded. They turned to other undefended areas of the city, committing every kind of violence and plunder, robbing and burning what they could not carry. The damage in the area around Via Dante was particularly serious, affecting Jewish-owned industries (liquor factories, sawmills, small craft factories, and a large garage). The looters then left for other areas, attacking individual Jews and destroying and burning their houses and shops, as well as a synagogue which had been plundered and burned in 1945.[71] Violence started up again the next day, though to a lesser extent, since the British had declared a state of emergency and, more promptly and decisively than in 1945, deployed the force to disperse the rioters and restore order. During these encounters a Jew apparently threw a bomb at a police van. The Arab religious and lay leaders made an appeal for calm that contained a harsh condemnation of the violence and an admonishment not to forget that it was everyone's duty to "show the world that the Libyan population is capable of taking responsibility for governing itself and that it respects order."[72] Toward afternoon on June 13, order was largely restored, though tension remained very high. Outside Tripoli, with the exception of Suq al-Jum'a, where the houses of the Jews were completely plundered, no remarkable incidents occurred during the two days, though in the two preceding weeks some Jewish peddlars crossing the hinterland had been killed, so that most other peddlars stopped making their regular trips to fairs and small towns.[73]

According to the British administration's official count, there were thirteen Jews and three Arabs killed, twenty-two Jews and thirteen Arabs seriously injured. Thirty-eight Arabs, sixteen Jews, one Italian, and one policeman were lightly injured.[74] The Jewish sources show higher figures, especially for the Arabs. Fourteen Jews were killed, including seven old men, six women, and one child; twenty-two were seriously injured and about a hundred lightly, and one woman raped. According to the most reliable Jewish sources, about thirty Arabs were killed and many wounded.[75] An initial estimate gave the number of homeless Jews who had taken refuge in the *hara* and the refugee camp of Port Benito as 1,600. Damage to homes, shops, workshops, and livelihoods was colossal, about three hundred families being completely ruined. The number arrested, including about ten Jews, was ninety: forty for looting, twenty-nine for rioting, four for assault, nine for incendiarism, seven for possession of arms, and one for rape.[76]

On June 14, the mufti, accompanied by the chief rabbi, visited the *hara* to express his solidarity and calm people down. He did not succeed and aroused bitter protests and shouts of "We want Italy, which has always protected the weak." In the afternoon an emergency meeting of the notables of the two communities, again initiated by the British, was called to see how calm could be restored. At the end of the meeting the following appeal was issued:

> The regrettable incidents which have just been committed by irresponsible elements who take no account of political, social, or material interests, even less so religious and humanitarian concerns, and which have caused innocent victims, cannot fail to rebound to the great moral and material discredit of Libya itself.
>
> We who are meeting here wholeheartedly deprecate such acts and associate ourselves with the profound regret expressed by all sensible people, who maintain that relations within the population, whether among individuals or communities, is the best way to attain well-being, peace, and the future which we all aspire to; this future cannot come to pass unless there is a guarantee of security and mutual respect for individual and collective rights.
>
> In the future we shall not sit idly by as the rabble which has several times sullied the name of our Country rages, though we shall discuss every effort in close collaboration with the Authorities, which we shall keep informed of any possible threats to disturb public order and the peace of the population.
>
> We shall ask the Authorities to crush with an iron hand anyone who dares violate the sacred principles of that friendship, which for generations has characterized relations between Arabs and Jews.
>
> In the meantime, the representatives of the Authorities who have attended our meeting have assured us that they will not fail to take severe measures against anyone who we claim constitutes a danger to public order. And never again will we allow public safety to be violated.
>
> We trust that these disruptive elements will refrain of their own accord before they are touched by the inexorable punishment which will guarantee stable tranquillity for the population not only in the present but also in the future.[77]

But tension persisted for a long time. Sporadic incidents flared up throughout the summer. A bomb was thrown in Zlitin, blinding two Jewish children in the Jewish quarter. Then in Tripoli in November another bomb went off in front of an Arab shop. The British surrounded the *hara* and arrested thirty Jews for possession of arms. One of those arrested, Lillo Mahluf, a sixteen-year-old, killed himself on November 14 by throwing himself out of the window of the police office, apparently to escape interrogation. The next day the Jews of Tripoli proclaimed a twenty-four-hour protest strike.[78] In this climate of tension and overriding fear that the pogroms would be repeated, Jewish protests, international appeals, and hostility against the British increased, as well as aversion to the very idea of remaining subject to the Arabs in the future. The British were still held to be the covert instigators of everything and accused of applying double standards, one for Arabs and one for Jews, and of opposing Jewish emigration. On June 14, immediately after the pogrom, a group of forty-two Libyan and Italian Jews sent the representatives of the four great powers involved in the future of the former Italian colonies a memorandum in which, after denouncing Arab violence, they declared:

> We want the return of wise and firm Italian administration; otherwise we must ask you, who control our fate, for ships and transportation to emigrate *en masse* anywhere in the world where we can be assured of work, housing, and a future for our children, and where the tears we have shed for so many years may provide fertile moisture for a new life.[79]

A few weeks later, another group sent an open letter to the United Nations Security Council, ending with these words: "We make one cry to all free peoples: Set us free! Set us free! Set us free!" Here are the more significant passages:

> Our situation has become unbearable materially, economically, as well as morally. We live under the specter of the *pogroms*; our minds are full of fear at the danger that disorders may break out at any moment and the so-called irresponsible elements (in this territory no one is responsible), thirsting for blood and plunder, will assault us in our homes. Jews who are well-off have made themselves secure by building double steel doors, like those on safes, to protect themselves from possible attack, but we poor are bearing the whole brunt of this disorderly situation. We have knocked on all doors to escape from this hell on earth, but we have found that the local Authorities prevent all Jews from leaving the territory. No reason and no commitment—either material or moral—will allow us to leave legally with exit visas. Our only fault is being Jewish. It is worse for us than being in a concentration camp because there we would not have to think about how to feed our children, risk our skin, and fear attacks by evildoers, since the camp guards would protect us against assault.
> When we dare repeat and press our demands for exit visas the au-

thorities reply that if we do not give up this wish of ours there will be more disorders. Thus for fear of losing hundreds more lives and hundreds of thousands of pounds in looting and other damage, as happened in November 1945 and June of this year, we have to submit and wait for the day when we will be saved. . . .

This week the British Military Administration's spokesman said at a press conference that the exit restrictions for Jews originate with the Security Council provisions forbidding Jews to leave for Palestine. Now we ask whether the Security Council Order completely forbids any Jews to leave, so that he is deprived of the security to live in peace? We believe that the Security Council, if it has advised our Administration, wished the ban to apply only to those able to bear arms, not women, old people, and children as well.

This is an appeal to you, the Supreme World Organization, to help us, make our lives secure, and free us from this hell on earth where twice in a year and a half we have been assaulted by conscienceless bloodthirsty masses and have lost our lives and goods. Over 60 percent of our community is living solely on subsidies from our brothers overseas due to the loss of their capital in the looting. We ask you to order our Administration (rather than advise, since advice in this case will not be heeded) to open the gates for Jews who want to leave the country, have paid all government taxes they owe, and have no case pending, no conviction in court, and no debts to pay. We ask that old people, women, children, and even young people be allowed to leave if they want to live in other countries such as Italy, where they speak the same language and will be free of this hell.[80]

The insistence in these appeals on requesting the right to emigrate clearly shows the frame of mind of Libyan Jews after the pogrom of June 1948. Though the pogrom was more limited and less dramatic than those of 1945, fear, anger, hatred for Arabs and the British, and the desire to put an end to such a precarious situation, were even greater. This was so not only among the Jews of Tripoli but everywhere, even in Cyrenaica. In a few weeks a flood of poor, terrorized people poured from the hinterland and the coast to Tripoli in search of safety and a means of escape. From some places, such as Gharian, whole communities left, abandoning homes and land. On February 2, 1949, Britain (which three days before had recognized the State of Israel) raised the ban on emigration. Cyrenaica, then on the verge of winning independence, also emptied of Jews almost completely, even though due to Idris their situation was better there than in Tripolitania. By mid-1950, of the more than five thousand Jews who until a short time before had lived in Cyrenaica, there remained about three hundred, mostly in Benghazi.

Such an exodus preoccupied the Arabs as well, especially those in the hinterland who immediately felt considerable economic ill-effect. It was also viewed with concern by the Italians, since they knew they were liable to the same fate. Only a minority viewed it with favor, since they hoped to take over the businesses which the Jews had abandoned.[81]

Obviously, the greatest repercussions were felt by the Jews themselves and their organizations, which were obliged to deal with the appalling problem of this mass of refugees, most of them completely destitute. Some of them piled into the *hara*, some into the Old City, some into the closest areas of Tripoli, and some, the better-off, into the New City. They entered a situation which was very serious due to the general crisis in the country, the wounds which had not yet healed from 1945, and the fresh wounds of the latest pogrom. Completing the picture was the fact that since the British authorities had let it be understood that they would soon allow emigration again, many Jews who still had businesses began to liquidate them and sell all their possessions, even at half the value, so that they would be ready to leave. By early 1949 about a third of the Jews of Tripoli were living on assistance, in addition to the majority of refugees. In September 1950, when, as we shall see, almost twenty thousand had already departed, about two-thirds of those about to leave were receiving assistance.

Immediately after the pogrom the AJDC earmarked an emergency contribution of fifteen thousand dollars. Other funds and contributions came from other Jewish international organizations. But the AJDC bore the large part of the expenses to cope with the situation. It took on almost all expenses for direct and indirect assistance (first aid clinics, schools, etc.) for the entire period until emigration was allowed again and until it was over.[82]

Not all Jews merely waited for departure and prepared for it. There had already been cases of clandestine emigration after the 1945 pogroms. Some young women had resorted to fictitious marriages with soldiers of the Palestinian Brigade; some young men enrolled or pretended to be soldiers of the Brigade; some had embarked as fishermen on Italian fishing boats which let them off in Sicily. Between July 1948 and January 1949 these cases became much more numerous. According to the most reliable figures, there were about 2,500 cases of clandestine emigration, generally young men who were impatient or wanted to get to Israel to fight. Many tried to reach France or Italy via Tunisia, but were arrested by the French authorities and sent back. Others entrusted themselves to the waves in any craft they could find, or bought passages on merchant or fishing ships leaving from Tripoli. To do that it was often necessary to bribe policemen, Arab and British, who were responsible for port control; in other cases it was possible to take advantage of the benign propensity of some BMA officials to look the other way. Many of those who succeeded in reaching Italy stayed there. About six hundred went on to Israel.[83]

More than nineteen months passed in this atmosphere heavy with fear, poverty, repressed bitterness, and, above all, waiting. Then on February 2, 1949, came the great moment: official authorization for anyone who wanted to leave. The director of the Alliance school and a few days later secretary of the WZO Executive Tripoli Committee, in charge of emigration to Israel (set up on February 18), Haim Abravanel, captured that moment which had been so long awaited:

> On February 2, 1949, the British authorities gave official approval for Jews to leave. It was snowing for the first time in Tripoli and under the white flakes blown by the wind thousands of poor Jewish wretches ran toward the street where the police offices were, the Municipality and the Community offices, to get their passports at last. At the same time they were selling, liquidating everything: furniture, business assets, work tools, etc. Without even knowing how they would reach Israel, unless it was through Italy, they wanted to leave immediately. In a few days over eight thousand passports had been issued. An indescribable excitement reigned everywhere and especially in the Jewish quarter, the *hara*. The authorities were deluged in the incessant and determined throng animated by a single desire: to leave Libya.[84]

In fact only a few were able to take immediate advantage of the reopening of emigration: those who were better-off and those who wanted to go to Italy to stay or in order to try to travel on to Israel. The most reliable information shows that this individual emigration amounted in the first half of 1949 to a little under 2,000, 1,500 of whom immigrated to Israel via Italy.[85] For the mass of Jews, Israel was still far away, a reality which had hardly crystallized out of a dream.

The initial WZO Executive plans called for immigration to Israel, *aliyah*, to amount to 7,000 a year. But when Baruch Duvdevani, the official sent by the Israeli government to take charge of Libyan *aliyah*, arrived in Tripoli, the Community leaders told him right away that such a level was impossible. Many more than that, about 30,000, almost everybody, wanted to leave. Holding them back for such a long time would have been inhuman, it would have meant very high expenses for assistance and danger to health. Above all, it would have been extremely risky, since, though it was not clear what political future the United Nations would decide on for

Libya, there were many signs that the most probable solution would be independence. In that case anything might happen, from the closing of emigration to further pogroms. With such a prospect, it was necessary to make arrangements for emigration *en masse* as soon as possible. The question was discussed, as well as with Duvdevani, with Izhak Reffael, the Aliyah Department official sent for the purpose from Jerusalem, and with an envoy of the World Jewish Congress. Finally it was agreed that there would be no restrictions on immigration. The first departures were on April 5, 1949.[86]

In the first year of WZO Executive activities, up to March 16, 1950, almost all the Jews of Cyrenaica (3,276) left for Israel, many from the hinterland and the coast of Tripolitania (3,714),[87] and the first batch of Jews from Tripoli (9,372), a total of 16,362. At the same time the WZO Executive was engaged in several other activities connected with mass emigration. Its medical efforts were extraordinary. Thousands of individuals were given medical checkups, treated, and in many cases cured, so that they would be able to face departure, the sea voyage, and integration in Israel under the least distressful conditions.[88] Considerable help was also given to those who were still awaiting their turn. Besides efforts in health and education (much of the teaching was devoted to Hebrew), the greatest effort in this respect was probably directed at the young, and children in particular.[89] The WZO Executive dealt with other problems with the help of local Jews (the contribution of Sion Nemni was very important). It tried to deal with the obstacles that prevented some emigrants from leaving and limit the economic losses of such a large number of hasty departures. A service was begun to solve the problems of those whose departures were held up by pending debts, unpaid rents, unfinished jobs, and so forth. The CABI Olim organization [Administrative Committee for the Immovable Assets of Emigrants] was set up to prevent those departing from having to sell off their property at any price (thereby depressing the market even more). It paid the leavers half the value of their property and promised to sell it when the time was ripe at the best price. In the meantime it took care of the property and, through underground channels, since exporting capital was illegal, sent the profits to the owners who had emigrated.[90] Nor should one forget what was done—due especially to Nemni—to ease the adjustment and initial integration of the immigrants in Israel, especially those who were received in transit camps. Efforts were made to help them solve their problems, particularly those resulting from the situation of inferiority in which, like the majority of Sephardic Jews, they found themselves in relation to the Ashkenazim who had immigrated before them.[91]

By the end of the first year of WZO Executive activities[92] there were still 12,000 Libyan Jews waiting to go to Israel. A little over 1,200 had not applied to leave. Almost all of them had considerable interests, which they did not want to give up or sell at low prices. Leaving for Israel was a hard decision for them, and, if really obliged to leave, they would have preferred Europe, generally Italy. To have a complete picture of the situation, one must add a number of Jews who were European citizens. Most of these were also chary of Israel and hoped or believed that they would be able to stay in Libya.

At this point emigration turned into the WZO Executive's race against time. The Bevin-Sforza compromise, granting Britain trusteeship over Cyrenaica, Italy trusteeship over Tripolitania, and France trusteeship over Fezzan, was defeated in the United Nations on May 17, 1949. Instead, a resolution was passed on November 21 granting Libya independence by January 1, 1952, at the latest.[93] The problem became one of how to get everybody out who wanted to leave, before that date. "Libya will have its independence by January 1, 1952, at the latest; we hope that before that almost all the Jews will have left the country. . . ." This sentence in Abravanel's report of September 1950 synthesizes the whole drama of those days and the succeeding twenty-one months.

Faced with the definite prospect of an Arab government, some of those with considerable interests in Libya who had not applied to leave, or had applied more as an alternative than a conscious decision, also decided to go. What *Israel* said on October 5, 1950, is typical of the situation:

> In 1949 the flow of Jewish immigrants from Libya was largely composed of people from the poorer classes. Now, however, one finds even among the wealthier groups a growing desire to leave the country for Israel, and transfer to Israel their industrial plants and businesses. Now even among the young of the richest Jewish families there is greater interest in the Zionist movement for youth immigration.

After the United Nations vote on November 21, 1949, though departures continued in a regular way, tension was growing. Those who had not yet been able to leave were afraid of being caught in Libya when independence went into effect. Each ship leaving might be the last. A great deal depended on what the United Nations would do to protect the rights of minorities in the new state. That issue concerned only a minority, though—those who did not want to leave and, having a European citizenship, felt more secure. The majority took no interest; concerned only with finding safety before it was too late, they gave neither attention nor credence to Arab invitations. Arabs who were aware of the danger that the departure of the Jews posed for the Libyan economy were beginning to press more and more insistently for those who had not yet left to give up the idea and help in building the new, independent Libya.

In this climate, the end of 1951 arrived and authority was transferred from the British administration to the Libyan one of King Idris. Of the approximately 36,000 Jews who had been in Libya four years earlier, only some 6,000 remained, these mostly in Tripoli. Of them, 269 overcame the obstacles to their departures raised by the Libyan government and reached Israel the following August. In all, 31,343 Libyan Jews emigrated to Israel directly (via forty-two trips from Tripoli to Haifa) or indirectly, via Italy.[94] Who those were, who were left behind, and what were their state of mind and prospects, are related in a report dated December 18, 1951, from Nehemiah Robinson of the Institute of Jewish Affairs:

> The proclamation of Libyan independence marks the virtual end of a process which began with the end of the last war: the gradual disappearance of an ancient Jewish community.
>
> At present there are still about five to six thousand Jews remaining in Libya, most of them in the city of Tripoli. Emigration to Israel has been going on for many years, and those who have registered to emigrate are anxious to get out before independence goes into effect. It was previously stated that a few thousand Jews had decided to remain in the new Libyan state, but some of them are probably leaving soon, and it is now estimated that only about eight hundred have decided to remain in Libya. Two thousand are old and sick and thus cannot presently be transferred.
>
> Most Jews are fearful of the new regime, which it appears will be headed by the Muslim prime minister of the Libyan provisional government, Mahmud bey Muntasser, who during the war was pro-German. He recently appealed to the Jews to remain, but it is feared that Arab League pressure and the simmering anti-Jewish feelings may provoke renewed persecutions, the memory of which still lives in the minds of Libyan Jews. The National Congress Party appears to hope that it will win the elections which will take place next year in Libya. Mr Saadawi's spokesman is complaining that the activities of "Jewish agents" in Tripoli are having negative effects on the country's economy.
>
> The final decision of how many will stay in Libya will depend on the guarantees of the Jews' rights which are included in the documents constituting the Libyan state. Two years ago, the interests of the Libyan Jewish community were brought to the attention of the General Assembly by a spokesman of the World Jewish Congress, which is pursuing efforts to safeguard for the Jews remaining the rights necessary to maintain their traditional rights and to ensure their right to emigrate.

The recently issued Constitution does not contain provisions to safeguard the interests of the Jewish community and the right of Jews to free emigration with their belongings. Nor does the Constitution explicitly provide for the continuation of the Jewish community's autonomy in matters regarding marriage, divorce, and so forth.[95]

8. Libyan Independence
(1949–1951)

Any discussion of the situation of the Jews in Libya during the reign of Idris must start from the United Nations resolution of November 21, 1949, which approved Libyan independence and set January 1, 1952, as the deadline. Many of the legal and political bases for the Jews' situation were actually established—often implicitly—in the transitional phase of accession to independence before the transfer of power from the occupiers to the new Libyan state. This, in accordance with the November 21 resolution, occurred between the end of 1949 and the end of 1951, and was based on provisions included in the resolution.

The resolution approved by the U.N. General Assembly[1] stated that the constitutional basis of the new Libyan state was to be submitted to deliberation by the representatives of the "inhabitants" of Cyrenaica, Tripolitania, and the Fezzan, meeting together in a national assembly. They were to be assisted by a commissioner appointed by the United Nations and an advisory council consisting of ten members, the representatives of Great Britain, France, Italy, the United States, Egypt, Pakistan, Cyrenaica, Tripolitania, the Fezzan, and the "minorities in Libya." In anticipation of independence, the administering powers (Great Britain for Cyrenaica and Tripolitania, and France for Fezzan), in cooperation with the U.N. commissioner, were to initiate the necessary steps for transfer of authority to a duly constituted independent government.

The first step taken to put the resolution into effect was the appointment of the U.N. commissioner, in the person of the Netherlander Adrian Pelt. The second and more difficult step—due to differences among Libyan political and tribal forces and divergences of interest among the four minorities (Italian, Jewish, Greek, and Maltese)—was the formation of the advisory council. Since only one seat was reserved for the minorities, it was finally assigned to a spokesman of the largest and most politically significant minority, the Italians. However, it was necessary to find a representative jointly acceptable to the minorities and also the Arabs. This was no easy task, as is shown by the fact that Aurelio Finzi, the president of the Tripolitanian Court of Appeal, was originally singled out, and only in the second place did the choice fall on Giacomo Marchino, the vice president of the Economic Council of the Colonial Office, commissioner of the Agrarian Association, and vice president of the Savings Bank of Libya. This candidate was well respected, since he had generally succeeded in performing his difficult tasks without antagonizing any one of the four minorities, and had even on more than one occasion shown himself capable of asserting his independence from Pelt's policies.[2]

The negotiations to set up the advisory council were so protracted that its first meeting was not held until April 1950. Meanwhile, the British and French presented their plans for the future political and administrative organization of the Libyan state. The broad political goal of the British and French, which ultimately was to prevail despite strong opposition among the Tripolitanian Arabs and from the Arab states in the United Nations, was a federal state. Within this framework, Cyrenaica, Tripolitania, and the Fezzan would each wield the same amount of political power, despite the demographic and economic disproportions and unequal development of institutions among them. This solution had the result of markedly reinforcing the position and political strength of Cyrenaica and of Idris, who was closely allied with Britain, and further undermined that of the Tripolitanian nationalists. They were allied with the Arab League and Egypt and therefore with a political viewpoint opposed to British and French interests. The British plan accepted the principle that the minorities should be represented in the future national assembly. This was evident in the plan's early version and, what was more important, in the later form drawn up after the initial negative reactions of Tripolitanian nationalists. According to the British plan, the assembly (together with an administrative council) was to begin functioning within the year and draft the constitution of the new Libyan state.[3]

It is clear that during the earliest phase things were falling into a pattern far from unfavorable to the Jews. These developments accorded with their wishes and with suggestions that Jewish organizations which had shouldered the responsibility had been making since the summer of 1949 to the governments in London, Paris, Rome, and Washington. Organizations involved were the World Jewish Congress and the Consultative Council of Jewish Organizations,*

---

*Founded in New York in 1946.—*Trans.*

comprising the American Jewish Committee, the Anglo-Jewish Association, and the Alliance Israélite Universelle. They considered the Libyan question of supreme importance, since the solution found for Libyan Jews was sure to set a precedent to be applied in other Arab countries yet to achieve their independence. The Jewish organizations requested that during the period of transition to independence Libya should be ruled by a neutral power, and that minorities should be assured of representation so that they could express their views.[4] In practice both of these requests turned out to be less crucial than they had originally seemed. The choice of Adrian Pelt did indeed ensure that the agencies responsible for overseeing the preparation for independence were guided by a neutral figure who without doubt had the best of intentions toward the Jews. However, the commissioner almost immediately showed that he was mainly concerned with fulfilling his far from easy task in such a way as to avoid exposing himself to Arab and particularly Libyan accusations of piloting the independence process from a Western (or colonialist) standpoint. The commissioner also showed his basic desire to avoid difficulties and conflicts between himself and the Libyans regarding questions of "secondary" importance. From his point of view, the problem of the Jewish minority had been solved in general terms and in principle. The guarantees to ensure respect for these terms, rather than being embodied in precise constitutional and legislative measures, acceptance of which would have been difficult to obtain from the Arabs, were substantially left for the future. They were to arise from Libya's long-term need, after independence, for a clean record in order to be admitted as a member of and to receive aid from the United Nations and affiliated international organizations. The minorities' right to participate directly through their own representatives in drafting the future constitutional and juridical bases of the state was in practice reduced to an insignificant level: Marchino's good offices and skill in political dealing. Moreover, Marchino had to protect the interests of four different minorities and, being an Italian, was inevitably inclined to give priority to the problems of his fellow-Italians. He would also try to prevent any single minority's particular viewpoint from leading to a conflict which might jeopardize the others' chance of solving their own problems. More generally, it cannot be overemphasized that, though in principle it was right for the issue of the Jews to be merged with those of other minorities, from a political point of view the decision soon turned out to be far from satisfactory, both because the problems of the four minorities differed concretely, and above all, because of the suspicion which rankled in the Arabs against the Italians and which led some political leaders to justify Arab intransigence toward Jews by the need to view the minorities as a single problem and prevent the Italians (the largest minority, more than four times the other three put together) from continuing to influence Libyan life, while turning other minorities against the Italians and Jews.

One thing now clearly emerges from documentation on the long and tortuous process leading up to Libyan independence. Marchino's private archives, which contain reports on his meetings with Idris and important Tripolitanian political figures, reveal it particularly clearly. It is the determined, albeit always concealed and even verbally denied wish of the majority of Arab political groupings to exclude the Jews from the political life of the future Libyan state. This was the wish not only of the political organizations, but clearly also of Idris. The amir of Cyrenaica does not appear to have personally nourished any particular hostility toward the Jews. In his political strategy, though, the Jewish issue was certainly secondary, and not such as to induce him to oppose the major Tripolitanian parties or give the Arab League additional cause for suspicion and hostility toward him. This was all the more true at a time when he was still only king-designate, and the choice between federalism and a unitary state was still under discussion, so that he could not afford to displease the Tripolitanians. They accepted him only as long as they believed that they could not achieve Libyan independence without him. They saw Idris, as the Arabic saying goes, as the dog whose tail they had to hold on to so as not to drown. Hence Idris had to maneuver backstage in order to include the terms of the Universal Declaration of Human Rights in the Libyan constitution to protect the Jews, while maintaining a cautious and ambiguous position on political rights for them. On the one hand, he hoped to appear liberal by granting the Jews of Cyrenaica both active and passive suffrage, in the certainty that their very modest numbers would make this concession of no practical consequence. On the other hand, he wished to justify his alignment with the Tripolitanian extremists in terms of the need to avoid losing contact with them and prevent them from falling under the influence of the Arab League. In 1950, Idris received leaders of the Jewish community and gave them reassurances regarding their "rights"; Prime Minister Muntasser likewise reassured them at the end of 1951 when independence was proclaimed; on the latter occasion the director of the Jewish Agency's Tripoli office was also invited. Idris' real position emerges from what he said in 1949 in a secret meeting at the Mehari Hotel in Tripoli with Duvdevani, the Jewish Agency representative, to the effect that the Libyan Jews would receive his protection, but he could see no future for them in Libya.

Some Arab leaders did not wish, and others were unable, to adopt an openly anti-Jewish stance. The Jews who wanted to stay in Libya were a minority of the total, but they were the richest and economically most active. Apart from the damage which an anti-Jewish stance would have caused the country's economy, leading to a total exodus of essential energies and capital and the criticism which this would have provoked in the traditional elite, such a stance would have alienated too many sympathizers of the new Libyan state and would thereby have placed it in an untenable position at the United Nations. This organization had raised the minorities issue in its resolution of November 21, 1949, which included, in a somewhat vague form, the question of minorities' representation in the National Assembly as "inhabitants" in Libya. We can understand why the leaders of the larger Arab parties refrained as long as they could from showing their cards. In their encounters with Pelt, Marchino, and the other Western members of the advisory council, these parties even showed a willingness to consider including a Jew among the Tripolitanian representatives to the National Assembly. The National Congress Party aired the idea of assigning a seat on the administrative council to the Jewish minority, as indigenous to Tripolitania. Their position with regard to the Italian minority, though equally ambiguous, was more cautious. It was extremely important to the Italian minority to have its own representative, particularly since its large numbers and geographical spread made it certain of being able to provide representation in the future. The National Congress Party and other smaller political groups were against direct, popular election of the members of the National Assembly. They gave the argument—partly justified and partly specious—that the elections would have to be held under occupation and thus could not be truly free elections. The party succeeded in gaining the support of the Italians, hence of all the minorities, for its point of view, and promised them in return a place in the National Assembly.

The first proof of the insincerity of these declarations and promises came in mid-1950. The advisory council had decided to create a preparatory committee, called the Committee of Twenty-One, since it had seven members for each region of Libya. It was entrusted with resolving the problems of the composition and functioning of the National Constituent Assembly, which was to draw up the constitution. The new committee did not include a representative of the minorities. According to the agreements, Marchino was to participate, and his name had been put forward by the majority of the political groupings entrusted with proposing the seven Tripolitanian members.[5] On the argument that he was a foreigner, he was in the end excluded from the advisory council. In his stead there was a Muslim, even though in the earlier discussions the Arabs had let it be understood that a Libyan Jew would have more chance of being accepted than a foreigner. In fact, this was the occasion on which the Arabs began to support the idea that the term "inhabitant" used in the U.N. Resolution of November 21, 1949, should be understood not in a broad but in a narrow sense. They understood it not in the literal sense, as almost certainly it was used by the U.N. General Assembly and as currently accepted in international legal terminology,[6] but in the sense of "indigenous Libyans."[7] This distinction significantly emerged just as the administrative council decided to deny voting rights to "foreigners." Pelt accepted the decision despite Marchino's repeated protests to the advisory committee and the United Nations.[8] The importance of the distinction is obvious, not only for Italians, Greeks, and Maltese, but also for Jews. Most Jews who wanted to remain in Libya were "indigenous" but also "foreign," since they held Italian, or sometimes other, citizenship. The way was opened to any interpretation of their effective status and thus to a whole series of discriminations in the present and, more important, the future. Despite this, authoritative Arab figures continued for some time to talk about including a Jew (obviously, not a "foreign" one) as one of the Tripolitanian delegates to the National Assembly.[9] Even Pelt, talking with A. S. Karlikow of the American Jewish Committee in mid-August, thought there would be a Jewish delegate. The commissioner said that the possibility was not to be excluded, since the Arabs' interest lay in using the Jews as a pawn against the Italians, by showing that they were distinguishing between the "real" Tripolitanian minority (the Jews) and the "false" minority (mainly the Italians). The Arabs might also think that the Jews, being aware of the Arab ploy, would in the end refuse to be represented so as not to alienate the Italians. It is impossible to say whether Pelt really believed what he was saying, or whether he was saying this merely to gain time, forestall outside interventions which might make his task even more complicated, and shift all responsibility to the Arabs. It is worth recording, though, that what he said gave Karlikow the impression that Pelt would not do much about the issue of the rights of the Jews. He seemed to agree with the Arabs' position, and believed that a position like the one the Jews had had under the Ottomans (obviously, in his view, the best to which they might aspire) could be guaranteed merely by inserting, as Idris proposed, "entire sections from the Human Rights Charter."[10]

In fact, as everything would have led one to expect, both the Jews and the minorities as a whole, just as they were excluded from the Committee of Twenty-One, were also excluded from the National Constituent Assembly. As usual, they were given the general assurance that the exclusion did not necessarily mean that minorities would also be denied political rights in the future.[11]

The National Assembly's first task, begun on November 25, was to choose a monarchical and federal system for the new state, and to designate Idris as king. With the exclusion of minorities from the assembly and the opening of its first session, the political history of the Jews of Libya entered a new and decisive phase dominated by the problem of what the constitution laid down for minorities in general and the Jews in particular.

To Idris and the Tripolitanian political groupings linked to him at the time, the solution seemed clear. For political groups in Cyrenaica and the Fezzan the problem of Jews hardly arose, because in those regions the Jews and other minorities were sparse, nonexistent, or completely dependent on Idris. The solution was to insist on a restrictive interpretation of the term "minorities" in the U.N. resolution of November 21, 1949, and distinguish clearly between *foreigners* and *national minorities* indigenous to Libya. The Greeks, Maltese, and especially Italians had to be considered foreigners for all intents and purposes, and thus denied political and associated rights (such as the possibility of official posts), while their economic influence had to be restricted. Despite this, there were many political and economic reasons why it would have been inadvisable for the Cyreanican and Fezzanese Arabs to provoke an exodus of Italians, not least among them their need to secure the votes of the Italian representative and Marchino in the advisory council in favor of the federal solution.[12] Typical is the decision taken in the administrative council in January 1951, in connection with bidding for contracts, that 60 percent of the capital of companies bidding had to be Arab-Libyan owned. The Jews in particular had to be considered as a national minority, and had to be exploited as such in the United Nations and before the Western governments. At the same time, the Arabs thought they had to make the Jews choose between the status of foreigners and that of Libyans, obliging them to either give up political and associated rights or the foreign citizenship which most of those wanting to stay in Libya possessed. The Arabs would recognize the Libyan citizenship—either ipso facto or upon request— of all Jews born in Libya or who had resided there for a certain time, the length of which depended on the political grouping, as long as they renounced any foreign citizenship or, upon reaching the age of twenty-one, did not opt for it.[13] Finally, as regards constitutional guarantees, hardly anyone was willing to go beyond what Idris had previously suggested—that is, including the human rights approved by the United Nations in the constitution of the new Libyan state. Other, more precise guarantees, if they ever came into being, would be included in normal laws which might be issued later on after the declaration of independence.

Despite this very restrictive Arab position, basing himself on the letter and spirit of the U.N. resolution of November 21, 1949, Marchino initially tried to insist on political rights. He later realized that he had the support of neither Pelt nor many of his fellow-members of the advisory council and that insisting on this would only hinder negotiations on other issues. In the end he tacitly accepted the basic Arab view, and merely tried to render the insertion in the constitution on human rights as broad and precise as possible. Marchino based his argument on the United Nations' application of human rights in the statute of the city of Jerusalem and the provision for a federation of Eritrea with Ethiopia. At the same time Marchino was trying to make the inclusion of human rights as binding a commitment as possible, through an explicit reference to the U.N. Declaration of Human Rights. In negotiations concerning the regulations on citizenship, he supported the requests given to him by the minorities and the optional use of the Italian language in government and legal matters for a period of ten years, since Italian was the tongue most used in relations among the minorities and the most widespread after Arabic. For this purpose Marchino drew up the following memorandum of requests to be included or at least taken into account in the drafting of the constitution:

BASIC RIGHTS

The Libyan Constitution shall guarantee all residents of Libya without distinction of nationality, race, sex, language, or religion, the enjoyment of human rights and fundamental freedoms, specifically:

(1) Equality before the law and equal protection by the law. No foreign company engaged in industrial, commercial, agricultural, crafts, educational, charity, banking, or insurance activities shall be subject to discriminatory measures.

(2) The right to life, liberty, and the security of persons.

(3) The right to freedom of opinion and expression, and the right to embrace and practice any belief or religion, including the right to teach the religion practiced and its prescriptions.

(4) The right to education.

(5) The right to free exercise of one's own profession within the limits of the law.

(6) The right to freedom of meeting and peaceful association.

(7) The right to the inviolability of dwelling houses and the prohibition of entering and searching them without a prior, specific permit issued by the authorities.

(8) The right to confidentiality of correspondence.

(9) No one may be arrested or detained except by the legal order of the appropriate authorities, unless in the case of flagrant and grave violation of the law in force.

(10) No one may be deported except as prescribed by law.

(11) The right to a fair, objective, and public trial in courts for everyone charged with a penal offense with all guarantees necessary for his defense.

"Appropriate courts" implies the request that the judicial College, excluding its President, include judges originating from the ethnic minorities in a number equal to the judges of different origin.

(12) The provisions of the penal code may not, in any case, be applicable retroactively.

(13) The right of freedom of emigration to any other country without loss of assets and with the faculty of transfer of movable assets and the personal goods and equipment belonging to the person emigrating.

(14) The right to submit petitions to the Head of State and to appeal to him to have any death penalty commuted.

(15) The inviolability of property. No one may be deprived of his property, particularly his contractual right, except in the manner determined by law and provided such person is awarded just compensation.

(16) The right to participate fully in the economic, financial, and social life of Libya, with no discriminations or distinctions to be made between citizens and non-citizens of Libya.

(17) The acquisition of Libyan citizenship shall confer the right to equal enjoyment of all the civil and political rights of citizens of the Libyan State, regardless of race, origin, language, or religion. Such status shall be considered to include the right to vote and be represented, to hold positions in public bodies, and to hold political office.

CITIZENSHIP

The clauses of the Constitutional Charter regulating the right to citizenship of the Libyan State should incorporate provisions corresponding to the following concepts:

(1) All persons of foreign citizenships and who at the coming into force of this Constitution have had their normal residence in Libya for a period of not less than ten years shall have the right to acquire Libyan citizenship provided they apply for it.

(2) All members of national or religious Minorities, who were born in Libya, shall have the same right, with the right to opt for their fathers' citizenship upon reaching the age of twenty-one.

(3) No restriction shall be exercised over members of national or religious Minorities [who were] born in Libya and possess Libyan citizenship who intend to request foreign citizenship.

(4) Residents of Libya who do not fall under the categories described in the preceding clauses (1) and (2) may acquire Libyan citizenship under reasonable conditions, which shall be specified in the Constitutional Charter.

(5) Libyan citizenship shall be granted to every inhabitant of Libya who does not possess any foreign citizenship.

THE RIGHT TO USE THE ITALIAN LANGUAGE

Noting that Italian is the language commonly used in relations among the various ethnic Minorities and is the most widespread, together with the fact that many members of the Minorities do not know Arabic, it is requested that for an appropriate period of time, which could be limited to ten years, the use of Italian be allowed in public offices, including legal offices and courts.[14]

Marchino wanted to facilitate and expedite the negotiations, avoid stalling on particular issues when a contrary decision had already been taken in the National Assembly,[15] prevent more intransigent Arabs from intervening, and probably keep a margin for maneuvering in order to protect Italian interests. He thus accepted the Arab view that it was better for the knottiest part of the negotiations—solving the fundamental problems before presenting them subsequently to the National Assembly—to be carried out unofficially and be based on "personal, mutual, and friendly understanding between the negotiators." These were Marchino himself; Halil bey Gallal, the chairman of the National Assembly working group responsible for drafting the section of the constitution dealing with the rights of the people; and Ali Assad bey al-Jerbi, deputy minister of foreign affairs in the provisional government. Thus, the Arabs got their way and the negotiations did not become official negotiations between two ad hoc delegations appointed by the National Assembly and the advisory committee of minorities.

One has to consider the almost complete lack of support for Marchino from Pelt and the Western members of the advisory committee and the intensive nature of the negotiations (carried out between June 11, 1951, and July 27 in a country house belonging to Marchino).[16] It is undeniable that the results that the minorities member achieved and which formed the basis of the subsequent deliberations in the National Assembly were significant. There too, Marchino continued pressuring Pelt and the members of the National Assembly's working group. Agreement on many points was easy after Idris' decision to refer to the Universal Declaration of Human Rights (though Arab delegates rejected its explicit inclusion in the constitution as being "superfluous"). On more politically sensitive points, though, the Arabs adopted an inflexible position aimed at keeping the constitution silent on the issues, thus not committing it in any way. Reaching a compromise on almost all questions, despite this posture, was a great achievement for Marchino. The solution was sometimes positive and sometimes a mere reference to the problems at issue in the constitution, even though dealing with them was left to the Organic Law of Tripolitania and particular laws.

After many discussions, the principle was accepted that foreigners should be deported only in accordance with the provisions of the law (Article 190 of the constitution). Compromise solutions were reached for the following problems:

(a) Making foreigners fully equal with citizens as regards civil rights, resolved in Article 191 of the constitution, which states: "The legal status of foreigners shall be prescribed by federal law in accordance with the principles of international law."

(b) The use of Italian and the right to set up schools and educational institutions in which teaching was done in the mother tongue, resolved by Articles 187 and 24 of the constitution, which stipulated that "cases in which a foreign language may be used in official transactions shall be determined by a federal law" and that "everyone shall be free to use any language in his private transactions or religious or cultural matters or in the Press or any other publications or in public meetings."

(c) Guaranteeing that all those who had a fixed residence in Libya on November 21, 1949, could continue their professional activities, and that contractual rights would be respected, both of these through Article 210 of the constitution, establishing that "unless they are inconsistent with the principles of liberty and equality guaranteed by this Constitution, all laws, subsidiary legislation, orders, and notices which may be in operation in any part of Libya upon the coming into force of this Constitution shall continue to be effective and in operation until repealed or amended or replaced by other legislation enacted in accordance with the provisions of this Constitution."

The most difficult compromise to reach was the one regarding citizenship. In view of its importance, it is useful to refer directly to the account of these negotiations which Marchino sent to the Italian representative on the advisory committee and the leaders of the Jewish, Greek, and Maltese communities. It reads:

> The most heated discussion was that revolving around Libyan citizenship. The minorities have requested that all foreign citizens resident in the country ten years prior to the date of promulgation of the Constitution should be admitted to Libyan citizenship without formalities and on simple request. This request was declared unacceptable unless supplemented by a second principle according to which foreigners opting for Libyan citizenship were not to enjoy political rights until the fifth year after acquisition of citizenship. For my part, I de-

clared that I could in no way agree to a proposal which sanctioned a principle contrary to the general custom of civilized states and which clearly reflected an attitude of distrust toward foreigners residing in the country, who in great part were deserving of recognition for their efforts in behalf of its progress and development. I expressed the conviction that the open distrust which lay at the bottom of such a principle would in general awaken doubts in those who intended to acquire Libyan citizenship and dissuade them from their intentions. I added that, above all, such a principle would needlessly compromise every honest aim at sincere collaboration between the Arab majority and the foreign minorities.

In a second phase of the discussion, the proposal was made to me to extend citizenship to resident foreigners who had lived in the country a period of ten years, starting from January 23, 1943. I also rejected this proposal because, in my view, it did not meet any of the objections raised against the first proposal and it repeated the negative attitude outlined above. Moreover, since it was clear from the proposal advanced that it was being intended to exclude, during the initial phase, all members of minorities in recent possession of citizenship from active participation in the political life of the country, I pointed out that such an intention was harmful because it tended to exclude from public affairs the very elements that were most mature and reflective. I concluded that I could see no reason why they were so unwilling to accept the simple formula proposed by us and which was in every way similar to that adopted by the assembly of the United Nations in its resolution on Eritrea.

Finally an area of agreement was found, based upon the understanding that Libyan citizenship would be conceded to foreigners requesting it and having had residence in the country for at least ten years before the date of promulgation of the Constitution; they would also have a right of option valid for two years, to be exercised from January 1, 1952, on. This too was a compromise solution which, practically speaking, will not enable foreigners acquiring citizenship to take part in the political life of the country during its first months of life, particularly in the elections of 1951. But I saw fit to accept the proposal of my honorable interlocutors, first and foremost because it would seem advisable that naturalized foreigners, especially Italians and Jews, should not be involved in the boiling political controversies now agitating the country, and in the second place, because I became thoroughly convinced that no more was to be obtained by further insistence.[17]

On one request the Arabs were completely intransigent—the freedom to emigrate. This was the freedom most dear to the Jews. Some wanted to leave and were afraid that they would not be able to do so before the proclamation of independence. Others wanted to stay but did not want to have the possibility of emigrating closed to them if the situation in Libya became such that they could not stay.

Having large investments in Libya, the latter were worried that they might not be able to liquidate them. Arabs were also very worried that the Jews might leave. A minority of Arabs were concerned for political reasons, because they wanted to prevent Israel from being strengthened, but the majority feared that Libya would be divested of energies and capital essential for its economy. They were worried above all that once the Jews had received the right to emigrate freely with their property it would also be given to the Italians, who were more numerous and more important for the Libyan economy.[18] This explains why Halil bey Gallal and Ali Essad bey Gerbi completely rejected all Marchino's arguments (not least that the right to emigrate and protection of property were specifically provided for in Articles 13 and 17 of the Universal Declaration of Human Rights).[19] Marchino's later efforts to raise the question within the responsible working group of the National Assembly (even the right to emigrate for a limited number of years) met the same fate.

The results of Marchino's negotiations with the Arabs aroused contrasting but mostly negative reactions among the Jews. These criticisms were so widespread and emphatic that their real basis should be assessed. With different tactics and a more determined attitude, could Marchino have got better results? Everything leads me to think that no more concessions could have been gained and thus the criticisms leveled against Marchino when the negotiations were over were largely unjustified and were an expression more of disappointment and worry about the future than of a calm and realistic assessment.[20] He was accused of having mainly protected Italian interests and of glossing over those of the Jews. Karlikow wrote on August 31, speaking partly on behalf of the Jews to his superiors in the American Jewish Committee in New York, that Marchino had "done fairly well . . . on general human rights issues; quite well on matters of particular interest to the Italians; and very poorly on the issues of particular concern to the Jewish community."[21] The Jews may have been right in reproaching Marchino, in my opinion, for perhaps reassuring them too much, before the negotiations had formally got under way, that the Arabs were well disposed and the prospects favorable for a successful conclusion[22] (though this belief was also widespread among the Jews).[23] Later, he kept them poorly informed about the progress of the negotiations. Though this does not relate directly to the negotiations, Marchino voted in the advisory council against including Libya in the sterling zone without asking the Jews' opinion beforehand. He thereby risked losing for them any vestiges of sympathy in London and thus making it more difficult to bring about an emergency intervention by the British government on behalf of the Jews. Other criticisms of Marchino were less well founded. They either related to issues having nothing to do with the constitution, so that raising them in that phase of drafting the constitution for the new Libyan state would have been very difficult, especially since requests regarding the constitution had been submitted not to Marchino but to Pelt through him, or they implied such a basic mistrust of the new Libyan state that merely raising them would have jeopardized the entire negotiations. Obviously, no one could realistically expect such a thing from someone representing not one but four minorities. Such questions were raised neither by Pelt with the Libyan leaders nor by the U.S. representatives in the United Nations. Even if these two criticisms of Marchino had been justified (particularly the first), before subscribing entirely to them, one must have a clear idea of the conditions in which the minorities member had to operate: the general political conditions already mentioned and those arising from the attitude of the Jews of Tripoli and their leaders regarding the problems and prospects which the negotiations opened up.

The primary sources from the Community of Tripoli are lacking for this reconstruction of the attitude of Jews. What can be deduced from material preserved in the archives of international Jewish organizations involved in the issue, particularly those of the American Jewish Committee, which played a predominant role, is enough to confirm that throughout Marchino's informal negotiations with Halil bey Gallal the Jews' position was neither clear nor firm enough to constitute a real point of reference for the minorities member.

Apart from a few individual and completely atypical cases, the Jews of Libya and their leaders, between November 1949 and January 1951, hardly took part in the actual political process leading up to Libyan independence. The minorities issue was left almost entirely in Marchino's hands. In this period it was the American, British, and French Jewish organizations and the World Jewish Congress which took all initiatives in the United Nations and in approaches to Pelt, the advisory council, and the various governments involved in the future of Libya. The same can be said for these organizations' contacts with the leaders of the Community of Tripoli and the most aware and active figures in Libyan Jewry. These contacts were so episodic and unconstructive that, in October 1950, the World Jewish Congress found itself in the predicament of having to submit a report on the Jews of Libya to the United Nations without having been able to consult Libyan Jewish leaders in advance. The same happened to the American Jewish Committee. From correspondence be-

tween the New York office and the Paris office as well as the AJC
Tripoli representative (Ruben Hassan, one of the few Libyan Jews of
Italian citizenship who were trying to come to grips with the issues)
it emerges that between late November and late December 1950 the
AJC tried several times to find out whether the leaders of the Community of Tripoli agreed in substance with the steps which it had
taken in the United Nations and the policy it intended to pursue in
the future, and whether they had any objections or proposals to add.[24]
    The foremost consequence of this passivity on the part of the
Libyan Jewish leadership is easy to guess. Precisely in those months
when the political and constitutional bases for the future state were
being laid down, when positions were being defined and the premises laid for future groupings and alliances, both internally and inter-
nationally, among the various political forces, the Jews of Libya were
out of the running. They thereby fueled the belief that they were excluding themselves completely, which could be interpreted as a sign
that they already considered themselves foreigners, and would resign themselves to whatever was going to be decided for them. They
also bolstered the belief that the Jews had no particular demands besides those shared by all minorities and thus that they had delegated
the whole affair to Marchino. Another consequence was less serious
only in appearance. It created a bad and confusing impression and
gave a crucial margin of maneuver to those who on an international
level and in the United Nations found it opportune not to commit
themselves regarding the future status of Libyan Jews. This consequence was that for over a year the Jews did not put a stop, by making a definite choice and taking responsibility for it, to the dualism
characterizing efforts on their behalf by Jewish organizations defending them. These organizations agreed on the basic goal of guaranteeing as well as possible the status of the remaining Jewish community in the future Libyan state. But the American Jewish Committee
(AJC) and the Anglo-Jewish Association (AJA) adopted partially diverse positions on what it was most important to ask for and get in
order to achieve the goal itself as well as on the general political
prospects of their work. The AJA functioned within the orbit of British policy prospects and had a more pragmatic and limited view of
the problem. Its main objective was not so much to win political
rights for the Libyan Jews (they were difficult to get from the Arabs
and almost useless, since the small number of Jews remaining in
Libya made self-representation unthinkable) as to protect as much
as possible the Jews' right to community and cultural autonomy (the
rabbinical court, schools, language, etc.). The AJA thought that
effective protection could best be ensured by the influence which

the British government would maintain on the Libyan government after independence. It would also be ensured, as Pelt also envisaged, by Libya's long-term need for economic and technical assistance from the United Nations and the major Western countries. The AJC saw the problem of Libyan Jewry as an important aspect (since it was a precedent which might turn out to be decisive) of the broader problem of the situation of all Jews living in Muslim countries. The AJC's main goal was to ensure that Libyan Jews would be able to enjoy complete civil and political rights and find a formula which would explicitly give the United Nations the right to intervene and enforce respect for these rights if the Arabs violated them.[25]

The Libyan Jews' passivity is not easy to explain. As far as one can understand, it had many causes, some of them apparently contradictory. An important report of late February 1951, from the Paris office of the American Jewish Committee, on the situation and prospects of Libyan Jewry,[26] tends to explain the passivity by the lack of strong and effective leadership. After Habib left office, no one wanted to undertake the leadership of the Community. Finally, after a long crisis, Moshe Nahum was elected president. He was a good person but certainly not endowed with the personality needed at such a difficult time. Among the rabbis there was the same lack of men who were up to the job, since many, including the best of them, had left for Israel. There is surely some truth in this explanation and the one which is in part its premise, namely, the impoverishment of abilities and energies caused by the exodus to Israel. The lack of leadership does not suffice, though, to explain the seriousness of the phenomenon and, above all, says nothing about the situation lying behind the passivity. It was because of this underlying situation that the phenomenon was such a serious one and that the exodus left such gaps. Among those who had left were some of the most aware and active figures in Jewish affairs; but, despite the exodus, there were still plenty of people in Tripoli capable (due to experience, culture, and social standing) of taking the reins of Libyan Jewish life. They would not be lacking in the future either, since they were largely members of the minority which had no intention of leaving. It is thus in the situation underlying the passivity that we must look for an explanation.

The predominant state of mind at this time among the mass of Libyan Jews has been described in the last chapter. For the majority, who planned to emigrate, what would happen in the future in Libya was of little importance and, in any case, did not concern them directly. Their main and often sole interest was how to leave in time, before Libya became independent, and if possible take their possessions with them. Some of them—at least on a psychological level—probably secretly harbored a certain resentment against those who did not intend to leave. The departing majority must have considered the others the "privileged ones" who, because of their economic and social positions, were able to stay, or resented that the others did not hear the call of Israel. Thus, the masses were generally uninterested in internal and international political developments involving Libyan independence not directly affecting their own chances of leaving. They were interested less in Community institutions than in those dealing with emigration and assistance to those waiting to leave.

The state of mind of those who intended to stay in Libya is harder to define. They were influenced by a whole series of psychological and cultural motivations, some originating in the past and some in reaction to the present. Some people, mainly old and without relatives, did not feel like beginning a new life in another country. Apart from this minority, most of those staying were, in contrast to those who wished to leave, the richest and most Westernized Jews, linked most closely to the Arab elite and also the Italian minority, with important economic interests in Libya and of foreign, usually Italian, citizenship. The choice they made was almost a compulsory one, often determined almost solely by not wanting to give up an economic and social way of life that would be difficult to build again elsewhere. According to the aforementioned American Jewish Committee Report of February 1951, at this time there were about 4,000 Jews intending to stay in Libya. Ony 500–750 of these were not rich or at least well off.[27] Three-quarters of them were citizens of Italy or some other Western country, and almost all looked at their own future with apprehension. Psychologically, this complex of factors led to a mixture of two contrasting emotions which eventually came to dominate their state of mind. These were mistrust and trust: mistrust of the Arabs' basic sincerity toward the Jews and trust in the ability of the Arab leadership, especially Idris, to realize that it needed the Jews. The Sanusi leader had the powerful factor working for him that he had never shown anti-Jewish feelings and in Cyrenaica, which he controlled, there had never been Arab pogroms. Libya would gain direct and indirect, internal and international advantages from a fair and liberal policy toward its Jewish minority. The Jews were economically active and dynamic, but numerically small, devoid of political ambitions, loyal, and not backed by any foreign interests. Culturally, the Jews more than any other minority were able to understand the country in which they always lived. They could act as a conduit to the other minorities, especially the

Italians, who, politically, would be the most difficult to integrate into the new Libya. Thus, on the level of behavior, there was a diffuse tendency to reinforce the motives for trust by being loyal to Idris, and to view as crucial the influence over him of all those who might reinforce his power and keep him under control. There was a strong tendency among these Jews to wait and see how the independence process would develop, without attracting attention to themselves and taking as few initiatives as possible. Translated into political terms, this line of behavior led most Jews to a kind of immobilism, concerning both Community life and the issues of the Community's future legal basis (for which the prevailing tendency was to maintain the status quo) as well as the future position of Jews in Libya. All initiatives were left to Marchino, who in his official capacity dealt with the problem from the point of view of all the minorities together. At most, the Jews would give their general consent to the federal solution, which Idris desired as much as the British and which was objectively meant to challenge the most extreme nationalist trends in line with the Arab League. But even this was done with some caution, without committing themselves too much, so as not to jeopardize the possibility of choosing in the future whether to join the new Libya as Libyan Jews or Italians.[28]

Obviously, not everyone shared this state of mind or the passivity that derived from it. Those who did not generally chose to work for emigration, which they considered at that time the most important and urgent matter. In such a situation, one should be surprised neither at the lack of energy and capable people from which the Community institutions suffered nor at the inertia and lack of political initiative which characterized them. In a psychological atmosphere such as the one which I have tried to describe, even those who did not share the general political inertia and who wanted to rescue Community organizations from it could do little. They were obliged to act in isolation, and there was a danger of provoking disagreements and internal schisms which would have serious consequences for the already precarious unity of Libyan Jewry.

In February 1951, after more than a year of almost total political passivity in which the Community went no further than a series of general contacts with Pelt and Marchino, it seemed for a moment as if the situation might change. Marchino urgently needed precise instructions for his negotiations with the Arabs. The American Jewish Committee, seeing that all its requests to the Community leaders had been in vain, decided to send two of its own representatives to Tripoli, Abraham S. Karlikow and André Chouraqui, to convince the Community to finalize its policy and draft its requests. The two envoys did this in a few days. When they left Libya, the Community's general political attitude regarding requests of a constitutional nature and other specific requests which it would submit to Marchino and Pelt had been decided on. The general political attitude was the same as the one which the AJC had adopted during contacts in previous months at the United Nations and with the governments involved. It had been decided with regard to requests concerning constitutional issues that Marchino would try to have the Universal Declaration of Human Rights explicitly inserted in the constitution. Regarding the legal basis of the Jewish Community, rabbinical court and schools, and related issues (holidays, language, etc.), after some uncertainty as to whether it would be appropriate or not to try to win back the rabbinical court's authority regarding inheritance, it was decided to maintain the status quo. The only new request was for full recognition until the end of 1964 of the existence and work of the CABI Olim. That was the date by which those agencies had to complete the sale of property they were administering and transfer the profits to the former owners. The AJC wanted to find a way to make the United Nations able to intervene effectively even after independence to guarantee respect for the conditions of Jews remaining in the country and thereby create a precedent which could be invoked in other similar cases. It decided to ask the United Nations to take official note of the articles in the Libyan Constitution relating to "basic human rights" and the "fundamental freedoms, to be applicable both to citizens and non-citizens in this nation." On the request of the Libyan government, the U.N. would set up a special permanent commission to receive complaints regarding violations of these rights and freedoms, investigate them, and make recommendations about them to the Economic and Social Council and the General Assembly. A special document was prepared for this purpose. Pelt was supposed to have the Arabs accept it, and the Libyan government was to present it to the United Nations in the form of its own resolution, as soon as Libya was admitted.[29]

There is no point in discussing the merits of these requests. Apart from a few nuances, those relating to basic rights were the same as those of other minorities. Those relating to Community organization and life were not of such a nature as to raise special issues, and could form a normal base for negotiations. Obviously, much could be said about the last one, particularly about its political absurdity and counterproductive nature. It lacked any serious premise providing for a decisive outside action against Idris and the National Assembly to oblige them to accept it. For the American Jewish Committee it would have the value of a first move toward resolving the question within the forum of the United Nations. For Libyan Jews, though, it had the defect of being no less than a declaration of a priori mistrust of the new Libyan state, and thus amounted to a provocation. So much so that Marchino merely forwarded it to Pelt, who never presented it. What is important to emphasize here is that, though all these requests were ready by the second half of February, they were not forwarded to Marchino until early April, and only after repeated inquiries by Marchino himself and the American Jewish Committee. It had been agreed with Karlikow and Chouraqui that the Community Council would see to the matter quickly. After the two had left, the Community leaders were seized by various doubts. Some members of the council proposed re-examining the demands, amending them, and reducing them in number so that they would not poorly dispose the Arabs by seeming too many. The council was summoned three times for this purpose, but each time lacked a quorum. Finally, on March 26, a meeting of about thirty prominent figures was held to read the Community Statutes which had to be sent to Marchino for his approval. The assembly took no decision, however, and appointed a commission to study the issue. Someone even proposed calling another meeting for a hundred people. And so early April arrived with nothing decided, and the requests approved in February were finally sent to Marchino just as they were, since he had communicated that he could not wait any longer.[30] These hesitations can certainly be explained by the weak authority exercised by Nahum and the council. They also show that the decision taken in February was less a real community decision than one practically imposed by the AJC envoys on a council incapable of expressing and sustaining its own point of view. It had tried to hide its own lack of ideas and its powerlessness by passively accepting both the political framework suggested by Karlikow and Chouraqui and all the demands which the various sectors and groups within Libyan Jewry were pressing. This also explains why, after the burst of pseudo-activity during those two months, the Community collapsed into its former passivity, precisely when it should have seized the day, and despite the American Jewish Committee's pleas to be kept up to date with the progress of Marchino's negotiations.

Though the Libyan Jews' criticism of Marchino for not adequately informing them of the outcome of his negotiations with Halil bey Gallal has some validity, the criticism appears in a new light. Considering the state of affairs in the Community leadership and the attitude of the Arab camp, it is realistic to ask whether the Community Council's being any better informed about the negotiations would not just have given rise to delays, obstruction, stalemate in the negotiations themselves, and an ultimate conclusion even less favorable for the Libyan Jews and perhaps, by reflection, for the other minorities. One may thus conclude that Marchino did well to avoid such risks.

The failure, after the Marchino–Halil bey Gallal negotiations were concluded, of subsequent attempts to improve the results, first in Tripoli, through Marchino and Pelt and with the Libyan provisional government directly, and then at the United Nations, proves that it was impossible to gain any more than Marchino had already gained.

Libyan Jews, as we have said, generally reacted negatively to the results of the negotiations. It is hard to say whether these reactions would have led to anything more if it were not for the American Jewish Committee. We know that the Community of Tripoli decided to express its disappointment officially to Marchino and ask him to press further a series of demands only after receiving a letter from Karlikow. The latter requested precise information on the terms of the agreement which Marchino had reached and pointed out some of the proposals which he considered most crucial. Karlikow asked Nahum to inform him if the Community had changed its views since February.[31] As the letter which Nahum wrote to Marchino on August 23 shows, the Community of Tripoli decided that four issues were of "maximum importance" and asked for negotiations on them to be reopened:

1. *Emigration*
We must insist on this vital issue. We would like emigration to be continued as presently in effect and in no way hindered as a result of economic and social, political, or tax considerations. If, despite all your efforts, you do not succeed in incorporating free emigration in the Libyan Constitution, then at least have it included in the provisional legislation, even as a special provision relating to the Jewish community.

2. *Use of Foreign Languages* (Primary School Education)
It is not clear from the paragraph on this subject whether you explicitly reached the same agreement as that concerning official use of non-Arabic languages or whether what is in the paragraph is your personal opinion.

Supposing that a similar transitional agreement was arrived at for primary schools as for official use of languages, we think that in this case the analogy does not respond to the real needs of the people. While after enough time has passed people may not need any other language than Arabic for official purposes, they can never give up in their own family life their own ethnic and national character. Primary education is practically an extension of the family, and no civil law can require families of a different ethnic and national origin to send their kindergarten-aged children to a school where the mother tongue is not the one they use. Those with the right to be considered residents, just as they must fulfill the duties of citizens, should have the right to be treated equally with others. One of the most basic and sacred rights is that to an elementary school at state expense in one's mother tongue.

We are thus requesting you to insist that the right be included in a permanent, constitutional form, not a transitory one.

3. *Specific Requests by the Community*

Please note that in our letter No. 117, dated April 1, 1951, we submitted to you, in addition to the Universal Human Rights, several requests of ours and specific proposals which we would have liked to see included in the Libyan Constitution. We find that none of these has been broached in your discussions.

(a) The status and rights, etc. of the Jewish Community;

(b) General charitable assistance to poor Jews;

(c) The right not to work and open businesses on Saturdays and religious and Jewish holidays;

(d) How the Jewish schools should function;

(e) The functions of the Rabbinical Court and the Statutes covering it;

(f) How the CABI Olim should function.

On all of the above we would appreciate receiving your explanations, and if these matters have not been discussed in Tripoli, we ask you to raise them without fail.

It is necessary that our requests be officially put forward in the appropriate quarters, and we ask you to make a point of them, even if you have the impression in advance that you may not succeed. Even though our requests may be rejected, it is necessary that they be put on the agenda and that there be a clear record of them in the minutes.

4. *Article 24 of the Fundamental Principles*

We would appreciate its being changed to read as follows: "Persons belonging to religions other than the Muslim may preserve the Personal Statutes and inheritance laws of their religion and/or nationality of origin if they so desire."[32]

Nahum's request no longer referred to a permanent United Nations committee to supervise respect for the rights and freedom of the Jewish minority. It was after the above request that Marchino[33] and Pelt, in September before the constitution was finally approved and promulgated (on October 7) and even afterward (with regard to nonconstitutional matters), made some last fruitless approaches to the National Assembly and the provisional government to try to obtain a revision of what had unofficially been agreed between Marchino and Halil bey Gallal. Just as with the previous contacts, the Libyan spokesmen completely refused to go beyond a general assurance that the Jewish minority could rest assured that all problems relating to the legal basis of the Community would be solved through a special law in accordance with its wishes and the principles fundamental for setting up the institutions of the new kingdom.[34] With regard to the freedom to emigrate, all Pelt was able to get was a vague assurance from the prime minister, Muntasser, that no obstacles would be put in the way of these departures.[35]

Even during this last phase, the greatest efforts were being made by the major Jewish organizations. Just before independence went into effect, they were trying to persuade Libya to accept explicitly the Universal Declaration of Human Rights. They were engaged in a last attempt to salvage the right to free emigration when the Arabs had rejected it. The organizations were trying to win recognition for the minorities' right of recourse to the United Nations if their rights should be curtailed. The World Jewish Congress sent the director of its political office, A. L. Easterman, to Tripoli in October to explain to the leaders of Libyan Jewry what the WJC intended to do. He was also supposed to contact Pelt and those who were working with him in Libya in order to get their support.[36] The main arena for these efforts was not Tripoli, though, but Washington and the United Nations. At the Sixth Session, in Paris, December 1951–January 1952, the General Assembly discussed the work of the Libya Commission and ratified Libyan independence, which was proclaimed on December 24, 1951.[37] The main protagonist of these efforts, besides the World Jewish Congress, was the American Jewish Committee. Since all its approaches to the Libyans and Pelt had been in vain, until the end it was trying to convince a delegation, specifically that of the United States, to propose a recommendation or similar initiative to give Libyan Jews a future right to appeal to the United Nations. Even among those who shared the AJC's concerns and realized how important the Libyan precedent would be for Jews of other Muslim countries, no one was willing to make an explicit commitment. Anyone doing it would have been exposed to the accusation of interfering in the internal affairs of the new state. The action would have aroused Arab hostility and might have rebounded against the Libyan Jews themselves. Some attacks from the Libyan nationalist newspaper *Al Libi* were already implying this. At that very time it accused the Jews of plotting, together with other foreign elements, against the interests of Libya. Thus even those who had seemed willing to make some reference to the problem within a general discussion, in the end either were silent (like the United States) or made such a cautious and fleeting reference that it could not lead to any real political debate (like Israel).[38] Some cautious contacts behind the scenes were more successful. It was probably after these that the Libyan prime minister, Muntasser, made the following declaration to the United Nations *Ad Hoc* Political Committee: "The new Constitution of Libya contains a section on human rights which makes it clear that the Constitution adopted in letter and spirit the fundamental principles of the Universal Declaration of Human Rights proclaimed by the General Assembly in this city in December 1948."[39] In and of itself, this statement did not amount to much, and was not even entirely accurate. But, for lack of anything better, Muntasser's words might still be useful when the question of whether Libya should be admitted to the United Nations came up. The statement might still bolster the hope that the Libyan government would settle the questions left pending in the way that it had promised and in a spirit of conciliation. The World Jewish Congress[40] and the leaders of Libyan Jewry[41] showed that they understood his declaration precisely in this sense.

9. From Idris to Qadhdhafi (1952–1970)

Full independence in 1952 opened a new and decisive phase in the history both of Libya and of the Jews remaining there. This is not the place to give minute details about domestic and international events which occurred during this period. It is enough to provide a few general indications to serve as a frame and sketch the main phases of the most recent history of Libya, from the kingdom of Idris to the republic of Qadhdhafi.[1]

The Sanusi kingdom's domestic and foreign policies started off on a cautious and moderate note. They were also marked by a lack of clear ideas, particularly with regard to what attitude the kingdom should take toward its Italian and Jewish populations. This vagueness partly reflected the basic way of thinking of the king and his closest advisers and partly resulted from the absence of a nucleus of leaders. The responsibility for this lies initially with the Italian colonial administration, but just as much with British military officials. The absence of other leaders allowed a power-holding group consisting of a few families to crystallize around the king. The most prominent family was that of Brahim Shelhi, who was already the king's confidant from his years of exile and was now his all-powerful adviser. These families lacked any real connection with the emerging reality of Libya, and several of them were fighting among themselves even to the point of bloodshed. The Sanusi regime's lack of policies was also partly imposed on it by circumstances. There were internal problems caused mainly by the profound socioeconomic and cultural differences between Cyrenaicans and Tripolitanians, the disagreements and rivalries to which these gave rise, and nationalist and pan-Arab ferment in Tripolitania. The dissolution of political parties immediately after independence and the expulsion of the most important nationalist leader, Beshir bey Saadawi, did not halt this nationalist unrest but merely made it less apparent and cohesive. Other problems were Libya's extreme poverty and the lack of trained Libyan professionals. Hostility and mistrust of the Sanusi monarchy in the Arab world led Idris to foster good relations with the West, particularly the United States, Britain, France (though the Fezzan problem dragged on until August 1955, when the French finally left), and, despite great opposition, Italy. In return for the help of the Western powers, the king granted the United States the use of a large air base in Tripolitania and Britain several air, sea, and land bases in Cyrenaica, to which the British transferred their Near Eastern strategic reserve forces. Without the help of these powers, of the United Nations (into which Libya was admitted on December 15, 1955), and of the Italians living in the country (who constituted the most progressive and dynamic group in the economy), Idris certainly would not have been able to overcome these difficulties.

Obviously, his policy created other new problems for Idris, particularly with regard to the most nationalistic Libyans and hard-line Arab countries, especially after the takeover in Egypt in July 1952 by Naguib's and Nasser's Revolutionary Command Council gave the entire Arab nationalist movement new vigor. A typical example of this tightrope policy was Idris' attitude toward the Arab League. As long as it was controlled by Abd-er-Rahman el Azzam Pasha (whose relations with the most extreme Tripolitanian nationalists were well known) and despite direct and indirect pressures on the government from within and without, Libya did not join. As soon as the powerful secretary-general relinquished his position, Libya submitted its application for membership and, having been accepted into the Arab League on March 28, 1953, adopted the position of the moderate countries—Saudi Arabia, Tunisia, and Morocco. Significantly, Libya's closest and warmest relations with Arab states besides its Arab League connections were, again, with Tunisia and Morocco, both of which were ruled by moderate Western-oriented regimes. Its relations with Nasser's Egypt soon became more difficult. In 1954 they deteriorated to such a point that the Egyptian cultural attaché was expelled for distributing "subversive" material and, it was said, even arms to the nationalists. The Egyptian leader did not look kindly on Idris' cordial relations with the British and Americans (especially after the Suez crisis in 1956, when Nasser accused Libya of allowing the British to use the Cyrenaican bases against Egypt), while it was to Egypt that the Libyan nationalist opposition was looking more and more. Egyptian technicians with their scarcely concealed air of superiority, with their tendency to interfere in Libyan political life and serve Egyptian interests more than those of Libya, aroused annoyance and suspicion. So much for Libya's foreign relations during the 1950s. In domestic politics, nothing very significant happened. Nevertheless, during those years Idris' position even in Cyrenaica was being undermined slowly but surely. This was due to the country's poverty and the numerous successive governments' inability to deal with it, differences between the various cabals (around which eventually much of the political life revolved and the elections were fought), and the broader rivalries between Cyrenaica and Tripolitania. Another cause was the growing influence, especially over the new intellectual, military, and young elites, of extreme nationalist, anti-imperialist, and pan-Arab clandestine parties. Finally, one should not underestimate the negative effects of the differences, jealousies, and secret maneuvers provoked by the king's advanced age and the lack of a direct heir to the throne. After the death of Idris' brother and designated successor, an heir acceptable to the group of families holding power and the various branches of the royal family could not be found. To show how serious these differences were it is enough to say that the powerful Brahim Shelhi himself fell victim to them, being assassinated by a young cousin of the queen. In addition to a death sentence for the murderer, this caused the entire branch of the royal family of which he was a member (since the queen was the king's cousin) to be excluded from succession.

An important change took place at the beginning of the 1960s. The foremost factor in it was the discovery and development of petroleum. The first fields were located in Cyrenaica in 1959. Other, richer deposits were found over the next few years. By 1968 Libya had the sixth largest reserves in the world (about 8 percent of total reserves), and about forty companies were operating about nine hundred wells on its soil. The oil extracted during 1970 amounted to over 162 million barrels. It was not long before consequences of the discovery of oil were felt. Though the serious problems related to the complete lack of technically qualified personnel in Libya persisted, the country with no lack of capital began to experience thorough economic and social change. While this fact bolstered Idris in the short run, it made his long-term prospects more precarious. In the new situation it was more difficult for him to justify his relations with the West and avoid closer inter-Arab solidarity. Within Libya, extreme nationalist, pan-Arab, and populist trends were gaining new vigor as a result of the new economic situation. Idris' position was also weakened socially and politically by the overwhelming amount of aggressive Nasserist propaganda, which had become an important element in the Arab world, both in general and in relation to Libya. To complete the picture, one must not overlook the negative effects of maneuvers and speculation regarding oil-drilling rights and the divisions and fierce struggles they produced within the Libyan leadership, the important families, and even the king's entourage. The first indications of the crisis wracking the Sanusi regime occurred toward late 1961, when a clandestine group associated with pro-Egyptian and Baathist views was arrested. Eighty-seven of those arrested, accused of a "communist conspiracy" to overthrow the monarchy, were sentenced in February 1962 to various terms. Between late 1962 and early the following year, Idris carried out a fundamental revision of the 1951 constitution, ending the federal basis of his regime and abolishing regional assemblies and governments. The meaning of his decision was clear: Idris was trying to centralize his power and restrain the Tripolitanians' ever-growing nationalist ferment. They were less closely connected than the Cyrenaicans to his person and family, had always longed for a hegemonous role in Libyan political life, and were more open to pan-Arab and Nasserist ideas. The 1963 constitutional reform, rather than solving the Sanusi monarchy's problems, merely gave it a breathing space. Moreover, it came after the murders of Buseiri Shelhi, the minister of palace affairs, and of General Mahmud Buqwaytin, commander-in-chief of the Libyan armed forces. These deaths deprived the king of two loyal collaborators and led him to make continual changes in the leadership and composition of the government, undermining its prestige and effectiveness. This was shown by the serious disorders and subsequent repression in January 1964. Idris' refusal to attend the summit of Arab heads of state in Cairo to solve inter-Arab differences was interpreted by nationalist and pan-Arab elements as coldness and hostility toward Nasserism and Arab solidarity. The disorders were suppressed, but all the same, from then on Libya was obliged to integrate its policy more with the Arab one and improve relations with Egypt. For the sake of these relations, Mustafa ben Halim, the Libyan prime minister, was obliged to visit Cairo twice in the same year. Any improvement in relations with Egypt was really in form only and merely slowed the Sanusi monarchy's fall, without stopping it. Bolstered by oil and the economic power it gave him, Idris might conceivably have achieved a *modus vivendi* with Nasser. But the situation was becoming more and more precarious as a result of clandestine activities by military and intellectual opposition groups and the influence in Libya of Egyptian radio broadcasts during those years. Under the daily radio barrage, nothing could prevent the Libyan masses, especially the young, from feeling themselves more and more part of the "Arab revolution" and looking on Nasser as the symbol of their redemption. In such an atmosphere, not even the resounding Egyptian defeat in the Six Day War of June 1967 helped Idris' position. On the contrary, the Israeli military success had the effect on many of increasing the intensity of nationalist passion and criticism against Idris' half-hearted support of the Arab cause and subjection to Anglo-American imperialism.

In view of this, the events of September 1–4, 1969, though for a moment they took everyone by surprise, should not really amaze us. They led to the fall of the monarchy and the seizure of power by the officers of the Revolutionary Command Council, and by Captain (soon self-promoted to Colonel) Muammar Qadhdhafi, the inspirer of the "revolution." The young officers had Nasser as their model. They had kept their plans secret, and some of them, such as Lieutenant-Colonel Saad-ed-Din Abu-Shureb, who had emigrated two years earlier under suspicion of subversive actitivites in association with Egyptians, were formerly military officers who had secretly returned to Libya for the occasion. The only cause for surprise can be the fact that Qadhdhafi and his supporters met hardly any resistance, even in Cyrenaica, where the Sanusi had a much older and surer power base (despite its weakening in recent years) than in Tripolitania. But even Cyrenaican compliance can be explained. First, the officers of the revolution waited until Idris was out of Libya to carry out their coup. Second, it is quite probable, though never absolutely proven, that another coup was expected a few days later. With Idris' consent, it was to eliminate the treacherous nephew and heir to the throne (and the declared enemy of the Shelhi family) the young prince Hassan Er-Rida. He was the son of Idris' late brother, and had been appointed successor only because there were no other heirs, due to the exclusion of the entire branch of the family which had been involved in the murder of Brahim Shelhi. Thus Qadhdhafi's coup was initially mistaken for the other one, and troops loyal to the king did not resist. The lack of resistance can also be attributed to the attitude of the heir to the throne; as soon as Prince Er-Rida was arrested by the soldiers, he hastened to renounce voluntarily all his constitutional powers and the post of viceroy which he was occupying during his uncle's absence from the country.

One needs to keep these events between 1952 and 1969 in mind in order to understand what was happening to the Jews in Libya during the Sanusi reign and the Libyan government's attitude toward them. Though initially moderate, the Sanusi regime subsequently became more and more restrictive and repressive, without reaching the extreme arrived at by Qadhdhafi's government. In order for us to understand the attitude of Idris and the group of Libyan leaders closest to him, one thing must be very clear. Despite the limits and motivations (both economic and in foreign policy) discussed above, the Idris position with regard to Libyan Jews was never rigidly hostile. Nor did this basic attitude change during the 1960s when, after the discovery of oil, the Libyan economy became less dependent on the contribution of Jewish business (according to the *Jewish Chronicle* of April 30, 1954, at that time the Jews controlled almost 90 percent of Libyan commerce) and the government was less tied to the Western powers. The sole real reasons for the increasingly restrictive and repressive Libyan government policy toward the Jews between 1952 and 1969 lie in (a) the radicalization of the Arab-Israel crisis which occurred during those years and its internal repercussions for all Arab countries; (b) the development of Libya's relations with the Arab League, Nasser's Egypt, and other Arab countries and the pressures which these countries could thus exercise on the Libyan government; (c) the parallel radical development (and also spread) of hostility toward Jews (as "foreigners," "rich people," and "Zionists") which the two previous factors gave rise to on the emotional and political levels among the masses and among the new Libyan elite.

In practice the various Libyan governments which succeeded each other to power during those years merely adapted their Jewish policy gradually to the "requirements" and "opportunities" dictated to them by external and internal circumstances. They were trying— and herein lies the great, bitter historical and moral lesson of the entire historical process—to play the card of their Jewish policy partly as a proof of their sincerity and identification with the Arab front and partly as a diversion and a means to meet popular and nationalist demands where they considered them least painful and damaging to their own power. In other words, the monarchy saw its Jewish policy as a handy sop for its critics and adversaries both abroad and at home. The best proof of this is in the dynamics of this policy.

The first year and a half after full independence went into effect was the best time for Jews living in Libya. They enjoyed normal conditions and looked forward to peace and prosperity. The Libyan government appeared willing to keep its promises and translate them promptly into the required legislation. About a hundred Jews were granted regular passports, valid for five years, in which the holders were defined, as specified under Article 8 of the constitution, as Libyan citizens.[2] No obstacles were raised to the departure of those who wanted to emigrate to Israel. The only difficulties involved certain belongings which the emigrants were not allowed to export. In almost all cases the objection was dropped when the emigrants bribed police officers in charge of control.[3]

In this situation the Libyan parliament's approval of a series of restrictions on the ownership of property by foreigners (which did not go into effect, since the king, concerned about possible economic repercussions for the country and diplomatic protests, refused to countersign them) and sporadic attacks against the Jews in some Arab newspapers⁴ did not worry the Jews. Most who had decided to stay in Libya thought that these incidents showed the Libyans' lack of experience in self-government or the traditional relationship between Arabs and Jews. They thus tended to underestimate them and to maintain that with time the situation would change and become completely normal. This would happen if the Jews for their part worked for normalization by encouraging a new type of intercommunity relations and especially personal relations with Arabs. They should not dramatize isolated episodes such as those mentioned and should behave, depending on their status, as either good citizens or good foreigners, dedicated to their work and devoid of any ambition or wish to participate or interfere in the political and administrative life of the new kingdom. In particular, the Jews should take care not to adopt any position regarding differences and jealousies between the various cabals and between Tripolitanians and Cyrenaicans, on which centered much of the country's political life.

This psychological attitude explains why already in this initial period—while the possibility still existed—most of the Jews who were not foreign citizens did not exercise their right to vote. They precisely wished to avoid taking any form of position in the struggle between cabals. This was true especially of Tripolitania. In Cyrenaica the situation was somewhat different since in this region differences between the cabals were less heated and the Jews were more integrated into the various groups. The psychological attitude also explains why the majority of Jews who had decided to stay in Libya took care to avoid giving any pretext for accusations of disloyalty toward the new regime. Thus most of them, and the Community authorities, tried to reduce to the minimum and keep strictly within the bounds of the "acceptable" their relations with Israel. They kept their distance from the few Zionists and pro-Zionists (mostly young people) who had remained behind. When the government's attitude toward Zionists began to change, they minimized and did not protest particular expressions of the change. A typical example is the Tripoli Community's refusal, in order to avoid accusations of sending money to Israel, to contribute ten million lire (one-third of the amount needed) asked of it to enable forty old and sick people without relatives or possibility of work to emigrate.⁵ Another is the passivity with which they received the decision of the government of Tripolitania to close the Maccabee Club, held guilty of "antipatriotic activities." It was the only pro-Zionist organization still active,

though, after the departure of Max Varadi in 1951, it had been reduced almost exclusively to sports and recreational activities.[6]
   This psychological attitude influenced not only political behavior. In various forms and to various extents, it influenced practically
all Libyan Jewish life, setting off a process within the community of
rapid shedding of many traditional forms of life and progressive at-
omization of its unitary fabric. In Tripoli, where the majority of Jews
were concentrated (out of a total of four thousand who had not left,
only three hundred lived in Benghazi and very few, generally pre-
cariously, in other smaller centers), the *hara* in a short time became
a Muslim quarter. The vast majority of its inhabitants had left for
Israel, and those who had decided to stay, as soon as they could manage it, moved into the European quarters of the New City. They did
this not only to live more comfortably, but also to break with their
past and integrate better into their "real" social context. An article
published in mid-August 1957 in *Israel* brings out the changes which
this attitude had brought about in only a few years:

Today the Jews of Libya are all concentrated in Tripoli, in the new part
of the city, and have completely European habits, facilitated by the relative comfort in which they find themselves. They all speak Italian in
addition to the Tripoli dialect, which is a local barbarization of Classical
Arabic. They lead private and family lives, enveloped in a somnolent
petty bourgeois atmosphere which sees no further than its own city.
   There are no group Jewish activities of any sort. They are explicitly
forbidden by the government, which a year or so ago on some pretext
ordered the closing of the Maccabee Club. The temperament of the
Jews of Tripoli also excludes the possibility, since from spiritual in-
dolence or personal interest they have quickly grown used to the habits
and requirements of the new Libyan kingdom: they live like others and
bit by bit are losing their own individuality, if it ever existed.
   What has been said might appear strange to anyone who passes on
Friday evening along Giaddit Istiklal, the main street where most of
the city's activity goes on, and sees the long, melancholy rows of shut-
ters lowered for the approaching Sabbath. The shops all belong to Jews:
perfume-sellers, dealers in fabrics, haberdashers, closing out of respect
for the religious tradition which was still very lively in the last generation. The half-darkness into which the streets are plunged due to all
those shuttered windows gives some idea of the economic contribution
which the Jews make for the country: but this is not surprising. Something which appears to reveal the still living Jewish consciousness is
no more than a gesture which falls into the country's conformist habits, benevolently tolerated by the Sanusi government: on Fridays the
Muslims close, on Saturdays the Jews, and on Sundays the Catholics—

thus the already slow life of the city never closes down altogether.

The young no longer pay even this tribute to religion: as employees in government offices or American companies, caught up in practical everyday life and general absenteeism, they are assimilating to the rest of the population, almost without noticing it.[7]

In this climate, the first restrictions were adopted by the Libyan government in early 1953 just as it was applying for and being granted Arab League membership. The restrictions—suspension of the postal service to Israel, closure of the Aliyah Offices, and expulsion of Meir Shilon, the Jewish Agency representative—did not give rise to much concern. Nor did the stopping, soon after, of emigration to Israel. It became clear that the Libyan government, rather than really stopping emigration, wanted to make a gesture "for the principle" and, though it prohibited direct departures for Israel, did not oppose departures "via Italy." In this second phase, what alarmed some people most was that the Libyan government, which until then had issued normal passports to anyone who applied, began (on the pretext that they had to await the completion of formalities relating to citizenship) to refuse passports and instead grant a temporary travel document valid for a single trip and bearing no indication of citizenship. For anyone who had to go abroad, this created considerable difficulties with the authorities of the other country. Moreover, it did not auger well for the future. The specific issue of passports became more serious in 1956–1957, when it became almost impossible to renew expired passports issued five years before. The juridical situation of Libyan Jews also worsened, since the question of passports showed the government's wish to stop considering as ipso facto Libyan citizens the Jews who did not have any other citizenship, and to subject them (as occurred under the law of April 17, 1954) to a naturalization process, which contradicted the government's commitments and was clearly discriminatory. Despite its seriousness, not even this act provoked any formal protest on the part of Libyan Jews. Only two initiatives were taken, since the Arab reaction to them dissuaded others from taking legal steps. They took the form of cases brought in court by individual Jews defending their right to be considered full Libyan citizens.[8] Only international Jewish organizations—the Alliance Israélite Universelle, American Jewish Committee, and World Jewish Congress—tried to denounce the situation, mainly through the diplomatic channels of the Western powers and some European and American newspapers.[9]

It is not easy to say to what extent this passivity on the part of those concerned and the scant echo outside Libya of these initial acts of discrimination affected the Libyan government and made it believe that it could turn the screws again. It may have thought that such acts would not give it many problems with the West, while it would be able to appear to the Arab League less moderate, less subject to the great powers, and could appease internal opposition groups and the most vehemently anti-Israel and pro-Nasser public opinion. What is certain is that these initial actions in the second half of the 1950s were followed by a series of others which grew more and more serious. The first one obliged those who wanted to emigrate to Israel to ask for authorization to emigrate "to Italy" purely and simply, and not "via Italy" as they had done for the last three or four years. This formula initially worried the Italian government a good deal, since it feared that the emigrants would settle in Italy. In order to solve the problem, a direct agreement between the Italian government and the Jewish Agency was necessary, by which the government agreed to accept all Jews coming from Tripoli "through Mr. Sion Nemni," who was responsible for *aliyah*.[10] The following year, on March 30, 1957, the Libyan government began enforcing the boycott against Israel, discussed since January 1953 and officially announced in January 1956,[11] but until then inoperative. A special law forbade "any individual or corporation to make personally or indirectly an agreement of any nature whatsoever with institutions or persons residing in Israel . . . or with persons representing them" or "to deal with national and foreign companies or institutions who have interests, subsidiary branches or general agencies in Israel" or to export goods to countries "where the [Relation Officers'] Conference is convinced that they re-export them to Israel." The same law also forbade registration of "immovable property dealings concluded with the aforesaid institutions or persons even if the registration concerns dealings previous to the enactment of this law. An exception, however, shall be made in the case of dealings confirmed before the 1 Jan., 1953."[12] On the heels of this law and completing its work, Jews living in Libya were prohibited in succeeding months through various provisions from maintaining direct or indirect relations with Israel or with Israeli entities, with a penalty of eight years in prison and fine of ten thousand lire. Another provision required anyone having powers of attorney relating to the property of those who had emigrated to Israel to inform the authorities. In addition the practice was introduced of requiring German suppliers to declare that none of their receipts would go for reparations which Germany owed to Israel. A special office was set up to confiscate from any merchant (Jew, Muslim, or foreigner) any goods bearing emblems even resembling the star of David. Finally, on De-

cember 31, 1958, a decree by the president of the executive council
of Tripolitania, referring to an Italian law of 1931, ordered for un-
specific "reasons of public order" that the council of the Community of Tripoli be dissolved and replaced by a Muslim special commission.[13] Despite commitments originally made to Marchino, the
Libyan government had not provided a new legal basis for the Community. According to the 1931 law, the commissioner could hold responsibility for no longer than a year, but powers were no longer to
revert to any council.

These provisions had serious psychological and practical consequences for Libyan Jews. Approaches by the international Jewish organizations to the British, French, and particularly the U.S. governments were to no avail.[14] For many Jews the boycott had serious
repercussions. It particularly affected medium-sized businesses.
One report from late 1957 spoke of a "disastrous" economic situation, and another from more or less the same time assessed the
number of poor Jews at about half the total Jews of Tripoli not possessing a foreign citizenship.[15] The boycott thus affected the already
far from flourishing overall economic situation of the Community
itself. Despite the departure to Israel of many of the poorest Jews, the
Community had been in dire straits for some years. Besides normal
expenses, it had to cover many extraordinary ones, such as the reconstruction of the cemetery and a new synagogue, since of the
thirty-five existing ones only two were not in the abandoned *hara*.
From year to year the Community found it harder to cover its deficit
through emergency voluntary donations, as the government became
more and more slow to grant authorization for collecting them. In
this situation the 1957 legislation caused the internal differences on
"political" issues (the attitude toward Zionism, toward the government, etc.) to burst out into the open. These differences had gradually alienated the most active and responsible elements in the Community (such as the *aliyah* representative, Sion Nemni, in 1955),
while provoking general discouragement, spreading absenteeism,
lack of interest in Community life, and increasing fear. The result,
since the members could not make the Community function normally, was a crisis in the Community Council and resignations. The
consequences were fortunately mitigated by the selflessness of a few
individuals who took over the task of carrying on what little Community life could function in such a situation. Effraim Barda, in particular, an Italian citizen, between 1960 and 1967 kept the meager
Community life going and dealt with the most urgent issues: the
school, the cemetery, and relations with the government and the
Community commissioner. A few Italians, bolstered by their posi-

tion as foreigners, managed the crucial institutions such as the CABI Olim. The Libyan government requisitioned the most important Jewish school and in April 1960 also closed the school of the Alliance Israélite Universelle, despite the protests of UNESCO. The Italian consulate helped by opening another school and meeting all the expenses, including the support and salaries of the Hebrew teachers.

A gradual improvement in the situation did not begin to come about until 1962. But it was shadowed with much uncertainty and concern about the future, so that by the end of 1963 it was thought that one-fifth of Libyan Jews, if they could do so without undue losses, probably wanted to emigrate.[16] Several circumstances combined to give rise to this wish. The most important were as follows:

(1) After the provisions of 1956–1958, contrary to what many feared, the Libyan government passed only one more measure specifically directed against Jews: on March 21, 1961, a special law stipulated that "all goods and property in Libya belonging to organizations or persons resident in Israel or connected to them by citizenship or professional affiliation" were to be "sequestered" by the government. The measure was certainly a serious one; its psychological effect was largely dispelled, however, since many people had been expecting it since 1956, and especially since it affected those who had left for Israel rather than most Jews who had remained behind. Besides this law, several other measures affecting the Jews were adopted in 1960 and 1961. Non-Libyans, whether physical or juridical persons, were prohibited from buying real property (May 24, 1960); commercial franchise-holders were prohibited from holding more than ten franchises each (affecting about four hundred Jews); in solidarity with the Algerians, the boycott was extended to France. These measures, though harmful, hurt not only Jews but also in some cases all foreigners or everyone living and working in Libya. They reflected a logic which was certainly censurable and worrying, due to the nationalism on which it was based, but had nothing to do with anti-Semitism. They thus provoked less reaction than the measures taken in previous years had among the Libyan Jews. Moreover, they came at a time when, due to the discovery of oil, the country's economic situation and even more so its prospects for the future—despite a thousand other negative indicators—were looking bright. At the same time, the prospects of the Libyan Jewish community, which normally was especially active and able to take advantage better than any other group of new situations and conditions, were also improving. Over less than six years, the Jewish community's economic situation went from the "disastrous" condition of 1957 to one in which half of its members might be described as "well off"; there

were cases of Jews being "very wealthy," and, of even more significance, there were no more than forty families on Community assistance.[17]

(2) The running of the Community of Tripoli by a commissioner turned out in practice to be much less disastrous than the Jews had feared. There was broad-ranging collaboration between the special commissioner and the Jewish leaders, three of whom made up a commission to support the commissioner. Their joint efforts enabled the Community to function fairly well, even receiving donations from the Arabs for poor Jews. Everyday relations between Jews and Arabs on the whole did not deteriorate at the time and stabilized at an acceptable level. The Jews were still the victims of the traditional scorn and petty intolerance of the Muslim populace (expressed in the usual baiting and hotheadedness of the youth, often using a Jewish funeral as a pretext). Hostility to Jews showed no sign of lessening among the new Arab elite. The newspapers which it inspired were conducting systematic intimidation against the Jews, trying to isolate them and frustrate important Jewish commercial enterprises. This hostility was growing at the same pace as Nasserism and spreading to other levels, particularly the traditional Arab elite where personal and business relations with Jews had been improving.

(3) Taking advantage of the new situation brought about by the discovery of oil and Idris' new need to develop good relations with the West and get help to exploit the discoveries, in the early 1960s the international Jewish organizations began to exert more intense and systematic indirect pressure on the Libyan government to turn it toward a more lenient attitude, conforming with the promises it had made prior to independence. These efforts generally took place on two levels. First, the organizations denounced in the international press the slights, discrimination, and attacks[18] to which Jews were subject in Libya, to the point that the Libyan authorities were obliged to defend themselves and try to refute the accusations being leveled against them.[19] Second, the organizations asked Western governments and the United Nations to approach the Libyan government. The American Jewish Committee, whose president, Louis Caplan, made a personal brief visit to Tripoli in the summer of 1961, was particularly active in this respect. The AJC denounced the system of discrimination under which the Libyan Jews lived and demanded respect for the agreements made with the United Nations and embodied in the constitution. Moreover, on the basis of information from Libyan Jewish and Arab sources and the Comité des

Egyptiens Libres in London, it repeatedly pointed out that since late 1960 former Nazis had been entering Libya from Egypt and had, it alleged, been put in charge of the Libyan government's Jewish policy.[20]

(4) In view of this situation, the leaders of Libyan Jewry in 1961 decided that the time had finally come to approach Idris directly. Some of them still had faith in him and feared what might happen when he died, believing that, despite appearances, he was a moderate and not personally hostile.[21] They met in March in Tripoli and founded a committee of five members (Lillo Arbib, Hai Glam, Clemente Habib, Angelo Nahum, and Pinhas R. Naim) to represent the Jewish Community of Tripoli before the government. The committee prepared a petition which it presented on June 1 to Prime Minister Sayed Mohammed Otman El Sed. It requested (a) recognition of Libyan citizenship for all Jews born or residing in Libya and having no other nationality; (b) the right for Jews to administer directly their own religious and charitable institutions; (c) reconstitution of the rabbinical court; and (d) authorization to bring from overseas a chief rabbi and the teachers and textbooks needed for the Jewish schools.[22]

This initiative seems to have had no results for several months. The Libyan government did not react to it in any way, and gave the impression that it was letting the petition drop without even a reply. Then, thanks to the discreet but determined indirect efforts of the international Jewish organizations, a few new facts began to raise the hope that there would be a positive result. The organizations persuaded Adrian Pelt, the former U.N. commissioner, who had been invited to Libya to attend the tenth independence anniversary festivities, to make some cautious inquiries of the Libyan authorities.[23] The issuing of passports was somewhat liberalized, particularly for people traveling for business or not accompanied by their families. Confronted with applications for whole families, the usual attitude of the officials in charge was to issue only one or two passports, so that a "hostage" would remain in Libya and make it less likely that the other members of the family would not return, or to ask for some money as a deposit. Also, Libyan Jews living in Tunisia would be issued a document declaring that the bearer was not a Libyan citizen, thus enabling the person concerned to register as a stateless person.[24] At the same time, the Libyan authorities began to pressure prominent Jewish figures to formally deny in the United Nations the accusations of anti-Semitism being made against Libya, implying that, in return, the authorities would grant some of the Jews' wishes. With some heart-searching, the Jews decided not to take up these offers. The most political Jewish leaders realized that accepting the offer would have led to the Jewish organizations' becoming indifferent to Libyan Jewry, and thus to their losing the only real help on which they could count.[25] A firm stand toward the Libyan government might eventually persuade it to barter the concessions for the Jewish leaders' denial, in order to shake off the doubts and hostility of the Western world and thus avoid obstacles to the assistance and investment which were essential to the government. The best proof of the accuracy of this reasoning lies in what happened between June and August 1962. In June, precisely a year after the Jewish leaders had submitted their petition, a group of them were received in Beida, Cyrenaica, by the Libyan prime minister. He assured them that the requests they had made the year before would soon be examined and given "benevolent" consideration. Indeed, on August 8, after the cabinet had officially considered the requests, it issued a communiqué which, though silent on the other demands, did recognize that, in accordance with Article 8 of the constitution, Libyan Jews not possessing any other nationality were deemed to be Libyan, and municipalities were authorized to issue the appropriate certificates. At the same time, with the obvious intention of making the decision less distasteful to extreme nationalists and the hard-line Arab governments, a royal decree was issued stipulating that anyone who had had "relations with Zionism at any time" (even by visiting Israel after the declaration of Libyan independence) or had "at any time worked on behalf of either the moral or material strengthening of Israel" was liable to have his Libyan citizenship revoked.[26] Just over a month later, on September 15, a government communiqué stated that the measure adopted the year before regarding the "sequestering" of possessions of persons and organizations which had moved to Israel was now being put into effect.

The August 8, 1962, communiqué provided a formal arrangement for their juridical status which most Jews in Libya found quite satisfactory, despite the fact that they soon learned that the government's decisions existed only on paper. This arrangement lasted until June 1967. Obviously, the satisfaction can be understood only in terms of Libyan realities.[27] In a non-Muslim, noncommunist European or American country, the situation would have been completely unacceptable. Even discounting the attitude of the Muslim populace and the new Libyan elite toward the Jews and the measures which the government had taken in previous years against the Jews or all foreigners, after August 8, 1962, the Jews did not find any change in some conditions. Getting passports (especially for those who could not give "valid" reasons or wanted them for whole families) became less difficult, but certainly not easy. Similarly, nothing changed in practice regarding the real possibility of Jews occupying official positions. The same can be said for a series of issues affecting business. Difficulties in exporting money legally increased the risks for those who tried to do it illegally. The obstacles which for years had been hampering the free development of many activities persisted. Almost all Jews who were doing business on a fairly large scale, owned considerable real estate, or were involved in the oil industry continued the practice of having an Arab associate, which they had adopted in previous years to circumvent some of these obstacles. Despite all this, and despite the fact that many, as in the past, still felt "hemmed in and watched"[28] and worried about the future, especially the post-Idris era, on the whole the five years following the government communiqué of August 8, 1962, were a period of relative calm for Jews living in Libya. There were continual rumors (often echoed abroad) that further restrictive measures were imminent and even that the situation would be overturned, explaining the tendency to abstain from any form of Libyan political life. However, these five years allowed the majority of Jews to devote themselves more securely to their businesses. They developed (especially in some sectors of the oil industry) and achieved an important position, even though it may have been secondary within the economy of Libya, particularly Tripolitania. The secure climate lasted until the last few months before the ultimate crisis of June 1967, until a communiqué—whose legal and political terms were never fully clarified—to lawyers and legal offices made it particularly impossible for Jews to sell real property. Some saw this measure as just another turn of the screw, others as a way of preventing the wealthiest and most enterprising Jews from departing.

The relative calm and prosperity were confirmed between 1962 and 1967 by formal acts on the part of official government spokesmen. These statements did not commit the government at all, but were no less meaningful and encouraging for those to whom they were directed. This atmosphere explains why the dramatic events of June 1967 took the Jews by surprise. That month marked the decisive turning point in the Libyan situation toward the crisis in the Sanusi monarchy two years later and practically the end of the Jewish presence in Libya. Even the most pessimistic (or one might say realistic) of the Jews—those aware of the dark cloud gathering above their heads as the Arab-Israeli conflict worsened, Nasserist tendencies in the Arab world grew stronger, and Idris' power weakened —were caught by surprise. The balancing act which Idris was performing to survive and ensure a place for himself between the more

radical Arab states and the Western powers and between Nasserists
and moderates came to occupy center stage in Libya. The period was
also characterized by a constant anti-Zionist and anti-Jewish—often
openly anti-Semitic—campaign waged by extremist newspapers
(*Ar-Raid* and *At-Taliya* in Tripoli, *Al-Hakika* in Benghazi) and even
some pro-government papers. The PLO opened many offices serving
mainly as centers of anti-Jewish propaganda, while from Egypt and
Syria came a continuous flow of anti-Jewish broadcasting and pamph-
lets, such as *The Jews in the Koran*, which even quoted passages of
Hitler's *Mein Kampf* with approval. These facts aroused concern
and indignation; largely underestimated, they were considered the
price that Idris had to pay his critics and adversaries, letting them
give vent to their extremism and activism while still "behaving" and
staying within his control.

The cause and pretext of the June 1967 events in Libya was the
outbreak of the Arab-Israeli crisis in another open conflict of arms,
the Six Day War. The first signs of it in Libya appeared on Friday,
June 2, when the mullahs began to proclaim a holy war and gave sermons to this effect on the radio. Almost at the same time, a week of
propaganda for the Palestinian cause was proclaimed for June 5–12.
Under pressure from Nasserist groups, the government had to join
in; it declared in the name of Idris that Libya was "in a position of
defensive war" and was ready to help in the liberation of Palestine.
After the government had taken this position, the Italian, Greek,
and Maltese minorities expressed their support for the Palestine
week. Even the Jews, in a vain attempt to avert the danger hanging
over them, sent Idris a telegram of solidarity, emphasizing their neutral position and loyalty to the king. Thus, as the atmosphere grew
more and more tense, the morning of June 5 arrived, and news came
of the Israeli army's opening of hostilities. Demonstrations, riots,
and violence immediately began.[29] Mobs of Arabs stirred up by extremists began running through the streets of Tripoli shouting anti-
Israeli, anti-Jewish, and anti-imperialist slogans, hunting down Jews
and attacking their shops and homes. Some of the main city streets,
where Jewish and Italian shops were more numerous, were almost
completely plundered and set on fire. The police, taken by surprise,
could do little. Jews still living in the *hara* were evacuated and, together with other Jews gradually arriving from the New City, taken
to police stations, barracks, and thence to the Gurgi camp on the
outskirts. Only the proclamation of a state of emergency and curfew
prevented the situation from escaping entirely from the authorities'
control (significantly, the minister of the interior was replaced by a

special ministerial committee) and finally, without stopping the rioting and violence, managed to restrain them. They continued, sporadi-
cally, until June 9, and were aimed generally at Jews and foreigners,
particularly civilian or military Americans. The military authorities
of the Wheelus Air Base were obliged first to evacuate their own citizens to the base itself and then to airlift them to Europe. Individual
acts of violence were still occurring on June 12. In 1945 and 1948, it
will be remembered, the British and Muslim religious authorities,
once the height of the violence was over, tried to calm people down
and encouraged the formation of joint reconciliation committees.
Following that example, on June 8 Lillo Arbib approached the mufti,
Sheikh Abd-er-Rahman el Galhud, and asked for his help in convening a meeting between representatives of the communities and in re-
establishing security and calm in the city. His request received no
reply; nevertheless, the following day the tone of the preachers in
the mosques became less violent.

Giorgio Fattori, the first Italian correspondent to reach Libya
after the events of June 5–9, reconstructed them as follows. His accounts clearly indicate their basic character, certainly anti-Jewish
and anti-Western, but in essence anti-Idris:

> This time all of Tripoli seems to have caught fire; even though the vic-
> tims of the manhunt were once again the Jews, it was more than racist
> fury. It was an attempt at revolution which the government has had dif-
> ficulty in quelling with fifteen thousand police and several thousand
> soldiers . . . It all began during the morning of June 5, a Monday. Sun-
> day had been a day like any other. A successful party had been held at
> Georgimpopoli in honor of the winners of a bridge tournament and
> there had been much festive coming and going from the beaches. At
> nine o'clock on Monday morning Radio Libya announced that Egypt
> and Israel were at war and suggested that people stay at home. But tens
> of thousands of transistors had been tuned in to Radio Cairo for days. It
> was now inciting Libyans to revolt, murder the Jews, throw the Ameri-
> cans out of Wheelus Base and out of Tripoli. The first groups of demon-
> strators flocked to the center at about ten o'clock. According to many
> witnesses, the orders were being given by Egyptians and Syrians work-
> ing here. It all looked organized. Some youths ran through the city
> streets marking the doors of Jewish houses with white chalk . . . The
> shops began burning. In the Old City and the center, at Shara 24 Di-
> cembre and Shara Istiqal, the most important streets in Tripoli, Italian
> and Libyan shops, but particularly those of Jews, were burned. There
> were fires everywhere. The demonstrators shouted for Nasser and
> some were seen spitting on portraits of Idris, the king of Libya. Three
> Jews were stabbed to death under the terrified eyes of foreigners.

The police reacted in the afternoon, when the city was already in chaos and terror. They began to evacuate Jews from the Old City and bring them to the Gargaresh barracks near Tripoli. Their efforts seemed hesitant at first. "My shop was being sacked and plundered for a whole day," an Italian told me, "before the police raised a finger." On Tuesday Radio Cairo excitedly announced that American aircraft were on their way from the Tripoli base to bomb Egypt. A furious crowd on the promenade attacked the house of a Jewish family. An American truck which happened to be passing was stopped and destroyed. The two soldiers were wounded and barely escaped lynching.

The curfew and intervention of soldiers in force gradually reduced the impact of the revolt. Jews who had not been taken to the barracks barricaded themselves in their homes, sought refuge in the homes of friends, and were also helped, it is true, by Libyan families. Two girls were taken out under a blanket in the back seat of a car. A woman who had just had a caesarian operation was practically stolen away from the hospital and taken to safety. But every so often someone was caught and quickly had his throat slit. On Wednesday, June 7, some shops were still burning. In the afternoon an American helicopter flew back and forth over Georgimpopoli at a very low altitude. That was the signal; the Americans living in the quarter left it en masse and took refuge in the military base. Six thousand women, children, and non-essential servicemen were transported to Rome, Wiesbaden, and Spain.

Many Europeans, and even some Americans, had in the meantime sought refuge in the hotels in the center, which were protected by police cordons. The final exodus from Georgimpopoli took place on Thursday, when rumors came that the people of Zawia, the town which has sent a record percentage of Libyan volunteers for Nasser's army, were planning a march on Tripoli. "I was going by car to Zawia to see what had happened at my building site," an Italian engineer told me, "when I was stopped by a line of police and made to turn back. Down the road I could see a cloud of dust and I thought there had been an accident. Instead it was the people of Zawia, armed with sticks and knives, marching toward Tripoli." The encounter between the soldiers and the Zawia extremists caused eight deaths, but the attack was repulsed. That was the turning point in the revolt. Panicking Europeans besieged the airplanes. In one week, besides the Americans, seven thousand people left. An emergency Alitalia airlift was begun to repatriate Italians since the police were now in control of the situation. The amount of destruction and burning began to be reckoned up . . .

More than a hundred Jewish shops have been destroyed.

On Friday there were no more demonstrations, but Jews were still being killed. Besieged in their homes, every so often someone would try to reach a more secure hiding place or get some food. Tragedy struck mainly the poor Jews, those who have neither means nor outside support. A girl tried to get to the market wrapped in a barracan with her face covered like an Arab woman. She was recognized and killed on the spot. On Saturday afternoon an old Maltese, Sammud, was mistaken for a Jew and stabbed eight times. Last Sunday I went to the place where the two American soldiers had been wounded. There were only soldiers and police to be seen in the city, and everything appeared to be under strict military control; but at the same time in a street in the center a Jew was being knifed.

How many have they killed? No one knows exactly, the figures disagree; perhaps seventeen, perhaps many more. Six thousand Jews live in Tripoli. Over a thousand are safe, for the time being at least, in the Gargaresh barracks, and hundreds with foreign passports (including all the Italians) are being protected by their embassies. Three or four thousand remain and are hiding in the city. The police prevent their houses from being attacked but do nothing to help them. They have been barricaded in for thirteen days. There are children, and many are old and alone. If they go out to look for bread or medicine, they risk being killed.

Tripoli is regaining its calm . . . The curfew has been changed to eight-thirty in the evening, traffic is starting up again, but many windows in the city stay closed. Behind them are the *hudi*, the Jews: cut off from everyone, they wait for they know not what.[30]

The Libyan government, like the Tripoli and Benghazi newspapers, tried to minimize the seriousness of the riots. According to the government there were a total of four deaths in Tripoli—two Arabs (a man and a woman), one Christian, and one Maltese. Other sources, both Jewish and Western, put Jewish victims alone at fifteen dead and thirty wounded. The number of victims in fact was probably higher. On June 7 two whole families (those of Shalom Luzon and Emilia Baranes Habib), thirteen persons in all, were taken away from Tripoli by a Libyan official (subsequently sentenced by the Sanusi authorities, then absolved by the revolutionary government) on the pretext of leading them to safety in a camp where Jews were being assembled. He slaughtered them somewhere outside the city. The same sources related that between one and three Jews died in Benghazi, but this is less certain. On June 5 there were also demonstrations and riots there against Jews and the British, though they were less serious than in Tripoli. Many shops and stores were set on fire. After some initial hesitation, the police took the situation in hand, and the riots ended much sooner than in Tripoli.[31] In Benghazi, as in Tripoli, to save the Jews from further violence and to prevent the unpredictable consequences that another outbreak of xenophobia might have for the monarchy, the Libyan authorities put all the Jews of Benghazi in a camp near the city. On June 20, 1967, over a week after the last attacks, Cesare Pasquinelli, the Italian ambassador to Libya, who was one of the people most active during and after the riots in saving Libyan Jews (as he had previously done in 1942–1943 for French Jews), wrote to his brother in Italy as follows:

> The government has the best of intentions, but it was overwhelmed from the first day by a Nasserist rabble. Now the police have taken the situation firmly in hand, but unfortunately public opinion is entirely with Nasser, and even more so after the defeat [in the Six Day War] than before. Israel has done marvelously, but here it is the Jews (a few thousand of them) who have to pay for it by being hunted down by the mob if they leave their homes. The police has had to keep many of them in barracks to protect them; the others are in hiding. It is incredible that we must still see this after the Nazi infamy . . . I am spending my time in discussions with the Libyan ministers to get their help. Up to now, the ministers have been well disposed.

These few lines summarize the critical situation of Libyan Jews after the riots and violence: the threat that still hung over them, and caused most of them to stay indoors for many days, in hiding, or in the Gurgi camp,[32] and the terror which they still felt. Though the Libyan government had good intentions, it was unable to restore security or even enable funerals to be held for the victims. It is not surprising, then, that for the vast majority of Jews the only possible solution seemed to be to leave Libya and seek refuge in a safe country. As soon as they could do so, about fifty people left for Tunisia, but for the majority the goal was Europe, and specifically Italy. This was due to Italy's proximity, the close relations which the Jews had had with it, and the readiness and selflessness with which the Italian diplomats set to work to make the exodus possible. All other problems became for the moment secondary, from the problem of business interests and assets being left behind in Libya to the more general one of what would happen afterward. Going back to Libya, emigrating to Israel, staying in Italy or some other Western country, and how to make a living: all that was put off for the future; for the time being, what counted was finding safety and escaping from further pogroms, which were quite probable.

The first official step was taken by Lillo Arbib on June 17. He sent a message to Prime Minister Hussein Mazegh asking him "to allow Jews so desiring to leave the country for a time, until tempers cool and the Libyan population understands the position of Libyan Jews, who have always been and will continue to be loyal to the State, in full harmony and peaceful coexistence with the Arab citizens at all times." The government quickly agreed: the emigration office started work on June 20 preparing the documents necessary for departure. Once again, this is not surprising. In view of the situation in Libya at the time, the solution was the best one for Idris. It would prevent a repetition of the violence which had discredited him in the eyes of Westerners; at the same time, by eliminating the main object of popular hatred it made further riots less likely, assuaged the most unruly, and, above all, deprived his internal and external foes of a powerful weapon against him and his throne. Nor should the fact be underestimated that, in view of the urgency of arranging the departures, more than one aspect of the departures was either resolved to the advantage of the Libyan government or was left vague, also to the government's advantage. The government found itself in the fortunate position of being able to choose at a later time the solution most opportune to it, when the domestic and international situation would have cleared and it could make the most of what had happened in the meantime. An example of the first sort was the measure authorizing those leaving to take with them only twenty pounds sterling a head, instead of the three hundred normally allowed. This was justified on the basis that otherwise the burden on the Libyan economy would be too heavy, and that the Tripoli head office of the Banco di Roma, the only bank authorized to exchange Libyan pounds, did not have enough foreign currency. The most serious case of the second sort was that the government left vague perhaps the most important aspect of the entire operation: whether the move overseas was to be considered temporary or permanent; in other words, whether those leaving would be able to come back and reclaim their rights as citizens or foreign residents without any difficulty or whether the departure in some way altered their juridical status in Libya.

The exodus took a little more than a month. By September there were just over 100 Jews left in Libya, all of whom were in Tripoli except 2 in Benghazi. The vast majority—just over 4,100—went to Italy. From the Gurgi camp, other assembly points, and their homes (where until then they had remained practically imprisoned) the Jews of Tripoli, together with the Jews of Benghazi who had been brought to Tripoli, went to the port and the airport, many of them escorted by the police to protect them from possible attack. Thence, with only their personal luggage, they boarded ships and aircraft provided, thanks to the Italian government and embassy which did all they could to help, by the Società di Navigazione Tirrenia [Tirrenia Navigation Company] and Alitalia, and set off for Naples and Rome.

The task of receiving the Libyan Jews and helping them in Italy was taken on by the American Joint Distribution Committee. They were received not as temporary exiles, as they would have wished, but as refugees under the aegis of the United Nations High Commissioner for Refugees. With the help of the United HIAS [Hebrew Immigrant Aid Society] Service, the AJDC assumed a large part of the expenses of the operation and all aspects of relations with international organizations. The Union of Italian Jewish Communities took care of relations with the Italian authorities. The Jewish Aid Committee (Deputazione Israelitica di Assistenza—DIA) of the Community of Rome took care of the refugees in the capital, while the AJDC itself cared for the rest. The refugees themselves appointed their own emergency committee (Raffaello Fellah, Lillo Arbib, Vittorio Halfon) which took on all responsibilities for representing the Libyan Jews in dealings with other organizations.

Some of the refugees—230 families in all, about 1,200 people—largely Italian citizens, thus those with a good chance of setting themselves up on their own, the better-off and those possessing funds and interests in Italy or other countries, made their own arrangements as soon as they arrived without even getting in touch with the Jewish aid organizations. According to information available,[33] 162 families established themselves, initially at least, in Rome, 53 in Milan, 8 in Leghorn, 4 in Florence, 4 in Latina, and 1 in Genoa. Another 200 families, consisting of 988 people, mostly Libyan citizens, were temporarily housed in three camps provided by the Italian government at Latina, Capua, and near Naples. It was this group which subsequently provided the main contingent of the more than 1,000 who left Italy for other countries, especially Israel. Finally, a third group—amounting to 1,887 people, comprising 365 families, 8 from Benghazi and the rest from Tripoli—went to Rome. One-sixth of these families said that they had no need of assistance, while responsibility for the rest was assumed by the DIA, which gave them money and helped them to get settled and find work and schools for their children. Among these, after a year 105 families (578 people) had left for Israel, 7 for the United States, and 7 had returned to Libya. The general intentions and aims of only a few of those remaining are known: in September 1968 about 100 families were about to leave for Israel and 9 for the United States; 20 had decided to stay in Italy, 30 were undecided between Italy and Israel, and 11 had not yet made any decision, but appeared to be leaning toward staying in Italy. At around this date the emergency committee was disbanded and the Community of Rome set up an aid commission, to integrate Libyan Jews into the Community and solve related religious and aid problems.

Among these three groups into which the mass of refugees to

Italy were divided, we only have precise information—due to the DIA reports—on the third, the group which went to Rome. Though the information is incomplete, these reports provide elements enabling us to form a clearer idea of the Libyan Jews as a group. The least complete data relate to the juridical status of the Jews. It is known only in the case of 169 families: 122 possessed Temporary Travel Documents, 18 had Libyan passports, 10 had Italian passports, 9 Tunisian, 7 British, 2 French, and 1 Moroccan. Sociocultural information is more abundant. According to a DIA report:

> Among the 1,887 people interviewed by the Rome Committee (DIA), only three (one aged fifty and two in their eighties) had a university law degree and only one of these had ever practiced; three people practiced as lawyers without having a degree, but openly and legally, since they had been authorized to do so by the Libyan government when the state acquired independence from Italy.
>
> The generation born between 1930 and 1940 has largely attended intermediate schools. Some of the younger members have diplomas in drafting or accounting, but it has not been possible to indicate a significant number of people practicing these professions. Among the older generation, basic or retrogressive illiteracy is widespread.
>
> One may speculate that the minimal attendance at secondary schools (beyond the elementary level) is due in part to compulsory attendance (enforced between 1938 and 1944) on the Sabbath, which went against a strong commitment to religious observance. More generally, the lack of interest in culture in a scholastic sense or as a means of acquiring knowledge is a Libyan trait affecting the Jews despite their study of Hebrew and attachment to tradition, which, however, they practice in a magical and superstitious way.
>
> Families consist of an average of 5–6 people, and the birthrate is high. This puts a burden on the parents, even though the patriarchal concept and organization of the family allows for division of responsibilities.
>
> The women study little, do not work, marry young, and are responsible only for domestic matters. Within the family the woman's opinion prevails and often is of a decisive nature which belies her very feminine or modest appearance; it is she who determines what course the family follows.
>
> The men are materially responsible toward their families but play little part in their children's education: their prestige within and outside the family is in proportion to their productive capabilities.
>
> In less progressive families the woman obviously depends on the man, who takes all decisions on his own and provides for needs to the extent he can or wishes to; in more progressive families the woman has more intellectual independence but shares little in material responsibilities.
>
> Libya does not have a regular army and is only now preparing the

laws to establish one; so no citizen has done military service . . . In practice no one has ever done military service because a Jew holding the passport of another nationality did not go to his country in order to do service or, in the case of British citizens, did not have the obligation.

The information provided by the WZO Executive shows that the group is characterized by much ill health: there are cases of diabetes, hypertension, heart disease, obesity, gout, gynecological problems due to numerous pregnancies too close together, glaucoma, the consequences of trachoma, and in children cases of anemia and malnutrition.

Some psychosomatic problems evident on arrival have now subsided: cases of anxiety, headache, and insomnia.

The most prevalent activity in the group, one can say the only one, is commerce. This was the best way to make a living in Libya, especially during the last ten years, after the oil boom and consequent presence of the American oil industry, "the American base."

Commerce was practiced on every scale and showed some typical characteristics of colonial countries: each shopkeeper would sell many, even dissimilar lines, with domestic appliances and American-style furniture predominating. Land speculation was very widespread, both building lots and sites for drilling for petroleum and other hydrocarbons.

The Jewish colony lived in considerable comfort and even the more modest Jews, those from the Old City, who were most integrated into the country, lived quite independently.

Reaction to the dramatic event which has changed the course of their lives has been extremely measured and dignified. Those who decided to stay in Italy and later return to Tripoli or Benghazi to retrieve some of their assets have not asked for any more aid. They have taken and adapted to any kind of work, though finding it has not been easy, for several reasons:

(1) There was little work available in the Italian market.

(2) They did not have work permits because they were foreigners or stateless persons.

(3) They lacked professional qualifications.

Though they were used to independent work with high economic incentives, they have accepted what has happened to them, are full of confidence in their own resources, and are determined to rebuild the affluence they have lost. The confidence and optimism characterizing the group seem to originate in the Libyan Jews' ability to commit themselves to work and the absence of a tradition of assistance or at least of overprotection . . .

During the school year 1967–1968:

—7 children went to kindergarten;

—104 children attended elementary schools;

—58 children attended intermediate schools;

—13 young people attended accounting schools;

—2 young people attended draftsmanship schools;

—28 young people attended ORT* vocational training courses;
—5 young people attended *liceo* [secondary school preparing for university];
—3 young people attended the university, and 1 graduated in chemical engineering.

Though almost everyone attended and learned little from elementary and intermediate Jewish schools, the number of failures is quite low. The administrators took into account the Libyans' change in school and educational system, the fact that children coming from the camps were changing for the second time, and especially their probable emigration. In other schools many pupils at all levels had to take their examinations again in October. From information provided by the parents, though, it appears that school grades were generally not outstanding; as we have already observed, this probably derives from not being used to the environment.

It emerges from the same report that when they arrived in Italy most of the refugees in the Rome group did not know what the future might hold. There was a widespread belief that a permanent return to Libya had to be excluded and the most probable solution would be emigration to Israel.

However, some people in the group expected that the Arabs would think again in view of an exodus which deprived them completely and suddenly of the economic operators holding most of the investment and representing the focus due to their knowledge, experience, and initiative, of the country's future economic growth.

The problem facing most of them was how to recuperate their holdings in Libya, especially since the initial approaches by the emergency committee on this subject to the Libyan government and the Libyan embassy in Rome did not lead to any positive result.[34] After a petition had been sent to Idris at the end of August,[35] the situation began to open up in October, probably due to a press campaign in Italy and in the British and American Jewish press. The embassy began to renew Temporary Travel Documents, and the Libyan government authorized the export of £300 for each family of one person, £600 for families of two or more persons, and £750 (in three allowances) for each child of school age. These measures led a very few to return permanently to Libya and a considerable number to

*A Jewish organization for training in crafts and technical skills, founded in Russia in 1880. The Russian name has been given the English equivalent of Organization for Rehabilitation through Training. See *Encyclopedia Judaica* 12:1482–1483.—*Trans.*

return temporarily to put their affairs in order, liquidate and take to Italy as much as they could. It emerges from the information available that, by August 1968, members of 127 Libyan Jewish families undertook 267 trips to Tripoli and 2 to Benghazi and that, of the 169 families for which data are available, 130 succeeded in recuperating (by going personally to Libya or entrusting others with the task and giving them a percentage) some or all of their property (103 of these even got back their household goods and cars) and 4 their household effects alone, while 103 * did not manage to get back everything. By that time 163 of these families were living off their own resources, and had no more need of aid from Jewish organizations.[36] Obviously, though this information is significant, it gives only an indication. It covers a limited sample of refugees and, since it relates to those receiving DIA assistance, covers largely families which had generally left property and capital in Libya which were quite modest and thus more easily recuperable. In economic terms the major problem of recovery did not involve these families so much as those which had left major interests and conspicuous fortunes in Libya, which were often more difficult to liquidate in a short time. Recuperation by the wealthy continued in various forms and using various expedients (with the self-interested help of the big Arab merchants who wanted to take over the Jews' assets and clientele) up to the military coup in September 1969.[37] In view of the excellent conditions which existed for recuperating small assets, their owners were well satisfied. Shops and apartments sold easily, since they were much in demand (especially shops, which the Libyans considered "gold mines" if they could be managed by Italians). The story was very different for Jews with much property and wealth in Libya. Shops formed a minor part of their assets. One can say with certainty that when the Sanusi monarchy fell, though by then there were few Jews left in Libya, their assets and interests were still considerable. This applies both to those who were still living there and had decided to stay, and to those who were "commuting"—in other words, those who had really left, but would return to Tripoli every so often for a while to take care of their businesses and liquidate gradually. According to the Jews of Libya Association [Associazione Ebrei di Libia], Jewish assets in Libya in 1969 amounted to $350–400 million. The assets were actually larger than they appeared, since some of them were no longer under Jewish names, but were listed under the names of Arab individuals or companies which lent their names or had formally taken them over.

*This should perhaps read 35.—*Trans.*

This already precarious situation finally collapsed as a result of the military coup d'état in September 1969.[38]

When it took over power, the Revolutionary Command Council, headed by Colonel Abu-Shureb, solemnly announced that it would respect international treaties adhered to by the monarchy and confirmed the new Libya's support for the Human Rights Charter. Just over a month later, Abu-Shureb was replaced as president of the Revolutionary Command Council by Qadhdhafi. On October 16, the latter proclaimed the five points on which the new regime was to be based: "The expulsion from Libyan territory of any foreign presence; absolute positive neutrality; an enemy to enemies, a friend to friends; national unity as a step toward Arab unity; the permanent elimination of political parties."

What this meant in practice for the just over two hundred Jews remaining in Libya quickly became clear:

> The men were rounded up and taken to police stations, where they were threatened at gunpoint and subjected to all kinds of maltreatment; current accounts were blocked without any arrangement or justification; people were summoned for questioning by officials. These sessions would end with an endless and laborious tour around the entire city until they had to rush home at impossible hours, when the curfew had already begun, with all the dangers associated with breaking it. Giulio Hassan, the son of the wealthiest Jew, was sent to prison.[39]

In this atmosphere, on October 31 *Ar-Raid*, which had become the official organ of the new regime, took up arms by declaring itself the interpreter of public opinion. It began a vast press campaign against the Jews, in which other Libyan newspapers soon joined. Its campaign had two main points, each of which was soon destined to become reality. The first was a request for the immediate confiscation and "restitution to the people" of the assets of Jews who had left Libya after the June 1967 war "and who have been fighting against us and have been our enemies from time immemorial." The second point concerned the Jewish cemeteries, which, according to *Ar-Raid*, should be destroyed:

> It is the unavoidable duty of the city councils of Tripoli, Benghazi, Misurata, etc., to remove their [the Jews'] cemeteries immediately, and throw the bodies of their dead which, even in their eternal rest, soil our country, into the depths of the sea. Where those dirty corpses are lying they should put buildings, parks, and roads. Only thus can the hatred of the Libyan Arab people toward the Jews be satiated.

Although the new provisional constitution promulgated on December 11, 1969, adhered to the principle of the equality of all citizens before the law,[40] the new year opened for the Jews still living in Libya, and for those who still had interests there, not to mention affection for Libya and memories of it, with the gloomiest of outlooks. Many Jews who still lived there or happened to be there and who had passports hastened to leave. A few months after the military coup, there were only about a hundred left,[41] mostly old people without relatives. The number was destined to diminish even more during the next few years, reaching less than forty in 1972 and sixteen in 1977.* These are the Jews whom, in November 1973 in Paris at a meeting with European intellectuals, journalists, and political figures, Qadhdhafi brandished to prove his assertion that it is possible for Jews who are friendly to the Arabs to live peacefully in Libya and be protected by his government.[42]

A series of measures against Jews were in fact adopted in 1970 and, Qadhdhafi's assertions to the contrary, put an end to the Jewish presence in Libya.

The first official measure (following the de facto refusal to grant exit visas) occurred with Law no. 14 of February 7.† By this law the Revolutionary Command Council extended the Sanusi law of March 21, 1961, concerning assets of those who had left for Israel, to those who had moved "permanently" overseas. As two communiqués, one of the following day and one of March 7, explained, the measure implied that as of the date of the new law it was not "permitted for anyone to draw up any contract of lease or sale or any other deed relating to the funds and properties" which were "under sequestration." That was obvious, but in addition Jews resident abroad "must be considered as having left the country permanently, except where the person concerned shall show a certificate to the contrary issued by the Passport and Immigration Department." The latter was a legal absurdity, since the burden lay on the Jews to provide the proof, but made issuance of the document the prerogative of a body of the Libyan state. Moreover, it was not specified by which criteria it would be determined whether residence overseas was to be viewed as temporary or permanent. Beyond these legal subtleties, the real meaning of the law for the new government was soon made clear, since the authorities immediately began to "sequester" the assets of all Jews who had left in 1967 and had not returned to settle

---

*By 1982 there were only about ten Jews left, including one family (Raffaello Fellah, personal communication).—*Trans.*

†Law no. 14 of 1970 regarding a System for Administering Certain Funds and Properties, *Official Gazette*, no. 8, p. 15.—*Trans.*

again in Libya, and to require all Jews requesting temporary exit and re-entry permits, without distinction, to submit the statement declaring their funds and properties required by the new law for anyone who had settled "permanently" overseas.

In the face of such serious events, a group of Jews from Tripoli who had fled to Italy sent the Libyan government petitions on March 25 and May 5, 1970. The petitions criticized the discriminatory nature of the law and emphasized that none of the Jews who had left Libya had settled overseas permanently[43] (though the Libyan authorities were deliberately using the term "Israelite"—which in Arabic is the same as "Israeli"—instead of the term "Jew"*). Neither communication received any reply, unless one can consider as such the issuing, on May 9, 1970, of Law no. 57,† which listed by name about eighty Jews whose funds and properties were being "placed under the administration of a Sequestrator General." Article 1 of the new law stipulated:

> By Resolution of the Revolutionary Command Council the names of certain individuals residing abroad may be added [to the appended schedule] if their absence from Libya is intended to be permanent or if they engage in activities harmful to the security and safety of the State. Absence with no intention of returning shall be deemed to be an absence for a period exceeding six months without an acceptable excuse.

A few days later, on May 28, a letter arrived in Rome from Tripoli addressed to the "Libyan Jewish Community." It bore no letterhead nor official seal. It was signed by one of the better-educated and more moderate members of the RCC, Raid Abdul Munham el-Huni** (now in voluntary exile in Egypt due to differences with Qadhdhafi), and reads as follows:

> I have received your letter dated May 6, 1970, in which you express your concern about your present position. If there is one thing we can assure you of, it is that we are not racist, and are not among those who approve racism, and that you may return to Libya as soon as possible, upon which the Law of Sequestration will cease to apply to anyone who returns here.

*Meredith O. Ansell et al., *The Libyan Revolution: A Sourcebook of Legal and Historical Documents* (Stoughton, Wisc.: Oleander Press, 1972), p. 124, used the term "Israeli" in its English translation.—*Trans.*

† See ibid., pp. 219–223, Law no. 57 of 1970 on the Administration of Funds and Properties of Certain Individuals, for an English translation.—*Trans.*

**For more information on el-Huni, see Omar El Fathaly et al., *Political Development and Social Change in Libya* (Lexington: Heath, 1980), pp. 43, 46, 47.—*Trans.*

In the face of such a disconcerting and ambiguous initiative, the Libyan group in Rome decided to contact the Libyan embassy there and inform the Libyans that, as a proof of their good will and in order to restore some confidence in it among the Libyan Jews, the government in Tripoli could at least begin by revoking the "sequestration" of assets of those who were still in Libya.

The last step in the process of practical elimination of the Jews from Libya was taken by Qadhdhafi on July 21, 1970. On that day the RCC passed three laws marking a radical turning point in Libyan history. In the first law the RCC, "in the firm conviction of the Libyan people that the time has come to recover the wealth of its sons and ancestors usurped during the despotic Italian government, which oppressed the country in a dark period of its glorious history, when murder, dispersion, and desecration constituted the only basis on which the Italian colonizers stole the people's wealth and controlled its resources," stipulated "notwithstanding the fact that the State instead of the people is requesting compensation for damages suffered during the Italian occupation . . . restitution to the people of all immovable assets of any sort and of movable assets attached to them owned by Italian citizens." The second law prohibited (except with special approval of the council of ministers) the issuing of further "licenses, permits, or authorizations to Italians to practice commerce, industry, any trade or craft, or any other activity or work" even by renewing those already in force.[44] These two laws were put into force in record time, by October of the same year.[45] Through them, all Italians living in Libya were deprived without compensation of all their assets and expelled from Libya, even if they had been living there for decades or had been born there. A third law of the same date was intended to close the books on the Jews. All their funds and properties already "under sequestration" (and those of fourteen Arabs and Catholics) were subject to "restitution to the people." What made the measure against the Jews—whatever their citizenship—different from those against Italians was the absence of a "historical" preamble. The law did recognize the right of those expropriated to receive compensation, though there was nothing about when and how they would receive it. Here is the text of the third law:

> In the Name of the People
> The Revolutionary Command Council:
>   In view of the constitutional notice dated 2 Shawal 1389, corresponding to December 11, 1969, and Law no. 6 of 1961 making the assets of certain Israelis subject to sequestration;

In view of Law no. 57 of 1970 on the administration of funds and properties of certain persons;

Upon the proposal of the Minister of the Interior and the Minister of the Treasury and approval of the Council of Ministers,

has promulgated the following law:

Article 1. The funds and properties of the persons subject to the sequestration provided for under Law no. 6 of 1961 and Law no. 57 of 1970 and whose names are listed in the attachment shall be restituted to the State.

Article 2. Compensation is due to the persons indicated in the preceding article for the funds and properties passed to the State. Such compensation shall be determined by one or more commissions to be established by order of the council of ministers under the chairmanship of a member of the magistracy of a grade no lower than presiding judge or chief prosecutor, first grade.

The appointment of the chairman of the commission shall be made by order of the Minister of Justice, without further formalities. The decisions of the commission shall be ratified by the council of ministers.

Article 3. Compensation owed in accordance with the previous article shall be paid by means of government bonds which may be encashed within fifteen years.

If the Minister of the Treasury so proposes, the Council of Ministers shall, through its own order, determine the procedures for issuing said bonds, their denomination, and how they shall circulate and be used.

Article 4. The Ministry of Housing shall take possession of the properties and unbuilt land, while the General Institute for Agricultural Reclamation shall take possession of all lands, agricultural and reclaimable in uncultivated or desert areas, which have passed to the State. Each of these institutions shall arrange to administer whatever has been assigned to it as the representative of the State, while the Sequestrator-General, as the State's representative, shall administer other assets taken over by the State.

Article 5. The Ministries of the Interior, Justice, Agriculture and Agricultural Reclamation, Housing, and the Treasury, shall execute this law, which becomes effective upon its promulgation and shall be published in the *Official Gazette.*

The Revolutionary Command Council: /s/ Qadhdhafi, Mch. Magareif, Abdussalam Gallud, Moh. Gedei, Dr. Giuna Scriha, Moh. Rabihi. Promulgated on 18 First Gemadi 1390, corresponding to July 21, 1970.

The fact that the measures against Italians and against Jews were adopted at the same time leaves no doubt as to the intention of the RCC. Having cleared the British bases out of Cyrenaica in March and the American bases out of Tripolitania in June, the measures constituted Qadhdhafi's achievement of the first of the five points in his October 16 program: the expulsion from Libyan territory of all traces of foreign presence. According to this logic, it is significant that the July 21 measures affected all forms of Western presence in Libya, from the cultural to the religious. They required the closing of the Italian Cultural Institute of Tripoli and all Italian schools still existing in Libya, as well as the confiscation of church properties and religious educational institutions, and left only two churches, one in Tripoli and one in Benghazi. The discrimination between Italians and Jews flouted all the commitments which Libya had made to the United Nations and in the 1956 Italian-Libyan Agreement. Italians were subject to expropriation without compensation with the explicit claim that Libya should get compensation from Italy. The Jews suffered expropriation but were promised compensation. The official explanation lies in the "historical" preamble to the measure against Italians which, significantly, does not exist in the one against Jews. On a "historical" plane then, the RCC did not consider the Libyan Jews to be identified with colonialism. It recognized in practice that they were a component of Libyan reality prior to colonization and independent of it. The reference to the law of March 21, 1961, established a clear connection, not only juridical but also political, between the measure itself and the Israel boycott, thus with the Arab-Israeli conflict. Such a connection is doubly significant. It protected the measure from any accusation of racism or anti-Semitism, clarifying the meaning of the letter which el-Huni had sent two months before to the Libyan Jews who had taken refuge in Italy and preparing the ground for the declaration by which, three years later, Qadhdhafi "opened the doors" of Libya to Libyan Jews and Jews from other Arab countries who had emigrated to Israel. It also tended to establish a sort of indirect logical relationship between the Arab-Israeli conflict and the commitment to compensate those expropriated, implying that as long as the former lasted, the latter would not be settled. This is indirectly confirmed by the fact that, while all compensation has consistently been denied to the Jews, some non-Jews subject to the same law of July 21, 1970, have subsequently been freed from the sanctions, allowed to return to Libya, and had their assets restored. Obviously, a connection of this sort may represent a principle, but may also conceal a hope of creating divisions or at least divergent positions between the Jews, thereby undermining support of Israel and affecting a portion of foreign public opinion.

The July 21, 1970, law in practice marked the end, after over two thousand years, of the Jewish presence in Libya. The fact that a few Jews still remained shows only those individuals' material and psychological inability to leave the country, and extreme fatalism.

The main part of what had been Libyan Jewry was already living in Israel. The vast majority, having overcome considerable initial difficulties—material, psychological, and cultural—adjusted well. This is particularly true when they are judged in relation to the average of Jews originating in Arab countries; it is less true in relation to the country as a whole and in relation to Ashkenazi Jews. The younger generation, those who left Libya very young or were born in Israel, have few of the characteristics of Libyan Jews.[46]

The integration of Libyan Jews in Israel does not fall within the limits of this study. Another book would be needed to deal with it, one which could only be written by an Israeli scholar or someone able to carry out the necessary field research. For present purposes, some information may give a general idea of how this integration took place and some stages in its development. Between 1949 and 1952–1953 the life of Libyan immigrants was anything but easy. It was particularly difficult for the Jews of Tripoli to adapt (due to their numbers and socioeconomic and cultural characteristics) to a situation so different from the one from which they originated. After this first stage, integration was relatively easier and less traumatic and on the whole more successful than that of other North African communities. It was made so by the Libyan Jews' longstanding familiarity with hardship, their low and medium economic and social standard, their strong solidarity deriving from an equally strong attachment to the values and customs of their own tradition, the traumatic experience of the pogroms, the widespread knowledge of Hebrew among the immigrants (though it was a classical, almost biblical Hebrew), and the vigorous efforts, carried out by an ad hoc organization created by Frigia Zuarez and Sion Nemni, the Yahadut Luv [Libyan Jewry], to provide assistance and help in overcoming difficulties in acclimatization. The very small number of Libyan Jews who have left Israel (about fifty for Italy and one family for Australia) is an important proof of this. Moreover, during almost the entire first twenty years, there were no cases of rebelliousness and criminality (those cases which have occurred in the last decade involve the new generation born in Israel). Another sign of successful integration is the large number of "mixed" marriages, that is, outside the Libyan community. Those who were from small towns and the hinterland of Libya were generally steered quite soon toward agricultural communities. In this way a large number of Libyans became active modern farmers, and today constitute the entire or preponderant population of some *moshavim* [cooperative communities of smallholders]. Jews from Tripoli were mostly housed temporarily in reception camps (Beit-Lid, Tel Litvinski, Mahane Israel, Mabarat Bat-Yam, etc.) as large as towns, where life was very hard. As time went on, and as other arrangements were found for the inmates, some of these camps were closed. Those who had lived there often moved to nearby locations (for example, from Beit-Lid to Netanya); other camps grew into urban centers themselves (the case of Bat-Yam is typical) or became suburbs of nearby towns (as Mahane Israel became for Tel Aviv). The Jews of Tripoli generally had to give up their traditional occupations; most of them took jobs as laborers, particularly in construction. As the years went by, many of them managed to become small- and medium-scale builders and contractors. Relatively few of the immigrants studied and entered the professions. A few entered political life (two, Frigia Zuarez and Sion Halfon, becoming Knesset members); others made their careers in the army (the present deputy head of artillery and military commander of the Jerusalem area are Libyans). On the whole, most Libyans have clearly improved on their situation, even though those who were in business in Libya—and they were many—generally did not find an opportunity to take it up again and have had to turn to other work. In politics, most Libyans support the non-extremist religious parties, while fewer support Mapai and even fewer Mapam, the revisionist and liberal parties. The younger generation is now completely integrated, not very religious, but quite attached to its own traditions.

Outside Israel, the countries to which Libyan Jews emigrated were the United States, France, Britain, and above all Italy. Though after the events of 1970 some Jews who had fled to Italy in 1967 left for Israel or other countries, Italy still has the most cohesive community—after Israel, of course—of Libyan Jews.

The group living in Italy today numbers about two thousand, counting Italians and Libyans. Its economic situation can be viewed as good or average, with a few quite wealthy individuals. Apart from a few cases, it has integrated well into both secular and Jewish Italian life. Within the community, there are several psychological attitudes. There are two dividing lines which often cross and intersect: one based on generations and the other of a "nationalist" sort. Both are reflected in the Libyan Jews' way of viewing their recent history and viewing themselves in relation to the Libya, if not of today, then of a possible future. The elders and Italians have no doubt that the best period of this century for Libyan Jewry has been the Italian period, and tend to minimize its negative aspects. Many of them see peaceful coexistence with the Muslims as practically impossible, at least in the short and medium terms. As for the future, they see the subject of Libya in practice closed, whatever political developments may occur within the country. The younger generation (but not the youth, who in general are fast becoming Italianized and frequently tending toward rapid assimilation) and the real Libyans think very differently. Most of them feel themselves to be still Libyan in substance. Despite everything, they do not view the Sanusi period negatively and would return to Libya if the necessary conditions existed. Beyond their memories and attachment to the land of Libya and to their past, both recent and distant, if anything is held in common by the vast majority of the two groups, it is the same negative evaluation of the British role in Libya after 1943 and in particular during the pogroms of 1945 and 1948. Most Libyan Jews attribute them directly to British plans to remain in Libya and date the decisive change in Arab-Jewish relations from the British period.

In December 1971 a group of Libyan Jews living in Italy, including several members of the ad hoc defense committee formed after the Qadhdhafi government adopted its first anti-Jewish measures, founded the Associazione Ebrei di Libia [Jews of Libya Association]. Some of its main promoters were Raffaello Fellah, Vittorio Halfon, and the brothers Joseph and Simone Habib. The association's aim is to protect the spiritual and material interests of the refugees in relations with the Libyan government and coordinate the various groups spread around the world (a similar organization has been founded in Israel). The AEL has been active, in addition to its approaches to the Libyan government, in relations with the Italian government.[47] Though it was especially active in the first few years, later on the mistrust and resignation of many, together with the majority's traditional lack of participation in community affairs, have greatly reduced the association's activeness. It now survives almost solely through the personal sacrifice of a few individuals. It was active in approaching countries which had citizens among the refugees (Britain, France, and the United States), the U.N. Commission on Human Rights, the large Jewish organizations, and in general any politicians or journalists who, it was thought, might have some influence over Qadhdhafi. In this framework, there were even some contacts with Libyan exiles of Sanusi origin. The results of these contacts have been quite disappointing and amounted merely to a series of expressions of sympathy. Among the governments, Britain barracaded itself behind the impossibility of doing anything concrete, the United States replied clearly that its intervention would have no effect, and France let it be understood that it did not wish to jeopardize its own relations with Qadhdhafi for the sake of a few Jews. The best results were achieved in economic matters. They were restricted to refugees who, not being Libyan citizens, could receive total or partial reparations from their own governments.

294 From Idris to Qadhdhafi

The AEL has had several contacts with the Libyan government in recent years, through the Libyan Embassy in Rome and by letter. In 1971–1973 these contacts related to two issues. They were the compensation[48]—or at least some advance portion of it[49]—envisaged under the law of July 21, 1970, and the issue, particularly dear to all Libyan Jews from the religious, humanitarian, and family points of view, of protecting Jewish cemeteries and synagogues. Other contacts followed these more recently, after Qadhdhafi's declarations inviting Jews from Libya and Arab countries in general to return to their countries of origin. There were no results regarding either issue. The Libyan government in fact always refused to take any positive action, even as a means of showing its good will, to meet the requests. Regarding the assets, it limited itself to general assurances that the matter would be taken care of and similarly general suggestions that the Jews should be patient for the time being. Its attitude was more negative with regard to cemeteries and synagogues. As soon as the AEL heard what was being planned, it approached the government to avert the destruction of Jewish cemeteries, or, at least, allow the necessary religious procedures to be carried out.[50] Despite this, the largest Jewish cemetery in Tripoli was leveled and replaced partly by a road and partly by a port depot. This was justified by the need for urban development, affecting Catholics and Arabs as well as Jews (an Italian and a Muslim cemetery were also destroyed) and thus excluding discrimination against Jews. Five smaller Jewish cemeteries in Tripoli and others in sixteen other places in Tripolitania were also leveled. There is no precise information on the cemeteries of Cyrenaica, but it is probable that they suffered the same fate. Despite the initial formal assurances transmitted through the embassy in Rome, this outrage was committed without giving the families involved any chance of transferring the remains, a chance which was offered to the Italians. In memory of the departed, in 1977 the AEL had a monument erected in the Jewish area of the Verano cemetery in Rome. Finally, the synagogues have been transformed into mosques or used for profane purposes such as cultural clubs. Forty-four synagogues and places of worship in Tripoli and eighteen in sixteen other places in Tripolitania have been destroyed, transformed, or closed down. Such an attitude on the part of the Libyan government certainly does not give the refugees hope for the future. Nor do there appear to be any definite possibilities for a change in the situation. The "historical philosophical" arguments and implicit conditions which Qadhdhafi himself attached to his invitation to the Jews to return to their countries of origin seem to leave no room for hope. The position of the Libyan head of state is clear in its own way and can be summarized as follows:

(1) "Islam was ordered for everyone and was the last of the divine messages"; it "was ordered for all peoples"; "it is the religion which makes no distinction between white and black, between Arab and non-Arab, except in the name of religion."

(2) "Judaism itself is responsible for any oppression which may be inflicted on the Jewish people, since any action is without fail followed by a reaction in another place."

(3) It thus follows that, though the presence in Palestine of Jews "who went to Palestine before 1948" is acceptable, the presence of those who went later is not, since they were no longer subject to oppression. If they were oppressed in some Arab countries, the Jews "must have committed in Palestine some act against the Arabs which caused an adverse reaction against them. That is the same as saying that the Jews committed particular acts which were then turned against them."[51]

In view of Qadhdhafi's position, it is obvious that anyone accepting his invitation to return to Libya (or any other Arab country of origin, as long as it shares the Libyan leader's view) would in practice be accepting Qadhdhafi's "philosophy." That Jew would thus be not only opposing Israel but, clearly, acknowledging the "guilt" which, according to Qadhdhafi, makes Judaism responsible for any oppression committed against the Jews.

Notes

Translator's Preface

1. Mair José Benardete, *Hispanic Culture and Character of the Sephardic Jews*, 2d. ed. (1952; New York: Sepher-Hermon, 1982), p. 23.
2. Frantz Fanon, *Les Damnés de la terre*, with a preface by Jean-Paul Sartre (1961; Paris: Maspero, 1968); translation: *The Wretched of the Earth*, trans. Constance Farrington (New York: Grove Press, 1965).
3. Albert Memmi, *Portrait du colonisé, précédé de Portrait du colonisateur*, with a preface by Jean-Paul Sartre (1953; Paris: Payot, 1973); translation: *The Colonizer and the Colonized*, trans. H. Greenfeld (New York: Orion, 1965). Idem, *L'Homme dominé*, (Paris: Gallimard, 1968); translation: *Dominated Man: Notes towards a Portrait* (New York: Orion, 1968).
4. Norman Stillman, *The Jews of Arab Lands* (Philadelphia: Jewish Publication Society, 1979).
5. Guido Fubini, "Il rifiuto arabo-islamico," *La Rassegna mensile di Israel* 48, nos. 1–6 (January–June 1982): 179–188.
6. S. D. Goitein, *Jews and Arabs* (New York: Schocken, 1964).

Introduction

1. Ismail Chemali, *Gli abitanti della Tripolitania* (Tripoli, 1916), p. 64.
2. Cf. S. Applebaum, "The Jewish Revolt in Cirene in 115–117, and the Subsequent Recolonisation," *Journal of Jewish Studies*, no. 4 (1951): 177–186.
3. Cf. M. Simon, "Le Judaïsme berbère dans l'Afrique ancienne," *Revue d'Histoire et de Philosophie Religieuse*, no. 1 (1946): 1 ff. and 105 ff.; and esp. no. 2 (1946): 138 ff.
4. Salo Baron, *A Social and Religious History of the Jews*, 2d rev. ed. (New York: Columbia University Press, 1952–1960) 3: 172. Cf. also, more generally, G. Vajda, "L'Image du juif dans la tradition islamique," *Les Nouveaux Cahiers*, nos. 13–14 (1968).
5. For the history of Tripolitania, see Ettore Rossi, *Storia di Tripoli e della Tripolitania dalla conquista araba al 1911* (Rome: Istituto per l'Oriente, 1968); for a rapid excursus from an Arab viewpoint, Mohamed Ben Massaud Fusceika, *History of Libya from Ancient Times to the Present* (in Arabic) (Tripoli, 1961). For the history of the Jews, see Haim Hirschberg, *A*

History of the Jews in North Africa (trans.) (Leiden: Brill, 1974), esp. Ch. 11. For Jewish religious life and customs, see Mordechai Hakohen, *Gli ebrei in Libia (Usi e costumi)* trans. Martino Moreno (Rome, [1928]); idem, *The Book of Mordechai: A Study of the Jews of Libya*, ed. and trans. Harvey Goldberg (Philadelphia: Institute for the Study of Human Issues, 1980).

6. For the Karamanli period, in addition to Rossi, *Storia di Tripoli*, see R. Micacchi, *La Tripolitania sotto il dominio dei Caramanli* (Intra, 1936).

7. Solomon Grayzel, *A History of the Jews from the Babylonian Exile to the Present*, 2d ed. (Philadelphia: Jewish Publication Society, 1968), pp. 730 ff.

8. *Viaggi di Ali Bey El Abbassi in Africa e in Asia dall'anno 1803 a tutto il 1807* (Milan, 1916) 2: 165.

9. Micacchi, *La Tripolitania*, pp. 231 ff.

10. See Nahum Slouschz, "La Tripolitaine sous la domination des Karamanlis," *Revue du Monde Musulman* 3 (November 1908): 440 ff., esp. 448 ff.

11. F. Coro, "Una relazione veneta su Tripoli nel Settecento," *Rivista delle colonie italiane*, December 1930, pp. 1092 ff., esp. p. 1097.

12. M. Scaparro, *L'artigianato tripolino* (Tripoli, 1932).

1. Ottoman Rule

1. For the later Ottoman period, besides Rossi, *Storia di Tripoli*, see F. Coro, *Settantasei anni di dominazione turca in Libia (1835–1911)* (Tripoli, 1937), and A. J. Cachia, *Libya under the Second Ottoman Occupation (1835–1911)* (Tripoli, 1945).

2. On the cave dwelling communities of Gharian, see Harvey Goldberg, *Cave Dwellers and Citrus Growers: A Jewish Community in Libya and Israel* (Cambridge: Cambridge University Press, 1972).

3. Harvey Goldberg, "Ecologic and Demographic Aspects of Rural Tripolitanian Jewry: 1853–1949," *International Journal of Middle Eastern Studies*, 1917, pp. 245 ff.

4. AAIU, Libye-Tripoli, I, C. 12, J. Hoelfer, May 16, 1900; David Littman, "Jews under Muslim Rule in the Late Nineteenth Century," *Wiener Library Bulletin*, nos. 35–36 (1975): 71. [This passage is based on Littman's translation, with modifications.]

5. Comando del Corpo di Occupazione della Libia, Uff. Politico-Militare, *Censimento della Tripolitania del 3 luglio 1911* (Tripoli, 1912).

6. Statistics on the Jews of the Regency of Tripoli prepared in the early sixties by Giuseppe Toledano and published in the *Bulletin de l'Alliance Israélite Universelle*, 1861, pp. 12 ff., give partial data which are still very interesting regarding socio-professional activities. According to these statistics, there were about 5,835 Libyan Jews, subdivided as follows:

Tripoli	4,500	Anivas	150
Misurata	200	Zlitin	125
Benghazi	200	Gharian	100
Mesellata	150	Tajura	80
Jebel	150	Derna	30
Zawia	150		

Among the Jews of Tripoli, only 1,276 had definite jobs; there were also 1,974 unemployed women and children; 1,200 poor people, beggars, and other unemployed; and 50 invalids. Breakdown according to work was as follows:

1 chief rabbi	40 stove repairers
4 rabbinical judges	35 carpenters
17 rabbis	25 builders
11 students	4 blacksmiths
20 shopkeepers	15 dyers
37 manufacturers	20 wood utensil makers
15 silk goods makers	10 shoemakers
50 ribbon and braid makers	35 tailors
5 button makers	40 butchers
200 ribbon makers	2 scribes
7 turners	3 customs agents
70 druggists	8 moneychangers
30 tavernkeepers	50 spinners
11 unskilled laborers	200 'improvisors' (strolling
5 bakers	entertainers)
29 barkeepers	10 sorceresses
8 cookshop keepers	3 midwives
8 food merchants	20 porters
18 peddlars	20 servants
63 jewelers	25 cleaners

7. Ettore Rossi, "La colonia italiana a Tripoli nel secolo XIX," *Rivista delle colonie italiane*, December 1930, p. 1063.

8. A. Festa, *Scuole per indigeni in Triopolitania* (Tripoli, 1931); F. Contini, *Storia delle istituzioni scolastiche della Libia* (Tripoli, 1953).

9. In the technical and economic sector it was also Arbib who, in 1881, set up the first hydraulic press for esparto-processing.

10. See H. F. von Maltzen, *Reise in den Regentschaften Tunis und Tripolis* (Leipzig, 1870), p. 340, which also testifies that in Tripoli the cases of Jews being publicly flogged "by officials as well as by citizens" without their being able to resist, were far from infrequent.

11. On the Alliance, see N. Leven, *Cinquante ans d'histoire: L'Alliance Israélite Universelle (1860–1910)* (Paris, 1911–1920), 2 vols., G. Ollivier, *L'Alliance Israélite Universelle (1860–1960)* (Paris, 1959); André Chouraqui, *Cent ans d'histoire: L'Alliance Israélite Universelle et la renaissance juive contemporaine (1860–1960)* (Paris, 1965).

12. Up to 1866 the main spokesman and activist on the Tripoli committee was Giuseppe Toledano, eventually succeeded by Saul Labi and Maïr Levy. Besides working through the Alliance headquarters in Paris, the committee worked directly through and on European consuls in Tripoli, either to persuade them to influence local Ottoman officials or, in some cases, to restrain their "despotism" or anti-Semitism toward their Jewish subjects. The consuls had very broad powers which they frequently exercised, as Toledano said in one of his letters to Paris on July 31, 1861 (AAIU, Libye-Tripoli, I, C. 12), as "omnipotent autocrats." The committee concerned it-

self with almost all the issues involved in the situation of the Jews. It was involved in the most serious ones and, in its early years, even the minor issues, as long as they had something to do with Muslim fanaticism against the Jews. As stipulated in the Alliance Statutes, issues involving trade and economics were excluded, although some people would have liked the committee to be involved in these also; in 1869 there was a brief but heated disagreement on the subject between the Tripoli and Benghazi committees. Contacts were also established around 1870 with the Anglo-Jewish Association. They were less important, though, than those with the Alliance. For information on them, see *Report of the Anglo-Jewish Association, 1871–1872, 1876, 1879, 1880,* and *1887* (London, 1872–).

13. The budget of the Community of Tripoli in the 1880s could count on a total income of about 50,000 francs, originating from (a) the tax on meat, (b) the voluntary merchants' tax on exports,* (c) the sale of *mitsvot* in the synagogues, and (d) donations. This amount was barely enough, and in some years not enough, to cover: (a) tax for exemption from military service, (b) synagogue expenses, (c) assistance for poor invalids, (d) living expenses for the Talmud Torah students, (e) charity to the poor, (f) expenses for *dayanim* and rabbis, and (g) assistance and travel expenses for foreign Jewish travelers. The cemetery administration was independent and likewise barely sufficed. See "Israélites de la Tripolitaine," *Bulletin de l'Alliance Israélite Universelle,* no. 14 (1889): 107.

14. AAIU, Libye-Tripoli, I, C. 13, T. Sutton to Alliance, April 22, 1901.

15. On the living conditions of the Jews of Amruss, two interesting accounts were sent to the Alliance on March 14, 1904, and June 15, 1906, by a woman teacher, M. Avigdor, and a woman traveler, Anna Rabbinovitz, who had visited the small towns near Tripoli (AAIU, Libye-Tripoli, I, C. 18–19). The first of these gives this chilling description:

"A feeling of horror and sadness gripped me as I set foot on the ground. At the sound of the carriage, in the space of a minute a considerable crowd clustered around us. There were women in a very indecent get-up, almost all of them blind in one eye; ragged children, almost indescribably filthy and with dirty faces in which only their eyes could be made out; old people and men, all of repulsive appearance, hemmed us in. We had great difficulty in passing through those dirty, narrow alleys in which a sickening odor made us hardly able to breathe. The *hara* of Tripoli which are known for their filth seem like boulevards in comparison with these quarters full of filth, in which the eye cannot find a clean spot to rest on.

"This small village is almost entirely inhabited by Jews. Our coreligionists are quite uncivilized; to look at them one would think one was in primitive times and the most barbarous at that. They lead an extremely miserable life, since great poverty prevails amongst them.

"Most of the Jews live off the meager profits of selling eggs. The rest go

*Hakohen, *The Book of Mordechai,* p. 171, mentions "a merchant's tax of one part in a thousand on the value of goods imported," called the *khaba,* according to Goldberg.—*Trans.*

en masse to Tripoli to hold out their hands. They can be seen every day in a group, begging for charity. The poor wretches are happy when they receive a crust of bread or a bite of food . . . Near the synagogue is a small room that serves as a refuge for about twenty boys and is called the Talmud Torah. Upon entering this so-called Talmud Torah, we had to close our noses and ears in order to stay for a few minutes in this place which was horrifying to see because of the dirtiness of the classroom and the sad appearance of the pupils. The boys were sitting on the ground huddled together howling and bellowing like small wild animals. At a distance, seated on a low stool, was a pathetic old man holding in one hand a Hebrew book and in the other a huge stick. To my great surprise, I learned that he was the teacher. This wretched rabbi was shouting fearsomely; despite this, his pupils were not listening to him at all and went on shouting and running around the classroom. He told us that he was very poor. His pupils' tuition charges were only twenty centesimi a month and, he added, they could not all pay regularly.

"Though these boys were at least sheltered in a poor room, the girls were all running around in the street."

16. See Sutton, report cited in note 14.

17. AAIU, Libye-Tripoli, I, C. 19, Anna Rabbinovitz to Alliance, March 18, 1906.

18. For the religious practices of Libyan Jews, see Hakohen, *Gli ebrei* and *The Book of Mordechai*. The observations of European travelers are also significant: e.g., Manfredo Camperio ("the Jews' fanaticism is so extreme that they will even refuse a last sip of water to a dying man on religious holidays") and P. Bettoli (who was struck by the "amazing" number of religious holidays, about eighty a year), in *Pionieri italiani in Libia: Relazioni dei delegati della Società Italiana di Esplorazioni geografiche e commerciali di Milano (1880–1896)* (Milan, 1912), pp. 40, 140. According to Camperio again, (ibid., p. 237), in 1880 the chief rabbi of Tripoli was a "liberal and cultured man," but his efforts to moderate the "blind fanaticism" of his coreligionists constantly failed.

19. See "Israélites de la Tripolitaine," *Bulletin de l'Alliance Israélite Universelle*, no. 31 (1906): 107. The entire article, which reproduces passages from a report sent to the Alliance central committee by Nahum Slouschz of the Sorbonne, and which he prepared during a research trip in Morocco and Tripolitania, should be seen for the documentation and clarification which it provides on the condition of Tripolitanian Jews at the beginning of the twentieth century. See also Slouschz's *Travels in North Africa* (Philadelphia: Jewish Publication Society, 1927), pp. 3 ff.

20. On moneylending, see Francesco Coletti, *La Tripolitania settentrionale e sua vita sociale studiate dal vero* (Bologna: Zanichelli, 1923), passim; Giuseppe Bevione, *Come siamo andati a Tripoli* (Torino, 1912), p. 263.

21. See Comando del Corpo di Stato Maggiore, *Manualetto per l'ufficiale in Tripolitania* (Rome, 1911), p. 27.

22. Camperio, in *Pionieri*, p. 11, recalls that in 1881 someone in an "authoritative position" in Benghazi told him: "Here and in Tripoli the Jews

own camels, horses, and stores full of merchandise, gold, and silver, and they are millionaires."

23. Ibid., p. 236.

24. Though referring to the first decade of Italian occupation, for the Jews' role as intermediaries, see E. S. Artom's illuminating observations, which will be referred to again, in his report, "L'importanza dell'elemento ebraico nella populazione della Tripolitania," *Atti del primo congresso di studi coloniali di Firenze (8–12 aprile 1931)* 4: 116 ff., esp. p. 118.

25. On an individual basis, the tax was quite low. But many Jews could not pay. Hence the decision of the Community of Tripoli to meet the expense itself. But the total figures were considerable, and the Community was not always able to pay. In 1903 this situation led to a serious crisis. The Ottoman authorities, which should have received not only the amount for the current year, but also that of the previous year which had not yet been paid, made about twenty arrests as a warning, and provoked a sort of protest strike on the part of Jewish shopkeepers and craftsmen. Finally, due to the decisive intervention of the Italian consul, who informed the Ottoman authorities that he would hold them responsible for any losses which might occur to Italian interests due to the trade stoppage, a compromise solution was found. The tax was reduced overall, and charges were subdivided according to taxpayers' incomes (among 3,825 taxpayers, it was ascertained that only 867 were able to pay it in various proportions, from half to seven and a half times). See AAIU, Libye-Tripoli, I, C. 15, M. Levy to the president of the Alliance, June 14, 1903, and December 8, 1902.

26. Earlier on there had been a couple of cases of accusations by Catholics against Jews of mocking Christ during the Easter period by going around with crowns of thorns on their heads. See AAIU, Libye-Tripoli, I, C. 1, and E. Labi, "Il miracolo di Bengasi," in *Yahadut Luv*, ed. F. Zuarez, A. Guetta, Z. Shaked, G. Arbib, and F. Tayar (Tel Aviv, 1960), pp. 203 ff.

27. What happened in the Jewish quarter of Idder is typical of the attitude of some of the local authorities and their venality. A few years after the first time that the synagogue of Misurata was plundered, the Jews (who to feel more secure had abandoned almost half of their houses and were living together, up to four or five families per house, in the remaining houses) managed to have night watchmen guarding their quarter. In 1896 these guards were suddenly removed. When the Jews protested, they were posted again, but only after the Jews had agreed to make a contribution of three napoleons to the *qaimaqam*. After three days the guards were removed again, and the *qaimaqam* informed the Jews that they had to pay five napoleons for the purchase of a plot of land on which to build barracks in the quarter. The Jews paid joyfully, but the barracks were not built. In consternation, the Jews of Misurata then turned to the chief rabbi of Tripoli and the Alliance, appealing for help. As one may read in their petition to the chief rabbi, they considered the Arabs who were their neighbors "our most implacable enemy," and, if it were not that their synagogue would fall into the hands of their "enemies," they were ready, in order to flee from the continual robberies and violence to which they were constantly subject, to

leave their dwellings and settle elsewhere. In this climate, the plundering of 1897 took place. The following day the Jews of Misurata went to the *qaimaqam* to protest and demand justice. He asked them whom they suspected. When they replied that they did not know of anyone and that he should ask the leaders of the tribes, the *qaimaqam* pretended to understand those words as an accusation and arrested some Arab chieftains. He soon released them, though, after having them pay him some contributions. It is easy to imagine what the consequences of this were for the Jews: in order to avoid reprisals, many of them decided to abandon the city. Others, who were terrified, once again appealed to Tripoli and Paris for help. See AAIU, Libye-Tripoli, I, C. 11.

28. AAIU, Libye-Tripoli, I, C. 7. [From a letter by Saul Labi, president of the Tripoli regional committee, to Adolphe Crémieux, president of the AIU, Paris. Based on a partial translation by Littman, "Jews under Muslim Rule," p. 69.]

29. Ibid.

30. Ibid., I, C. 11, and Littman, "Jews under Muslim Rule," pp. 69–70. [Based on Littman's translation.]

31. AAIU, Libye-Tripoli, I, C. 14.

32. Ibid., I, C. 20.

33. Some of the relative correspondence, covering the years 1900–1904, is preserved in CZA Z/1/311, 350, 359. Another appeal was made to Vienna in 1901 by Jacques Soufir de Félix, a merchant of Tripoli (ibid., Z/1/316).

34. CZA A 36/68. [Translated from the French original.]

35. See Theodor Herzl, *The Diaries of Theodor Herzl*, trans. Marvin Lowenthal (New York: Grosset, 1956), pp. 426–427; U. Nahon, "Le lettere di T. Herzl a Felice Ravenna: Il viaggio di Herzl a Roma nel gennaio 1904," in *Nel centenario della nascita di Teodoro Herzl* (Venice-Rome, 1961), p. 36; and G. Romano, "I rapporti di T. Herzl coi soinisti italiani," in ibid., p. 57.

36. See *Report on the Work of the Commission Sent Out by the Jewish Territorial Organisation under the Auspices of the Governor-General of Tripoli, to Examine the Territory Proposed for the Purpose of a Jewish Settlement in Cyrenaica* (London, 1909). The news of the JTO's interest in Cyrenaica aroused interest and discussions in the Italian press. Some feared that Britain was behind it. Opposing Italian colonial expansion in Libya, they considered the JTO a weapon in the hands of their opponents who held the opposite view and said that Libya would solve Italy's economic problems. A short notice, "Il territorialismo ebraico, l'imperialismo italiano e la Cirenaica," *Il corriere israelitico*, June 30, 1911, is significant in this respect. Following the lead of an article in *La voce* ("L'illusione tripolina," May 18, 1911) which made lengthy reference to the JTO report, the Jewish periodical wrote: "It is strange that the JTO Jewish expedition, so infertile from a Jewish point of view, should be destined to have an influence on Italian foreign policy."

For further information, see ASMAE, Segreteria generale (1908–1913), c. 38, fasc. 564, "1909: Banco di Roma, Azione inglese in Tripolitania; Colonizzazione israelitica in Tripolitania e Cirenaica." It is interesting to note that in January 1912 the JTO plans were suddenly taken up again at the time of the Italian-Turkish War. The Italian ambassador in Vienna was indirectly approached in order to find out the Italian attitude toward possible Jewish colonization in Cyrenaica. Di Sangiuliano let the initiative drop, though, sending instructions to the ambassador in the Austrian capital to respond by assuring the Jews that the Italian government was favorably disposed toward them, but could not involve itself in specific issues as long as there was a state of war with Turkey. See ASMAE, Segreteria generale (1908–1913), c. 48, fasc. 807, "Colonie di ebrei in Tripolitania."

37. Rossi, *La colonia italiana*, p. 1060.

38. Bevione, *Come siamo andati*, p. 27.

39. Perhaps V. Cottafavi, *Nella Libia italiana: Impressioni, studi, ricordi* (Bologna, 1912), pp. 68 ff., sensed this to some extent. While affirming that all the Jews without exception favored Italy, he explained this by the fact that they had "suffered greatly" under the Turks, and, in particular, he observed that "enthusiasm and collaboration" would come with time, implying that he did not regard their favoring Italy as the expression of a positive feeling but rather the consequence of the sufferings and discrimination they had gone through.

2. Italian Occupation (1911–1916)

1. See, e.g., just after the Italian occupation, W. K. McClure, *Italy in North Africa: An Account of the Tripoli Enterprise* (London, 1913), pp. 277 ff.

2. For how the Italian occupation happened, see Francesco Malgeri, *La guerra libica (1911–1912)* (Rome: Edizioni di storia e letteratura, 1970); S. Romano, *La quarta sponda: La guerra di Libia, 1911–1912* (Milan, 1977). For military aspects during 1911–1912 and subsequent years, see Ministero Affari Esteri, Com. Documentazione dell'Opera dell'Italia in Africa, *L'Italia in Africa*, Serie storico-militare, Part 1, *L'opera del'Esercito*, vol. 3, Massimo Adolfo Vitale, *Avvenimenti militari e impiego: Africa settentrionale (1911–1943)* (Rome: Istituto Poligrafico dello Stato, 1964) [referred to henceforth as Vitale, *Africa settentrionale*].

3. G. Lattes, "Tripoli italiana," *Il vessillo israelitico*, October 1911. See also most of the issues between October 1911 and late 1912 of *Il vessillo israelitico* (Casale Monferrato), *La settimana israelitica* (Florence), and *Il corriere israelitico* (Trieste). In the climate of euphoria created by the Italian-Turkish War, a "Preghiera per la salute del re e per la vittoria degli italiani a Tripoli" [Prayer for the King's health and for an Italian victory at Tripoli] was distributed. It invokes a divine blessing on Vittorio Emanuele III and on "our Italian brothers who are fighting in the city of Tripoli and around it to liberate that Country from its oppressors and set right all the wrong that they have done."

4. See U. Nahon, "Una lettera di Giolitti del 1912 su gli 'israeliti delle nuove provincie italiane'," *La rassegna mensile di Israel*, September 1972,

pp. 430 ff.; and "Una lettera dell'On. Giolitti al *Vessillo*," *Il vessillo israelitico,* August 1912. For the supposed persecution of the Jews of Benghazi, see "Gli ebrei e l'impresa italiana," *Il corriere israelitico,* November 30, 1911, including two denials by the president of the Community of Benghazi, Effraim Halfon; for the Rhodes incident, see *La settimana israelitica,* June 14, 1912; September 12 and 20, 1912.

5. See, e.g., F. Coppola, "Israele contro l'Italia," *L'idea nazionale,* November 28, 1911.

6. For an overall view, see Renzo De Felice, *Storia degli ebrei italiani sotto il fascismo* 3d ed. (1961; Turin: Einaudi, 1972), pp. 54 ff.; for a detailed view, see "La guerra e l'antisemitismo," *La settimana israelitica,* December 1, 1911, and M. Bolaffio, "Il momento antisemita," ibid., January 19, 1912.

7. See, e.g., G. Lattes, "Gli ebrei di Tripoli," *Il vessillo israelitico,* November 1911.

8. The Community of Tripoli officially joined in December 1912, and the Community of Benghazi soon afterward.

9. It was established by a legislative provision of June 13, 1912, that the chief rabbi had to be of Italian nationality. It is impossible to say for sure whether the Italian authorities wanted to appoint one speedily or whether, content at having established the principle, they preferred not to make the appointment, while they awaited the provisions establishing the Statutes of the Community of Tripoli.

10. When the Italian occupation took place, the chief rabbi of Tripoli had been in Salonica for nearly three years, apparently due to the Community's economic difficulties. His functions had been taken over by the acting chief rabbi, Elia Raccah. See ASMAE, Segreteria generale (1908–1913), c. 46, fasc. 700, "Rabbino di Tripoli."

11. See the interview, "Cose di Libia," which Rabbi Dario Disegni gave to *La settimana israelitica* (April 3, 1914) on his return from a visit to Libya. He speaks repeatedly of the "misoneism of the vast majority of the numerous indigenous rabbis"; "they are horrified at all the novelties of European civilization and see all Italian rabbis, whoever they are, as worse than reformers—actual destroyers."

12. For the events involving the chief rabbi of Tripoli, see AUCII, fasc. "Tripolitania," 1911 ff.

13. Typical of this last point is a hint which a lawyer, Sullam, made at the afternoon session, May 12, 1914, at the headquarters of the Congress of Jewish Communities. The minutes read: "Refers to anti-Semitic episodes which have taken place in Tripolitania. Says that it is necessary to orient ourselves toward doing what is necessary in order to save them, *because anti-Semitism might cross the sea.*" Also: "The rich Jews, those who are afraid to give money for Jewish causes because they do not want to look less Italian, should be shown that helping the Jews of Tripolitania to improve themselves will have its repercussions in the motherland" (AUCII, "Congresso delle Comunità Israelitiche Italiane, Roma: maggio 1914").

14. See AUCII, fasc. "Tripolitania." For Margulies' position, see the interview which he gave to *La settimana israelitica,* January 3, 1913.

15. See AUCII, fasc. "Congresso delle Comunità Israelitiche Italiane, Roma: maggio 1914," afternoon session, May 12.

16. ACS, Ministero della Real Casa, "Ufficio del I° Aiutante di campo generale di S. M. il Re," Sezione speciale, b. 3. The *Manualetto per l'ufficiale in Tripolitania*, prepared in 1911 by the General Staff, reads more simply: "The Jews control a large portion of commerce; they are willing to accept domination by any country, and indigenous people treat them with contempt" (p. 22).

17. Some of these expressions must have been frankly ostentatious, going by what General Tommaso Salsa, commander of the Tripoli garrison, wrote to his wife: "And this evening another party, which is of course being given by Jews again. They seize every occasion to show off and remedy the inferior condition in which they were kept by the Arabs and Turks" (E. Canevari and G. Comisso, *Il generale Tommaso Salsa e le sue campagne coloniali* [Milan, 1935], p. 390).

18. See what Domenico Caruso, director of the Civil Service in Tripoli, wrote on this subject on January 6, 1912, to the chief secretary of the prime minister's office: ACS, Presidenza Consiglio Ministri, Gabinetto, 1912, b. 397, fasc. T 1–2.

19. ACS, Ministero della Real Casa, "Ufficio del 1° Aiutante di campo generale di S. M. il Re," Sezione speciale, b. 7: Ministero Guerra, Div. Stato Maggiore, "Bolletino di notizie riflettenti le operazioni in Tripolitania e Cirenaica," January 8, 1912.

20. A reference to these complaints, though limited to the statements "of some Arab leaders hostile to the Jews" which were being challenged, was included in the communiqué released by the Italian Jewish Universities Committee after the Colombo mission to Libya: see *La settimana israelitica*, January 9, 1913, and *Il vessillo israelitico*, January 15, 1913. According to some Italian Jews in Libya, the change in attitude toward the Jews was the result of unspecified "local Jesuit intrigues" and a campaign by the Italian church press. See AUCII, fasc. "Tripolitania," letter from Bianca Arbib Nunes Vais to A. Sereni, mid-June 1912. This interpretation is not credible, though.

21. For a typical example of this overdramatization of every episode, see *La settimana israelitica*, November 21, 1913, which reports a protest by "many Jews of Tripoli" at the fact that on the occasion of the king's birthday Jewish leaders were not invited to the parade and reception offered by the governor.

22. For the text of the relevant decree, see *Il vessillo israelitico*, July 1912, pp. 219 ff.

23. ACS, *Presidenza Consiglio Ministri, Gabinetto*, 1912, b. 398, fasc. T. 7. The same source, esp. b. 400, fasc. T. 10, contains many other documents from the Office of the Director General of the Civil Service and subordinate offices, concerning the Jews of Tripoli and Libya. Caruso's concern about a foreign presence and "infiltration" can be seen in his letter of January 6, 1912, cited in note 18, clearly showing his hostility to any concession

to the AIU: "The Alliance schools are French and they spread French influence and civilization, while our interest is to spread our civilization by teaching our language and spreading knowledge of our history."

The Committee of the Jewish-Italian school in Tripoli, and its director, Giannetto Paggi, though for somewhat different reasons than Caruso, shared his opinion. See Paggi's letter to Anselmo Colombo, March 5, 1912: "There is an institution here which, if it had not distorted its aim, might also have been very useful: it is the Alliance Israélite. But it spends its money on schools which are no use, first, because in out state schools young people can get a much more complete and contemporary education; second, the teaching of French here, thanks to our soldiers and sailors, has seen its day; and, third, poor people need to learn a trade in order to earn their living. All the young Jews who attended Italian schools and speak our language have easily found work; the others . . . are shining shoes . . . in French" (AUCII, fasc. "Tripolitania").

Finally, it should be noted that Giolitti must have shared this opinion. This can be deduced from a letter to Minister Di Sangiuliano (at that time colonial issues were still dealt with by the Ministry of Foreign Affairs; the Ministry of Colonies was not set up until November 20, 1912) dated January 14, 1912, in which Giolitti supported Caruso's request to reopen the Libyan schools as soon as possible so that the Alliance would not win the advantage. See ACS, *Presidenza Consiglio Ministri, Gabinetto,* 1912, b. 397, fasc. T. 1–2. In subsequent years the effort against the Alliance (which the nationalist press had made its target since before the occupation; see *La settimana israelitica,* August 25, 1911) was developed to the point that in 1914 the land on which its Tripoli school stood was expropriated with the excuse of the new city plan, and the Ministry of Colonies declared itself unable to provide another plot in exchange, saying that there was none available.

24. It was not only the most modern and enterprising Libyan Jews who were optimistic about the usefulness of the Libyan Jews for the Italians, but also some of the leaders of the Italian committee. E.g., in October 1912, when the colonial authorities appointed a commission "for the pacification of the Arabs," Anselmo Colombo right away wrote to Angelo Sereni in the following optimistic terms: "And so we must clearly show that the most suitable elements for insinuating [acceptance of the Italians] into the minds of the Arabs are the Jews, who are looked on better than the Catholics and have better relations with the Arabs due to the many types of business they do with them." See AUCII, fasc. "Tripolitania," letter dated October 18, 1912.

25. "The Jew has a greater spirit of enterprise and initiative, and why not also foresight? Among the indigenous people, the Jews were the best prepared to receive the new sovereignty because much of the Jewish population, taking advantage of our schools, learned Italian before the occupation. And it is the Jews who, sensing now more than before the necessity and advantages of knowing Italian, flock to the Italian schools." See ACS, Presidenza Consiglio Ministri, Gabinetto, 1912, b. 397, fasc. T. 1–2, "Relazione

sulle scuole italiane in Tripoli," drafted in April 1912 by the director of the civil service in Tripoli, Domenico Caruso, and sent to the chief secretary, prime minister's office, May 2, 1912.

26. Ibid.

27. For the Rattazzi Law and general legal aspects in Italy see G. Fubini, *La condizione giuridica dell'ebraismo italiano: Dal periodo napoleonico alla Repubblica* (Florence, 1974), pp. 23 ff.

28. This helps to explain the general favor with which the decree was received. Typical of it is the commentary ("Per gli ebrei della Libia") made by *La settimana israelitica*, March 15, 1912.

29. See, e.g., *Il corriere israelitico*, March 15, 1915; *Israel*, December 29, 1921.

30. The decree of August 26, 1916, approving the regulations by which the Community of Tripoli would function, stipulated:

"Article 2: With regard to Jewish subjects of Tripolitania and Cyrenaica, justice is dispensed by the Rabbinical courts in suits for any amount, with regard to civil status, family law, and religious practices.

"The courts' decisions become enforceable upon approval by the regional judiciary.

"Disputes between Jewish subjects relating to inheritance law may be brought to the attention of rabbinical courts, but the relevant decisions must be submitted for confirmation by the regional judiciary.

"If confirmation is refused, the case may be submitted to the Court of Appeals.

"With regard to Jews who are Italian citizens or foreigners, rabbinical courts have authority only in religious matters; the courts' decisions have no legal effect in this respect.

"Article 3: Appeals against the decisions of rabbinical courts may be submitted to the court which delivered the decision being questioned.

"The time limit for filing an appeal is fifteen days from the date on which the decision was issued, if this was done in the presence of the parties, or otherwise from the date on which they were notified.

"A decision may not be enforced while an appeal is pending. When the court has heard the chief rabbi of Tripoli regarding interpretation of Talmudic regulations, it shall deliver a decision which is definitive except for the procedure established for providing for enforcement.

"Article 4: The members of rabbinical tribunals, in the number fixed by tradition and local customs, shall be rabbis who are Italian citizens or subjects, indigenous to Libya, members of the respective Communities, and not less than twenty-five years of age.

"The Governor may suspend this regulation on condition that the applicant was born in Libya."

For an opinion on this, see U. Ajò, "Il Tribunale Rabbinico di Tripoli e la recente legislazione," *Israel*, April 5–17, 1917.

31. During the period immediately following the Italian occupation, about 2,000 Jews were living in Benghazi (according to the medical census of 1914, there were 1,862 in four hundred families spread all over the city),

almost all of them in trade. Benghazi had two synagogues (four a few years later) and a cemetery. There were another 350 or so Jews in about seventy families living in Derna, which did not have a Community organization. The Benghazi Jews, like all Libyan Jews, were very religious, but at the same time "very eager to become civilized." "Conscious of the needs of modern life, avid for culture, and eager to improve their intellectual condition," they already sent their sons to the Italian schools under the Ottoman government, and many of them knew Italian. See P. Mei, *Gli abitanti della Cirenaica: Studio etnico-antropologico* (Rome, 1914), pp. 47 ff. For further information regarding the second decade of the century, see U. Tegani, *Bengasi* (Milan, [1922]), pp. 56, 122, 126, 134, 156 ff. According to this author (p. 155), Jewish relations with the Arabs were traditionally tense, though superficially they were good because of continuous economic relations. "There has been no amalgam of Jews and Muslims, despite their lengthy contact. Mutual ill will, deep and insurmountable, thus broods between them, originating in the clear disparity of race, religion, and customs, and finding new sustenance in the Italophilia openly expressed by the industrious sons of Israel, who in any case are usually the devoted subjects of any government. They thus form a caste distinct from the population. They are controlled by the officials of the Jewish community which is subordinate to Tripoli in religious matters and whose highest figures in Benghazi are three rabbis and a chief rabbi."

32. For all documentation relating to the regulations, see AUCII, fasc. "Tripolitania," 1914–1916.

33. The government point of view emerges clearly in the following conclusions in a memorandum drafted by the Ministry of Colonies probably for the Romanin-Jacur Commission, which was responsible for preparing the formal organization:

"In summary:

"1. All Jews, whether Italian citizens or subjects or foreigners, born in the district of the association, to be established by the University itself, or who have resided there for at least three years, shall have the right to belong to the Jewish University. Jews who have not yet completed the three years of residence, or are passing through Tripoli, may not be excluded from religious ceremonies and may also, if the University considers it appropriate, take advantage of the charitable institutions run by this University.

"2. Foreign Jews, whether citizens or subjects of another State, may belong to the University, enjoy all the rights of the other members of the fellowship regarding participation in religious rites and receiving charity, and the right to be buried in the Jewish cemetery, but shall be excluded from appointment of officials and may not be appointed to official positions.

"3. Jurisdictional powers exercised directly by the University or the rabbinical court may as a norm apply only to Jews who are Italian subjects, never those who are citizens. Thus they shall never be applicable to Italian citizens nor as a norm shall Article 44, Clauses A, C, and E, of the Draft Statutes apply to foreign citizens and subjects: the first and last clauses shall not apply because they cover family relations encompassed by the civil code, and the second clause because it entrusts the rabbinical court with a right of surveillance over members of the religious community which, insofar as it is unspecified, exceeds the responsibility of a purely religious authority; though such surveillance may be admissible in a primitive society, it cannot be applied to individuals belonging to the people of the ancient European civilization, persons whose freedom of action should have no other bounds than those prescribed by the law, to which all citizens of every religion are subject.

"N. B. For Italian subjects who are Jews, a religious marriage contracted according to Mosaic Law is valid under civil law and is recognized as such by the State, thus divorce is also recognized. For Jews who are Italian citizens, marriage must always be regulated in accordance with our civil code.

"The above is the text of Art. 44 [of the Draft Statutes]. In addition to the functions which the governing authorities may grant the rabbinical court, it is responsible for:

"(a) guardianship of orphans who are minors;

"(b) application of religious sanctions;

"(c) the protection of public morals;

"(d) ascertaining whether the conditions required under Mosaic Law for declaration of divorce have been met."

34. The first request was based on the following arguments, besides maintaining that the foreigners resident in Tripoli were few and all devoted to the Italian cause:

"(a) to avoid schisms between fellow Jews;

"(b) to avoid excluding from the Community certain worthy persons who until now have played an energetic role in it;

"(c) to avoid depriving the Community of some good and competent people who in the past and for some time have controlled its destiny, either as council members or as presidents, and who might continue to contribute;

"(d) so that the Community may receive higher contributions and income."

The leadership backed up these arguments with the point that unless foreigners were admitted, local rabbis would be discouraged from pursuing a higher education. The committee, which had given its support to other small requests by the Community, opposed both, since it was certain that they would be rejected.

35. For the various phases of the 1914–1916 revolt, see Vitale, *Africa settentrionale*, pp. 85 ff. As a result of the revolt and the precarious living conditions which it caused, in late 1915 two thousand Jews "of most impoverished condition" left the hinterland and arrived in Tripoli (where they received help from the Alliance as well as other sources). See *La settimana israelitica*, November 25, 1915.

36. During the war, in 1917–1918, a few thousand Libyans, including eight hundred Jews, were enlisted or mobilized in the civil mobilization service in Italy. Most of these Jews were deployed in Northern Italy in war industries (such as the Ansaldo). Due to a combination of climate, food, low salaries, and the problem of Sabbath observance, these Jews had a hard life.

The Italian Jewish Universities Committee was obliged to intervene with the military authorities in order to have the conditions agreed on respected and resolve several cases caused by the dissatisfaction and insubordination of enlisted Libyan Jews. See AUCII, fasc. "Tripolitania," 1917–1918; ACS, *Carte Ameglio*, b. 13.

37. Typical of this is a letter sent just after Italy had entered the war by Quintino Guetta on behalf of a group of young Tripoli Jews to the local newspaper, *Nuova Italia*. He complained that a manifesto issued by the Alumni Association to praise Italian participation in the conflict, though it spoke of wars to liberate unredeemed lands and wars to redeem oppressed nationalities, omitted "any mention of the rebuilding of the Jewish state in Palestine, for which Zionism is working all over the world and many thousands of young Jews are shedding their blood to reach the goal for which they have yearned for over eighteen centuries." See *La settimana israelitica*, June 24, 1915.

38. Reliable and meaningful data on the economic composition of Libyan Jewry at the time of the Italian occupation are lacking. It is thus impossible to go beyond what has usually been stated, i.e., that the Jews (Italians, Libyans, and foreigners) controlled much of local trade and the economy. Some information may be deduced (though only quantitative aspects regarding some of the activities which were more important from a Western point of view) from the *Prima guida turistico-commerciale di Tripoli italiana* (Venice, 1912), published by the Istituto Italiano per l'espansione commerciale e coloniale.

39. It is interesting to note that these episodes were used by the Italian Jewish press to rebut accusations of being pro-Turkish coming from the nationalist press. See, e.g., A. Levi-Bianchini, "L'italianità degli israeliti di Bengasi," *Il vessillo israelitico*, December 1912.

40. According to the report by Anselmo Colombo prepared on his return from his visit to Libya in late 1912, in Amruss all ninety-five houses inhabited by Jews were seriously damaged, and in Zanzur many houses were ransacked and the *sepharim* and holy books were burned. By late 1912, of the approximately two hundred families (almost all craftsmen) previously living in Amruss, only about forty remained, and in Zanzur only five or six of the seventeen or twenty of a year before.

41. The firm of Halfalla Nahum suffered particular damage to its property and activities all over the territory. Compensation requests submitted to the Italian authorities show that direct damage amounted to over 130,000 lire (ASMAI, *Libia*, p. 118).

42. According to a study by the Italian civil service in early 1912, in Tripoli Community charity helped 1,861 people (132 sick, 329 invalids, 616 indigent, 697 widows and their children, 87 orphans who had lost both parents) with an annual expenditure of over 42,500 lire. See ACS, Presidenza Consiglio Ministri, Gabinetto, 1912, b. 398, fasc. T. 6. To appreciate these figures one must consider that the Community included about 8,500 people in Tripoli City (where most of those receiving help were). These 8,500 were joined in late 1911–early 1912 by another 2,000 refugees from the hin-

terland. The Community's income came mainly from the tax on meat, which yielded about 60,000 lire per annum.

43. ACS, *Carte Ameglio*, b. 20, fasc. "Banco di Napoli. Tripoli."

44. The most outstanding case during the initial period was the prison sentence of two years and four months given to Aron and Effraim Halfon, the owners of an important Benghazi firm which had the confidence of the colonial authorities, for whom it worked in food supply and coastal transportation. Accused in 1913 of corruption, fraud, and smuggling, the brothers were not sentenced by the military court of war of Benghazi until March 1916, because the investigation and trial were long drawn out due to the difficulty of proving the complicity of those they dealt with (an Italian corporal was sentenced to seven years and four months). See ASMAI, *Cirenaica*, p. 149/1-8, "Inchiesta contro Ditta A. E. Halfon."

45. The attitude of the military, especially that of the officers, toward the Arabs was characterized in general—and more and more so as the revolt spread—by great political shortsightedness and "great hostility, resentment, and hatred," which led to the Arabs all being treated as enemies without distinction. Thus the Jews were greatly appreciated, not only for the efficiency and punctuality with which they performed services, but also as friends. See ASMAI, Libia, p. 122/6-52, "Situazione politico-militare (1915)." The quotation is from a report dated July 29, 1915, by the commander of the Tajura garrison. For the "very grave errors in indigenous policy" committed by the military authorities, see in the same fascicle the personal and confidential circular sent by the governor, General Ameglio, to all officers and officials of the colony and the telegram sent three days later by Minister Martini to Ameglio.

46. On the religious and historical issue of the Sabbath for the Jews, see Augusto Segre, "Il sabato nella storia e nella tradizione ebraica," *L'uomo nella Bibbia e nelle culture ad essa contemporanee: Atti del Simposio per il XXV dell'Associazione Biblica Italiana* (Brescia, 1975), pp. 79 ff.

47. It is significant that an Italian rabbi such as Disegni should become the spokesman for these complaints, in the interview in *La settimana israelitica*, April 3, 1914. Speaking of the situation in Tripoli and the reasons why the situation of the Jews could not be viewed as entirely positive, he said the following about the Sabbath issue:

"Among 'external' causes, one must unfortunately include the hostile attitude of government circles and much of the immigrant Italian population. This is almost entirely composed of Sicilians. Almost all the officials, especially those in the lower ranks, are Sicilians too. Almost all these Sicilians harbor real ill will toward the Jewish population and show it often in acute expressions of petty tyranny, injustice, and rudeness.

"Thus on Sunday mornings in the customshouse, conversations such as the following one often take place: 'Why didn't you come yesterday and take away your merchandise?' 'It was Saturday, that's our holiday.' 'Don't give me your Saturday! Yesterday was your Saturday, today's our Sunday. Get lost!'

"The Arabs as a group are neither well disposed nor hostile, but feeling that they have the support of the officials, they are throwing their weight around. When disagreements arise between Arabs and Jews, and an official has to intervene, there is never a time when the question is not quickly put, 'You're a Jew, aren't you?' with a sneer that leaves no doubt that the issue has already been decided in the mind of the speaker against the Jew.

"On the whole the Community leaders do not seem very disturbed by this situation, which they think is a temporary one; but perhaps they are not weighing it accurately. The government, in order to win over the few rich Jews and important people, treats them with favor, but lets dislike spread and rampant injustice be committed against the Jewish masses. All this is certainly very bad, if for no other reason than that it fosters the conviction among the Jews that in order to ingratiate themselves with their new masters they must lose their own traditions and customs.

"It is therefore necessary that we undertake a campaign, with tact but firmness, on behalf of justice and our own dignity. The Jewish leadership should be the first in this, since we cannot now leave it to the young people who are willing but isolated and weak and are those who, inside themselves, suffer the most from this state of affairs."

See also the short leader article, "Il sabato intangibile!" *La settimana israelitica*, June 24, 1915.

48. See *Israel*, November 2, 1916.

49. The polemic spread from Libya to Italy. See "Il fatto di Bengasi nel suo significato generale," *La settimana israelitica*, October 9–16, 1914, substantially agreeing with the traditionalists: only the Jews themselves should have the guardianship of the Torah; concentrating solely on the theme of the Italian "motherland" was unacceptable; "such a secondary" event as "the change in rule over Libya" was not to be identified with the redemption of the people of Israel; the Jews had had their own "motherland" at Cyrene, which the Romans had "crushed."

50. This is what Giannetto Paggi, the new headmaster, said to Anselmo Colombo on March 5, 1912, about the new Community leadership which was forming:

"Though I have not written to you, I have been talking with some of the notables of the Jewish Community here, and this is what I found out: there is an embryonic administration; it is led by the Italian Jewish notables, i.e., Comm. Ernesto Labi, Cav. Isach di H. Hassan, Meborath Hassan, etc.; there are others capable of forming a serious administrative council, such as Halfalla Nahum, Alfredo and Mario Nunes Vais, and others; but someone has to dispel the truly oriental apathy and egoism developed to the nth degree. Everyone knows how to shout: I will take responsibility; things go well as long as people only have to accept positions, but getting something done is another kettle of fish.

"Moreover, you showed me that the soul of an administration is a good secretary. There is none here and it is impossible to find one among the indigenous Jews. We will have to catch one among the Europeans and pay him well, and he will also need to know Arabic, at least the Arabic spoken here . . ."

See AUCII, fasc. "Tripolitania."

51. On the figure of Nhaisi, see *Israel*, August 8 and October 10, 1918, on the occasion of his unexpected death in 1918 before he was thirty.

52. See Nhaisi's letter on this subject, published by *La settimana israelitica*, May 21, 1915. The weekly commented that the letter clearly showed "an incipient conflict between the youth and the Community leadership, a conflict between the opposing ideas of Jewishness and Europeanism." "If such is the case," the Florentine journal wrote, without concealing its sympathy for the former, "few debates can be more fertile than this one, if it is conducted on the right level."

53. See in this connection Aron F. Gomel's attack (in a letter to *La settimana israelitica*, November 25, 1915) on the Community leaders because of the spread of begging:

"There are hundreds of wretched people, dirty and ragged, who go around from shop to shop, from house to house, dragging behind them their daughters and sons, tattered, half-naked, and girls of thirteen or fourteen who are learning, at the most precious time in their lives, to hold out their hand for charity! This sad scene is repeated immutably every Friday, without anyone bothering to raise his voice and shout in order to stop such a scandal which, in our name, cries shame on our race.

"What kind of an impression do we give here in the Colony of our brotherliness and our proverbial solidarity in the face of such things?

"Let the head of the Community awake, then, let his colleagues in the administration act and not let time intervene before they bring such a state of affairs to an end, since it exists nowhere except in Tripoli.

"There are so many ways to put an end to this shame and help those unfortunate people, so that they do not need to expose themselves to the suffering, humiliation, and, alas, occasional derision to which beggars are subject.

"Could not the Community tax all those shops and distribute the proceeds fairly among those unfortunates, while prohibiting poor people from going around asking for charity?"

In the same vein, though expressed in more general terms, Elia Nhaisi had already requested in the same journal (August 12, 1915) that the Community set up courses in Italian, so that it would be possible for more Jews to find work.

54. See, for the complete texts, *La settimana israelitica*, September 16, 1915.

55. See, for the complete text, *ibid.*, October 21, 1915.

56. See ibid., October 7, 1915.

57. Nothing was done either by the office of the director of the Civil Service or by the Ministry of Colonies. This can be argued on the basis of a confidential report to the governor dated October 9, 1915, from Giacomo Tedesco, examining the civil authorities' policy toward the indigenous population, both Arabs and Jews. With regard to the Jews, Tedesco wrote: "It is

not believed that the civil authorities have changed their attitude toward the Jewish population, because it does not appear that the complaints of a considerable group of dissidents has been held against them. They were holding against the Community leaders their complete passivity or lack of control over matters in the general interest, because of hidden motives of personal interest. They are complaining also, in this respect, that the issue of the Statutes for the Jewish Community has still not been settled." See ACS, *Carte Ameglio*, b. 19.

58. See *La settimana israelitica*, September 22–30, 1915.

3. Arab Revolt and Italian Reconquest (1916–1931)

1. Comprehensive studies of the Arab revolt and Italian reconquest of Libya do not exist. There are numerous Italian accounts of the military operations. A synthesis of these is provided in Vitale, *Africa settentrionale*, pp. 85 ff.

2. On the Sanusis, see E. E. Evans-Pritchard, *The Sanusi of Cyrenaica* (Oxford: Clarendon, 1949; reprint, 1963); M. F. Shukry, *al-Sanusiya: Dayn wa-Dawla* (Cairo, 1948).

3. For the text of the Basic Law and of the governor's decrees to implement some parts of it, as well as the decree-law of October 31, 1919, which, with few variations, extended the Basic Law to Cyrenaica, see Torquato Curotti, *La Libia* (Borgo San Dalmazzo, 1973), pp. 89–105 and 87–88.

4. In the absence of a real historical study of these events, see—with due caution because of its nationalist position and apology for Volpi— Raffaele Rapex, *L'affermazione della sovranità italiana in Tripolitania: Governatorato del Conte Giuseppe Volpi (1921–1925)* (Tientsin: Chihli Press, 1937); on Amendola's governorship, Renzo De Felice, "Amendola ministro delle Colonie," in *Giovanni Amendola nel cinquantenario della morte, 1926–1976* (Rome, 1976), pp. 161 ff.; C. Filesi, "Giovanni Amendola e la questione Cirenaica," *Rivista di studi politici internazionali* January– March 1977, pp. 77 ff.

5. See Rapex, *L'affermazione*, p. 101. A telegram from Volpi to Minister Girardini on December 18, 1921 (ASMAI, Ufficio cifra, Tell. in arrivo, sub data), is also significant. It denies rumors of supposed Jewish sympathy for the Arab cause: "Y. E. has already heard from Commr. Belli that some Jews here are said to be in touch with Jewish Socialist representatives for disruptive purposes, either for the Socialist aim of making us abandon the colonies in general or the aim of the said local elements to help internal plans for amirates or similar political arrangements believing that the said Jews' trade with the hinterland will benefit thereby. This Government has discovered nothing specific to indicate this. In fact, Commr. Halfalla Nahum, previously appointed leader of reactionary local Jews, and recently returned from a lengthy trip with his family to London and Paris, has a correct attitude of devotion to the Government alien to such initiatives."

6. See M. Sani, "Politica ebraica in Tripolitania?" *La vita italiana*, October 1921, pp. 292 ff., esp. p. 294.

7. Artom, "L'importanza," (cited in Ch. 1, no. 24), pp. 118 ff.

8. Camera di Commercio Industria Agricoltura per la Tripolitania, *Indicatore-Annuario del Commercio, dell'Industria, dell'Agricoltura in Tripolitania* (Tripoli, 1924). The Chamber of Commerce was founded in October 1921. In 1923, five of its members (Salomone Giuili, Felice Hassan, Juseph Barda, Messaud Hassan, and Abramino Forti) and its treasurer (Salomone Nahum) were Jews.

9. E.g., there was strong Jewish participation in the Unione Tripolina company for esparto trade and processing, one of the largest in the country. Before the Italian occupation there were four firms dealing with esparto, three with Jewish and one with British ownership. The Banco di Roma took over that of Eugenio Arbib; Perry Bury and Co. sold its plant to P. Nahum (then H. di P.). In 1920 the Banco di Roma and the two Jewish firms Nahum and M. di J. Hassan amalgamated into the Unione Tripolina. There were also companies with Jewish participation in the tuna-fishing industry. Several fisheries were not productive, though, in 1922–1923, since they had been seriously damaged by the rebels. One of the largest of these, at Marsa Zuaga, was managed by a Nahum. See Rapex, *L'affermazione*, pp. 413 ff.

10. There were also the following firms: one brickworks, three glassworks, one plumbing manufacturer, and three machine repair shops.

11. Here is a list of firms registered in the second category (classes 4–6) with the Tripoli Chamber of Commerce (F = foreign, I = Italian, L = Libyan):

Arbib, Ruben (F)	four businesses, one class 4, three class 6; trade with Nigeria and Sudan; import-export; commercial franchises; grocery
Barda, Juseph (L)	two class 4 businesses: import-export; grocery
Barki Fratelli (L)	two class 6 businesses: import-export; bric-à-brac dealing
Curiel, Rafaello (F)	one class 4 business: henna
Curiel, Raffaello and Arbib	two class 4 businesses: import-export and grain
Debasc, Hammus di B. (F)	three class 4 businesses: import-export; grain; grocery
Debasc and Nemni (L)	two class 4 businesses: import-export; grocery
Forti, Abramino (I)	two class 6 businesses: import-export; grain
Gehan, Hlafo and Gabriele (L)	two class 6 businesses: trading; hide dealing
Gehan, Huatu (L)	three class 6 businesses: trading; wool and leather export; henna
Giuili, Salomone di M. (L)	two class 6 businesses: import-export; woven work
Giuili, Scialom di M. (L)	two class 6 businesses: import-export; woven work
Habib, S. L. (F)	two class 5 businesses: import-export; grocery

Haggiag, Simeone (F)	one class 4 business: import-export
Hannuna, S. di M. (L)	two class 6 businesses: import-export; woven and handmade work
Hannuna, Vittorio di M. (L)	three class 6 businesses: import-export; trading; woven and handmade work
Hassan, Aron (L)	three class 6 businesses: trading; leather and wool export; woven and handmade work
Hassan, Isac di Haim (I)	one class 4 business: import-export one class 5 business: trade with Nigeria and Sudan
Hassan, Jacob di Haim (I)	four class 4 businesses: import-export; grocery; leather and wool export; henna
Hassan, M. di J. (I)	two class 4 businesses: import-export; leather and wool export
Hassan, Messaud (L)	three businesses, one class 4, two class 6: trade with Nigeria and Sudan; import-export; woven and handmade work
Hassan, Pace (I)	three class 6 businesses: trading; henna; ostrich feathers
Hassan, Umberto (I)	two class 6 businesses: trading; grocery
Hassan, Vittorio di M. (L)	three class 4 businesses: import-export; henna; woven and handmade work
Hatuma, Davide (L)	two class 5 businesses: trading; livestock and butchery
Labi, Enrico fu Isacco (L)	two class 5 businesses: import-export; commercial franchises
Mimun, Hammus (L)	two class 5 businesses: import-export; henna
Nahum, Abramo (I)	three class 4 businesses: banking; import-export; henna
Nahum, Elia (L)	four class 5 businesses: boatbuilding; import-export; henna; leather and wool export
Nahum, Halfalla di P. (I)	three class 4 businesses: import-export; trade with Nigeria and Sudan; woven and handmade work; plus the only Jewish farm (olive, citrus, and fruit groves) in the Tripoli area
Nunes Vais, Abramo (I)	one class 6 business: franchises and commissions
Raccah, Abramo di E. (L)	three class 4 businesses: import-export; grain; leather and wool export
Tayar, G. di M. (F)	two class 6 businesses: import-export; henna

12. See AUCII, Comitato, letter from the secretary to Felice Ravenna dated February 8, 1931, (the multimillionaire was Halfalla Nahum). A draft

note for Mussolini, prepared soon after by Ravenna, states: "One-third of the population consists of ragged indigents, one-third of poor people, and one-third covers the levels in between the poor and about fifteen wealthy families" (AUCII, fasc. 33).

13. The 1931 census was exhaustively studied by R. Bachi, "Gli ebrei delle Colonie Italiane: Note statistiche sul censimento 1931," *La rassegna mensile di Israel* (January–February 1936, pp. 385 ff. For the 1928 census, one should consult Camera di Commercio Industria e Agricoltura della Tripolitania, *I risultati del Censimento industriale e commerciale in Tripolitania al 15 ottobre 1928–VI* (Tripoli, 1930). For the electoral rolls of the Community of Tripoli in 1930, see ASMAI, Libia, p. 31 (1930–1935).

14. Bachi, "Gli ebrei delle Colonie Italiane," pp. 389 ff.

15. The difference of ten between Tables 6 and 7 is due to difficulties in assigning categories due to the problem of nationality. See note to Table 3 in the census.

16. In 1914 the Muslim population of Tripoli amounted to 19,907; in 1924 it was below 21,000; but by 1931 it had reached 42,654.

17. Bachi, "Gli ebrei delle Colonie italiane," p. 393, shows that the Jewish population of Tripoli and Benghazi in 1931 fell into the age groups shown in Table N-1. It emerges from the same study that the average size of a Jewish family in Tripoli was 4.38 (in the rest of Tripolitania, 4.25; Benghazi, 4.48; the rest of Cyrenaica, 4.45). People married young, and 73.3 percent of children (in Benghazi 77.8 percent) lived with their parents (pp. 394 ff.).

18. The nineteen taxpayers contributing most were:
Borgas Da Silva, Giuseppe (merchant), and Hatuma, David (property-owner)
1,300 lire
Nahum, Halfalla; Nahum, Clemente; Nahum, Scialom; and Nahum, Emilio (merchants)
1,000 lire
Nahum, Maurizio (merchant)
800 lire
Curiel, Victor (franchise-holder), and Nemni, Raffaello (merchant)   700 lire
Abta, Scialom; Barda, Jusef; Haddad, Jacob; and Hassan, Hlafo (merchants)
600 lire
Arbib, Jacob; Arbib, Nuatu; Barki, Jusef; Benjamin, Moses; Haggiag, Simenone; and Hassan, Angiolino (merchants)   500 lire

19. The figures are from Contini, *Storia delle istituzioni scolastiche della Libia,* passim, esp. pp. 37 ff. and 77 ff. The Jewish public schools were established in 1939, just after the Fascist racial laws were extended to Libya. In general the Jews were among the best students, even compared with Italians. See, e.g., Regio Instituto Tecnico—R. Scuola Complementare—Tripoli d'Africa, *Annuario 1927,* vol. 5 (Rome, n.d.), pp. 44 ff., esp. pp. 46 ff.

20. See A. Ciotola, *Un venticinquennio di organizzazione sanitaria in Libia* (Rome, 1937); Gov. Gen. Libia, Ispettorato Centrale di Sanità, *Relazione per l'anno 1939* (Tripoli, 1940).

21. Rapex, *L'affermazione,* p. 66.

22. For the first case, see "Da Tripoli: Un'assoluzione," *Israel,* September 6, 1923. For the second case, see ASMAI, pos. 150/27, fasc. 127, "Nahum, Eugenio." In the first instance Nahum was sentenced by the special

TABLE N-1. *Age Structure of Jews in Tripoli and Benghazi, 1931 (per thousand)*

Age	Tripoli		Benghazi	
	Males	Females	Males	Females
Up to 5	149	145	135	132
5–10	149	138	129	139
(0–10)	(298)	(283)	(264)	(271)
10–20	195	208	228	221
20–30	175	182	206	195
30–40	131	129	128	128
40–50	82	82	81	90
50–60	63	57	55	44
Over 60	55	58	39	52

court of Zawia on December 10, 1922, to ten years' imprisonment and confiscation of assets; subsequently, in May 1923, he was acquitted on appeal, as the court decided that the crime ascribed to him was not prosecutable.

23. Ottone Gabelli, *La Tripolitania dalla fine della guerra mondiale all'avvento del fascismo* (n.p.: Intra, 1939) 2: 24, 28.

24. A typical example is Amendola's visit, as minister of colonies, to Libya in July 1922. He visited the Jewish quarters of Tripoli and Benghazi, receiving many demonstrations of popular support and statements of loyalty to Italy from the religious and lay leaders of the two Communities. Moreover, in Benghazi, he responded to a petition submitted to him by the local Zionists "expressing Italy's support and sympathy for the Zionist movement and reconfirming the government's firm position toward Zionism." See *Israel*, July 13 and 20, 1922.

25. A telling example of this is that in the summer of 1921 the Italian authorities in Tripoli forbade the showing—organized by the Circolo Sion and previously permitted by the authorities in Benghazi—of a film on Herzl's life. The official reason given was that the censor had not given approval; in fact, the step was taken to avoid offending the Arabs. See AUCII, fasc. "Corrispondenza 1921," R. I. Barda to A. Sereni, July 28, 1921.

26. Festa, *Scuole per indigeni in Tripolitania*, p. 53.

27. The latter was probably the origin, or at least one of the causes, of several incidents, some violent, which occurred in and around Benghazi in 1921–1922 (two Jews were killed, probably in the course of being robbed). See *Israel*, April 14, May 12 and 26, 1921, and May 18, 1922.

28. AUCII, "Corrispondenza avv. Ravenna 1932," July 25, 1932.

29. AUCII, fasc. "Tripolitania," H. Nahum to A. Sereni, March 10, 1920.

30. AUCII, fasc. "Bengasi," 1920.

31. AUCII, fasc. "Corrispondenza 1929," A. Monastero to the president of the Consortium of Italian Jewish Communities, September 19, 1929.

4. Life in the Jewish Community

1. As in previous chapters, reference will be made in this chapter to the Comitato delle Università Israelitiche Italiane [Italian Jewish Universities Committee], the Consorzio delle Comunità Israelitiche Italiane [Consortium of Italian Jewish Communities], and the Unione delle Comunità Israelitiche [Union of Italian Jewish Communities]. For the convenience of the reader who may not be closely acquainted with Italian Jewish affairs, it should be stated that the three names refer to the same organization at different periods in its juridical and administrative development. The designation Committee was used up to 1920, when after its being granted the status of juristic person, the designation Consortium was bestowed on it. The name Union was in turn given to it in 1931 following the new law (linked to the legislation regarding permitted religions) on the position of Judaism in Italy within the framework of the Fascist state. For further information cf. R. Frau, "Appunti sul regime giuridico delle Comunità Israelitiche in Italia dallo Statuto sino al R.D. 30 ottobre 1930, N. 1731," in *Studi economico-giuridici* (University of Cagliari, 1969); also De Felice, *Storia degli ebrei italiani sotto il fascismo* (cited in Ch. 2, no. 6), pp. 102 ff.

2. Artom, "L'importanza dell'elemento ebraico" (cited in Ch. 1, no. 24), p. 121.

3. I. Sciaky, "Tripoli ebraica," in *La rassegna mensile di Israel*, April 3, 1926, p. 268.

4. Ibid.

5. "Gli ebrei di Tripoli in una conferenza del Rabb. Mag. Dr. Artom a Firenze," in *Israel*, September 21, 1922.

6. A consequence of this psychological attitude was the particular sensitivity of the Libyan Jews as a community with regard to all aspects of their relations with the Italian administration. The administration's actions were watched and judged through a constant comparison between its policy toward the Jews and its policy toward the Arabs. Artom's statements on the subject are typical:

"The Tripolitanian Jewish population, which feels and in many ways shows a profound sense of gratitude to the Italian government, because of its efforts in the spheres of peace, civilization, well-being, and justice, nevertheless becomes alarmed and distrustful whenever it perceives in some new legal provision or some new government measure anything which might, or which it fears might in any way run counter to its beliefs or religious observances. This and this alone can sometimes make it believe that 'Things were better in the bad old days.' Another rather delicate question is the comparison which Jews sometimes feel induced to draw between attitudes toward them and attitudes toward the Arabs. They feel themselves to be, and on the whole actually are, above the Arabs from the moral and civic points of view; in the period of domination by local tribal leaders and by the Turkish government, they were used to being looked on as below the level of the dominant population. Today they feel hurt and offended when it appears that the Italian Government gives greater respect to the Arabs' religious practices and rites than it gives to those of the Jews" (Artom, "L'importanza dell'elemento ebraico," p. 120).

7. See "Gli ebrei di Tripoli" (cited in note 5 above).

8. Artom, "L'importanza dell'elemento ebraico," p. 117.

9. I. Sciaky, "Visioni tripoline," *Israel*, November 26, 1925, suppl. According to a census made at the request of the Union of Italian Jewish Communities in 1934, there were five private Jewish libraries in Tripoli accessible to the public: one with 1,200 volumes, two with 1,000, one with 500, and one with 300. The oldest dated from 1813 and the most recent from 1901.

10. For a history of Libya during the Italian occupation, with particular reference to economic, political, and social development, see Claudio G. Segre, *Fourth Shore: The Italian Colonization of Libya* (Chicago and London: University of Chicago Press, 1974); for the same period from the Arab point of view, Shukry, *al-Sanusiya* (cited in Ch. 3, n. 2); idem, *Milad Dawlat Libya al-Haditha: Wathaiq Tahririya* (Cairo, 1957).

11. See "Gli ebrei di Tripoli."

12. First the pro-Zionist and later the Zionist groups made a point of criticizing such cases. Besides the article by Nhaisi, "Questioni vitali dell'ebraismo libico" (in *La settimana israelitica*, September 8, 1915), see, e.g., the petition (written by Nhaisi himself) from the Circolo Sion to the Italian Jewish Universities Committee, published almost in its entirety by *Israel*, June 27, 1918.

13. See the Circolo Sion petition cited above.

14. See Sciaky, "Visioni tripoline"; "Gli ebrei di Tripoli." Useful information can also be gleaned from a letter which Rabbi Artom wrote on April 5, 1931, to Felice Ravenna to describe the state of education in Tripoli ("anything but satisfactory, whether viewed from the Jewish standpoint or from that of general education") and propose his own plan of reform (AUCII, "Questioni scolastiche"). What Vittorio Levi, an Italian member of the Community of Tripoli's charity committee, wrote to Ravenna was even more pointed: "Two thousand five hundred children learn sheep-like, by rote, Talmudic texts of which they can obviously understand neither the doctrine nor the poetry, under the guidance of *shamashim* [beadles] masquerading as teachers. They are characterized by dirty nails, long beards, and the traditional stick. This goes on for eight or nine hours a day on premises which the goats of our Calabria would hardly be able to stand, and where light is feared and given out grudgingly! These schools thus breed candidates for tuberculosis or, at best, undernourished beings bearing the marks of the *galut*" (AUCII, "Corrispondenza 1932").

15. The elementary-school-age population of Tripoli in 1929 was estimated at about 3,000—2,000 boys and 1,000 girls. Of the boys, 1,150 attended the Talmud Torah, 500 the rabbinical schools; about 50 were being educated in the family or privately. About 350 Talmud Torah students were attending state schools as well. Another 321 attended the Italian Jewish school set up on an experimental basis two years previously. Finally, there were about 500 girls attending state schools. See the President of the

Talmud Torah to the Community of Tripoli, September 31, 1929, in AUCII, fasc. 15.

16. The most serious measure, even though it was later rescinded, was perhaps in October 1922 when the postal service stopped hiring Jews, justifying itself on the basis of the difficulties in which it found itself since it had already hired many Jews and they did not want to work on the Sabbath. See AUCII, fasc. 21.

17. In July 1922, in order to reach a settlement with the Community, which maintained that it could not take on the financial burden of an Italian chief rabbi, Volpi, the governor of Tripolitania, recognized the post of chief rabbi as part of the civil service, and thus to be financed from the budget of the Ministry of Colonies.

18. In early 1931 Governor Badoglio told Commissioner Disegni that he was not averse, if it would solve the issue of the rabbi's appointment, to considering the possibility of making the chief rabbi a sort of mayor of the Community. See AUCII, fasc. 12. The following year, with Felice Ravenna, Badoglio considered doubling the chief rabbi's stipend, as long as the Communities would do the same (AUCII, "Corrispondenza 1932").

19. *Israel*, June 27, 1918.

20. The Italian authorities opposed the appointment of S. Z. Margulies as chief rabbi in 1918 because he was a former Austro-Hungarian citizen. In the Fascist period they particularly required that the chief rabbi be neither too conservative and traditionalist nor too actively pro-Zionist.

21. To assess Artom's role, particularly the importance he gave to the cultural problem in relation to the state of Libyan Jewry, see his appeal to the "Jews of Tripolitania" of August 15, 1920, and his platform speech of January 29, 1921 (fully recounted by *Israel*, February 10, 1921). The following passage in his appeal is especially significant:

"Remember, my dear brothers, that as regards education you, who are rightly seen as a model through your strict observance of so many Jewish practices, should be inferior to no one in the upright morality of your way of life nor in your precise and rational knowledge of the law and language of Israel.

"Nor should you keep apart from non-Jewish culture, which is now essential if you want to lead an independent and acceptable way of life. Culture, both Jewish and secular, must be fostered among you and extended to groups of people who, through awe of ancient prejudices and ingrained habits, until now have been deprived the great benefits which it brings. I should like to give a word of brotherly advice to the young people. Remember that the true progress of Jewish culture depends especially on your zeal in respecting our law and everything Jewish. You would lead the Community to ruin if, dazzled and seduced by the apparent spendor of alien civilizations, you abandoned, even in the slightest particular, the eternally living and salutary norms of Jewish life. It is up to you to show that Israel can merge the demands of its age-old law with the best which modern civilization has to offer."

22. From a letter by Artom to Angelo Sacerdoti, dated April 28, 1933, and dedicated to the issue of a rabbi for Tripoli, one learns that good relations with the Italian authorities lasted as long as the latter believed that Artom would go along with their plans for assimilation. A crisis occurred when the authorities realized that the chief rabbi had no intention of doing so (AUCII, "Corrispondenza 1933").

23. A long letter which Artom wrote in August 1926 (when his return from Tripoli as chief rabbi was being planned) to the president of the Consortium, Angelo Sereni, summing up his experience in Tripoli, includes the following:

"The confusion existing in the Community for intrinsic reasons was increased by D. L. [Decree-Law] 26.VIII.1916 n. 1145, containing the regulations governing the Jewish Community of Tripoli. While these regulations are flawed in many respects, they are patently absurd as regards the position of chief rabbi. Though one article (no. 33) is dedicated to the chief rabbi, all provisions of the regulations omit the chief rabbi's function. They establish that the various Community services should be run by the committees, of which the chief rabbi is not a member and which are not obliged to have any relation whatsoever with the chief rabbi; hence the chief rabbi's participation in running the Community is, according to the aforesaid regulations, entirely voluntary and dependent on the wish of the committees. Whether for the reasons mentioned above, or because of the spirit of individualism which rules many of their members, these committees never solicit his participation. Not only this, but when I comment on their work or ask to be kept informed of discussions which I believe fall within my authority, they reply that the regulations give the committees, not the chief rabbi, full responsibility for managing individual services of the Community.

"Because of this attitude, during the three years and more when I held office, I was *never* asked to solve questions of ritual, my opinion was *never* listened to, except purely for purposes of information, on issues involved in religious services, education, or charity, either by the council or by the committees, I *never* participated in hiring or dismissing Community officers, while decisions relating to ritual were *frequently* taken without my even being informed, and I was called on *almost daily* for matters completely outside my responsibility, such as requests to oppose decisions taken by the judiciary or orders of the security or planning authorities. Characteristic and instructive in showing the concept the Jewish Community of Tripoli had of the function of a chief rabbi is the fact that, while appointments to positions invested with religious authority, such as the judges in the rabbinical court, were considered irrevocable, the chief rabbi's appointment was not so considered. According to the Community, the chief rabbi should be appointed for a term which is not too long so that, as is explicitly stated, the council members should not permanently commit their successors" (AUCII, fasc. "Corrispondenza 1926").

24. A clear indication of this struggle was given at the convention of the Italian Jewish Universities Committee and chief rabbis held in Milan,

July 10–11, 1922: "A personal struggle is going on in Tripoli between Halfalla Nahum's party and another one: they are fighting between them and ruining the Community. The rabbi's appointment is one of the questions at issue. It is held that the Community can carry on without a chief rabbi, with only its local rabbis, who since they know the local dialect are best suited for certain functions. The rabbinical court should be composed of local rabbis . . ." (AUCII, fasc. "Congresso 1925," minutes, fols. 21 ff). Among public positions, see *Israel*, which was favorable to Artom, esp. in the article "La crisi rabbinica di Tripoli," July 6, 1922; letters under the same title, October 18, 1923; and Artom's letter to *Israel*, published on November 8, 1923.

25. *Israel*, October 21, 1930, and esp. AUCII, fasc. 12.

26. For Disegni's activities, see *Israel*, November 27 and December 24, 1930; January 20, February 13, and March 13–20, 1931.

27. In the late 1920s the problem of the rabbinical court became critical, after the Community leaders—as usual, partly for practical reasons and partly for reasons of power—established that the judges did not have to be rabbis (appointed for an indefinite term) but could be chosen (for a specific term) by the Community council from those eligible to be its members. That step provoked "serious differences in views between the mass of Jews and the Community council and even among the judges themselves" and deprived the court of its moral authority. See *Israel*, June 6, 1930.

28. See AUCII, fasc. "Il Congresso delle Comunità Israelitiche Italiane (marzo 1933)"; and *Israel*, March 24–30, 1933.

29. Sciaky, "Tripoli ebraica," p. 269.

30. For the problem as a whole, see AUCII, fasc. "Tripolitania" and "Questioni scolastiche."

31. See AUCII, fasc. "Tripolitania."

32. For the founding of the Talmud Torah in Tripoli and its early years of activity, see *Bulletin Igdil Thora Bie* (Tunis, 1897), which also lists contributions which the school received.

33. See H. Nahum, *Discorso inaugurale del nuovo Gran Consiglio della Comunità Israelitica (Tripoli, 11 agosto 1917)* (Tripoli, [1917]), pp. 15 ff, esp. p. 17.

34. More or less lively polemics continued throughout the 1920s and later, without producing any result. The first important reform was carried out in 1931, when girls were admitted to the school. More radical reforms were not carried out until 1937.

35. See AUCII, fasc. "Tripolitania," Communiqué No. 2 from the Community of Tripoli, March 27, 1920.

36. "Intorno al problema scolastico a Tripoli," *Israel*, January 5, 1922, still supported the idea of an Italian-Jewish school in the terms set forth in the Nahum plan, which was later abandoned in favor of the idea of a school within the state system:

"An appropriate means to attain the goal would be to set up an Italian-Jewish elementary school for the time being and later perhaps also an intermediate school, with qualified Jewish teachers. The Italian school curriculum for that level would be taught, while the basic elements of Jewish culture would be imparted, and teaching would be carried out in Italian and Hebrew alternately as soon as it was feasible.

"The school would obviously be subject to the supervision of the government education authorites which would cover, either entirely or in large part, the expenses for running it.

"It is not difficult to persuade oneself of the effectiveness of this procedure. One has only to think that if it were carried out the two biggest obstacles to many Jews' attending Italian schools and the only reason why those who attend do not do so earlier would be removed. These reasons are the reluctance of many Jewish families to put their children in a non-Jewish environment at an early age, fearing that they will be exposed to religious principles opposed to Judaism, and the fear—certainly well-grounded—that young boys absorbed into a secular educational system will completely abandon their Jewish studies, thereby failing in one of their most important religious duties. One would also avoid a serious pedagogical problem. As I have noted, in order to avoid contravening the precept regarding religious study, most Jews attending Italian schools go, when they can, to the indigenous schools as well; the radical difference in methods and lack of coordination between the two educations can only be bad for the pupils and reduce the profit they gain from both systems.

"Finally, one other consideration should not be glossed over. The indigenous Jewish population often has the suspicion, which is not always either unfounded or unjustified, that the Italian government keeps it in a position of inferiority to the Arabs which it knows it does not deserve: to put the Jews on a level with the Arabs in education would produce in them great satisfaction and gratitude toward the government."

37. See G. Amendola, *Discorsi politici (1919–1925)* (Rome, 1968), pp. 135 ff. (July 18, 1922).

38. It is reproduced, under the title "Proposte per l'adattamento dei programmi vigenti nelle scuole italiane alla scolaresca ebraica di Tripoli," in *La rassegna mensile di Israel,* 1926.

39. See "La questione della scuola ebraica a Tripoli," *Israel,* November 11, 1926.

40. See the essay by Angelo Piccioli in Luciano Zùccoli et al., *La rinascita della Tripolitania: Memorie e studi su quattro anni di governo del conte Giuseppe Volpi di Misurata* (Milan: Mondatori, 1926), p. 287.

41. In Benghazi and other towns the problems were the same, but generally less critical, due to the far smaller numbers of Jews or fewer differences between them. In Benghazi in 1934, besides the Talmud Torah, there was a Jewish school attended by fifty pupils in six classes (three lower-level classes in which only religious education was taught, and three upper-level classes in which Hebrew language and Jewish history and culture were also taught from textbooks from Palestine). In Barce, Apollonia, Derna, and Tubruq, there were courses of purely religious education.

42. On the origins of the Circolo Sion, established in accordance with the program of the Zionist Congress of Basel, see, in addition to the second chapter, C., "Il movimento sionista a Tripoli," *Almanacco Annuario della Tripolitania 1922 "El Gerid"*, pp. 63 ff. For the club's activities (as well as those of the later Zionist Organization of Tripolitania [OST]) see *Israel*, which always followed it with support and attention, esp. the issues for April 22 and December 21, 1916; December 6, 1917; January 7, June 10, and October 31, 1918; October 6 and December 11, 1919; October 7, 1920; and January 7, 1924. On Libyan Zionism in general, see F. Zuarez and Y. Rubin, "Le origini del sionismo in Libia," in *Yahadut Luv* (cited in Ch. 1, n. 26), pp. 129 ff.

43. The first *chalutz* [pioneer, settler] from Tripoli was Elia Fellah, a member of the Circolo Sion, in 1921. He was followed by others, mainly masons, who generally had considerable difficulty in finding work and adapting to the hard life in Palestine, so much so that later on the OST planned to buy a piece of land in Palestine and build a house to receive immigrants from Tripoli. See *Israel*, February 8, 1923; January 17, 1924; and April 30, 1925. Between 1933 and 1938 about forty families emigrated to Palestine, as well as about twenty young members of the Ben Yehuda.

44. For further details, see *Israel* (which initially opposed the Concordia e Progresso, but later came around to the idea of an agreement), May 25 and June 22, 1922; April 26 and May 17, 1923; and March 13, 1924.

45. The aims which the OST set itself in its statutes were the following:

"(a) To cooperate in the Jewish effort in the Diaspora and to support in every way possible the historical aspirations of Israel and the reconstruction of a Jewish Eretz Israel;

"(b) To awaken and enlighten the consciousness of the Jews of Tripolitania with the ultimate aim of imbuing them with the idea of the unity of Israel and a desire for its spiritual and national realization;

"(c) To set up Zionist groups in places around Tripolitania where Jews are living and to direct their activities and functioning;

"(d) To represent Jewish aspirations and national organization vis-à-vis the colonial authorities;

"(e) To seek the cooperation of all other Jewish organizations in Tripolitania and to act in accord to support and protect Jewish interests and promote the national reawakening of the Jews of Tripolitania;

"(f) To influence local Italian public opinion so as to encourage more understanding between the two peoples and win the Italians' growing sympathy for Jewish national aspirations;

"(g) To publish the newspaper *Deghel Sion* in Judeo-Arabic;

"(h) To take the most appropriate steps to spread Jewish culture and Hebrew language among Zionists, in order to win over the minds of Jews not only broadly but also deeply;

"(i) To act in conjunction with similar associations, local Jewish Communities, and other organizations, so that every group will set up courses in Hebrew, classes, and lectures;

"(*l*) To create a central library with a reading room and small local libraries to help people to study Jewish history and civilization;

"(*m*) To support associated groups morally and, if possible, financially." See *Israel*, February 18, 1926.

46. One result of these differences was that, in 1926, some members of the Maccabee Club broke away. Besides sports, in the meantime it had begun drama and put on many very successful shows. One hundred of the 260 members also wanted to have recreational activities (dances, parties, and gambling). They founded a new club, Gioventù Israelitica Tripolitana [Tripolitanian Jewish Youth] (GIT), which functioned for just over four years, then was obliged to cease activities due to financial difficulties.

47. See Organizzazione Sionistica della Tripolitania, Sez. Culturale "Ben Jehuda," Scuola "Hattikvà," *Opera svolta negli anni 5692–5693* (Tripoli, 1934); *Israel*, October 26, 1933.

48. *Israel*, October 18, 1934; December 13, 1934; July 9–16, 1936; and January 7–14, 1937. There were examinations at the end of the courses before passing to the next level. At the end of the first session in 1933–1934, 202 pupils passed (99 boys and 103 girls), 57 had to repeat (24 boys and 33 girls), and 90 failed (18 boys and 72 girls).

49. The expression is taken from Nahum's platform speech (*Discorso inaugurale*, p. 32) at the opening session of the Community council elected in 1917.

50. Ibid., pp. 9, 24 ff.

51. A typical example is the manifesto "To Voters" spread around Tripoli by the Circolo Sion at the time of the December 15, 1918 elections and published in *Israel*, December 23, 1918:

"Brothers!

"For the second time in a few months you are called to the important task of electing your representatives on the Council of the Community.

"The time for contests between personalities is past: today you must choose between two programs.

"What are these two programs?

"Ours is well known: we want to defend our tradition; spread education, especially Hebrew language and Jewish history; strengthen the Jewish national consciousness. We have faith in our people's glorious past and want to prepare it for its great future, soon to come.

"The largest Jewish organizations in America, Russia, Britain, and Italy are behind us.

"What is the opposing program? It is not even a program: its greatest shortcoming is that it is not even a program. Just because they are rich and enjoy greater social influence, some men think that they have the right to be called to lead our Community. But what do they want to do with it?

"What direction do they want to lead it in?

"They do not know, and do not care about knowing. They do not know, or pretend not to know, that without a strong culture, without respect for tradition, without national consciousness, Jewish life will collapse. This would not be the first case: other great centers of Jewish life, such as Tunisia, have been ruined within a few years by administrators who were incapable of Jewish idealism.

"We must not allow that to happen to us.

"We must want to increase and pass on to our children the glorious heritage received from our parents. If we do this we know that we are fulfilling our duty as Italian citizens, citizens of that great country which together with its allies has declared itself in favor of the rebuilding of a Jewish national home in Palestine.

"Anyone betraying Zion is, today, betraying Italy!

"Voters!

"Would you be traitors? Do not have regard for rich men or poor, but let yourselves be guided by the idea alone; then you will be able to say that you have done your duty toward your people."

52. See "Il programa della Comunità di Tripoli," *Israel*, September 24, 1917. The article, attacking Nahum's platform speech of a month earlier, provoked a long and energetic reply from Nahum (*Israel*, November 22, 1917), opening with this somewhat exaggerated but generally accurate picture of the accusations which were being made against him by the Circolo Sion and which *Israel* had seconded:

"This is what the editors of *Israel* imagine about us and our Community: In Tripoli there are Jewish plutocrats who dominate the Community. They are conservative, domineering, and don't care how things go as long as they run them, avoiding change, avoiding innovations. All they want is to hold power without any problems. They don't want any interference from outsiders: thus they put off, delay, and draw out the appointment of the Italian chief rabbi by taking refuge behind a stupid (*sic!*) shopkeeper's excuse, the state of the budget. On the other side there are many young people full of enthusiasm and idealism, blessed with energy and wisdom, led by a martyr for Judaism who is persecuted by the autocrats—a martyr of great culture and genius who with his followers wants to break the chains binding the future of Jewish life in Tripoli, and is determined to shatter this unjust and illegal oppression. He is struggling and will continue to struggle and is already on the right path, and destiny and the future smile on him. He was elected with broad support to the new Council, and now with him consciences are being aroused. The new president of the Community, chosen by bargaining and with the blessing of both parties, wants to keep a foot in both camps, above all keep within the circle, count on the votes of the angels and the devils, and thus, wherever he can, he tries to reconcile, always thinking of the power of the plutocrats and always trying to avoid displeasing them. He certainly fears them: thus he is a fearful soul. He would like as chief rabbi someone who would keep both sides happy, and would not even mention the date when he would be appointed, for obvious reasons. But his greatest mistake is that he does not take into account the Circolo Sion, which has shaken up Jewish lethargy in Tripoli and is reawakening lost souls. This forgetfulness is really unpardonable! It is due to thoughtless obsequiousness toward the conservative party; nor is his slight nod toward a "pied-à-terre" in the world for the Jews any help. His Zionism is an underhand kind which, so that it should not be seen coming in through the door, will come in through the window, keeping up appearances with one side and throwing sand in the eyes of the other.

"This is no doubt what the editors of *Israel* think about our Community. They should not be surprised or shocked, but the truth is not like that at all. Here is the truth:

"There is no plutocratic conservative party in Tripoli, a party created and held together to dominate Community affairs. In fact, painful as it is to say so, until a little while ago everyone was completely uninterested in anything to do with our administration.

"On the other hand, most of the members of the Circolo Sion are still very young, very inexperienced in public affairs, lacking in knowledge of real social and moral problems, far removed from observing and finding solutions for the demands of practical life. They are dominated by their president, share his ideas, follow his principles; like him, they are infatuated with unadulterated Zionism and believe they have attained the ideal when they raise the Zionist flag or sing "Ha-Tikvah." What is more, for their own use and consumption they decided to consider themselves the party of opposition to the constituted Jewish authorites; they have attacked them in various kinds and ways, and have become the more obstinate the more the authorities failed to pay them heed.

"I do not want to judge whether the last council, of which I was initially a member, did right or wrong in paying no attention to this group of young people, and not organizing it and giving it wise and prestigious leaders. One thing is certain: that since the Circolo Sion was founded, its president has not enjoyed the sympathy of most citizens, whether because of his obstinate position; or the letters he has sent to the Jewish press, almost all of them based on prejudice and personal animosity; or the self-importance which he gave himself among less intellectual elements, always with the thought of opposing the Community leaders, who would not bend to his wishes.

"The Circolo Sion members, due to their good intentions and the Jewish ideals inspiring them, deserve consideration and respect. However, they should choose their leaders carefully, and should try to merge Jewish energies to obtain the strength that comes from union; they should try to show that they are a support and help to the leaders of the Community; they should be deferential to them and deserve their trust; above all, they should understand that idealism is not an end in itself, and that to attain their ideal they must get things done in practical life. They ought to understand that even in the best of cases, continual Zionist propaganda and activity in Tripoli, even carried out by the best elements in the Community, remains on the level of a mere ideal; it remains purely a feeling which all Jews who have not fallen away feel profoundly in their hearts. Tripoli is not a capital, where public opinion, the press, and propaganda can influence the achievement of age-old aspirations. Important and truly effective movements in New York, London, some Italian centers, and elsewhere evolve slowly and more maturely.

"If the young people of Tripoli really want to be useful to Zionism, if they want to give moral support to the vast efforts of Zionism around the world, even under the sign of the Magen David, they must give their energies to improving themselves and their fellow Jews, develop their own activities in good deeds, in educating Jewish youth, in contributing to firm unity among Jews; they must show other citizens, the government, and the world that our race deserves to take back its position on the globe, with the support of all civilized nations, first and foremost that of Italy.

"Zionist commemorations and propaganda are and will remain sterile when the spirit and arm are not tempered, when the Community is not directed at practical welfare and in full accord with the civil and political guidelines which govern it."

For further information, see *Israel*'s comment on Nahum's response (in the same issue)—on the whole quite mild, except with regard to the coolness of the new president and leaders toward Zionism; see also Elia Nhaisi's reply to Nahum (*Israel*, February 7, 1918). It should be noted that, while *Israel* supported the Circolo Sion, the *Vessillo israelitico* supported the leadership.

53. AUCII, fasc. "Tripolitania," H. Nahum to A. Sereni, June 23, 1919.

54. In *Israel*, June 27, 1918, see the aforementioned petition which the Cricolo Sion sent the Italian Jewish Universities Committee to point out how serious a situation it was, defend its own policy, and indirectly censure the actions of those who had resigned; see also the newspaper's commentary favorable to the petition; the September 2 issue contains the response to the Circolo Sion (extremely vague and evasive) by Angelo Sereni writing on behalf of the committee; and the October 31 issue has the Zionist program for the upcoming elections.

55. *Israel*, February 20, 1919.

56. Ibid., November 17, 1921.

57. Ibid., January 17, 1924.

58. It was on this occasion that the Zionists were eliminated from the Community organizations. In his flexibility, and perhaps in order not to lose the support of some of the Zionists at least, in 1925–1926 Haggiag had drawn on the administrative and technical assistance (especially in education) of Isacco Sciaky, a trustee of the Italian Zionist Organization in Libya. However, when Haggiag resigned from the post of president, the substitute acting president, Salomone Giuili, brusquely expelled Sciaky, thereby putting an end to Zionist "interference" in running the Community. It is possible also that the still smoldering differences within the Zionist movement in Tripoli (related to the elimination of the Circolo Sion and formation of the OST) and rivalry between general Zionists and revisionist Zionists (with whom Sciaky sympathized) may have played a role. These differences died out only in 1928–1929, when the most flourishing period began for Libyan Zionism. For the "Sciaky case," see *Israel*, September 16, 1926; AUCII, fasc.

"Tripolitania" and "Corrispondenza 1926." For internal differences within Libyan Zionism, see *Israel*, November 19, 1925; March 11 and 29 and November 1 and 11, 1926; January 21 and October 20, 1927. To appreciate the background of political and Community affairs against which the Zionist recovery was taking place, it is useful to read what the secretary of the UCII wrote to Felice Ravenna on July 25, 1932, on the basis of a conversation he had had that same day with Babani Meghnagi, the secretary of the rabbinical court:

"Local Zionism is going well now: its present leader, a certain Fargion from Benghazi, makes a point of not getting involved in electoral wrangling, and cultural work is making progress: over 200 young people have started using Hebrew in their daily lives" (AUCII, fasc. "Corrispondenza 1932").

59. In a long report from Alberto Monastero, the special commissioner, to Badoglio, dated August 13, 1929 (see ASMAI, posiz. 150/31, fasc. 144, "Libia: Comunità Israelitica in Libia, 1928–1929"), one reads:

"Discontent and disorder have grown from when the administration of the Community was taken over by Cavaliere Haggiag, initially as president of the council, and later, after some members of the council resigned, as government commissioner. His appointment greatly surprised the majority of the community and those who had criticized Haggiag. It created unease and despair because it was seen as a proof either of that man's power, or of the government's indifference to the community. In fact Haggiag, an authoritarian and selfish man, ran the community as he liked, without any concern for public opinion or for the improvement, progress or well-being of individuals or institutions. He surrounded himself with relatives or faithful disciples, ignored every provision of the law, and lost the sympathy and cooperation of the best people on the council. His arbitrary methods were encouraged by his appointment as governor commissioner following the weakening and dissolution of the council, and since then there has been an increase, if not in his acts of despotism and favoritism, certainly in the discontent and suspicion of the rank and file . . . The majority was aware of his personal abilities, but could not stand his despotism and complained that the Community's interests had been abandoned. From being a public concern, the Community's institutions became Haggiag's private domain, run for the psychological and perhaps economic benefit of his followers. He certainly never gave any account of what he was doing and was obviously excessively anxious for a position that almost everyone else has avoided. I have reason to think that Haggiag, a powerful banker involved in many organizations, aimed at winning a predominant position of patronage over the Community, either in order to maintain and extend his own interests, or from ambition and the will to rule, since he was not lacking in political ambitions, which seemed to him well founded when the rumor and vision arose that there might be a local parliament which perhaps would send representatives to Rome. An obstacle to these hopes was his situation as a French subject, which he had acquired by choice upon reaching the age of twenty-one, as the child of a Turkish subject who became French and then Turkish again. He had already made arrangements so that he could claim

332 Notes to Pages 107-109

Libyan Italian citizenship, by having the French consulate publicly deprive him of his citizenship. His lengthy tenure as the head of the Community would no doubt win him metropolitan citizenship without delay. This is the key to the determined efforts of Haggiag, who, moreover, is not thought capable of noble, altruistic, or patriotic sentiments."

60. Haggiag's view of the revision of the regulations emerges clearly from his letter to Angelo Sereni dated February 18, 1927 (AUCII, facs. "Corrispondenza 1927"). According to Haggiag, the mass of Tripoli Jews was not ready for a representative system; moreover, many who were taxpayers and voters were such only because their tax had not been collected in the past and their votes helped a particular "party." He had already dealt with this second aspect by reducing the number of taxpaying voters from about 1,800 to about 800. He thought that the electoral system required of the voters a certain level of education. If the number of voters were reduced, the council might also be reduced from 30 to 7-9 members. Sereni agreed with "the need to amend the Community Statutes, which had turned out in practice to be too progressive for a community which was still too Oriental"; it is difficult to say whether Sereni was really convinced of this or had been influenced by Haggiag. See "Verbale della riunione del consiglio del Consorzio del gennaio 1926," in AUCII, fasc. 10/493. Whatever he really thought, a telegram from the Libya Office of the Ministry of Colonies to the governorate of Tripolitania, dated September 4, 1926, shows that Sereni supported Haggiag's appointment after the latter had resigned the presidency and taken the post of government commissioner. He considered Haggiag suitable for the post, and able "to bring about, in full accord with the government [of Tripolitania] reforms which should be introduced in the Community Statutes to ensure that they will function in a regular fashion" (ASMAI, Posiz. 150/31, fasc. 144, "Libia: Comunità Israelitica in Libia, 1928-1929" [actually covers 1926-1931]).

61. *Israel*, July 11, 1929, and, for the electoral campaign, June 20, 1929.

62. *Israel*, August 6, 1929; ASMAI, posiz. 150/31, fasc. 144, "Libia: Comunità Israelitica in Libia, 1928-1929," esp. Badoglio to Direz. Gen. Africa Settentrionale del Min. delle Colonie, July 22 and August 17, 1929.

63. AUCII, fasc. "Corrispondenza 1929," F. Nahum to A. Sereni, July 30, 1929.

64. ASMAI, posiz. 150/31, fasc. 144, report, August 17, 1929 (cited in note 62 above).

65. Ibid., telegram from Badoglio to Minister De Bono, August 7, 1929. Badoglio states that the appointment "met full approval Jewish Community." However, Jewish sources show that many Jews—especially among the masses—were against having an *arel* [uncircumcised] head of the Community (AUCII, *Comitato*, letter from the secretary to F. Ravenna, dated February 8, 1931 [based on a conversation with Rabbi Disegni]).

66. This concern was already a lively one in 1926. The then governor, De Bono, expressed it when he replied to Minister Di Scalea's "reservations" at the suitability of appointing a non-Jewish commissioner, as the Libyan colonial authorities proposed, with the suggestion to put off the

whole problem until after the 1916 statutory reform and "to carry on for now with the existing rudimentary administration" (ibid., P. Di Scalea to Government of Tripoli, September 13, 1926, and E. De Bono to Ministry of Colonies, September 17, 1926). The concern emerges clearly in a telegram from Minister De Bono, dated August 5, 1929, in which he expressed "some reservation" about appointing a non-Jewish commissioner and asked for futher information about the situation and the incidents which had occurred during the elections, in order to be well "informed about a question which, like all those related to the Libyan Jewish communities, is followed with great attention in metropolitan Jewish circles" (ibid.). The aforementioned reports by Badoglio on August 17 and by Monastero to Badoglio on August 13, sent to Rome ten days later, are replies to this telegram.

67. In August the elections were held for the bodies governing the Community of Benghazi. According to Badoglio (who had already expressed the opinion that "system cannot be applied in Cyrenaica either"), there were "inconveniences and requests to annul the election results" which were soon accepted, though without any need for a non-Jewish commissioner (ASMAI, posiz. 150/31, fasc. 144, Badoglio a Ministero Colonie, July 30 and August 23, 1929).

68. Some of Monastero's comments in the aforementioned report to Badoglio of August 13, 1929, are significant in this respect. Monastero characterized the Haggiag administration as "unsystematic, almost a family type of administration" (by "family-type" is meant not only personalistic but lacking any bureaucratic structure and ignorant of modern accounting and public administration systems), but he quickly added that this "had partial precedents and pretexts in the more or less family-type systems practiced by the Community before it." Regarding Community affairs as a whole, Monastero commented: "it cannot be said that the Community has ever had a period of full administrative organization, order, and tranquillity; until the Italian occupation there was a series of crises due to resignations by administrators or removals of them by the government at the request of community members, and accordingly the *system prevailing from 1916 until now has been administration by the government commissioner.*"

69. After these incidents, when Ravenna visited Tripoli to get his own idea of the situation, he asked Badoglio whether he thought the elections should be held again, since not all members of the administrative commission had the sympathy of the Jewish masses. Badoglio replied that, though "with all due caution" he was not against them, the time was not yet right; first an Italian chief rabbi should come; then after a few months, when they thought the Community was "ready," he would proceed to call elections (AUCII, "Corrispondenza, 1933," F. Ravenna to A. Pacifici, August 21, 1933).

70. ASMAI, posiz. 150/31, fasc. 144, and fasc. 145, "Libia: Comunità Israelitica in Libia, 1929–1935," passim.

71. R. Habib to Rabbi Disegni, March 5, 1931, AUCII, "Corrispondenza, 1931."

72. To give some idea of the accounts of the Community of Tripoli at

the time, here is the balance sheet covering the period January 1–September 7, 1931, issued by the special commission three months after Monastero began running the Community:

INCOME

I. Balance forward from fiscal year 1930		
1. Reserve funds as of January 1, 1931	29,909.43	
2. Remaining assets from compulsory taxes	9,430.00	
		39,339.43
II. Property revenues		
4. Income from real estate		10,432.05
III. Proceeds from religious services		
5. Synagogue *mitzvot*	21,446.40	
6. Tamid [daily offerings]	1,319.05	
8. Matzah [unleavened bread] oven	2,000.00	
		24,765.45
IV. Miscellaneous taxes and dues		
9. Tax on dowries	17,220.50	
11. Burial tax	15,338.00	
12. Dues on tomb construction	3,562.00	
13. Rabbinical court dues	1,314.00	
14. Tax on meat	245,269.00	
16. School fees	4,453.50	
17. Choir dues	2,252.25	
19. Liquor tax	190.00	
		289,599.25
V. Legacies and donations		
20. Interest on Arbib, London, legacy		10,064.00
VI. Miscellaneous proceeds and collections		
22. Cemetery offerings	397.55	
23. Ritual bath collection box	347.10	
25. Donations for food and clothing for poor students	6,265.00	
26. Sick fund coupons	1,650.00	
28. Miscellaneous offerings and *mishebera-chot* for the Talmud Torah	3,016.40	
30. Home collection boxes for the Talmud Torah	1,148.25	
		12,824.30
VII. Contributions from the government and other agencies		
31. Reimbursement for portion of rabbinical court rental	1,562.50	
32. Reimbursement of rabbinical court operating expenses	1,562.50	
33. Reimbursement expenses for assistant teachers	15,000.00	
34. Contributions from various agencies	16,500.00	
		34,625.00

VIII. Extraordinary and special proceeds
  35. Private donations to the Community   6,441.25
  36. Fines   196.00
  37. Miscellaneous occasional   6,119.00
                                                               12,756.25
IX. Obligatory taxes
  38. Obligatory contribution paid by savings   60,430.22
      bank account 1931
X. Clearing transactions
  39. Clearing transactions   7,250.00
                                          Total income: 502,085.95

EXPENDITURES

I. Property expenses
  1. Maintenance of rental properties   652.60
  2. Real estate taxes   518.65
  3. Maintenance of properties for public use   6,015.15
     (synagogues, hospice, Talmud Torah)
                                                                7,186.40
II. Recurring expenditures for synagogue worship
  4. Rental of synagogue premises, Dahra and   5,220.00
     Bel El
  5. Synagogue lighting to end of May   10,527.10
  6. Officiants, assistants, *tokeim bodkim*   5,679.95
  7. *Shamashim*   3,091.15
  8. Synagogue furnishings   3,178.00
  9. Consumption items   5,158.20
  10. Mizvot collection office expenses   2,884.40
  11. Chief Rabbi's stipend contribution   5,391.00
  13. Ritual bath   296.60
                                                               41,426.40
III. Extraordinary expenses for synagogue worship
  14. Construction of third sanctuary Dar Zet-   8,630.00
      lau and renovation of the three sanctu-
      aries
  15. Repair of synagogue electric light fixtures   375.00
                                                                9,005.00
IV. Religious education
  17. Stipends for Talmud Torah and advanced   81,490.00
      Talmud class teachers
  18. School meals and clothing for poor pupils 12,688.75
  19. Fixed student grants   4,125.00
  20. Grants for students in Italy   11,100.95
  21. Stipends for Etz Haim rabbis   20,145.00
  23. Grants and clothing for choirboys   4,222.50
  26. Bookbinding costs   721.00
  27. School fees collection office expenses   427.65
                                                              134,920.85

V. Charity

28. Cash grants (Hilluk)	45,000.00	
29. Cash grants for emissaries*	7,139.00	
30. Passover wheat	17,211.00	
31. Petty charity expenses	11,614.60	
32. Clothing and barracans	448.00	
33. Doctors' fees and medicines	10,058.40	
34. Food and grants for poor invalids (Bekor Holim sick fund)	26,557.80	
35. Dowry funds	500.00	
36. Grants awarded by lot	1,500.00	
37. Subsidies to the educational charitable society, Jewish Women's Association, Alliance Israélite	1,200.00	
38. Cook and nurse employed by Hospital	4,760.00	
39. Care of poor invalids		
(a) Grants	7,318.50	
(b) Meals	288.00	
40. Legal counseling in rabbinical court cases	1,700.00	
		135,295.30
VI. Burial		
41. Cemetery employees	15,640.00	
42. Materials for tomb construction	5,107.40	
43. Gifts to gravediggers, etc.	2,178.55	
		22,925.95
VII. Meat		
44. Meat production employees		9,000.00
VIII. Administration		
45. Administrative employees	26,360.00	
46. Ushers	4,930.00	
47. Rental of Community premises	3,791.50	
48. Printing and stationery	3,741.95	
49. Telephone, postage, and telegraph expenses	1,134.30	
50. Tax collection	1,300.60	
51. Commission on rent collection, etc.	192.95	
53. Furniture, furnishings, and typewriter	2,875.75	
54. Tips to administration employees	3,212.50	
55. Rabbinical court expenses	2,229.55	
		49,769.10
IX. Pensions		
56. Pensions to former judges, teachers, ushers		10,166.00

*This item might alternatively refer to cash payments related to legacies. —*Trans.*

X. Contributions
  57. Contribution to farm   30,000.00
XI. Liabilities remaining from fiscal 1930
  58. Cash debts in course of payment   22,496.10
XII. Clearing entries
  60. Clearing entries   12,050.00
XIII. Unforeseen expenditures
  61. Unforeseen expenditures   17,844.85

                                    Total expenditures: 502,085.95

The special commission commented on the account:

"We thought that it would be useful to give you an account (closed on September 7) showing you the financial situation of the Community which His Excellency the Governor has entrusted us with administering.

"The figures speak for themselves and we thus wish to add only a few general remarks.

"Income was as predicted; voluntary donations such as *mitzvot* and other offerings reflect the general crisis and have been few, jeopardizing the Community's regular financial situation.

"Expenses for building maintenance, religious services and education, meat, the cemetery, and general administration corresponded to expectations.

"Expenditures for charity have been much higher than expected. They have made heavy demands on the Community budget, so that after only eight months of the fiscal year the amount allocated has been almost used up already.

"The contribution to the farm has been lower than projected. However, government contributions amounting to about 9,000 lire have not yet been paid in, and we can expect an excellent tobacco harvest and good proceeds from the sale of about fifty head of cattle purchased for breeding. Most of the fairly high unforeseen expenditures were incurred for the celebrations in connection with the visit of Their Highnesses the Prince and Princess Royal" (AUCII, "Corrispondenza 1931").

73. For an overall picture of Monastero's administration, see "L'amministrazione della Comunità israelitica nella relazione del Commissario straordinario," *L'avvenire di Tripoli*, July 7, 1931, and, for more detail, *Relazione finale del Commissario straordinario governativo Comm. Dott. Alberto Monastero sulla gestione della Comunità israelitica della Tripolitania dall'agosto 1929 al maggio 1931* (Tripoli, 1931).

74. Nahum, *Discorso inaugurale*, pp. 24 ff; "L'Assemblea generale del Circolo Sion (24 settembre 1918)," *Israel*, October 31, 1918; September 22–29, 1926.

75. *Israel*, January 2, 1930. Significantly, the commentary concluded as follows:

"The Jewish Community of Tripoli may be grateful to its special commissioner for having succeeded in such a short time, by wise administration, in setting to rights its shaky financial situation, so that the consider-able amount of one hundred thousand lire was saved to be used for this worthy end. The Jewish Community of Tripoli, which has suffered so much from internal discord, should finally learn from him that, when the special administration ends, with discipline it can have wise and strong leadership."

Israel's approval and overall opinion are all the more significant since a few weeks earlier, on November 17, 1929, an article whose overall tone was quite harsh toward Libyan Jews had appeared in *Il gazzettino* of Venice, causing some commotion and concern. The planned clearing of the *hara* and turn to agriculture were seen in it as working together and necessary to solve the "Jewish question." Any fusion between Italians and Jews (in con-trast to that between Italians and Arabs) was thus seen as impossible (AUCII, fasc. "Concessione agricola Principe di Piemonte").

76. *Israel*, November 1, 1934. For further information on the conces-sion, see *Relazione finale* (cited in note 73 above), pp. 12 ff.

77. Some Jewish farms were set up in Libya between the mid-1920s and mid-1930s. These initiatives were taken by Italian rather than Libyan Jews. Badoglio's requests to the owners of these farms that they employ Jew-ish labor went unheeded: except in a few cases, Libyan Jews did not like agricultural work (AUCII, fasc. "Concessione agricola Principe di Piemonte" and "Corrispondenza 1933").

78. There are many indications of this in correspondence between Tripoli Jews and the Union of Jewish Communities; many letters criticizing the Community leaders were sent to Rome, especially in 1933 when the First Congress of the Union was being planned and in progress (AUCII, "Corrispondenza 1931, 1932, and 1933").

79. AUCII, fasc. "Corrispondenza avvocato Ravenna 1932," July 25, 1932.

80. AUCII, fasc. "Appunti su situazione Tripolina (1933)."

81. The appointment of Lattes as chief rabbi had great importance in this context. After the earlier disappointing experiences, especially the Balbo-Castelbolognesi crisis [see Chapter 5], the presence of a chief rabbi en-dowed with the qualities and diplomacy necessary to win acceptance from the Italian authorities, Community leadership, the vast majority of local rabbis, and crucial sectors of the traditionalist masses, removed tension and re-established balance in the situation. It provided the Community leaders with the legitimacy necessary for their views on various issues to be ac-cepted, while it helped to restore good relations between these leaders and the Union of Jewish Communities in Rome. Besides the specifically politi-cal aspect—remedying the lack of rabbis and firmly establishing better rela-tions with Balbo—a new chief rabbi had been asked for by the leadership in Tripoli ever since the Balbo-Castelbolognesi crisis. In July 1935 Alberto Fresco, one of the members of the administrative commission, raised the question, rather directly but with great realism and sensitivity, in a conver-sation with Angelo Sereni which the secretary of the Union summarized in the following words to Ravenna, its president:

"The Commission would like the Jews of Tripoli to develop, and the

Rabbi's rigidly orthodox attitude has turned out to be opposed to this development. The basic problem of the core of Jews in Tripoli remains to be solved. After trying three times, it has to be decided whether to leave them to themselves, or whether it is not necessary and urgent to find a rabbi who would be capable of restraining overly radical change and finding a balance between the demands of present-day life and those of a commitment to Jewish life" (AUCII, fasc. 11/A, secretary of the Union to F. Ravenna, July 11, 1935).

5. Relations with the Italian Authorities

1. One indication of this is the contributions in considerable amounts made by many Jews to the "loan of the lictors" (*prestito del littorio*)* (*Israel*, February 4, 1927) and especially to funds collected for the ONB† (*Bollettino ONB*, September 15, 1928) and, in 1935, to the collection of "gold for the motherland"** (AUCII, fasc. 11/A). Other indications are the contacts between young Jews in Tripoli and the Fascist youth organizations and, even more, the fact that even the Talmud Torah schools did not judge it inappropriate to take the initiative of inviting Fascist gerarchs and the latter were not ashamed to visit the schools (see, e.g., *Rivista delle colonie italiane*, June 6, 1931, pp. 480 ff., which refers to an "academy" organized by the Talmud Torah School of Benghazi in honor of D. M. Tuninetti, the National Fascist Party's special commissioner for Cyrenaica).

2. For these problems, see De Felice, *Storia degli ebrei italiani*, pp. 92 ff., 103 ff., 163 ff.

3. AUCII, fasc. "Questioni scolastiche," subfasc. "Colloqui": Ravenna-Mussolini Conversation, January 17, 1933.

4. For the whole affair, see "Contro una sentenza della Corte d'Appello per la Libia," *Israel*, July 28, 1921 (giving the Community's position complete approval), and AUCII, fasc. 21 and "Tripolitania."

5. See his statements as minister of colonies, at the opening session of the commission for reform of the statutes of the Libyan Communities, AUCII, fasc. 26, memorandum dated July 1937.

6. Some Italian Jews also belonged to the Fascio of Tripoli. One of them was Francesco Provenzal, the first director of the Fascist weekly, *Libia fascista*, which began to appear on February 8, 1923.

7. Many of the Italian Jews living in Tripoli were worried about how the situation was developing. After the August incidents, some of them

---

**Il fascio littorio*, a symbol of power in the Roman Empire, was made part of the emblem of the Fascist state on December 30, 1926.—*Trans.*

†Opera Nazionale Bolilla, a national organization for physical and moral education of youth, established on April 3, 1926. It was named after the Genovese who began the revolt against the Austrians in 1746.—*Trans.*

**The League of Nations imposed economic sanctions against Italy in connection with the Ethiopian War in October 1935. In November and December, the government collected gold for the motherland.—*Trans.*

were even afraid that the Fascists were checking their mail (AUCII, fasc. 21, B. Nunes Vais to A. Sereni, October 21, 1923).

8. This attitude was particularly common in the colonial bureaucracy, which zealously enforced the regulations to the letter (even those which had fallen into disuse when the Basic Law was passed, if they had not been abrogated, and those which remained formally in effect but applied only to exceptional situations of law and order). The bureaucracy was also sensitive to some Fascist calls for a new "style" and new "dignity" in its relations with indigenous people. A typical consequence of this was that, in Cyrenaica and particularly in Benghazi, a tendency emerged in 1923–1924 to consider local Jews, particularly non-Europeanized Jews, as being on the same level as the Arabs and to revive some old restrictive measures, such as those forbidding natives and prostitutes from riding in public carriages and from attending the baths and cinemas of the metropolitans. The Community of Benghazi appealed against these measures first, on May 14, 1924, to the secretary general of the governing authorities of Cyrenaica and then, on June 12, 1924, to Angelo Sereni, the president of the Committee of Jewish Communities. The first appeal concentrated on the injustice of considering the Jews on the same level as the Arabs: "Though the local Jewish population consists partly of people born in Benghazi, it has always distinguished itself from the Arabs both through civil development and political behavior. This has deeply hurt the local Jews, who would never have believed that the proofs of total loyalty and faithful attachment to the Motherland which they have given could be so ignored as to put them on a level with a population of backward civilization like the indigenous Arabs, with whom the Jews now find themselves at odds precisely because of their differing attitude toward Italy.

"Hurt by this incident, the Jews of Benghazi ask that their attitude toward Italy serve once and for all to distinguish them from the Arabs, since they form a population in which there are many metropolitan Italian citizens, foreign citizens, and subjects and individuals whose civilization is no lower than that of the Italians themselves."

In the second appeal, the protest was more explicit, circumstantiated, and political:

"Though, since the Italian occupation and throughout 1922, the Government of Cyrenaica has always considered the Jews of our Community as a separate element, from 1923 until the present a new concept about it has gradually emerged, culminating in recent provisions which have seriously disturbed our Community. The new concept which we have noticed is the following: making a distinction between metropolitan Italian citizens and Libyan Italian citizens, and including Jews among the latter.

"It began with the distinction being made at official receptions and other public functions. The Jews no longer appeared as a separate group, but were mixed in with the Arabs. The council's efforts to correct the situation were useless. Next a campaign was waged by the local press to get rid of all government employees who were not metropolitan Italian citizens, leading in fact to the dismissal of some Jewish employees.

"Finally, on May 14 last, Italian drivers were forbidden to take in their carriages indigenous people and prostitutes, according to the licences granted to them by the authorities."

Despite these protests, the provisions were not annulled for many years, though they were applied less and less strictly. An approach by French diplomats in 1931 on behalf of Algerians and Tunisians who were forbidden access to bathing facilities on the Giuliana beach (but not other beaches) also failed. The provisions were not annulled until 1935, on the initiative of Minister Alessandro Lessona, who raised the idea to Mussolini in the following terms:

"The criteria for rigorously distinguishing indigenous people from metropolitans and excluding them from all expressions of European social life derive from a policy adopted under very different conditions of public order from those prevailing now and in the general framework of a policy of severe repression of unruly populations.

"In the present period of full normality, which Y. E. is encouraging with measures aimed at raising the material and moral level of indigenous populations, it appears that the aforementioned rules ought to be revised, in the way that you consider most suitable to the present situation.

"That would also prevent an imbalance between the two colonies, since broader views have already been applied in Tripoli, as well as disharmony with the systems applying to indigenous populations in the other areas of North Africa under European administration."

For a complete account, see AUCII, fasc. "Bengasi" p. 21; ASMAI, "Libia," p. 31, 1930–1935.

9. For the whole episode, see ASMAI, pos. 150/27, fasc. 127, "Nahum, Eugenio." Other individuals involved in the affair had their sentences annulled and were expelled only later, when Badoglio became governor.

10. See AUCII, fasc. 12 and "Tripolitania"; also "Una lettera del Rabbino Maggiore Dott. Artom," *Il corriere di Tripoli*, September 18, 1923 (the letter was published with a harsh editorial comment refusing in effect to take Artom's arguments into account); and "Che cosa succede a Tripoli?" and "Dopo i fatti di Tripoli," *Israel*, October 4 and November 1, 1923. The first article in *Israel* expresses the reactions of Italian Jews: "The facts which have been definitely recorded and the vocabulary of the extreme Fascist newspapers which we have read with our own eyes (even when we discount any information which we have not been able to verify completely) leave no room for doubt. It is clear that the general attitude of some Fascists toward the entire Jewish population of Tripoli is based on the most openly expressed scorn and contempt for any consideration of the Jews' dignity and rights."

11. In September, after they had been informed of the incidents, Senators Romanin-Jacur and Polacco privately approached Federzoni, the minister of colonies, in Padua. He gave them "the broadest assurrances" that the disorders would not occur again, but also expressed the hope that Zionist propaganda would be "toned down." He said that in Libya the propaganda was spread "in a way damaging to harmony among the various elements of

the population." The initiative had been requested by Angelo Sullam, who, reporting on it to Angelo Sereni on September 29, added his own comment on Federzoni's opinion about Libyan Zionist propaganda: "The Jews would agree that this is true." See AUCII, fasc. "Tripolitania." It was almost certainly as a result of the Federzoni meeting that the Consortium in early 1924 sent Rabbi David Prato to Tripoli to reorganize the local Zionist movement. The Consortium hastened to inform the president of the Tripoli Community that Federzoni was about to visit Libya and recommended that he make sure that "the welcome he receives from the Jews will express their love of Italy." See AUCII, fasc. 21 and "Tripolitania," and, for an account of Federzoni's visit to the *hara* (where he was received amid great expressions of enthusiasm by the president of the Community, to whom he made a gift of two thousand lire for the poor), *Israel*, February 28, 1924, and *Corriere di Tripoli*, February 10, 1924. At the same time Federzoni made a donation of twenty thousand lire for reconstruction of the synagogue of Zlitin.

12. N. Placido, *La riconquista della Tripolitania: Scritti e polemiche, 1922–1923* (Tripoli, 1928), pp. 78 ff, which reproduces the article on the demonstration published in the *Corriere di Tripoli* on November 9, 1923.

13. See Ministero Affari Esteri, *I documenti diplomatici italiani*, series 7 (1922–1935) 4: 369 ff. For further information on subsequent developments in the Italian diplomatic position, see ibid. 5: 163 ff., 216 ff., 295, 344 ff., 368.

14. See AUCII, fasc. "Bengasi" and 21.

15. See AUCII, fasc. "Concessione agricola Principe di Piemonte," H. Nahum to M. Donati, January 14, 1930.

16. For documentation on the legislative reform, apart from indications to the contrary, see ASMAI, posiz. 150/31, fasc. 144 and 145, "Libia—Comunità Israelitica in Libia, 1928–29 and 1929–35."

17. In Federzoni's mind (see AUCII, "Corrispondenza 1927," A. Sereni to S. Haggiag, June 5, 1927), a first step along this road was represented by the Organic Law for the Administration of Tripolitania and Cyrenaica of June 26, 1927 (*Official Gazette*, June 28, 1927), which, in Article 56, deprived the rabbinical courts (but not the Muslim courts) of authority in matters of inheritance and transferred it to Italian courts. Though it was well received by the rich and Italianized Libyan Jews, the measure met with great hostility among the majority of Libyan Jews, due either to the traditional reasons or to the difficulty of applying Italian law in a situation like the Jewish one, where divorce was permitted and cases of men having two wives were not rare. Hence a series of approaches were made (generally through the Consortium) to have the regulation annulled or at least changed (so that the decisions of Italian courts would be based on Jewish law). Once the new juridical system covering this point had gone into effect in October 1928, there was a further wave of dissatisfaction, lasting for several years, especially among the Jews of Benghazi (AUCII, fasc. "Corrispondenza 1928," esp. 63).

18. *Official Gazette*, August 4, 1928.

19. One of the few observations which the Supreme Council of the

Colonies made concerned membership of the Libyan Communities in the Union of Italian Jewish Communities. Both the Union and the Council were concerned about the practical and legal difficulties resulting from the Union's being under the control of the Ministry of Justice and the Libyan Communities under that of the governor. The Union vainly tried to find a solution to the problem by appealing directly to the good offices of Minister Alfredo Rocco. As far as its activities in Libya were concerned, the Union thus had to answer to two separate agencies. Some of the supporters of the idea of founding an independent union of Libyan Jewish Communities subsequently referred to the incongruity of this. Related to these plans were those concerning the establishment of the office of chief rabbi of Libya and of a superior rabbinical court for Libya. In 1934–1935 the Union of Italian Jewish Communities favored these, since it hoped that thereby the long-standing problem of the appointments of the chief rabbis of Tripoli and Benghazi could be solved by appointing one Italian chief rabbi, while giving more authority to the rabbi of Tripoli. All three plans were favored by the Jews of Tripoli (especially the first, which the leaders of the Tripoli Community thought would raise Misurata and Derna to the level of autonomous Communities) but opposed by those of Benghazi, worried about their own Community's autonomy. The colonial authorities were not against the plans, since they hoped to take advantage of them to unify everything under the Communities and rabbinical court of Tripoli. However, since Rome was not in agreement, everything was shelved. See ASMAI, posiz. 150/31, fasc. 145, "Libia—Comunità Israelitica in Libia 1929–35"; AUCII, fasc. 11/A, 32 and 63.

20. *Official Gazette,* August 19, 1931. Some changes to the law were introduced in 1935. They concerned the composition of the arbitration commission provided for under Article 28 to settle controversies regarding Community tax assessments and the composition of the administrative commission. According to the 1931 law, employees of the Community or of institutions administered by or affiliated with it, their relatives up to three times removed, and persons having any kind of economic relation to the Community could not sit on the commission (Article 9). This, especially in Benghazi, made it exceedingly difficult to find qualified people legally able to hold official positions (AUCII, fasc. 26 and 63). The 1935 amendments corrected the situation by eliminating some of the incompatibilities.

21. ASMAI, posiz. 150/31, fasc. 45, "Libia—Comunità Israelitiche in Libia, 1929–35," Ministero Colonie a Badoglio, December 9, 1933.

22. AUCII, fasc. "Corrispondenza rabbino Castelbolognesi," F. Ravenna a G. Castelbolognesi, November 22 and December 2, 1933.

23. AUCII, fasc. "Corrispondenza avv. Ravenna: 1933," A. Sacerdoti a F. Ravenna, July 12, 1933.

24. Badoglio's correspondence with Mussolini and De Bono gives numerous testimonies to this. E.g., he saw the Sanusi as "either stupid or immoral, or both at the same time" (to Mussolini, June 24, 1929). The following passage from a letter of his dated June 20, 1920, to De Bono is typical: "First I must assure you that the Sanusiya is a bunch of gangling idiots.

Ridha, for example, has not yet plucked up the courage to come and see me. He is crestfallen, and consoles himself by eating like a pig, listening to a phonograph for hours on end, and mating. He has got three wives pregnant!" (ASMAI, posiz. 150/21, fasc. 90, "Sottomissione dei rebelli della Cirenaica [1929–30]"). For a summary of Badoglio's actions in Libya, see P. Pieri and G. Rochat, *Pietro Badoglio* (Turin, 1974), pp. 590 ff.

25. ASMAI, pos. 150/21, fasc. 90, "Sottomissione dei ribelli della Cirenaica (1929–30)."

26. Ibid., Mussolini to Badoglio, November 10, 1929.

27. For further details, see AUCII, fasc. "Questioni scolastiche," subf. "Colloqui," the report of the March 21, 1933, conversation between Ruben Hassan and Felice Ravenna, and fasc. "Corrispondenza avv. Ravenna," report by the secretary of the Union, dated July 25, 1932, to Ravenna on the secretary's conversation with Babani Meghnagi; also fasc. 11/A, "Relazione dell'attività dell'Unione delle Comunità Israelitiche Italiane del periodo dall'aprile 1933 al giugno 1934."

28. "Every Friday about five hundred Jewish beggars go around even to Arab, Greek, and Maltese businessmen. They categorically refuse to stop, considering it their sacred privilege, the honor which they bring to the Jewish people being left to the imagination. Swarms of pseudo-rabbis, would-be Talmudists, and wizards complete the picture, respected, obeyed, and feared" (V. Levi to F. Ravenna, February 5, 1932, in AUCII, fasc. "Corrispondenza 1932").

29. Ibid.

30. Between the late 1920s and the mid-1930s, relations between the Libyan Communities and the Union of Italian Jewish Communities, never very serene, went through several times of tension. The most serious crisis happened in early 1933, when the issue of Sabbath observance in the schools arose. Between accusations and counter-accusations, (even involving Angelo Sacerdoti, the Rabbi of Rome), matters reached a point where the Tripoli leaders accused those of the Union of behaving like a doctor trying to "make a diagnosis and treat a seriously ill patient without ever having seen him" and the Union in reply accused them of using a tone "inappropriate to the kind of relations which from a hierarchical point of view ought to prevail between the Union and Jewish Communities in the Kingdom and the Colonies." See AUCII, fasc. "Osservanza sabato a Tripoli." A few months later there was a public echo of this crisis at the Union's first congress. Ruben Hassan, the delegate from Tripoli, suggested that "Italian Jewry pay more attention to Libyan Jewry." See AUCII, fasc. "Congresso delle Comunità Israelitiche," minutes of the March 19, 1933, meeting.

31. The proposal was made for the first time in a long memorandum and budget covering the commission's planned activities for the next year, sent to Badoglio on January 15, 1932. It concludes:

"If we want to ensure that this rebirth takes place, if we want to give it enough impetus so that in a few years it can be considered a fact, only one measure, in the view of this Commission, is necessary: military service.

"Only by introducing military service will Italy be able to improve and use [this resource of] faithful subjects, make them into citizens who will be ready tomorrow for the military defense of the Colony and of the Motherland wherever they may be needed, as their fellow Jews in Italy have always been; only through military life, that superb temperer of body and soul, may the young generation achieve the physical and moral improvement which will surely bring benefits in the social and economic fields."

A similar proposal, formulated in almost the same terms, was put forward three and a half years later on a similar occasion, on June 27, 1935. It is interesting to note that Felice Ravenna also suggested this in July 1933. It is difficult to say whether the president of the Union was acting from conviction or in order to ingratiate himself and give concrete proof of the loyalty and faithfulness of Libyan Jews toward Italy. After the previous month's incidents between Arabs and Jews, he was visiting Libya to get his own idea of the situation and meet Badoglio. The governor answered the proposal in the negative, stating that "the Jewish community of Tripoli is not yet ready for military service" and adding "in view of the far from friendly relations between Arabs and Jews, it would be dangerous to give arms to the Jews, whom the Arabs consider cowardly. Bloody fights would be provoked and would lead to serious consequences." Badoglio continued with a malevolent gibe, regretting that the offer of military service had been put forward "when the occupation of the Colony has already been completed in its military aspect." See AUCII, fasc. "Corrispondenza 1932," 63; and "Appunti su situazione tripolina," report dated July 30, 1933, from F. Ravenna to the Union on his trip to Tripoli, July 19–25, 1933.

32. *Israel*, December 9, 1930.

33. Rabbi Artom gave the following embarrassed account at the Union congress: "One family asked me if I thought it would be advisable for these boys to come and study in Italy. In my reply I tried to beat about the bush, as we say, by hinting at the problems of the school year having already begun, the differing syllabi, etc., so that I would not have to mention that here the Jews for many years, unfortunately, have been used to going to school on the Sabbath. I was trying to play for time, hoping that there will be a better arrangement in Tripoli by the time the next school year comes around" (AUCII, fasc. "Congresso delle comunità Israelitiche" minutes of the March 19, 1933, session).

34. According to the leaders of the Tripoli Community, the judges of the rabbinical courts were obliged by twenty or so excited people to sign these protests practically under threat of force. Nevertheless, one of the judges refused, and the president later on stated that he signed under the threats which were made to him while he was ill in bed (AUCII, fasc. "Osservanza sabato a Tripoli," A. J. Arbib, on behalf of the administrative commission, to F. Ravenna, February 10, 1933).

35. The Union made similar inquiries in Rhodes and Salonica. It learned that in all these places no exemptions were made for intermediate-level pupils. Only in Algeria, under certain conditions, the parents were allowed to have their children excused. All Jews (in Rhodes even the rabbi's children) attended schools on the Sabbath in the normal way; anyone who

did not want to go to school on the Sabbath attended the Alliance or Community schools rather than public schools (AUCII. fasc. "Osservanza sabato a Tripoli").

36. Ibid.

37. Ibid., A. Sacerdoti to A. J. Arbib, January 31, 1933. Castelbolognesi's reaction expressed in a letter of February 13, 1933, to Felice Ravenna is also typical: "In religious matters the demands of the intransigent orthodox hold . . . even when they represent a minute minority" (ibid.).

38. The author of the statement was Raffaele Harbib, who sent it to Alfonso Pacifici, the editor of *Israel*, who used it after shortening it a little (AUCII, fasc. "Osservanza sabato a Tripoli," A. Pacifici to F. Ravenna, January 13, 1933).

39. Ibid., A. Pacifici to the Union and F. Ravenna, January 29, 1933, and, for concern aroused in the Union by the sequestration, De Angelis to Pacifici and Ravenna to Pacifici, January 27 and March 26, 1933, respectively.

40. Ibid., note by F. Ravenna, dated February 8, 1933; also (fasc. "Corrispondenza rabbino Castelbolognesi"), F. Ravenna to G. Castelbolognesi, February 11, 1933, in which the president of the Union commented, "Unfortunately the situation has been compromised by the hasty submissiveness of the administrative commission in maintaining that complete Sabbath observance is just the dream of a few orthodox Jews; as a result I have been confronted with far greater difficulties than there would have been if the issue had not already been discussed and decided without our participation."

41. For all these events, see AUCII, fasc. "Corrispondenza 1933," and "Corrispondenza avv. Ravenna"; also "Cronache Tripoline: Spiacevoli incidenti," *Israel*, June 22, 1933.

42. AUCII, fasc. "Corrispondenza 1933," F. Ravenna to U. Nahon, June 20, 1933, and U. Nahon to F. Ravenna, June 27, 1933.

43. On the Ravenna-Castelbolognesi mission, see AUCII, fasc. "Appunti su situazione tripolina"; "Osservanza sabato a Tripoli"; "Corrispondenza avv. Ravenna"; also the account in *Israel*, August 3–10, 1933.

44. AUCII, fasc. "Osservanza sabato a Tripoli"; "Corrispondenza rabbino Castelbolognesi"; 54 and 11/A, "Relazione dell'attività dell'Unione delle Comunità Israelitiche Italiane nel periodo dall'aprile 1933 al giugno 1934"; also *Israel*, February 15–22 and October 18, 1934.

45. Renzo De Felice, *Mussolini il 'duce'*, vol. 1 (Turin, 1974), pp. 285 ff.

46. *Israel*, January 25, 1934, which also contains the text of the manifesto issued on January 14 by the administrative commission and the chief rabbi:

"Jews of Tripoli! On Monday at 9 A.M., H. E. Air Marshal Italo Balbo, the new Governor of Libya, will arrive in Tripoli.

"The Jewish population received with great joy the news that the heroic trans-Atlantic aviator, with his illustrious name and youthful enthusiasm, was to govern this Colony in the name of H. M. the King of Italy, by appointment of the Duce. We wish to give H. E. Italo Balbo an enthusiastic welcome! As a sign of rejoicing, close your workshops, offices, and shops and come one and all to give the new Governor, the member of the Quadrumvirate of the March on Rome, the first auspicious salute with your unanimous applause."

47. For one of these attacks, which occurred a few weeks after Balbo's arrival in Tripoli, see De Felice, *Storia degli ebrei italiani sotto il fascismo*, p. 142.

48. For a detailed picture of Italian colonial policy in Libya from 1934 to the Second World War, and of Balbo's activities, see Segre, *Fourth Shore*, pp. 82 ff.

49. The expansion of their economic activities did not affect the geographical distribution of Libyan Jews. The 1936 population census shows this clearly (see Table N–2).

50. According to the 1931 census, only six families, consisting of 24 persons, were working in agriculture in the Province of Tripoli; according to the 1936 census, the number had risen to forty-two families (237 people) in the Province of Tripoli and two families (8 people) in the Province of Benghazi.

51. According to the 1936 census again, the distribution of Libyan Jews according to the occupation of the head of the family was as shown in Table N–3.

TABLE N-2. *Geographical Distribution of Libyan Jews, 1936*

Zuwara	736	Agedabia	53
Zawia	566	Benghazi	3,098
Zanzur	117	Soluq	5
Tripoli	17,196	Barce	281
Amruss	1,313		
al-Azizia	1	Benghazi Province	3,437
Castel Benito (Tajura)	174		
Nalut	41	Beda Littoria	5
Gharian	419	Cirene	25
Yafran	375	Apollonia	75
		Derna	322
Tripoli Province	20,938	Tubruq	240
		Port Bardia	45
al-Khums	745		
Qusabat	404	Derna Province	712
Tarhuna	95		
Zlitin	607	Mudizia di Brach	2
Misurata	838	Mudizia di Horr	14
Beni Ulid	58	Fezzan	16
Syrte	341		
Misurata Province	3,088		

SOURCE: Istituto centrale di statistica, *VIII Censimento generale della popu-lazione*, vol 5 (Rome, 1938), pp. 80 ff.

52. For Table 12, see *Annuario generale della Libia, 1940–1941*, vol. 19, ed. Consigli e Uffici dell'Economia Corporativa della Libia (Spoleto, 1940), pp. 147 ff., 296 ff., 403 ff., and 478 ff. Particularly in the commercial sector, the same firm was often active in several trades. The number of firms was thus less than that of activities shown in the table. Table 13 is based on the tax rolls, in AUCII, fasc. "Tripoli 1931–38."

53. In the early 1940s in the Province of Tripoli there were at least four joint-stock companies owned by Libyan Jews (Soc. An. Imprese Generali, for export-import, real estate transactions, contracts, and miscellaneous supplies, owned by H. Nahum and with assets of 280,000 lire; Soc. An. Italiana Distilleria Agraria, for alcohol distilling, owned by A. Arbib and with assets of 600,000 lire; Soc. Valorizzazioni Industriali Agrarie Tripoline, owned by E. Gutierrez and S. Nahum; Unione Tripolina, for vegetable horse-hair production and export, owned by H. Nahum, and with assets of 1,500,000 lire); six limited partnership companies (R. Hannuna e C.; E. Labi; La Libica; La Mandataria; Hammus Iss. Raccah; Serussi Messaud e C.); four individually owned limited companies (F.lli Gadzinski; Vittorio Hassan; Halfalla Nahum; Tayar G. di M.); and ten general partnerships (Isacco Barda e F.llo; Consorzio fabbricanti Buha; Bedasch Hlafo e Rahmin; Gadzinski e Ballini; Galamin e Barda; Leone Habib e F.llo; Haggiag Zachi e David; Hannuna e Meghnagi; David Nahum; Sion Seror). During the same period in the Province of Benghazi there were at least ten general partnerships owned by Libyan Jews. In the Province of Derna there were another four at least. Obviously, these

TABLE N-3. *Geographical Distribution of Libyan Jewish Population According to Occupation of Heads of Families, 1936*

Area	Total		Farming, Hunting, Fishing		Industry		Shipping and Communications	
	Fam.	Ind.	Fam.	Ind.	Fam.	Ind.	Fam.	Ind.
Province of Tripoli	4,848	21,019	50	237	1,859	8,566	133	624
Tripoli City	4,012	17,286	42	203	1,560	7,266	93	443
Province of Misurata	710	3,100	4	22	214	944	4	22
Misurata Town	203	838	—	—	53	229	1	3
Province of Benghazi	767	3,472	2	8	196	874	12	62
Benghazi Town	695	3,121	2	8	175	787	10	52
Province of Derna	153	714	—	—	40	165	1	1
Derna Town	55	322	—	—	12	64	—	—
Southern Military Territory	7	16	—	—	5	10	—	—
Total for Libya	6,485	28,321	56	267	2,314	10,559	150	709

Fam.: families.
Ind.: individuals.
SOURCE: Istituto centrale di statistica, *VIII Censimento generale della popu-lazione*, vol. 5 (Rome, 1938), p. 92.

data cover only companies which have been identified and, more importantly, make no mention of Jewish participation in companies the major
part of whose capital did not come from Jews. See *Annuario generale della
Libia, 1940–1941* 19: 138 ff., 396 ff.

54. For the high birthrate among Libyan Jews as a group and comparisons between Tripoli and Benghazi, see *Notiziario demografico*, no. 11
(1937); also R. Bachi, "La demografia dell'Ebraismo prima dell'eman-
cipazione," in *Scritti in onore di Dante Lattes* (Città di Castello, 1938),
pp. 258 ff. A result of this birthrate was the extraordinary growth which Libyan Jewry experienced during the 1930s: from 24,024 in 1931 to 28,191 in
1936 and 30,387 in 1939; in less than a decade there was thus an increase of
over 26 percent (compared with a growth among the Muslim population of
less than 15 percent). By June 30, 1939, the Libyan Jewish population was
distributed as follows:

Province of Tripoli: 22,498
Province of Misurata: 3,369
Province of Benghazi: 3,653
Province of Derna: 863
Fezzan: 4

In order to arrive at the total Jewish population of Libya, one must add
figures for Italian and foreign Jews living in the colony. Precise figures are
lacking, though. The only ones available date from January 1, 1934, and
cover only Tripoli: at that time there were 510 Italians, 1,260 French citi-

Trade		Liberal Professions and Crafts, Religious Functions		Public and Private Administration		Domestic Work		Non-professional		No Occupation Indicated	
Fam.	Ind.	Fam.	Ind.	Fam.	Ind.	Fam.	Ind.	Fam.	Ind.	Fam.	Ind.
1,710	8,405	72	348	146	672	87	137	756	1,920	26	110
1,288	6,404	61	296	141	648	87	137	719	1,804	21	85
387	1,818	12	62	9	31	3	5	66	142	11	54
115	516	3	20	7	22	—	—	23	46	1	2
350	1,775	17	78	42	197	14	26	131	443	3	9
309	1,546	15	70	41	196	14	26	126	427	3	9
97	488	3	10	4	20	—	—	8	30	—	—
37	234	1	2	1	6	—	—	4	16	—	—
2	6	—	—	—	—	—	—	—	—	—	—
2,546	12,492	104	498	201	920	104	168	970	2,535	40	173

zens and subjects, 310 British citizens and subjects, and 80 Jews of other nationalities. See ASMAI, "Libia," p. 31 (1930–1935).

55. According to a table prepared in 1942 by the Ministry of Italian Africa (ASMAI, "Libia," p. 25) the population of the Municipality of Tripoli increased under Italian occupation as shown in Table N-4.

56. *Annuario generale della Libia, 1939–1940* (Spoleto, 1939) 18: 99 ff., 352 ff.; 19: 129 ff., 394 ff.

57. A series of attempts were made to develop the silver and ivory crafts. These included founding a colonial school for gold and silver work, establishing production cooperatives, and setting up a committee as part of the Community of Tripoli to study, in cooperation with the Italian authorities, problems of production and marketing systems for the products. See *Israel*, February 14, 1935, and AUCII, fasc. 32, "Missione Castelbolognesi," "Relazione dell'attività svolta in Tripoli dal novembre 1934 a tutto maggio 1935," written by Gustavo Castelbolognesi after his return to Italy.

58. Balbo was probably not very concerned at differences between Arabs and Jews. They must have seemed to him to be ultimately reconcilable, in view of the Jews' and Arabs' harmony of interests. This is indicated by what he said to Vittorio Emanuele II during the king's visit to Libya in 1938: "The Arabs keep on shouting, but they need the Jews as much as they need bread and air to breathe. Look, here in Libya they fight, hate each other, and curse each other; but they back each other up all the time" (N. D'Aroma, *Venti'anni insieme: Vittorio Emanuele e Mussolini* [Bologna, 1957], p. 267). That does not alter the fact that Balbo thought that, if the Jews became Italians to all intents and purposes, and merged with the other Italians, these differences would also come to an end.

59. AUCII, fasc. 32, "Missione Castelbolognesi," G. Castelbolognesi to F. Ravenna, December 18, 1934.

60. ASMAI, posiz. 150/31, fasc. 145, "Libia—Comunità Israelitica in Libia, 1929–35," I, Balbo a Direz. Gen. per le Colonie dell'Africa Settentrionale—Ministero delle Colonie, January 12, 1935.

61. AUCII, fasc. 54, F. Ravenna to G. Castelbolognesi, January 5, 1934. On the basis of this meeting the Union asked the Community of Tripoli to prepare a petition to present to Balbo as soon as he arrived in Libya.

62. *Israel*, December 7, 1933.

63. It can be seen in AUCII, fasc. 54. The criteria indicated were largely the same as those adopted for the Ben Yehuda schools. In support of its negative evaluation of the public schools, the report observed that fewer pupils attended both Jewish schools and state schools—changing in favor of the latter—as they reached the higher grades: in the third elementary level there were about eighty attending both schools, in the fourth there were thirty, less than ten in the fifth, and only two in the first technical level.

64. For further details, see the complete text of the letter by which, the same day, Castelbolognesi apprised Felice Ravenna of the meeting, reproduced in De Felice, *Storia degli ebrei italiani sotto il fascismo*, pp. 523 ff.

65. AUCII, fasc. 32, "Missione Castelbolognesi."

66. De Felice, *Storia degli ebrei italiani sotto il fascismo*, pp. 199 ff.

TABLE N-4. *Population of the Municipality of Tripoli, 1913–1942*

	1913	1931	1938	1942
Italians	9,000	21,756	39,098	45,042
Muslims	19,000	41,040	46,743	84,322
Jews	10,500	14,754	18,437	18,892
Foreigners	4,500	3,888	3,879	3,567
Libyans of other religions	—	—	—	179

SOURCE: Ministry of Italian Africa, 1942 (ASMAI, "Libia," p. 25).

67. For these events, see AUCII, "Missione Castelbolognesi," esp. "Relazione dell'attività svolta in Tripoli dal novembre 1934 a tutto maggio 1935"; also *Israel*, March 21, 1935, which quickly challenged the interpretation given by the newspapers of Tel Aviv and Cairo.

68. AUCII, fasc. 32, "Missione Castelbolognesi," Castelbolognesi to the Union, February 21, 1935.

69. For these events, see AUCII, fasc. 32, "Missione Castelbolognesi," esp. "Relazione dell'attività svolta in Tripoli dal novembre 1934 a tutto maggio 1935," and fasc. 11/A.

70. ASMAI, El. III, box 89, fasc. 281, subf. "Comm. Dott. Gustavo Castelbolognesi," Balbo to S. E. Il Capo del Governo, Ministro delle Colonie, May 31, 1935. Mussolini approved the measure in a note dated June 17, 1935.

71. The text of the communiqué, which was sent from Rome, read as follows: "Some foreign newspapers have wrongly interpreted and commented on the removal of Prof. Gustavo Castelbolognesi from the post of chief rabbi of the Jewish Community of Tripoli.

"First, what has been published should be rectified. It has been said that the said Professor has been 'deported.' The rabbi is perfectly free in Italy.

"The reasons for the removal of Castelbolognesi are the following. He had been chief rabbi of the Jewish Community of Tripoli for less than two years, but does not seem to have been able to keep his distance from the local Jews, who are still attached to old customs in contradiction to the spirit of modern civilization, and practice rituals considered outdated by European Jewish communities.

"In view of some episodes of religious intolerance and considering that such a situation was liable to give rise to disturbances in the Jewish community, jeopardizing public order, the local Governor decided that he could no longer avail himself of the services of Prof. Castelbolognesi."

See ASMAI, El. III, box 89, fasc. 281, subf. "Comm. Dott. Castelbolognesi."

72. For further information, see AUCII, fasc. 63, memorandum sent by J. Jona to F. Ravenna, dated September 23, 1935.

73. AUCII, fasc. 32, "Missione Castelbolognesi," and fasc. 11/A. Sig-

nificantly, the president of the Union did not inform the leaders of the Community of Tripoli in advance of his trip and had no contact with them.

74. On this topic, see De Felice, *Storia degli ebrei italiani sotto il fascismo*, pp. 117 ff.

75. Balbo, telegraphing the Ministry of Colonies on December 6, 1936, to describe the events of the first day that the ordinance went into effect, gave these telegrams great importance: "I believe that without such incitement the episode would have passed without incident." See De Felice, *Storia degli ebrei italiani sotto il fascismo*, p. 525. Balbo's reaction in turn provoked an approach—personally ordered by Galeazzo Ciano—by the Italian consul in Jerusalem to the chief rabbi attributing to his "unacceptable intervention" the fact that the Libyan authorities found themselves obliged to "strictly enforce the law." See ASMAE, Palestina, b. 16, 1937, subf. "Agitazioni ebraiche in Palestina per i provvedimenti del Governo della Libia." Also in connection with the telegrams from the chief rabbi of Eretz Israel, see an article, "Cronaca nera ebraica," *L'avvenire di Tripoli*, December 7, 1936. It blames "the infractions and transgressions of a small proportion of lesser individuals among the local chosen people" on the chief rabbi's intervention. Moreover, it refers to the "influence" of the Jewish International, "which with its Muscovite and Spanish occupations seems to have time to make trouble in Tripoli as well." The article continued with a violent attack on the "petty scheming being carried on in Tripoli by that character, Mr. Chief Rabbi Castelbolognesi, who was unceremoniously kicked out of the Colony, and none too soon, even though he was an Italian citizen and a member of the Fascist Party." The article blamed his policies for spreading among the local rabbis scorn for the authority of the state, and praised the Arabs for their serious, understanding, and correct behavior. One of the two chief rabbis of Tel Aviv—probably after his colleague had been approached by the Italian consul in Jerusalem—also approached the Italian consul general in Jerusalem on February 19, 1937, on behalf of the Libyan Jews, though he used different terms. This is the consul's account of the meeting to Rome:

"Yesterday the Chief Rabbi of Tel Aviv came to Jerusalem and asked me to receive him. After making declarations of friendship and loyalty to Italy, he asked me to forward the request that the ordinance of the Governor General of Libya be applied by allowing anyone who so desired to observe the Sabbath. The Jewish authorities would exercise no pressure over those who feel able, as in many countries of West Africa, to work.

"The Chief Rabbi added that he had prevented a planned demonstration against our institutions in Tel Aviv.

"I replied to the Chief Rabbi in the same way as I had replied to other persons on other occasions, merely adding that he should take care not to get involved in partisan maneuvers aimed at creating nonexistent causes of complaint against the last country which freely accepts Jews."

See ASMAE, "Palestina," b. 16, 1937, telegram dated February 20, 1937.

76. AUCII, fasc. 83.

77. The following day, on November 27, 1936, *L'avvenire di Tripoli*, reporting on the audience, gave Balbo's reply as follows:

"The Governor, upon the insistent requests of members of the Community, replied that it is not possible for him to change a measure which is only intended to bring Tripoli into line with the cities of the Motherland. The Governor repeated his invitation to the Community members to campaign among their fellow-Jews to persuade them to adapt to the rhythm of our times, working harder and abandoning their respect for old traditions which require frequent long periods of idleness, leading to disastrous consequences for the family finances. Finally, he pointed out that those who wished to persist in the irritating observance of old customs could do it in complete freedom and tolerance if they left the new city and moved back behind the old walls."

78. *L'avvenire di Tripoli* of December 8, 1936, described as follows "the just punishment dealt out yesterday to some recalcitrant Jews":

"Yesterday, in the early afternoon, following the fruitless attempt at rebellion against the hierarchy, of which we spoke in Monday's *Avvenire di Tripoli*, on the part of a minority of the local Jewish population, in the square in front of the Tobacco Factory, just and timely punishment was meted out to some of the most typical of the malefactors. In accordance with the law, the regulations, and local custom regarding the subject in relation to the Libyan indigenous population, ten strokes of the *kurbash* were given to two disobedient Jews, Sion Barda fu Abramo and Nhaisi Saul di Nessin. A third, Benedetto Meghidesc fu Vittorio, who had been determined by medical examination to be unfit for the punishment due, was exempted: his punishment has been changed to three months' imprisonment.

"With exceptional clemency, a punishment which was moral rather than material in nature was provided for: those punished, in fact, experienced hardly any physical harm from the flogging, which had an important meaning as an example. The public event naturally attracted to the square and its surroundings a large crowd composed of metropolitans, Arabs, and even, for the record, some Jews.

"It should also be said for the record that a German Jew living in Tripoli who had been expelled from Tunisia shouted "Cowards!" at the Arabs present.

"This Jew, a certain Wolfgang Pinner, was immediately handcuffed and taken to the Prison together with the Jews who had been punished and with whom he had inappropriately expressed his rash solidarity.

"There is no need to add that the entire population of Libya received the administration of justice yesterday with the most complete, absolute, and legitimate satisfaction."

79. Prato had already approached the Italian diplomatic authorities in Egypt right after the publication of the ordinance of November 14 and had pointed out the negative repercussions which it would have on Mediterranean Jewish communities. See AUCII, fasc. 54.

80. De Felice, *Storia degli ebrei italiani sotto il fascismo*, p. 525.

81. Ibid., p. 526.

82. During 1937 the Ministry of Foreign Affairs followed with lively and constant interest political developments among Jews in North Africa (Tangiers, Morocco, Algeria, Tunisia, Egypt) and Palestine. Significantly, the ministry's longest and most important reports on the subject were sent to the Ministry of Colonies, which forwarded them to the governor of Libya. The reports paid much attention to Italian and Libyan Jews (of whom there were many in Palestine), who, moreover, had an attitude which gave no cause for complaint.

83. There were a number of Fascist Jews, particularly in Benghazi, where the number of Libyan Jews who had taken Italian citizenship was proportionately higher than in Tripoli. Among Benghazi Jews, Raul Fargion in 1937 was appointed to become the administrative secretary of the local Fascist federation and at the beginning of 1938 became a member of its federal directorate (AUCII, fasc. 74; for further information, see *Israel*, January 2, February 20, March 19–26, May 7–14, 1936; March 11, 18, and 25 and April 15, 1937; and May 27, 1938).

84. In Tripoli (where he visited part of the *hara*), Benghazi, and Barce, Mussolini was received by the Jews with expressions of friendliness and even enthusiasm. The Community of Tripoli presented him with a richly worked golden Hanukkah lamp inscribed "To Benito Mussolini from the Jews of Tripoli with deep gratitude and devotion." The chronicle of the Duce's visit to Tripoli, written by Felice Nahum and given great prominence in the March 25, 1937, issue of *Israel*, ended as follows:

"Even some persons close to the Duce believe that the welcome which the Jews of Tripoli gave him was one of the most important paid him in this triumphant visit to Italian Africa, a visit which will live in the memory of our people. Everyone had the feeling that not just a new era but a new history was dawning for these lands and all their inhabitants, without distinction of race or religion. The new age of work, peace, and development will take on an even faster and more intense pace, and the Jews of Libya will contribute with their intelligence and industry to the effort for civilization and progress and the affirmation of the Italian Empire in the Mediterranean and in the world."

In May of the following year, the king was also received by the Jews of Tripoli with expressions of friendship. See *Israel*, May 27, 1938, which gave less prominence to the king's visit than it had to Mussolini's.

85. *Israel*, March 25, 1937, and AUCII, fasc. 32, A. Lattes to G. Zevi, March 22, 1937. It is typical that *L'avvenire di Tripoli*, which, on March 18, 1937, gave Mussolini's visit much space and printed in full the rabbi's greetings, did not report the Duce's words, merely writing that he was "very touched by the expressions of their devotion." According to a witness, Roberto Arbib, Mussolini said:

"I am more than convinced of the loyalty and energetic industriousness of the Jewish people of Libya and Italy and I beg to assure them that they have no cause for concern and that Italy considers the Jews as being under her protection and that they will continue to receive the same treatment granted to all Italian citizens; there is no racial or religious discrimination in my mind and I remain faithful to the policy of equality before the law and freedom of worship."

86. For the arrival of Rabbi Lattes in Tripoli and the beginning of his tenure, see *Israel*, March 11 and May 6, 1937.

87. A certain underlying coldness persisted, especially on the part of Libyan Jews, who felt they had been disregarded by the Union (such accusations were made against the leaders of the Union by some Italian Jews as well, especially some of Fascist orientation). An echo of this state of mind can be gleaned in a July 1939 letter from Lattes to the Union in which, besides informing them that the Libyans would not be ready in time to attend a meeting called for three days later in Bologna for the delegates of all the Communities, he made this typical statement: "otherwise, not bad, when one considers that Jewish life in Tripoli is as a rule ignored by Italian Jewry" (AUCII, fasc. 31).

88. All information and letters used in connection with Lattes' work in 1937–1938 are to be found in his correspondence with the Union, AUCII, fasc. 32.

89. The tax increase led some taxpayers to begin the procedures necessary for abjuration of their membership in the Community. However, in almost all cases, Lattes persuaded those concerned to stop them.

90. On May 5, Lattes wrote to the Union: "The few rich people here and the merchant class, apart from a few against whom I am taking official steps, do their duty as Jews and more, since, in addition to the compulsory tax, they give generously. At the moment, with the help which they have volunteered, I am eliminating the shameful practice of begging. It is not possible to ask more than they are giving and it would not be unjust for sister Communities, especially those which have no poor people to support, to do something for us."

91. Among those wanting to take Italian citizenship were many employees of public institutions. There were many Jews working in them, as well as in the Tripoli branch of the Banco di Roma. After 1936 fewer Jews were hired and the issue was raised of whether or not public institutions could have regular staff members who were not Italian citizens (see ACS, PNF, "Situazione politica ed economica delle Provincie," b. 26, fasc. "Tripoli"). Thus some of the applications must have been made in order to secure jobs being held or in order to apply for jobs.

92. After Balbo arrived in Libya there were no more serious incidents between Arabs and Jews. A state of latent tension persisted and tended to express itself in varied ways, especially at football matches between the two communities (for such an incident, see *Israel*, February 20, 1936), so much so that these matches were eventually forbidden by order of the governor and local championships were reorganized within the communities. In October 1937, as the Palestinian question was worsening, a group of Muslim notables and ulamas, among them Prince Suleimen Karamanli, the qadi and

the mufti of Tripoli, two judges of the Supreme Shari'a Court, the president and director of the Waqf charity administration, and the director of the newspaper *El-Adil*, sent the following message (signed by a thousand people) to Mussolini:

"To H. E. the Grand Duce. In the face of the calamity which is befalling our Muslim brothers in Palestine on their own beloved soil, and all Islam in its sanctuary, which represents the first of the two (Mecca and Jerusalem) and which has been the homeland of the Arabs from the most ancient times and of Islam since its dawn, we Muslims of Libya address your excellency, O Grand Duce, with this energetic protest against the British government. It has not ceased dismembering the body of Islam and breaking the chains which link Muslims together, thereby spreading discord among them, sucking their blood, and taking over their possessions. And as if that were not enough, the British government has also struck at the holy Muslim land which has been the Muslims' property and home since the first century of Islam and in which they have lived during all this long period in perfect harmony and friendship with their neighbors.

"Having struck at that land, Britain gave it in fee to the Zionist Jews, from a feeling of bitterness against Islam and the Muslims, and in order to carry out an act of oppression and iniquity against those Arabs who sacrificed everything they had to consolidate peace during the world war, after Britain had made a solemn commitment and given its word of honor that it would support their cause and help them to win independence.

"But we see today that Britain does not keep its commitments and word and is aiming the last arrow in its quiver against Islam, in order to mortally wound it. Beloved Duce, it is to Your Government, which has accustomed us Libyans to being treated with kindness and assistance, and to You, who in many of your speeches have declared and shown yourself to be the friend of Islam and of the Muslims, that we present this protest against the wicked actions of the British government which we are denouncing. We pray you to take note of the feelings which animate us in the face of this painful fact, and we declare our full solidarity with our brothers in Palestine, before the whole world. Moreover, we pray you to stretch out your powerful arm to our Palestinian fellow-Muslims and protest on our behalf to Britain and the whole world.

"We take the occasion to express to Your Excellency our complete obedience, as always, with profound devotion." (ASMAE, "Gran Bretagna, Varie," package 19, "1923–1938".)

6. Fascist Racial Legislation and the War (1938–1943)

1. A letter dated December 22, 1938, from Aldo Lattes to the Union reads: "Here we are in the dark about everything that is happening in the Italian communities." See AUCII, fasc. 32.

2. De Felice, *Storia degli ebrei italiani sotto il fascismo*, pp. 254 ff.

3. In fact, though the measure referred explicitly to Libya, it hardly

concerned it. In practice, the foreign Jews who might have moved there were refugees from Germany, who had already been refused permission to enter Libya. The reasons were lack of work in the colony, so as not to deprive Italians of the few positions available; a desire not to displease the Arabs (Libyan Jewish communities had been forbidden since 1933 to collect donations for Jewish refugees from Germany, while Italian communities had not); and a desire not to harm the economic situation of Libyan Jews (since the potential immigrants would have been the poorest, those without any alternatives). Rather than having importance in itself, the reference to Libya indirectly emphasized the exclusion of Italian East Africa. For political and economic reasons, Mussolini initially played with the idea of sending a considerable number of Jews there. With regard to this idea and its possible repercussions for relations between Italy and its Muslim subjects, it is interesting that as soon as the viceroy of Italian East Africa, Amedeo of Savoy, heard of it, he telegraphed the Ministry of Italian Africa (the former Ministry of Colonies) to express his negative view of Jewish settlement in Eritrea or Somalia, where there were many Muslims: "My opinion is no, that it is absolutely inappropriate to encourage Jewish immigration to the Muslim countries of the Empire. It would provoke an inevitable reaction against us by the population, which is very sensitive about the Palestinian question."

If Jewish agricultural colonization was to be encouraged, the Duke of Aosta suggested, despite his doubts on the appropriateness of "installing unreliable elements" on the shores of Lake Tana, "adding new colonies to groups of Falasha Jews" in Ethiopia. If the idea was to increase trade and industry, "immigration could be allowed into non-Muslim highland regions." In both cases, "we should be very sure about the people to whom we are granting immigration" and "in any case strictly exclude non-Italian Jews." See ASMAI, Archivio di Gabinetto, file 70, (1936–1939), fasc. "Immigrazione ebraica in Somalia," telegram dated September 6, 1938.

4. For further details, see De Felice, *Storia degli ebrei italiani sotto il fascismo*, pp. 271 ff.

5. With R. D. L. [Royal Decree-Law] no. 70 of January 9, 1939, the four Libyan provinces became an integral part of the territory of the Kingdom of Italy. A special Italian citizenship was established for indigenous Muslims. It could be acquired on request, subject to the fulfillment of certain requirements. For the text, see Curotti, *La Libia*, pp. 126 ff. According to an internal Union memorandum, dated March 17, 1939, and probably based on news brought by Leone Hassan, though the switch to racism was followed by the little remembered January 9, 1939, decree, it was not welcomed by the Arabs. It was probably the rich and most politically educated who were concerned (to the point of refraining from buying land and starting construction) that sooner or later similar measures might be adopted against themselves. See AUCII, fasc. 34.

6. See Curotti, *La Libia*, p. 310. The main articles applied against the Italian Jews in Libya were Articles 10, 13, 14, and 21 of R.D.L. no. 1728 of

November 17, 1938. For the text, see De Felice, *Storia degli ebrei italiani sotto il fascismo*, pp. 562 ff.

7. For the discomfort of Europeanized pupils obliged to attend Jewish schools, see the Union memorandum dated March 17, 1939, cited [in note 5].

8. Typical of this are some questions asked by the Libyan authorities of the Ministry of Italian Africa and the prime minister's office in the initial weeks after the issuing of the measures applying to foreign Jews and those included in D. L. of November 17, 1938. See ASMAI, Archivio di Gabinetto, file 70 (1936–1939), fasc. "Israeliti," Memo for the Duce, November 10, XVII (1938); ACS, Presidenza del Consiglio dei Ministri, Gabinetto, 1937–1938, fasc. 3-2-2/5441-12.

9. De Felice, *Storia degli ebrei italiani sotto il fascismo*, p. 296.

10. ASMAI, Archivio di Gabinetto, file 70 (1936–1939), fasc. "Segnala-zioni—Varie."

11. Both documents have been published in De Felice, *Storia degli ebrei italiani sotto il fascismo*, pp. 368 ff.

12. The telegram which the Ministry of Italian Africa sent to Balbo on March 8, 1939, on this subject and the one sent the day before by the Ministry of Foreign Affairs to Italian Africa gave the reasons for the measure, stating that those concerned should be left "undisturbed" and arguing that the Directorate General of Demography and Race had not yet been able to examine their requests. In partial cancellation of this decision, four months later, on July 20, 1939, Balbo asked Rome to authorize him to expel "at the appropriate moment" a group of Jewish French subjects (Isacco Coen, Giacobbe Cohen, Raffaello Nuari, Rubin Baranes, Elia Baranes, Sion Seror, Leone Baranes, and Arturo Iurnò) who he was certain belonged to a spy organization operating in the port of Tripoli among Jewish customs clearance agents and shipping agents. See ASMAI, Archivio di Gabinetto, file 70 (1936–1939), fasc. "Israeliti."

13. Those interned, who were almost all over twenty-one, received 8–10 lire a day for support. At Tajura they could receive food from home; at Bu'ayrat al-Hasun foodstuffs were provided by the camp administration and the prisoners did their own cooking. See statement by Jacob Habib, in ACDEC.

14. ACS, Ministero dell'Africa Italiana, Direzione generale affari politici, b. 13, fasc. "Rimpatri stranieri dalla Libia."

15. Ibid. A note included there shows that in January 1942, 200 Jewish British subjects, out of a total of 1,821 foreigners evacuated, were sent to Italy.

16. Account by Jacob Habib in ACDEC.

17. ACDEC also contains eight accounts by Jewish British subjects who had been deported to Germany and escaped.

18. ACS, PNF [Partito Nazionale Fascista], "Situazione politica ed economica delle provincie," b. 26, fasc. "Tripoli," report to the Secretary of the PNF, Tripoli, October 27, XVIII (1940).

19. ASMAI, Archivio di Gabinetto, file 99/IX, fasc. "Varie—1941"; the

undated report was sent as a memo to the PNF inspector for Libya.

20. AUCII, fasc. 34, A. Lattes to the Union, September 11, 1939. There were cases in 1939 of Jews who, when the governing authorities charged the Fascio of Tripoli with organizing civilian mobilization, went and registered, saying that if it was necessary they wanted to do their duty as patriots.

21. For the issue of education, see AUCII, fasc. 34 and 35.

22. On this subject see the unpublished "Memorie" of Sion Nemni.

23. ACS, Ministero dell'Africa Italiana, Direzione generale affari politici, b. 7, fasc. "Propaganda antitaliana."

24. The fortnightly reports by the censorship office on correspondence being sent from Libya by Italian civilians and military personnel are a useful source of information on this subject (ACS, Ministero dell'Africa Italiana, Direzione generale affari politici, b. 14).

25. For events connected with the disbanding of the Maccabee Club, see Nemni, "Memorie."

26. A confidential report from the commander-general of the PAI, the colonial police, of May 2, 1941, to the Minister's Office of the Ministry of the Interior (ACS, Ministero dell'Africa Italiana, Direzione generale affari politici, b. 7) relates some of the events which occurred in Tripoli during April. On April 7 a certain Scialom Nahum was insulted. The event was distorted by those present, since Nahum was known to be a very polite person and gave no provocation. The aggressor justified himself "with the resentment aroused in him toward Jews when he heard that they had behaved badly toward the Italians in Benghazi." Two days later another Jew, Vittorio Levi, was punched and mistreated by persons unknown because when the war bulletin was read he did not stand up. The same happened shortly after to Rahmin Haggiag. Some officers from Benghazi, led by a barber, also mistreated Jews in Suq al-Turq. The same happened in the center of Tripoli on April 12 to Aldo Forti and Beniamino and Clemente Tamman, at the hands of a group including some air force officers. On the same day there was an attempt to force some Jewish shopkeepers to close their shops. Two persons received warnings for these incidents. In subsequent days provocations were committed against many Jews, including some leaders of the Tripoli Community. Following the air and naval bombardments during the night between April 20 and 21, 1941, the Jews were leaving the capital and seeking refuge in the hinterland. As Roberto Arbib wrote in his unpublished memoirs, "in the chaos and confusion there were many racial attacks against hundreds of Jews . . . The Fascists could not stand the sight of a single Jew." Many Jews trying to reach Zawia by train (including Halfalla Nahum, Rabbi Lattes, and Roberto Arbib himself) were forced to get off at Zanzur with the argument that they "stank."

27. It has not been possible to find official documents on the events in Benghazi of April 3 and 4, 1941. According to Jewish witnesses, a group of Italian civilians plundered Jewish shops, killing two Jews who tried to resist. See A. Guetta, "Three State Murderers," (in Hebrew), in *Yahadut Luv*, ed. Zuarez et al., p. 202.

28. ACS, Ministero Africa Italiana, Direzione generale affari politici, b. 7, confidential memorandum by Office of the Commander General of PAI, October 28, 1941, and March 17, 1942.

29. Ibid., memorandum by Office of the Commander General of PAI, July 30, 1941.

30. Interestingly, Fascist propaganda failed to take advantage of these episodes and was completely silent regarding them. Even in two publications, one official and the other semiofficial, on the British occupation of Benghazi and Cyrenaica and the crimes committed during them ("Che cosa hanno fatto gli inglesi in Cirenaica" ed. Ministry of Popular Culture [Rome, 1941], and G. Scalfaro, "56 giorni di 'civiltà' inglese a Bengasi" [Rome, 1941]), the Jews are referred to only in passing, to say that in the distribution of food and general relations with the population the British followed this order of precedence: Arabs, Jews, other races, Italians.

31. ACS, Ministero Africa Italiana, Direzione generale affari politici, b. 7, memorandum by Office of the Commander General of PAI, April 11, 1942.

32. Ibid., memorandum by Office of the Commander General of PAI, April 11 and 28, 1942.

33. Ibid., memorandum by Office of the Commander General of PAI, April 29 and July 23, 1942. The three sentenced to prison and those absolved were all under arrest.

34. G. Gorla, *L'Italia nella seconda guerra mondiale: Diario di un milanese, ministro del re governo di Mussolini* (Milan, 1959), p. 286, under February 7, 1942 (referring to the Cabinet meeting that day): "Ciano added that as the British withdrew in Cyrenaica they furiously destroyed the agricultural villages that Balbo had created. He said that the Sanusis and the Jews were particularly persistent in destroying and pillaging, and in reprisal Mussolini has ordered the Jews of Tripoli [correction: Benghazi] to be sent to a concentration camp at Gharian."

35. For this, see ASMAI, Archivio Segreto, file 113/VIII, and Archivio di Gabinetto, "Relazioni della PAI," esp. the reports by the police headquarters of Benghazi dated July 2, August 2, and September 2, 1942, and Tripoli, January 1, 1943. For life in the Giado camp, see Y. Hakmon, "The Exile at Giado," in *Yahadut Luv*, ed. Zuarez et al., pp. 197 ff.

36. For the text, see *Bolletino ufficiale della Libia*, June 2, 1942, and *Rassegna economica dell'Africa Italiana*, no. 8 (1942), pp. 421 ff.

37. *Rassegna economica dell'Africa Italiana*, no. 10 (1942), p. 534.

38. De Felice, *Storia degli ebrei italiani sotto il fascismo*, pp. 364 ff.

39. *Rassegna economica dell'Africa Italiana*, no. 10 (1942), pp. 536 ff.

40. For military operations on the Libyan front during the Second World War, see Vitale, *Africa settentrionale (1911–1943)*, pp. 241 ff. For life in the Sidi-Azaz camp, see A. Guetta, "Imprisonment at Sidi Azaz and at Buk Buk," in *Yahadut Luv*, ed. Zuarez et al., pp. 201 ff.

41. For futher information on the Sidi-Azaz camp, see Nemni, "Memorie." Many inmates in the camp tried to avoid working at all costs and if possible to return home. They resorted to wounding themselves and bribing

the camp officials. There were also incidents with local Arabs; during one of them a Jewish boy was killed.

42. ACS, *Presidenza del Consiglio dei Ministri, Provvedimenti legislativi, 1942, Ministero dell'Africa Italiana*, no. 17, "Disegno di legge riguardante limitazioni di capacità degli appartenenti alla razza ebraica residenti in Libia."

43. Article 3 stipulated that those Libyan Italian citizens should be considered of Jewish race who:

"(1) On January 1, 1942 XX, professed the Jewish religion, or were registered as members of Jewish Communities in Libya or showed some expression of Judaism;

"(2) Were born of parents or fathers of the Jewish religion, unless the father had professed the Muslim religion since prior to January 1, 1942 XX;

"(3) In cases where the father is unknown, was born of a mother of the Jewish religion, unless the mother had professed the Muslim religion since prior to January 1, 1942 XX."

Article 20 stipulated:

"The provisions of this law shall be observed insofar as they are applicable, also to foreign or stateless Jews, by treating citizens as metropolitan Italian citizens of the Jewish race, and subjects or protected persons as Libyan Italian citizens of the Jewish race."

44. Typical of this are Articles 6 and 7, which forbade Jews to act as guardians for minors or to employ servants who were either Aryan or Muslim.

45. Harvey Goldberg, "Ecologic and Demographic Aspects of Rural Tripolitania Jewry, 1853–1949," *International Journal of Middle Eastern Studies* 1971: 258.

46. For a detailed picture of the general situation, see Vitale, *Africa settentrionale*, pp. 315 ff.

47. In early 1941 the leaders of the Community of Tripoli, besides Chief Rabbi Aldo Lattes, were Umberto Di Segni, Alberto Fresco, Ruben Hassan, Raffaello Nemni, and Giorgio Calò (secretary of the administrative commission which also represented the Community on the municipal commission which prepared the list of poor people). In addition, there were six Jewish assessors appointed to the Tripoli Court of Assizes (Fortunato Barda, Umberto Di Segni, Mosè Haddad, Halfalla Nahum, Alfredo and Mario Nunes Vais), nine assessors serving the Court of Tripoli (two serving in Misurata and al-Khums respectively, four serving in Gharian and one in Malat), and two serving the Tripoli Juvenile Court (one each in Misurata, al-Khums, and Gharian). At that time the following organizations were still functioning: the Maccabee Club (president Roberto Arbib), later disbanded; the Ben Yehuda Association (president Sion Addad); the ADEI, the Jewish Women's Association, and the Women's Workshop (all three under the leadership of Lydia Nahum); and the Aguddat Torah Association (president Huato Hatuma). In early 1941 the leaders of the Community of Benghazi, besides Rabbi Hammaus Fellah, were Renato Tesciuba, Benedetto Buaron, Leone Cohen, Salomone Meiohas, and Alberto Treves. The assessors serving on the Court of

Assizes were Benedetto Buaron, Elia Fargion, Abta Mayer, and Renato Tesciuba. There were six more assessors serving the Court of Benghazi, two each serving Derna, Apollonia, and Tubruq, and four serving in Barce. Finally, there were five serving the juvenile courts of Benghazi (three) and Barce (two). The only organization functioning was the ADEI (president Jole Arbib). Precise information is not available on the composition of Community institutions in 1942. There was probably little change in Tripoli.

48. ACS, Ministero Africa Italiana, Direzione generale affari politici, b. 7, Telegram Superlibia a Comando supremo, January 27, 1943, and report, January 29, 1943, on the radio interception service (transmission at 0.05 hours, January 28, Press Nigh [Night?] press Sidney).

49. *The Times*, January 27, 1943.

50. A. Denti Di Pirajno, *La mia seconda educazione inglese* (Milano, 1971), p. 32.

7. British Occupation (1943–1951)

1. According to the official data of the British administration (British Military Administration Tripolitania, *Annual Report by the Chief Administrator on the British Military Administration of Tripolitania for the Period 1st January 1945 to 31st December 1945*, p. 53), when the Jews had returned to their places of residence and before the pogroms in November of that year again upset the distribution of Jews in Tripolitania—a total of 27,264 persons—their distribution by place of residence was as follows:

Zawia	776	Nalut	9
Zuwara	814	Mizda	15
Tripoli	19,330	Tarhuna	185
Amruss (Suq al-Jum'a)	1,563	Zlitin	788
al-'Azizia	19	Qusabat	418
Castel Verde	8	al-Khums	901
Tajura	223	Misurata	1,125
Gharian	502	Beni Ulid	84
Yafran	390	Syrte	114

Precise data are lacking for Cyrenaica: there were probably about 4,500 Jews, almost three-quarters of their number being in Benghazi and the rest in small towns, particularly Derna and Barce. For the Fezzan, under French administration, there are no figures. In 1943–1945 many foreign Jews who had been extradited to Tunisia or interned in Italy during the war and thence deported to Germany returned to Libya. According to the *Annual Report*, 1945, p. 11, 140 Jewish repatriates returned from Germany and Southern France in 1945.

2. For some cases of this sort involving Jews which came to light and the perpetrators of which were brought to justice, see *Corriere di Tripoli*, April 13, May 5, 20, and 21, and July 29, 1943. The most famous case was that of three well-known businessmen, Abramino Habib and Vittorio and Benedetto Arbib, sentenced respectively to two years, nine months, and six

months, for trying to sell the American military authorities piping removed from formerly Italian military stockpiles.

3. John Wright, *Libya* (New York: Praeger, 1969), pp. 189 ff. On the British administration of Libya, see Majid Khadduri, *Modern Libya: A Study in Political Development* (Baltimore: Johns Hopkins Press, 1963), Ch. 3; for the Arab point of view, see N. Ziadeh, *Muhadarat fi Tarikh Libya: Min al-Isti'mar al-Italy ila al Istiqlal* (Beirut, 1958), Ch. 7; Francis James Rennell Rodd, *British Military Administration of Occupied Territories in Africa during the Years 1941–1947* (London: HMSO, 1948).

4. A typical expression of the cordiality which in 1943 marked Jewish-Arab relations was a performance of the poetic drama *Joseph and His Brothers* which the Maccabee Club performed on October 24 in the Miramare Theater before the leaders of the two communities.* For the Jews' sympathy for the British in this initial period and their readiness to cooperate with them, see British Military Administration Tripolitania, *Annual Report*, 1943, pp. 15 ff, showing that many Jews agreed to cooperate even in fields repugnant to their religious sense (such as gravedigging) and even during the Sabbath.

5. *Corriere di Tripoli*, February 23, March 13 and 20, July 1, 15, and 31, 1943. The Maccabee Club, soon after being revived, was allowed by the British authorities to use premises previously used by the Italian Municipality and an area of 30,000 square meters near the sea, previously belonging to the Italian Corps of Engineers (and the materiel stored there, which was sold to the club at a very low price). In this area the club set up playing fields (football, tennis, basketball) and swimming facilities with a bar and restaurant.

6. For the participation of the Palestine Brigade and other Jewish units in operations in Libya and their role in Tripoli after the occupation, see L. Rabinowitz, *Soldiers from Judaea: Palestinian Jewish Units in the Middle East (1941–1943)* (London, 1944); W. Aron, *Wheels in the Storm: The Genesis of the Israeli Defence Forces* (Canberra, 1974). For brief information on youth organizations in Tripoli, see "Notizie della Tripolitania," *Israel*, November 28, 1946.

7. British Military Administration Tripolitania, *Annual Report*, 1945, p. 7.

8. Ibid., p. 9. The Libyan Jews' lack of political aspirations is also attested to in the general report, British Military Administration of Occupied Territories in Africa, *Report, 1941–1943, Presented to the Secretary of State of War to Parliament by Command HM* (January 1945), p. 25.

9. According to the British statistics (British Military Administration Tripolitania, *Annual Report*, 1945, Appendix N) there were 1,146 Jewish pupils in Tripoli in 1943–1944, 2,643 in 1944–1945, and 3,994 in 1945–1946. The numbers for the rest of Tripolitania were 288, 704, and 917. The

*In Hakohen, *The Book of Mordechai*, p. 53, Goldberg notes that this play, in Arabic vernacular, used a theme which was also a favorite Muslim tale. The play was recently revived and performed in Arabic by Libyan Jews in Netanya, Israel, in the summer of 1982.—*Trans.*

vast majority attended Italian schools. The Italian school for Jews of the Old City of Tripoli was directed by Emma Polacco, one of the noblest figures in Libyan Jewry, to which she devoted herself for almost half a century, playing an important part in clandestine emigration. The school opened again in October 1944 with ten classes in the Hebrew program (Hebrew syllabus and Italian language) and twenty-two classes in the Italian program (Italian syllabus and Hebrew language classes). After the November 1945 pogroms, the classes were reduced to ten, since many rooms were being used to house the homeless. However, a small school of three classes was soon opened at the refugee camp of Port Benito.

During the 1946–1947 school year those pupils who could not find a place in the Old City school were sent to the Principessa di Piemonte Italian school. In 1947–1948 and 1948–1949 these pupils went back to their former school which, in 1949–1950, with the financial help of the American Joint Distribution Committee (AJDC), was turned into a school and hospital.

10. For some public expressions of support and loyalty to the Allied cause, and Britain in particular, see *Corriere di Tripoli*, February 5, April 29, May 16, and September 3, 1943.

11. The first legal departures for Palestine took place in 1944. In that year Libyan Jews were assigned a batch of twenty immigration certificates. In order to use them the Community set up an Aliyah Office which assigned fifteen to large families and five to young people who, together with some young members of those families, went to Kibbutz Sde Eliyahu. A few months later another twenty certificates were issued. Twelve of these were assigned to members of the Hechalutz movement, three to other young Zionists, and the rest to persons outside the movement. Their departure was subject to many delays, however, since Egypt refused to issue them transit visas and the British administration for a long time would not grant approval to travel by ship. See "Notizie della Tripolitania."

12. A farm of about a hundred hectares was rented for the purpose. Initially ten, later up to sixty future emigrants were trained there. The Ben Yehuda asked for the Community's moral and material help in the project. At first the Community tried not to get involved at all and justified its refusal by lack of funds. Three council members, Sion Nemni, Yaacov Fargion, and Alberto Nunes Vais, finally persuaded it to support the idea. In November 1945 Arabs plundered and destroyed the farm. See S. Nemni, "Memorie."

13. On the economic crisis of 1944–1945 and the crisis in Arab-Jewish relations, the main documentation can be found in several reports on the November 1945 pogroms: (a) The report by the Community of Tripoli, "I tumulti anti-ebraici in Tripolitania 4, 5, 6 e 7 novembre 1945." This report was issued on December 31, 1945, and includes lists of names, statistics, press reports, official communiqués, notices, proclamations, etc. In AUCII, fasc. "Fatti di Tripoli." There are two English editions of this report: one unpublished, "Anti-Jewish Riots in Tripolitania," CZA, S/25/6457; and the other published in Jewish Agency for Palestine, *The Jewish Case before the*

Anglo-American Committee of Inquiry on Palestine (Jerusalem, 1947), pp. 392 ff. (*b*) The report drawn up by a Zionist agent at an unspecified date, but probably in view of the foregoing, for the Central Zionist Organization, "The Arab Anti-Jewish Riots in Tripolitania, 4–7 November, 1945," CZA, S/25/10.165. (*c*) The report in the *Annual Report, 1945*, of the British Military Administration for Tripolitania.

Useful for comments of a sociological sort is Harvey Goldberg, "Rites and Riots: The Tripolitanian Pogrom of 1945," *Plural Societies*, 8 no. 1 (Spring 1977); 35–56.

14. *Tarabulus el Gharb*, July 25 and August 29, 1944.

15. British Military Administration Tripolitania, *Annual Report, 1945*, p. 8.

16. On October 2, 1945, despite being under British control, the newspaper published an account of a meeting in Damascus between Muslim religious leaders who, referring to rumors of a possible partition of Palestine between Arabs and Jews, declared that "news of this sort aroused their scorn and led them to support any action aimed at eliminating the Jews from Arab countries." The Community of Tripoli pointed out to the British authorities how serious it was to publish this report.

17. British Military Administration Tripolitania, *Annual Report, 1945*, p. 10.

18. Except as otherwise indicated, the sources for reconstruction of the pogroms are the same as those indicated in note 13.

19. "In order to carry out the slaughter, the attackers used various weapons: knives, daggers, sticks, clubs, iron bars, revolvers, and even hand-grenades. Generally, the victim was first struck on the head with a solid, blunt instrument and, after being knocked down, was finished off with a knife, dagger, or, in some cases, by having his throat cut.

"In Zanzur and Amrus (Suk el Jouma) in particular, after having killed or injured their victims, the attackers poured benzine or petroleum over them and set them on fire, and ultimately those killed were so charred as to be unrecognizable. Grenades were used especially at Amrus (Suk el Jouma) against the synagogue as well as the houses. On some of the bodies signs of unimaginable cruelty could be discerned." ("Anti-Jewish Riots in Tripolitania," pp. 3–4.)

20. See Table N-5.

21. See Table N-6.

22. See Table N-7.

23. See Table N-8.

24. In order to meet the immediate needs of these thousands of victims the BMA allocated £10,000 in relief funds between November and December 1945. The Jewish Community of Tripoli considered that the assistance and measures taken by the British to help the victims were on the whole inadequate and too slow. A relief fund opened by the BMA with MAL 250,000 to which many Italians and British soldiers and some Arabs contributed collected MAL 2,372,010 by December 28. In connection with the Arab contribution, the *Annual Report, 1945*, p. 13, says "Arab monetary

support of a relief fund organised by the Administration has been tardy and inconsiderable. Impersonal charity is, however, uncommon among Arabs." A subscription among Jews collected MAL 2,150,000 by December 31, a paltry sum which can be partially explained by the general difficulties in which all Jews found themselves.

TABLE N-5. *General Summary of Those Dead, Succumbed to Injuries, and Missing in 1945 Riots*

Place	Children of Both Sexes between 1 and 7 Years	Boys and Girls between 8 and 15 Years	Young Men and Women between 16 and 20 Years	Men 21–60 Years	Men 60 Years and Over	Women 21–60 Years	Women 60 Years and Over	Total
Tripoli	—	1	2	16	7	7	2	35
Amruss (Suq al-Jumʿa)	8	3	3	7	5	10	2	38
Tajura	—	1	1	2	2	—	1	7
Zanzur	12	7	—	4	3	8	—	34
Zawia	2	2	1	2	3	1	2	13
Qusabat	—	—	—	3	—	—	—	3
Total	22	14	7	34	20	26	7	130

SOURCE: "Anti-Jewish Riots in Tripolitania," p. 12.
21. See Table N-6.
22. See Table N-7.
23. See Table N-8.

TABLE N-6. *Summary of Widows and Orphans from 1945 Riots*

Place	Widows	Orphans
Tripoli	12	32
Amruss (Suq al-Jumʿa)	3	16
Tajura	5	13
Zanzur	3	11
Zawia	4	13
Qusabat	3	7
Total	30	92

SOURCE: "Anti-Jewish Riots in Tripolitania," p. 13.

TABLE N-7. *Claims for Shops and Factories Plundered or Damaged in 1945 Riots*

Tripoli	
Retail shops of different wares	118
Retail shops of foodstuffs	24
Retail shops of groceries	43
Silversmiths and goldsmiths	101
Tailors	68
Forges	12
Watchmakers	3
Shoemakers	65
Electricians	3
Carpenters	12
Builders	1
Plumbers	2
Barber shops	8
Peddlars (various wares)	8
Bicycle repairs	2
Welders	3
Distilleries	4
Aluminum utensil factory	1
Tin factories	1
Tanneries	2
Agricultural concessions	3
Taverns	21
Various wares stores	228
Head office of Maccabee Club (partially)	1
Head office of Maccabee Club (sports field)	1
Head office of Jewish Boy Scouts	1
Total	736
Suq al-Jumʿa (Amruss)	
Grocery shops and different articles	8
Peddlars	5
Taverns	4
Tanners	20
Forges	8
Welders	4
Waggoners (privately owned cabs plundered)	6
Barbers	1
Total	56
Tajura	
Grocery shops and different articles	8
Taverns	1
Forges	1
Barbers	1
Total	11

TABLE N-7 *(continued)*

Zanzur	
Grocery shops and different articles	5
Total	5
Zawia	
Grocery shops and different articles	2
Taverns	2
Distilleries	1
Total	5
Grand total	813

SOURCE: "Anti-Jewish Riots in Tripolitania," p. 18.

TABLE N-8. *Claims Submitted for Compensation Resulting from 1945 Riots*

Tripoli		
356 claims for plundered homes	MAL	88,371,290
736 claims for plundered homes of different wares in detail and gross, factories, laboratories, stables, tanneries, various stores, agricultural concessions, head office of the Maccabee Clubs and of Jewish Boy Scouts		141,941,545
31 claims for assault and rape in the streets		955,175
7 claims for damage caused to private buildings		341,800
10 claims of the Jewish Community of Tripolitania for plunder and damage to synagogues of its property, 5 of which are in Tripoli and 4 in centers of the interior		7,558,278
Total in Tripoli	MAL	239,168,088
Centers of the Interior		
109 claims for plunder in Suq al-Jumʿa (Amruss)		8,088,755
94 claims for plunder in Tajura		11,226,265
1 claim for plunder in Qusabat		558,970
26 claims for plunder in Zanzur		4,487,652
47 claims for plunder in Zawia		4,702,022
Total in centers of the Interior		29,063,664
Grand total	MAL	268,231,752

SOURCE: "Anti-Jewish Riots in Tripolitania," p. 17.

25. *Corriere di Tripoli*, November 13–18, 21–25, 28–30, December 1–2, 5–8, 1945, and "Anti-Jewish Riots in Tripolitania," p. 30. On the basis of reports published in the press:

a. The accused included:

Arabs	Men	261
	Women	12
	Minors	16
		289
Jews	Men	6
	Women	0
	Minors	0
		6
	Total accused	295

b. Those sentenced included:

Arabs	Men	186
	Women	4
	Minors	14
		204
Jews	Men	4
	Women	0
	Minors	0
		4
	Total sentenced	208

c. Those acquitted or absolved included:

Arabs	Men	75
	Women	8
	Minors	2
		85
Jews	Men	2
	Women	0
	Minors	0
		2
	Total acquitted or absolved	87

SOURCE: "Anti-Jewish Riots in Tripolitania," p. 30.

26. *Corriere di Tripoli*, November 10, 1945. In the next few days the mufti, Mohammed Abul Assaad el Alem, issued a *fetua* (legal response) and a religious exhortation by which believers were exhorted to return what had been stolen to the Jews. See *Tarabulus el Gharb*, November 19, 1945.

27. On events in Cairo and Alexandria, see J. Schechtman, *On Wings of Eagles* (New York, 1961), pp. 184 ff.

28. British Military Administration Tripolitania, *Annual Report*, 1945, p. 14.

29. The report "Arab Anti-Jewish Riots in Tripolitania" (pp. 5–6) contains the following passage, which is quite significant since it is probable that the argument that the "leading Arab merchants" mentioned in the re-

port attributed to the "xenophobic Arabs" was the one that they actually made: "A group of leading Arab merchants, speaking to an American observer, declared that while they were loathe to admit it, they were convinced that had the Italians been in control of the territory no such outbreaks as had occurred would have taken place. The Italians would have quickly sent out shooting Carbinieri [*sic*] and that would have stopped any disturbance. The majority of the xenophobic Tripolitanian Arabs, these Arabs continued, are poor, ignorant and the absence of a strong hand during the riots made them feel that the government approved of the outbreaks."

30. British Military Administration Tripolitania, *Annual Report*, 1945, pp. 10, 13.

31. Ibid., pp. 9–10. Regarding the attitude of the Italians, the report commented (p. 15): "Italian employees in the administration have been very useful during the recent anti-Jewish disturbances, but not a few of the Italians fear that the disorders have been only a prelude to what might happen to them one day."

32. The *Annual Report*'s assertions that the Zionism of Libyan Jews was one of the causes of the pogroms had already been foreshadowed in private remarks by Brigadier Travers R. Blackley, Chief Administrator of BMA in Tripolitania, referred to in "The Arab Anti-Jewish Riots in Tripolitania," p. 6.

33. PRO, Foreign Office, 371/45394/8134.

34. "The Arab Anti-Jewish Riots in Tripolitania," p. 3. One may speculate whether one of the motives leading Arab nationalists to their action might have been the fact that a few weeks earlier the idea had been discussed in Europe and America of opening the doors of Tripolitania to massive Jewish immigration as a way of solving the difficult problem of what to do with the Jews from Central Europe without aggravating the crisis in Palestine. See "Anche in Tripolitania," *Israel*, November 15, 1945. The article also describes the reactions of Italian Jewry to the pogroms.

35. The "passively pro-Arab" tendencies of the British officials of the BMA were recognized even in an official publication such as Rodd, *British Military Administration of Occupied Territories in Africa*, p. 466: "In the riots it was apparent that, partly owing to the great Arab preponderance in the ranks and partly to their [the Tripolitanian police's] short existence as a body, they were not reliable unless under the supervision of British officers and they were inclined to be passively pro-Arab." The Jews denounced these tendencies several times, e.g., J. Gil, "Chanukka 5706 ben josheve la-mearoth be-Tripoli," *Al-Amizrah*, which refers to a meeting with the governor of Tripoli in which the governor accused the soldiers of the Palestine Brigade of introducing Zionism into Libya. General Parsons expressed the same opinion previously in his report dated April 19, 1944, in the Imperial War Museum, London, Maxwell Collection.

36. As an initial reaction to the dramatic events in Tripolitania, some even wondered whether Nazi or Fascist "influences" could be behind them. See PRO, Foreign Office, 371/45396/8134, the draft of the Foreign Office's reply to the World Jewish Congress.

37. As has often happened in similar situations, the main issue under discussion, the behavior of the BMA during the pogroms, was rapidly submerged in a number of minor issues—largely with less justification—concerning the BMA's behavior after the pogroms: its failure or lack of persistence in seeking out and punishing the culprits (in Italy, *Israel*, in "Tutti innocenti a Tripoli: L'incredibile condotta delle autorità inglesi," May 23, 1946, held that no one had been brought to trial), its insufficiency or delay in getting relief to the victims, its lack of concrete measures to enable economic activities to be started up again in the most devastated places and to protect the Jews from possible further outbreaks of popular xenophobia, etc.

38. PRO, Foreign Office, 371/45396/8134.

39. The harshest criticisms of the BMA were made by *P.M.* of New York* in a long article (reproduced by *Israel*, February 21, 1946) stating (1) that such violent incidents had not occurred "even during the last days of the Fascist regime, when the Italian authorities were spreading anti-Jewish propaganda"; (2) that the "main responsibility" for what had happened lay on the British Administration for civilian affairs in Tripoli; (3) that there was reason to suspect that the British military authorities intervened not at the request of the civil administration but on their own initiative "to stop those horrors from spreading"; (4) that, therefore, an international inquiry (that would investigate also the role played by former officials of the Criminal Investigation Department in Palestine now heading the police in Tripoli) was required; (5) that, nevertheless, "the disturbances in Tripoli, like those in Cairo, have provided British officials, who oppose the establishment of a Jewish national home, specious arguments to support their theses and violent motives to oppose any further immigration to Palestine."

40. After Libyan independence, during the Sanusi period, Libyan historiography adopted a similar attitude. See, e.g., Fusceika, *History of Libya* (cited in Int., n. 5), p. 71: "The Palestine incidents caused a riot in Tripolitania and Cyrenaica between Arabs and Jews. These regrettable incidents were caused by an error [the baseless rumors that some Jews had murdered the qadi and the mufti] and sensible Libyans were distressed by them and proceeded to put an end to the situation. The governing authorities punished the culprits." In the Qadhdhafi period the main responsibility has been attributed to "Zionist provocations," and it is insinuated that the incidents broke out "because of incitement by the British, for their own reasons, taking advantage of Arab hatred in Libya of the Zionist gangs." See the volume in Arabic dedicated to *The Centenary of the Municipality of Tripoli (1870–1970)* (Tripoli, 1970), pp. 283, 370, 374.

41. AAJC, preliminary report, dated January 13, 1949, by B. Segal on his mission to Tripoli.

42. "The Force was greatly outnumbered during the riots and severely handicapped by the lack of British personnel to lead the Libyan ranks.

---

*The date given for the *P.M.* reference (December 15, 1945) does not seem to be correct. The quotations have therefore been translated from the Italian. —*Trans.*

Largely owing to the lack of such leadership, the loyalty of some of the native police wavered and proved unreliable. Military assistance on a comprehensive scale was necessary to quell the disorders. Nevertheless, the Police made some six hundred arrests during the actual rioting, apprehending many of the main culprits" (*Annual Report*, 1945, p. 26). To explain the reality which lay behind the *Annual Report*'s term "waver[ing] . . . loyalty" we must turn to the Zionist report (p. 4):

"Arabs, Jews and British all agree that very many of the BMA police force: (1) helped the looters by turning their backs as the crimes were being committed; (2) participated in the looting; (3) did not protect Jews from attacks; (4) demanded bribes from some Jews in order to transport them from a dangerous section of the Old City to a safe place. One prominent Arab reported that he went to help his Jewish neighbour and was told by a policeman that it was none of his business and move along. As Brigadier Bertram Temple, Commander of Headquarters, Tripolitania Area, put it, "the police were disloyal"! He cited the case of Zanzur where on Tuesday night 48 hours after the initial outbreak in Tripoli City, 19 policemen and one British officer did nothing to disperse a crowd while nearly forty out of the total Jewish population of 120 were being murdered.

"The blame does not only lie with the rank and file of the police force. On Monday night the attack against Jews in Suk al-Juma resulted in 36 deaths. Four hours before the attack, the Sheikh of the community came to the police station and reported that the local Arabs were planning an attack on the local Jews. The officer in charge contacted police headquarters in Tripoli City, 4 miles away and asked for reinforcements and instructions. He repeated his call two times before the attacks commenced and once as they were going on, but he received no reinforcements and only instructions to keep his force barricaded in the police station as protection against the mob."

The police forces numbered about fourteen or fifteen hundred. They were mostly local Arab policemen with a very small number of Jewish policemen; the noncommissioned officers were also Arabs; the inspectors were partly local Arabs, partly "imported" Arabs, and partly British; the officers were all British.

43. *Corriere di Tripoli*, November 9, 1945.

44. This is proved by the BMA's first communiqué, published by the *Corriere di Tripoli* on November 6, 1945, in which the explosion of violence during the two previous days was defined as "disturbing" and described as "the work of irresponsible elements, who in most cases come from the Arab population."

45. *Corriere di Tripoli*, November 6, 7, 8, and 9, 1945.

46. Ibid., December 18, 1945.

47. Ibid., December 2, 1945.

48. AAJC, "Les Juifs de la Libye: Rapport rédigé suivant les indications et à l'intention du Secrétariat du Congrès Séphardi Mondial" (Tripoli, September 1950).

49. After the army re-established order, tension persisted for several months. The various measures which reduced and eventually abolished the curfew attest to this. Through these measures the military authorities sought to prevent occasions or pretexts for new incidents (e.g., the prohibition on November 14 against celebrations or parades in public places). The 1945 *Annual Report*, p. 14, provides direct testimony: "The inter-racial feeling, appearing so suddenly, still prevails, though on the surface every-day life has returned to normal." In this climate of tension Jewish life recovered slowly. Many Jews who had taken refuge in the *hara* or in camps organized by the British and who might have returned to their villages or houses in the New City or mixed quarters of the Old City delayed doing so (and many never returned). Two weeks after the end of the pogroms, on November 20, the president of the Community of Tripoli asked the British authorities "to institute armed military patrols, composed of British or mixed troops, in the streets and areas of the City of Tripoli in which housing and thoroughfares are used by both Arabs and Jews" and suggested allowing the authorities in other places to regulate patrols according to local conditions. The request was justified by the need to give confidence to those who had taken refuge in the *hara* and who otherwise would not return to their homes (see "Anti-Jewish Riots in Tripolitania"). There is also precise testimony in "The Arab Anti-Jewish Riots in Tripolitania": "British authorities have tried to get the territory and the Jewish populaton back to normal as quickly as possible, but the fear which has pervaded the Jewish population has thus far prevented this from happening. Two weeks after the outbreaks, those Jews whose shops were not destroyed still were afraid to open their shops, and many Jews whose homes were in predominately Arab neighbourhoods feared to leave the safety of their temporary shelter in the schools, synagogue or refugee camps."

50. AAJC, Report by Max Gottschalk, June 7, 1948.

51. The crisis was very serious in Cyrenaica as well. See *Israel*, March 13, 1947: "In Benghazi, Derna, and Barce the economic and moral conditions of the Jews have deteriorated so much that Renato Tesciuba, the president of the Community of Benghazi, has had to make an urgent appeal to the World Jewish Congress, pointing out the increasing unemployment and worsening health and requesting food and medical supplies." In 1947 in Cyrenaica, especially at Barce, there were also some sporadic attacks against Jews. Tesciuba—who had considerable popularity in the region and was a member of the Cyrenaican Parliament appointed by Idris—managed to get the president of the Cyrenaican National Front to have a firm and fair attitude on the part of the police, which at the time discouraged more serious violence.

52. See Nemni, "Memorie."

53. Among the various difficulties raised, those which aroused most protest from those involved were that the loans had to be for a four-year term instead of twenty years, as the Jews wanted, and that two guarantors were required for each borrower (AAJC, Preliminary Report, B. Segal).

54. Institute of Jewish Affairs, World Jewish Congress, Information Series, no. 11, April 1949, f. 4; CZA, S/20/555, "Report on the Jewish Community of Tripolitania," January 1949.

55. Ibid. For further views on the procedures, goals, and activities of the American Jewish Joint Distribution Committee, see Y. Bauer, *My Brother's Keeper: A History of the American Jewish Joint Distribution Committee, 1929–1939* (Philadelphia, 1974).

56. AUCII, fasc. 34, U. Nahon to R. Cantoni, April 2, 1948. In the report Nahon also discussed the school situation in Tripoli and some hinterland towns: "Since I have mentioned the schools I would like to tell you the emotion and satisfaction I felt when I visited the Hebrew school of Tripoli. It has two thousand pupils receiving all their instruction in Hebrew, apart from Italian and Arabic lessons of course. It is a magnificent effort which shows that "where there's a will there's a way." The teachers are mostly young people who themselves have not studied much beyond the fifth elementary level, but who have prepared themselves and carry out their task with devotion and enthusiasm. The school is located on the premises of the Italian school for Jews, which in an adjacent building educates another two thousand pupils, and which is a normal Italian elementary school with non-Jewish teachers, closed on the Sabbath and Jewish holidays and with classes in religion for girls. The boys attend the Talmud Torah for three hours every day. Those who attend the Italian school for Jews in the mornings go to the Talmud Torah in the afternoons, and those who attend the Italian school in the afternoons go to the Talmud Torah in the mornings. The Talmud Torah has also adopted Hebrew as the language of instruction. While in the *kutabin* * the children translate the Biblical verses into Arabic, here they translate them into Hebrew and the teacher asks them questions in Hebrew. Hebrew, then, is widely known in this community, at least among most young people under twenty. Starting on May 5, there will be a cafeteria funded by the Joint; many pupils it seems make the sandwich given out to them at break their main meal, while children in the interior collect orange peel from the garbage to nourish themselves. The poverty of the *hara* is luxury compared with conditions in the villages of the interior. I have visited two, Amruss having 1,200 Jews who are craftsmen or peddlars in the surrounding Arab villages. I have watched hammers and tongs being made for branding from scrap left over from the war. Having asked around, I concluded that they do not manage to earn 100 Italian lire a day. In Amruss the damage caused by the November 1945 riots, in which ten people died, is visible. Some form of school has only begun functioning again this year. It has three classes in cramped quarters crowded with over a hundred boys (girls, naturally, remain illiterate). Their acute intelligence, despite malnutrition and trachoma, manages to grasp the teachings of the Torah and whatever else is offered. For the last two months Dr. Viterbo has been giving them medical examinations and two nurses come every day to administer drops to trachomatose eyes. Perhaps, little by little, more of them will agree to

*Arabic word related to Hebrew *kitah*, "classroom."—*Trans.*

have treatment. There are no statistics for these communities, but I think that the figures for infant mortality and trachoma must be frightening . . . The other village which I visited is Tigrina, near Gharian, a hundred kilometers from Tripoli. There 330 Jews live in caves like troglodytes: in the same cave there are men, women, children, chickens, and goats."

57. There is clear information on two secret organizations, Aliyah Bet and the Haganah, in the unpublished "Memorie" of Nemni, who participated in both. Further information on the Haganah can be found in the accounts published in *Yahadut Luv*, Ch. 6, "In the Storm." Precise information is lacking on clandestine emigration via Italy and Tunisia. There are brief indications in the account by S. Zuriel, "Illegal Emigration," in Yahadut Luv, pp. 275 ff. In June 1948 Nemni wrote that emigration was "in full swing."

58. AUCII, fasc. "Fatti di Tripoli."

59. CZA, S/851/721, "Réponse au questionnaire de la Jewish Agency transmis avec sa lettre du 21/7/1949 n. 851/21/917, objet: Israélites du Moyen Orient," dated Tripoli, August 5, 1949. For an echo of Nahon's trip to Tripolitania and French North Africa, see U. Nahon, "Gli ebrei del Nord Africa," *Israel*, June 17, 1948.

60. Israel declared itself in favor of Libyan independence after a transition period under United Nations supervision. The Libyans should be free to choose the form of unification of Tripolitania, Cyrenaica, and the Fezzan they preferred, and they should be required to give precise guarantees for the rights of Italian residents and the Jewish minority. "L'atteggiamento israeliano in merito alla questione delle ex-colonie italiane," *Israel*, October 20, 1949. See also for the journal's uncomfortable comment, which reveals a mixture of discontent at the Israeli government's position and concern at the reactions which it feared would be aroused in Italy:

"We Italian Jews view with profound trepidation these initial international contacts between the State of Israel and Italy.

"We would naturally like any intervention by the State of Israel to be fully in the interests of Italy and any intervention by Italy to be in the interests of Israel. We fully understand that that is obviously not always possible, and it is precisely that fact which gives rise to our trepidation.

"Public opinion and the Italian government must understand that the State of Israel, only recently restored to independence after an age-long wait, is inevitably and necessarily the champion of the independence of all peoples, even the Arabs, which aspire to it and deserve it, and should weigh the merits of the case in an understanding way.

"Thus in the various and diverse issues concerning the former Italian colonies, the Israeli point of view on principle has to be on the side of those supporting independence. And so it is.

"We are pleased to note that, having said the above, the interests of Italy are explicitly given considerate and due attention by the Israeli government, and we are certain that it will subsequently defend these interests with sympathy and energy.

"Israel should realize and Italy should realize that they represent ancient civilizations, have vast common interests in the Mediterranean, and all possible reason to agree and cooperate in ever field. We profoundly hope that this will be the case, in colonial issues and in all others."

61. The Jewish elite continued to view Italy, despite everything, as a point of reference which it was difficult to give up, as is shown by many small facts. In January 1945, before the pogroms made sympathy and enthusiasm for Britain collapse, a new chief rabbi had to be found to fill the position left vacant the year before by Lattes' death. For this purpose, the Community turned to the chief rabbi of Rome. See AUCII, fasc. 32, Z. Habib to I. Zolli, January 21, 1945. In 1947 two young Jews from Tripoli were sent to study at the Rabbinical College of Rome (*Israel*, November 27, 1947).

62. A definite, though very secretive, step was taken in this direction by some Jews whose names are unknown right after the events of May 1946. In the archives of the Union of Italian Jewish Communities (fasc. "Fatti di Tripoli") there is a copy of it in the form of a "secret communication exclusively for internal use" dated Tripoli, June 10, 1946. It goes as follows:

"We are writing to express our opinion regarding the situation in Tripoli as it was under Italian rule, as it is at present under occupation, and regarding the best solution for the future:

"(1) The pre-Fascist Italian government brought this country progress, order, moral and material well-being, and, above all, security for the entire population.

"During the years of Fascism serious measures were taken against the local Arab and Jewish populations, which were morally and materially harmed by them; these measures were later intensified for the Jews through the racial legislation.

"(2) The British Military Administration, after bringing the joy of liberation from Nazism and Fascism, since the occupation until today has been inefficient in protecting order, justice, and balance between the various segments of the population. It has not shown enough understanding of the needs of the population, considering this territory as an occupied enemy country rather than a liberated friendly one, even though in fact almost the entire population of Arabs and Jews awaited and welcomed the British as liberators and friends.

"This attitude on the part of the British Military Administration led to disastrous consequences in work and the economy, which have largely affected the formation of the present situation of insecurity and unease.

"The unprecedented disorders of November 1945 have created in the various local communities a state of distrust and disharmony the effects of which are harmful to the country, and in the Jews a state of permanent terror.

"(3) It is our conviction that the Jews of Tripoli believe that a joint trusteeship by the Great Powers, with the participation of a democratic Italy, would govern the country with justice and firmness, give it internal security, and guide it toward the conditions necessary to carry out full independence, to which the Libyan people legitimately aspire.

"Such a solution would give the Jews the chance to participate actively in the progress and well-being of the country and, in restored harmony with the other segments of the population, the chance to peacefully develop their own ethnic, cultural, and religious characteristics and to contribute freely to the realization of the age-old Jewish national aspirations."

63. *Israel*, October 9, 1947.

64. AUCII, fasc. "Fatti di Tripoli."

65. R. Cantoni, "La Libia, gli Ebrei e l'Italia," *Italia Socialista*, July 25, 1947.

66. See *Israel*, May 27, 1948.

67. Article 23 of the Treaty of Peace with Italy established that "Italy renounces all right and title to the Italian territorial possessions in Africa." Libya, Eritrea, and Italian Somaliland would continue under their present administration pending their final disposal, to be determined jointly by Britain, the U.S.A., the Soviet Union, and France within one year from the coming into force of the treaty, in the manner laid down in the joint declaration reproduced in Annex XI to the treaty. This stipulated that if agreement could not be reached the matter would be referred to the General Assembly of the United Nations, and the Four Powers agreed to accept its recommendation and take appropriate measures for giving effect to it. The deputies of the foreign ministers would continue the consideration of the question and would also send out commissions of investigation to supply the necessary data on the question "and to ascertain the views of the local population" and submit their recommendation to the Council of Foreign Ministers.

68. For the broad outlines of the political and diplomatic events under discussion see P. G. Magri, "La questione delle ex colonie italiane (1947–1960)," in R. Salvadori and P. G. Magri, *Il trattato di pace con l'Italia e la questione delle ex colonie italiane (1947–1960)* (Parma, 1972), pp. 101 ff.

69. AUCII, fasc. 34, U. Nahon to R. Cantoni, April 2, 1948.

70. Perhaps a note dated April 1948 in AUCII, fasc. "Fatti di Tripoli," refers to this planned visit to Cantoni in Rome:

"No one more than us Jews desires independence, and we can thus understand very well the Arabs of Tripolitania who are struggling for this goal; however, it is necessary to be mature enough for independence and, unfortunately, the inhabitants of Tripolitania are not yet mature and therefore need someone to guide and prepare them.

"No native Tripolitanian has a degree to practice the liberal professions—there is no lawyer, doctor, engineer, etc.; those presently practicing are almost all Italians who are holding their positions pending the final decision regarding the future of the country.

"Moreover, the economy of Tripolitania is doubly tied to that of Italy, since the latter finds a market in the needs of Tripolitania, while raw materials from Tripolitania are sought after by Italian industry.

"There is a general conviction that all the inhabitants of Tripolitania hope for the return of the Italian administration, as a trusteeship on behalf of the U.N. the purpose of which will be to prepare the population to receive independence.

"In twenty years Italy has raised the living standards of Libyans from almost zero to that of the main European cities. It would thus not be just to deprive the population of this guide. With more balanced policies, Italy can still help the economy of Tripolitania to be fully productive."

71. AUCII, fasc. "Fatti di Tripoli," two reports on the pogrom of June 12–13.

72. *Corriere di Tripoli,* June 14, 1948, special edition.

73. AAJC, "Libya: Another Moslem State Established: Another Ancient Jewish Community Disappears," report dated December 18, 1951, by Nehemiah Robinson of the Institute of Jewish Affairs, World Jewish Congress, New York.

74. *Corriere di Tripoli,* June 15, 1948.

75. CZA, S/20/555, *Report on the Jewish Community of Tripoli,* January 1949. Other Jewish sources speak of about seventy Arab deaths. This figure was also quoted by *Israel,* June 17, 1948, "Il pogrom di Tripoli." *Israel's* report gives a good account (despite its triumphant tone and some hasty conclusions) of the enthusiasm that the armed resistance which the Jews of Tripoli put up against their Arab attackers aroused among local Jews and Jews outside Libya. *Israel* reports that order was restored "not by the British authorities, but by the Jews" with their "prompt, energetic, and most effective" reaction so that "today they are walking the streets of Tripoli with their heads held high, while the Arabs are prudently staying at home." Despite these exaggerations, it is clear that the Jews' armed resistance surprised the Arabs and the British by its success. The British informed the Community leaders that they were not "pleased" by it but had to admit that it was a case of "legitimate self-defense." See Nemni, "Memorie."

76. *Corriere di Tripoli,* June 15, 1948.

77. Ibid.

78. For these events, see AAJC, reports by B. Segal [cited in note 41] and N. Robinson [cited in note 73], and *Israel,* November 25, 1948.

79. See in AUCII, fasc. "Fatti di Tripoli," a signed copy. R. Cantoni, in his double capacity as president of the Union of Italian Jewish Communities and member of the executive of the World Jewish Congress, also approached the four great powers to request adequate protection for the Jews of Libya, guarantees that their rights would be respected in the future, and the right to emigrate. See ibid. The WJC also made another approach. As individuals or small groups, Libyan Jews took several similar initiatives; e.g., Ruben Hassan contacted Zachariah Shuster of the AJDC in early September to ask it to approach the U.S. government to return Libya to Italy (AAJC, memorandum from Z. Shuster to J. Wolfsohn, September 7, 1949).

80. For the complete text, see "Gli ebrei di Libia e il loro triste destino," *Israel,* November 18, 1948.

81. C. Focarile, *L'Italia in Libia* (Rome, 1950), p. 36; this is a collection of articles which appeared in April 1950 in the Rome daily, *Il globo,* by its special correspondent in Libya.

82. The documentation in AAJC is the basis of this.

83. AAJC, report by H. Abravanel, "Les Juifs de la Libye" [cited in

note 48]; Nemni, "Memorie"; the account by Zuriel in *Yahadut Luv*; and Schechtman, *On Wings of Eagles*, p. 141.

84. CZA, S/20/555, "Une Année de vie de l'OSE-Tripoli: 17 mars 1949–16 mars 1950," by H. Abravanel (April 1950).

85. World Zionist Organization, Jewish Agency for Palestine, *Reports of the Executive Subcommittee to the Twenty-Third Zionist Congress at Jerusalem (Ab 5711—August 1951)* (Jerusalem, 1951), p. 273.

86. For Duvdevani's account, see *Yahadut Luv*, ed. Zuarez et al., p. 297 ff.

87. See Table N-9.

88. In its first year of functioning the WZO diagnostic center registered 28,786 candidates for emigration. It took 29,062 radioscopies, 782 X-ray photographs, 18,397 Kahn tests, 1,599 Bordet Wasserman tests, and made 21,317 eye examinations. On March 16, 1950, there were 4,627 patients under treatment, while 7,327 had been treated and released (CZA, S/20/555, "Une Année de vie de l'OSE—Tripoli: 17 mars 1949–16 mars 1950"). The most active person in organizing the OSE health services was a non-Jew, Dr. Giuseppe Siclari, who later converted to Judaism.

89. For educational, cultural, and health services for youth, see CZA, S/20/555, "Situation actuelle des écoles juives à Tripoli," report dated February 1950.

90. In mid-February 1951 the CABI Olim was functioning in Tripoli and Benghazi. It was legally recognized and its two directors had been appointed by the two Community councils. They administered about 500

TABLE N-9. *Numbers of Jews Emigrating from Tripolitania Excluding Tripoli, 1949–1950, According to Community of Origin*

Community	Original Jewish Population	Emigrants
Misurata	912	510
al-Khums	902	463
Amruss	1,240	435
Zuwara	794	365
Yafran	391	364
Tigrina	464	335
Zlitin	604	308
Zawia	676	285
Tajura	202	152
Zanzur	(fled in 1945)	119
Qusabat	410	118
Syrte	180	115
Beni Ulid	85	85
Tarhuna	191	60

properties to a value of about 20 million MAL (about $118,235) yielding monthly returns of about 200,000–250,000 MAL (AAJC, "Libya a Crucial Testing-Ground for the Status of Jews in an Independent Moslem State," February 23, 1951, p. 5).

91. A typical example of these difficulties, also proving the attitude of some Israelis toward the immigration of the "ragamuffins" from Libya and Arab countries in general is the description published in early August 1950 in *Yediot Aharonot* (immediately taken up on August 17 by the Tripoli Jewish weekly, *Haienu*). Describing the arrival of a ship from Tripoli, the article emphasized the fact that the Libyan immigrants were squinting, crippled, and dressed in rags, and loaded down with dogs, cats, pigeons, and chickens, with the evident intention of selling them to the Israelis . . . As soon as the article became known in Tripoli, the Jews still remaining and the WZO Executive leaders were up in arms and protesting indignantly. Haim Abravanel spoke for all of them when he wrote a very firm letter responding to the author of the article, in which he reminded him of the sacrifices and suffering which these poor people had gone through, and how many of them before emigration was reopened had braved travail and danger to get out of Libya and reach Israel, certainly not to sell dogs and cats, but to return to the land of their fathers and fight for it.

92. For Zionist Executive activities, see CZA, S/20/555, and Nemni, "Memorie."

93. For the international aspect of the last phases of the Libyan independence process, see Magri, "La questione delle ex colonie italiane," pp. 123 ff.

94. World Zionist Organization Executive, Jewish Agency, *Reports for the Period April 1951–December 1955 Submitted to the Twenty-Fourth Zionist Congress in Jerusalem* (Iyar 5716—April 1956) (Jerusalem, 1956), pp. 81 ff.

95. AAJC, "Libya: Another Moslem State Established." [Translator has not been able to consult the English original of this report.]

8. Libyan Independence (1949–1951)

1. United Nations, *Official Records of the Fourth Session of the General Assembly: Resolutions, 20 September–10 December, 1949* (Lake Success, N.Y., n.d.), pp. 10 ff. For the whole process of Libyan independence, see Adrian Pelt, *Libyan Independence and the United Nations: A Case of Planned Decolonization* (New Haven and London: Yale University Press, 1970); Ismail Raghib Khalidi, *Constitutional Development in Libya* (Beirut: Khayat, 1956); and, more generally, Khadduri, *Modern Libya*, Ch. 4 ff.; S. Hakim, *Istiqlal Libya bayn Jam'iyat al-Duwal al-Arabiyah wal-Umam al-Muttahidah* (Cairo, 1965).

2. Pelt, *Libyan Independence*, pp. 202 ff, esp. pp. 204 and 207, 178 ff., and 183 ff.

3. Ibid., pp. 131 ff, esp. pp. 132 and 139.

4. Ibid., pp. 90 ff, and *Israel*, September 26, 1949. The most important approaches were made by M. L. Perlzweig of the World Jewish Congress, who later met with Pelt also, just after his appointment as U.N. commissioner. In these meetings the main specific demands, besides representation, concerned the need to guarantee the Libyan Jews special safeguards for their human, religious, and civil rights, specific guarantees for the religious and cultural autonomy of their Communities, and the right to emigrate with their assets if they so wished. See *Israel*, February 2 and 16, 1950.

5. The name of Giacomo Marchino was suggested by the Jewish, Greek, and Maltese communities, the Democratic League and Catholic Action (Italian parties), the Egypto-Tripolitanian Union Party, the Liberal Party, the Congress Party, and the United National Front (Arab parties). His name was not put forward by the Economic Front (a pro-Arab Italian party); the Labor Party (Arab); the Nationalist Party (Arab), which submitted only six names, leaving the seventh open for a minorities representative; nor by the Independence Party, the Kutla Party [Free National Bloc], or the Political Association for the Progress of Libya, which three parties did not submit lists because they were opposed to the principle of equal representation of Tripolitania, Cyrenaica, and the Fezzan. The Democratic League, Catholic Action, and the Maltese community submitted only Marchino's name. The Economic Front, the Greek community, and the Jewish community submitted names for all seven seats. The Jewish community, in addition to Marchino's name, put forward the names of Maurizio Forti and five Arab candidates (APM, Memorandum dated July 1, 1950).

6. This was the interpretation given to the term "inhabitants" by the *Ad Hoc* Political Committee of the United Nations (which became involved in the issue upon Marchino's request in January 1951) in its report (A./1457) submitted to the General Assembly [General Assembly Official Records, Fifth Session, 1950]. Paragraph 18 of the report states that "the word 'inhabitants' in paragraph 3(a) of the joint draft resolution [Resolution 289 (IV) of Nov. 21, 1949] was not intended to have a prohibitive meaning, excluding certain sections of the population from equal participation in the life of the new State, and that it was the desire of the Committee that adequate safeguards for the protection of the rights of minorities should be included in the future constitution of Libya."

7. Pelt, *Libyan Independence*, pp. 220 ff, esp. pp. 244 ff., 255 ff., 260 ff., 269 ff., 277, 282 ff.

8. See in APM, the statement included in the report on the advisory committee's June 23, 1950, meeting, and amendments to the draft report of the United Nations Commissioner in Libya to the Secretary-General, dated August 22, 1950 (A/AC.32/COUNCIL/W.4/ASS.3).

9. See in APM the statements to this effect made to Marchino by Beshir Bey Saadawi, the leader of the Congress Party, on July 4, 1950; to the U.S. representative on the Advisory Committee; and to Pelt on July 31.

10. AAJC, A. S. Karlikow, *Report on Geneva Trip for CCJO, August 14–22, 1950*, p. 6.

11. See, in APM, what Marchino wrote on September 13, 1950, to the

Italian representative on the advisory council relating what Beshir Saadawi and his political adviser Fuad Shukri had told him a few days before: minorities would be excluded from the Constituent Assembly; however, their party wanted to reassure him "as to the future" and tell him that Idris also, with whom Saadawi had met a few days earlier, "was similarly well disposed, likewise as to the future."

12. Another issue with regard to which the votes of the Italian representative and Marchino became important was whether or not, toward late 1951, Libya should be included in the sterling area (the group of countries whose currencies are tied to the British pound sterling). The Libyans themselves disagreed on it. Idris and the parties associated with him were for inclusion, while the nationalist opposition linked to Egypt and the Arab League opposed it. On October 12, 1951, in Geneva, Marchino voted against inclusion in the zone, maintaining that, since Libya was an agricultural country which needed to export, the customs facilities offered by Italy were more advantageous to it.

13. This position had already emerged clearly before the negotiations between Marchino and the Libyans began. See, in APM, the note dated January 30, 1951, on the statements regarding Mahmud Muntasser, chairman elect and from March 29, 1951, chairman of the council of ministers of the provisional Libyan government.

14. In AAJC, Annex II to A. Karlikow to American Jewish Committee Headquarters in New York, August 31, 1951. The first part of the list, "Basic Rights," was also set forth in another, more detailed document (Annex I, "Fundamental Principles"), which served as a basis for the negotiations and which was also attached to Karlikow's letter. [Translator has been unable to locate an official English version of Annex II. It is probable that the American Jewish Committee did not have it translated, though Annex I was translated into English and has been consulted for the first part of the quoted text.]

15. For issues connected with human rights and the demands which the minorities made to the National Assembly, see Pelt, *Libyan Independence*, pp. 563 ff. Ibid., pp. 902–921, has the final text of the Libyan constitution.

16. For a view of the process of the negotiations, see the summary of the report on them which Marchino gave on July 28, 1951, to the Italian representative in the advisory council, Baron Giuseppe Vitaliano Confalonieri (in APM, which also has a copy of another report, dated June 26, on the initial phase of negotiations), and, with few variations, on August 1 to the Jewish Community of Tripoli, which sent a copy of the report to the American Jewish Committee (in AAJC).

17. Ibid. [Translation based on that provided by American Jewish Committee, New York.]

18. Pelt, *Libyan Independence*, pp. 544 ff.

19. In AAJC, see the report [cited in note 16] by Marchino to Baron Confalonieri and the Jewish Community of Tripoli: "My interlocutors did not see fit, on the other hand, to consider our request for liberty of emigration, a principle which they admitted was of singular importance to mem-

bers of the Jewish minority. I was told that the matter would be regulated by the rules relative to issuance of passports and that it was not in keeping to make it the object of a constitutional principle. Moreover, it was declared that the Libyan State, in conformity with the practices of other states, was determined to reserve for itself completely the power to regulate emigration. Notwithstanding my insistence and my recalling the fact that such a principle (of free emigration) was common to democratic constitutions, from the English Magna Charta [*sic*] to the recent Statute of the Free City of Jerusalem, my interlocutors were unyielding and held to their point of view." [This passage is also quoted in a different English wording in Karlikow to Morroe Berger, AJC Headquarters, August 31, 1951, pp. 1–2.]

20. An indirect proof of this is that, in 1951, when the Community of Tripoli feared that, in connection with negotiations with the Libyan government to settle problems relating to Italian property in Libya, the Italian government would give up the building which was to be a school for about 500 Jewish children, the Community expressed its concern not to the Italian representative in Tripoli but to Marchino himself, by then a private citizen. He brought the matter to the attention of the Italian consul and emphasized the difficulties it would cause for the Jews of Tripoli if the Italians gave up the building. See in APM, Marchino to V. De Benedictis, June 4, 1955.

21. In AAJC.

22. In AAJC, Ruben Hassan to AJC, December 15, 1950: "Anyhow, also at this side the matter is very cleverly dealt with by Mr. Marchino who after his recent interviews with some of the Arab party leaders is at present in a very hopeful mood." Marchino to Karlikow, March 21, 1951: "The prospects seem favorable and the dispositions of the Arab political leaders seem to show a large sense of comprehension" [AJC trans.]; Marchino to G. Riegner, May 11, 1951: "I can assure you that on the Arab side I have found the best possible disposition. I have confidence that we shall shortly manage to arrive at some definitive decisions . . ." [no official trans.].

23. For these optimistic predictions, see, e.g., in AAJC, Hassan to Karlikow, April 3, 1951: ". . . the new Libyan Government has been formed; [its ministers] are all very well known, friendly and comprehensive persons and we are confident that under their rulership we can live peacefully" [English original]; Shuster to AJC, July 6, 1951: the secretary of the Community had written to him that Idris had received some Jewish leaders during his stay in Tripoli and had assured them of his support of Jewish requests for security, ability to work in Libya, and defense against discrimination; according to the secretary, "some Cyrenaican Jews told us that His Majesty is a very good man." Marchino met Idris as well, on May 29 when the king visited Tripoli. In his report on the meeting (in APM) Marchino wrote that the king-designate "assured me that he had arranged for prompt discussions to be held by the Constituent Assembly regarding the clauses concerning Minorities and expressed his confidence that the clauses adopted would be of satisfaction to the Minorities themselves."

24. See documentation in AAJC, esp. the report *Libya: A Crucial Testing-Ground for the Status of Jews in an Independent Moslem State,*

February 23, 1951; Shuster to Hassan, November 27, 1950, and Karlikow to A. Lasgove, December 27, 1950; also "Memorandum Concerning the Situation of the Jews in Libya Submitted by the World Jewish Congress to the General Assembly of the United Nations," October 20, 1950.

25. AAJC, Anglo-Jewish Association Foreign Affairs Committee, confidential report, undated, late October 1950; American Jewish Committee memorandum from Near East Committee, no. 3, October 12, 1950; Morroe Berger to Shuster, November 21, 1950, and Shuster to Hassan, November 27, 1950.

26. AAJC, *Libya: A Crucial Testing-Ground.*

27. Pelt, *Libyan Independence*, p. 544, also confirms that the majority of Jews who did not want to leave Libya were among the wealthiest.

28. It is significant that, according to the American Jewish Committee report of February 1951 [AAJC, *Libya: A Crucial Testing-Ground*], the approximately one thousand Jews having no other citizenship and wishing to remain in Libya sought some form of foreign "protection" (p. 5).

29. For the Karlikow-Chouraqui mission, see in AAJC, in addition to the report *Libya: A Crucial Testing-Ground*, documents summarized for Marchino and Pelt and the two accompanying letters sent to them by the council of the Community of Tripoli, esp. the letter to Pelt emphasizing the idea that the laws necessary for covering requests of a nonconstitutional nature should be approved before the constitution of the new state, so that subsequent official approval by the parliament would be only a formality.

30. AAJC, D. Jona (secretary of the council of the Community of Tripoli) to Karlikow, April 1, 1951; E. Weill (of the Alliance Israélite Universelle) to Karlikow, April 6, 1951; Karlikow to Nahum, March 27, 1951; Nahum to Karlikow, April 2, 1951.

31. AAJC, Karlikow to Nahum, August 16, 1951.

32. Ibid., Nahum to Marchino, August 23, 1951. See also the letter of the same day by which Nahum replied to Karlikow, sending him copies of the letter to Marchino and of Marchino's August 1 report on negotiations with the Arabs.

33. Marchino replied to Nahum's letter on September 25 with the following from Geneva (in AAJC):

"Dear Mr. Nahum:

"Please excuse the delay in replying to your letter of August 23; as you know, I have been continually on the move and this is the first opportunity I have had to answer you. I shall respond to what you wrote to me on an official basis on behalf of the Jewish Community point by point:

"1. *Emigration*

"I have verbally pointed out to you the insurmountable difficulties which I encountered during the conversations aimed at including in the Constitution of the Libyan State the joint request for freedom of emigration. Specific indications of these difficulties are contained in the report of mine which I have sent you.

"I have the impression that it would be very difficult to make the legislators shift from their opinion which is contrary to our views. Nevertheless,

I shall still insist on our point of view, with all possible energy and all my powers of persuasion.

"Your point that the desired clauses should be included in the transitory dispositions comes up against the same exception in principle as the one which the legislators put forward, since the fact that the clause in question is included among the transitory dispositions rather than the others does not diminish its effect and would definitively approve the principle which they do not wish to allow. The difficulties thus would be the same.

"2. *Use of Foreign Languages*

"I do not understand the precise implication of your point. It is necessary to emphasize first and foremost, and for the sake of better understanding, that no agreement has occurred on the official use of any language other than Arabic, which is the only language recognized in the organic law.

"The agreement arrived at referred to a recommendation to be included in the transitory provisions of the Constitution which would recommend that the regional organic law of Tripolitania would carry provisions and regulate, when it would be considered appropriate, the use of a language other than the official one. It is not specified that the use of a foreign language would extend to primary education. In view of the strong opposition which I encountered and overcame only with much trouble, I felt it appropriate to be content with acceptance of the principle without demanding broader application at that time and in that setting, since I feared that it would lead a hardening of the negative stance of the trustees of the National Assembly. The issue of education should be dealt with in a framework other than that of the Constitution as regards the language of instruction.

"3. *Specific Requests by the Community*

"With regard to these I wish to repeat and confirm what I have already expressed to you verbally, namely that the legislators have decided that the said requests are not of a sort which should be included in the Constitution, but rather covered by separate laws. I have been assured that in principle there are no difficulties with the Community's requests.

"4. *Article 24 of the Fundamental Principles*

"I am aware of the wish which you express to me in this respect. It seems to me, however, that the principle has already been embodied in a provision of the Constitution which, in its broad and general sense, may legitimately be interpreted as covering your request. Article 27 of the Draft Constitution reads: "Persons professing a religion other than Islam shall retain their personal status." In any case, I shall pursue the matter under discussion with all possible diligence. I am convinced that in general it will be extremely difficult to gain any more than has been already obtained and I hope that the discussions of the draft constitution in the National Assembly will not entail substantial changes to the portion of the constitution dealing with fundamental rights.

"The text of the draft constitution is not yet available in its entirety and will only be available when the Assembly is to discuss it. The U.N. Council for Libya, following a long discussion, asked this morning for the draft constitution to be made available to it for possible comments, and when this happens I plan to air all the good reasons lying behind our moderate demands . . ."

34. AAJC, Marchino to Karlikow, December 10, 1951.

35. Pelt, *Libyan Independence*, p. 822.

36. AIJA, minutes of the meeting of the council of the Community of Tripoli (broadened to include some important local Jews, including the Israeli immigration representative, Meir Shilon) with A. L. Easterman, October 24, 1951; Easterman to Pelt and Paul Cremona, political adviser, United Nations Mission in Libya, October 31 and November 6, 1951.

37. When independence was declared, the World Jewish Congress sent King Idris a message of congratulations and good wishes. After emphasizing the hope that Libya would be governed in full accord with the principles of the U.N. Charter, under the auspices of which it had been made into an independent state, the WJC stated:

"Inspired by lively sympathy toward the new state, the WJC strongly hopes that the government of Libya will fully recognize the minorities and the individuals composing them and, respecting their basic rights and freedoms, will serve as an example to other states, resisting any efforts and pressures from anti-democratic elements aimed at denying or restricting the rights and freedoms of all citizens" (*Israel*, January 10, 1952). [English text not available to translator.]

38. For the last stage in the advent of Libyan independence at the United Nations, see Pelt, *Libyan Independence*, pp. 843 ff., esp. 852 ff. For American Jewish Committee actions, see AAJC, esp. M. Berger to Karlikow, September 6, 1951; Shuster to W. Frankel, November 8, 1951; memorandum to Berger, November 30, 1951; Shuster to F. D. Roosevelt, Jr., December 17, 1951; Paris Office to Berger, December 17, 1951; Karlikow to P. Mangano (State Department), December 17, 1951; Karlikow to Marchino, December 18, 1951; Karlikow to Berger, January 4, 1952; Berger to Karlikow, January 8 and 21, 1952.

39. *Israel*, March 13, 1952.

40. The WJC issued a commentary in which, after welcoming the declaration as an important precedent for safeguarding the rights and interests of minorities, it stated:

"Mr. Muntasser's statement is fully in accord with the views which the World Jewish Congress has constantly expressed and with the many requests which our organization has made to the United Nations and to the Libyan authorities. The statement indicates that the promise made in the Libyan constitution, which guarantees the personal freedoms of non-Muslims, is being kept. It constitutes a genuine victory for democratic peoples, and the Jewish world will follow with great interest what Libya will do in the future to fulfill its commitment" (*Israel*, February 14, 1952). [English text not available to translator.]

41. See in *Israel*, March 13, 1952, the Italian text of Nahum's message to Easterman of the WJC:

"We thank you for the efforts which you have made on behalf of this community at the U.N. General Assembly in Paris. Your intervention and personal involvement have been crowned with success. The statement by Mahmud Bey Muntasser, the prime minister of Libya, has reassured all the Jews of Libya. They are convinced that this statement has been issued thanks to the efforts of the World Jewish Congress."

9. From Idris to Qadhdhafi (1952–1970)

1. For further information, see Khadduri, *Modern Libya*; Wright, *Libya*; Agnes N. Keith, *Children of Allah* (Boston: Little, Brown, 1965).

2. For the problem of passports and other issues, see L. Carpi, "La condizione giuridica degli ebrei nel Regno Unito di Libia," *Rivista di studi politici internazionali*, January–March 1963, pp. 87 ff.

3. Serious difficulties did not arise until August 1952, when the last group of emigrants was leaving. Customs officials checked their luggage closely and, finding forbidden belongings, confiscated them. For a moment it was feared that the people would be stopped from leaving too. Then the situation was resolved by allowing the emigrants to take only their hand luggage. Heavy luggage was handed over to the judicial authorities which, a few months later—due to the intervention of the British consul and particularly to that of Sion Nemni—allowed it to be taken out after a fine had been paid. See Nemni, "Memorie," and the polemical positions taken by the *Sunday Ghibli*, October 12 and December 6, 1952.

4. The harshest of these attacks appeared in the weekly *Al Libi*, October 20, 1952. It stated:

"The Jews living in Libya today represent a thin community of few numbers . . . They dominate the largest commercial and industrial activities and exploit all means with their skillful and enterprising methods . . . They call themselves Libyan citizens in order to exploit this status to attain their goals and interests . . . Could these Jews be sincere? We have never heard of a single Jew actively participating in the cause of our Country and we have never seen a Jew sacrificing his person or goods for the Country! And so what do they represent? The position of the Jews in Libya represents a form highly dangerous for the common cause of the Arabs and constitutes an insiduous disease in the body of the nascent Country . . .

"The Jews in Libya are a link of world Zionist policy, since their position is so mysterious. The indifference of these Jews has reached such a state that when the occasion arises for them to talk about the initiative in Israel they show pride in its revival and progress, without any concern for our feelings. The Jews in Libya—as in the rest of the world—believe only in the principle of amassing wealth and are faithful to no other country besides Israel . . . They tried very hard during the Italian regime to be Italians, wearing clothing like theirs, using names similar to theirs, speaking their language, imitating their customs and way of life, and together with the colonizers despising everything relating to the Arabs. We never heard about a single Jew wanting to send his children to the Arab schools . . . Every piaster that these Jews earn is a heavy brick of Arab blood building up Israel, and if they were allowed to arrange things as they would like they would move to Israel every facility for reconstruction in Libya and would demolish it and leave it in ruins in order to build up Israel."

The article was received with apprehension by *Israel* on November 6, and aroused a protest by the World Jewish Congress (see *Israel*, November 27, 1952).

5. See Nemni, "Memorie."

6. See in *Tarabulus el Gharb*, December 31, 1953, the letter by which Ali Eddib, the president of the legislative council of Tripolitania, informed the president of the executive council of the measure. After the Maccabee Club was closed, sports activities continued for a few years due to the personal initiative and efforts of Raffaello Fellah and Vittorio Halfon. They first tried to set up a new club; since they did not receive authorization from the Libyan authorities, they organized a basketball team which gradually inspired other teams. In 1959–1960, in order to avoid charges of separatism, they tried to have one of these teams join an Arab sports club. The attempt was not successful.

7. F. Nahum, "Ebrei di oggi in un paese arabo," *Israel*, August 29, 1957.

8. In 1954 two other episodes of discrimination occurred: the rabbinical court was abolished and, without any cause, the last four Jews serving in the police force were dismissed.

9. See esp. E. Nessler, "Quand les Arabes sont maîtres chez eux," *L'Information*, September 7–8, 1954.

10. Nemni, "Memorie."

11. *Israel*, January 29, 1953; January 19, 1956.

12. For more information, see Carpi, "La condizione giuridica degli ebrei," pp. 88 ff. [Quotations from English version in M. A. Nafa, *Libya: Company and Business Law* (London: Arab Consultants, 1976), p. 115.]

13. For the text of the decree, see *Israel*, January 22, 1959.

14. See AJWC and *New York Times*, January 21, 1959.

15. See AJWC, report, n.d., by Aldermann Moss. In order to evaluate the information fairly one must take into account the fact that from 1952 on the Jewish community of Tripoli continued to grow considerably. There was a high birth rate among poor families (in early 1963 the Jewish population of Libya amounted to 6,266, compared with the approximately 4,000 of 1952, of whom only about 400 lived in Benghazi, and almost 2,000 had foreign nationality, mostly Italian). Moreover, all figures quoted officially must be considered on the high side, since numbers were not removed (especially for Jews who had actually emigrated) due to omission, lack of precise information, or by intention.

16. AAJC, memorandum on the situation of Jews in Libya from the Paris Office to the Department of Foreign Affairs, dated Rome, October 23, 1963. In 1961–1963, about forty families, amounting to about 140 people, emigrated, mostly to Italy.

17. Ibid.

18. Some of the most significant attacks against Jews by the Arab press in this period were those by *Al Raïd* (August 15, 1960), *Tarabulus el Gharb* (August 17, 1960), *Al Libi* (August 19, 1960), and *Al Talise* (December 7, 1960). There also appeared in the Libyan press a letter signed "A Westerner" which was published in the *Tripoli Mirror* (a pro-government and pan-Arab English-language newspaper which occasionally published letters of criticism and protest and it seems for that reason was shortly after suppressed) on June 4, 1961. The letter took issue with an anti-Jewish article which the newspaper had published on May 21, written by a certain Prof. Zind, whom the letter called a Nazi and racist. The letter was published with an editorial introduction saying that only a Zionist could have written it. It was followed on June 11 by a lengthy commentary in a sarcastic and accusatory tone. The commentary said that from the French Revolution to the Algerian War the Jews had never fought for any cause except against the Arabs. The Jews had committed much worse crimes against the Arabs than those of the Nazis of whom so much was said. The article asked why the Jews did not protest the presence of Nazis and SS in the French troops fighting in Algeria or among the NATO forces or American racism against blacks. The conclusion was that Prof. Zind was not a racist since, if he had been, he would have hated not only Jews, but also Arabs, who are Semites too.

19. See the letter sent by the Libyan representatives in the United Nations to the *New York Times*, published on October 11, 1961. He was protesting against an article on the situation of Libyan Jews which had appeared on September 28. The letter asserted that Jews enjoyed full rights like all Libyan citizens, who had suffered the same persecution during the Fascist and Nazi occupation. It compared the situation in which Libyan Jews were living and those in which the Arabs of Israeli-occupied Palestine were obliged to live. For the reply by the American Jewish Committee, see *New York Times*, November 1, 1961.

20. See AJC *News*, October 28 and 29, 1961. For the former Nazis who were in Libya in 1961, the following names were put forward: Hans Eisele (regarding whom the Bonn government in 1959 had requested extradition from Egypt), Heinrich Willermann (Haim Fahoum), Hans Adler, and Bernard Bender (Ben Salem). See AAJC, Shuster to Simon Segal, November 13, 1961.

21. Both these assessments were also made outside the framework of Libyan Jewry. They were subscribed to by the Alliance Israélite Universelle and the Anglo-Jewish Association, and echoes of them can be found in the specialized press of the time, e.g., "Lybie: Instabilités et rivalités; La Vie économique est en stagnation," *L'observateur du Moyen-Orient et de l'Afrique*, July 27, 1962, pp. 15 ff.

22. Carpi, "La condizione giuridica degli ebrei," p. 90.

23. After his stay in Libya, Pelt sent Simon Segal a confidential memorandum. The former U.N. commissioner wrote that anti-Semitism, in the sense in which it is understood in the West, did not exist, but that there was strong feeling against Israel. It was not spontaneous but rather cold-blooded actions of an administrative nature taken by a special office conducting the

boycott against Israel. In the field of personal relations there was not much animosity against Jews. Arabs and Jews would meet privately, and he was impressed by the fact that a number of Libyan Jews were active members of the Tripoli Riding School. In Pelt's view, the new phenomenon of recent years was an atmosphere of xenophobia due to the fact that the new generation and many exiles of the Italian period who had returned were out job-hunting and thus were hostile to all foreigners—Italians, Greeks, Maltese, and Jews. (In AAJC.)

24. In AAJC, memorandum from the Paris Office to Sidney Liskofsky, dated July 17, 1962.

25. In AAJC, report attached to R. Arbib to Shuster, September 5, 1962.

26. Carpi, "La condizione giuridica degli ebrei," pp. 90 ff.

27. On this subject see the remarks in the AAJC memorandum of October 23, 1963, cited in note 16 above.

28. The expression was used in the memorandum sent on July 17 from the AJC Paris Office to Liskofsky. It should be noted that the same psychological climate extended to American Jews doing service at the U.S. air base, Wheelus Base. See S. Reinert, "U.S. Jews at Libya Air Base Live in Fear," *Herald Tribune,* October 26, 1964.

29. Except where specifically indicated, all information on the June 1967 incidents is taken from the confidential report, "The Anti-Semitic Riots in Libya of June 5th," written in July by Lillo Arbib, then president of the Community of Tripoli and a member of both the committee of three assisting the special government commissioner and the committee of five for the defense of the Jewish Community of Tripoli (in AAJC).

30. G. Fattori, "Paura e segreta tensione a Tripoli dopo giorni di sanguinose violenze," *La Stampa,* June 18, 1967.

31. On events in Benghazi, see G. Fattori, "Bengasi è calma, ma piena di paure dopo le gravi violenze del 5 giugno," *La Stampa,* June 20, 1967.

32. In order to understand the atmosphere during the days following the "restoration of order," it is significant that even the contacts between the members of the committee of five (Lillo Arbib was particularly active) with the special commissioner for the Community and the Libyan authorities took place by telephone until June 17.

33. All information on the departure and on settling in Italy between June 1967 and September 1968 is taken from the report "Relazione profughi ebrei provenienti dalla Libia," drawn up in September 1968 by the Rome Aid Committee [Deputazione di Assistenza di Roma] and preserved in AUCII. There are some figures and information on those who moved to Israel in F. E. Sabatello, "L'immigrazione dall'Italia in Israele (1969–1974): caratteristiche e integrazione," *La rassegna mensile di Israel,* May–June 1977, pp. 215 ff.

34. This concern explains why very few Libyan Jews in possession of Italian citizenship (only one out of the group in Rome) applied for the benefits provided by law to returning Italians. They were afraid that such action would prevent them from returning to Libya to liquidate their assets.

35. Here is the text of the petition, a copy of which is in AAEL:

"Rome, August 21, 1967

"To His Majesty King Idris Elawwal
  "Sovereign of the Kingdom of Libya
  "Tubruq
  "Humbly expressing our profound loyalty,
  "The undersigned, members of the Jewish community and Libyan and foreign citizens resident in Libya and temporarily domiciled in Rome, have the honor to address the following petition to Your Majesty:
  "1. Your Majesty,
  "Members of the Jewish community have lived in Libya for many centuries and since they saw the light of day have known no other homeland than Libya. The ties which they had to it and love for Libya led them to join the patriotic movements against colonialism together with their Arab brothers and to win the coveted honor of making a tangible contribution to the movements, so that some Jews were sentenced to death for it.
  "By recalling these facts, the community does not wish to maintain that it has reached a privileged position nor that it deserves special treatment; it reminds Your Majesty of them only in order to give concrete proof that the Jewish community has never had any Homeland other than its beloved Libya, as it has never had any Protective Throne other than Your Invincible Throne. Its ancestors were born in Libya and its fathers lived there and built their houses; everyone enjoyed the riches of Libya and found protection under its skies.
  "If some Jews do not possess Libyan citizenship—despite the fact that their ancestors were born in Libya and have lived there uninterruptedly for centuries—it is due to the fact that the authorities have not yet examined their applications though they were made years ago.
  "2. Your Majesty,
  "When the question of independence arose, the Jewish community voted in favor of it and fully supported the wishes of the Libyan people thereby fulfilling one of its most compelling duties, which is to show solidarity with its beloved Libyan brothers.
  "After independence was achieved, under Your beloved Throne, the community participated in establishing and stabilizing the national economy in all sectors and strictly adhered to the principles of the constitution and laws in force, while its sons lived as valid, loyal, and devoted citizens.
  "The Jewish community's relations with its Arab brothers have always been excellent. They show genuine collaboration; many commercial operations have been carried out by jointly owned companies.
  "This was so until the latest crisis, which was a general one.
  "3. Your Majesty,
  "As a result of the riots and events of last June, many shops belonging to the Jewish community were burned and destroyed. This was the work of riotous elements who are ignorant of the history of the community and forgot an important fact: that they were destroying the national economy.
  "After that, with the intention of protecting public order and lives, the authorities proceeded to gather a large part of the Jewish community in

camps set up for the purpose, and provided moreover for the Jews' protection and support.

"At the same time, the authorities were encouraging a large part of the community to leave the country temporarily, to leave the country where they had lived for centuries and in which, like all its sons, Arab and non-Arab alike, they had rejoiced with its joys and wept with its sorrows.

"All the procedures for that purpose were facilitated by the Government and the Police in order to protect public order and safeguard lives.

"These persons left with a re-entry visa and foreign currency amounting to twenty Libyan pounds for each person, and in some cases fifty pounds.

"Thus, the Jewish community—beside the serious damage suffered due to the destruction by the riotous elements mentioned above—has received only the paltry sum allowed upon leaving the Kingdom of Libya, after leaving behind its movable and immovable assets and money.

"4. Your Majesty,

"If we tried to describe to Your August Person our present situation, the trials which have led us overseas and our present patience, however much we described and outlined and illustrated, our pens and tongues would not be able to do justice to reality.

"We arrived overseas with only the twenty pounds, which is only enough for one or two days, while our children need clothing and our little ones—unaware of the odyssey in which they have been caught up—need nutritious food.

"Thus to the economic harm has been added the pain of finding oneself in a foreign country and faced with multiple difficulties with our children, babies, and wives, threatened by cold, hunger and the knowledge that any help—wherever it may come from—will last only for a day and not indefinitely.

"We have thus turned to the Libyan Embassy in Rome to ask that it arrange for an appropriate amount to be paid out of each one's account in Libya, or to be considered as a loan or assistance, and have also asked for an extension of the time limit (about to expire) for return to Libya for arranging our situation and also in consideration of the fact that the authorities have commendably offered all possible assistance in preparing the documents needed for departure.

"The Ambassador has assured us that he will give the matter his full attention and that he is awaiting official instructions.

"Since our absence from our country has exceeded all predictions, we have emphasized our wish to return to Libya to live there and continue to work with and for the country.

"5. Your Majesty,

"We are honored to submit this petition to Your Beloved Majesty because we have no one else to turn to besides Your Highness; our hope lies only in Your Majesty, may God protect You. Our absence from our Country (beloved Libya) has gone on too long and has consumed all energy in us, replacing it with disappointment and sorrow that we are witnessing the painful pilgrimage of our children through the streets of a city which they do not know and in which they are struggling to find sustenance.

"Our possibilities abroad are known, as are our activities and properties in Libya; our present situation could be compared to that of vagabonds, though the fault is not ours.

"The material harm is colossal for us, but it is also immense for the economy of Libya; our unease is increased by not knowing for how much longer we must suffer and what measures are to be taken with regard to us and our return to our beloved Country.

"Up to now our questions to this effect have received no reply. We are thus experiencing a painful drama: the people who yesterday constituted the backbone of commerce now see their activity reduced to trudging uselessly through the corridors of our diplomatic missions.

"6. Your Majesty,

"That is our present situation, as we have tried to describe it in brief for Your Majesty, to whom we appeal:

"(*a*) to arrange for all measures necessary to return the situation to its original state and thus give permission for us to return to our country to participate in its economic recovery with the loyalty and in the knowledge of being a favored son;

"(*b*) to grant an extension to the re-entry permits of those who have requested it, in order to allow them to re-enter Libya as well;

"(*c*) to arrange for payment of an appropriate amount in order to allow everyone to pay the debts incurred here.

"In conclusion, we pray to the Omnipotent for the continuation of Your beloved Throne, the eternal glory of the Nation, and to grant You, Oh beloved, dear, and just Sovereign, a long and happy life.

"Long live Libya. Long live the King. Long live the Heir Apparent."

36. According to the statement of Louis D. Horowitz, director general of the AJDC, in Geneva, February 15, 1968, on that date there were only 450 refugees still receiving assistance (AAJC, Bulletin no. 91, February 16, 1968).

37. In June 1968 a new law established new regulations covering the activities of Libyan businesses and required non-Libyan firms dealing in foodstuffs, textiles, and clothing to cease activities by July 31, 1969, and those dealing in other goods by July 31, 1970. This law was a powerful incentive to both Libyan and foreign Jews to liquidate their activities in Libya as far as possible.

38. For an overall, but balanced and incisive picture of the implications of the coup d'état and Qadhdhafi's military regime, see Jacques Roumani, "Libya and the Military Revolution," in *Man, State and Society in the Contemporary Maghreb*, ed. I. William Zartman (New York: Praeger, 1973), pp. 344 ff.

39. See in AAEL (which, except where otherwise indicated, contains all documents referred to in the last section) the report given by Joseph Habib in Rome on November 20, 1971, to the Jews of Libya Association. Giulio Hassan was held in prison, without any official charges being leveled

against him, for about three years, whereupon he was released and allowed to leave for Italy, without any explanation other than that the authorities had not been informed of his detention.

40. For the text of the new constitution, see Curotti, *La Libia*, pp. 239 ff. (Italian). [For English text, see Meredith O. Ansell et al., *The Libyan Revolution: A Sourcebook of Legal and Historical Documents* (Stoughton, Wisc.: Oleander Press, 1972), pp. 108–113.]

41. Institute of Jewish Affairs, *The Jewish Communities of the World* (London, 1971), pp. 14 ff. For the Arab point of view, particularly that of the PLO, on the situation of Jews in Libya (and a historical digression), see A. I. Abdo and K. Kasmieh, *Jews of the Arab Countries* (Beirut, 1971), pp. 79 ff.

42. See Press Office, Embassy of the Libyan Arab Republic, *Il simposio di Parigi: Incontro intellettuale tra Oriente e Occidente tra il Colonnello Moammar Gheddafi e un gruppo di illustri esponenti della Cultura e della Politica europea* (Rome, n.d.), p. 24: "Dozens of Jews are still living in my country today and receive assistance from the Libyan government if they are old or disabled. You may see for yourselves in Tripoli. We have given free benefits and monthly pensions for old age and for the disadvantaged."

43. The first of the two memoranda went as follows:
"ARAB REPUBLIC OF LIBYA
"To H.E. the Minister of the Interior and of Local Government
"Tripoli
"Your Excellency!
"After the customary greetings,
"The undersigned, whose names are listed beside each signature herein, wish to state to Your Excellency the following: the Revolutionary Command Council on February 7, 1970, decreed a law regarding the administration of certain funds and properties in Libya.

"This Law declares specifically that it applies to "Israelis" who have left the country (Libyan territory) for the purpose of settling permanently overseas.

"The Law also stipulated that:

"1. The Sequestrator General of Properties should take over the administration of such properties from such persons as provided for under Law No. 6/61.

"2. Any physical or juridical person within the Libyan Arab Republic and any Libyan overseas is required to submit a denunciation of all violations either written or verbal concerning the disposition of properties and all variations in the enjoyment of them and in joint and commercial companies, when one of the associates belongs to the group of persons to whom Article 1 of the law applies.

"In view of the above, it has become clear that the new law is no different from the previous measures except that it applies to persons who have left Libyan Territory and settled permanently overseas, as have those Israelis to whom Law No. 6/61 refers.

"Despite the clarity of the new Law, it has come to our notice that some officials of the Government Offices responsible maintain that the Law applies to all "Jews" whether Libyan or foreign citizens resident in Libya or abroad, regardless of the reason for which they may be overseas.

"In view of this situation, the undersigned have no other recourse but to turn to Y.E., as suggested by the Libyan Embassy in Rome. It is thus our honor to inform you of the following:

"1. The records of each of us show that at all times and on all occasions we have always been loyal to the Law of the land and on this occasion as well we wish to submit to the new Law and apply its provisions. We wish to avoid committing omissions and erroneous interpretations due to the way in which the Law is formulated;

"2. We are not ISRAELIS and have not left Libyan Territory to reside abroad permanently. We still preserve our residence in Libya, as the documents which each of us possesses will prove; we do not have permanent residence here, but are GUESTS, as the documents issued by the ITALIAN AUTHORITIES show.

"Thus, in order to avoid committing omissions or incurring suspicions which might put us in the position of breaking the said Law, even unwittingly, we the undersigned submit to Your Excellency this

PETITION

requesting clarification whether the said Law applies to all JEWS whether of Libyan nationality, stateless, or foreign nationality, having a stable residence in Libya.

"We declare here and now that we shall accept whatever interpretation Y.E. may give.

"We declare our address to be

Libyan Jewish Community
Via Garfàgnana Synagogue, Rome

and trust that Y.E. will reply promptly, allowing us to take the necessary steps in complete respect of the Law of our dear Homeland.

"Yours obediently,

"Rome, March 25, 1970,

"Raffaello Fellah, Vittorio Hassan, Angelo Nahum, Roberto Nunes Vais, Felice Mimun, Giuseppe Hassan, Frieda Nunes Vais, Vittorio Haggiag, Isacco Barda, Bondí Nahum, Pinhas Naim, Clemente Habib, by proxy Leone Habib and sons in liquidation, by proxy SAICIL in liquidation, by proxy Irene Habib Arbib, Alfonso Braha, by proxy Haddad di David Sons, Joseph Raccah, Vittorio Sasson, by proxy Sasson Abramo, Berhani Sasson, by proxy Eredi Scialom Nahum, Alberto Aidan, Hammus Halfon, Nessim Gean, Baranes Toni in Halfon, Abramo Mimun."

44. For further information, see Curotti, *La Libia*, pp. 414 ff.

45. On October 18, 1970, Qadhdhafi announced during what was said to be a spontaneous demonstration that 12,770 Italians had already left (almost all of those who were in Libya on July 21, since, according to the most reliable information, after Qadhdhafi's announcement there were no more than 2,300 Italians still in Libya, 1,800 of whom were there only temporarily for work) and that 37,000 hectares of land, 1,700 houses and apartments, 10 clinics, 500 factories, public, commercial, and professional premises, and

1,200 vehicles had been confiscated, and funds in banks to an amount of 80 million Libyan pounds frozen.

46. There are several sociological and economic studies on Libyan Jews in Israel; see the bibliography in Harvey E. Goldberg, *Cave Dwellers and Citrus Growers: A Jewish Community in Libya and Israel* (Cambridge: Cambridge University Press, 1972), pp. 193 ff.

47. By a law of December 6, 1971 (no. 1066), the Italian state granted an advance (of between 70 and 10 percent depending on the amount) on compensation owed to Italians whose property had been confiscated or made subject to restrictions by the Libyan government the year before. Before the law was passed, in May 1970, the Union of Italian Jewish Communities asserted that Libyan Jews who had never renounced their Libyan Italian citizenship (granted them in 1919 and 1927, for Jews in Tripolitania, and 1919 and 1934 for Jews in Cyrenaica) or had not received any other citizenship should be considered Italian citizens, since the Libyan government had never effectively granted Libyan citizenship. The principle was upheld by the Court of Milan in a decision of October 1973.

48. On July 27, 1972, the Jews of Libya Association collected an initial series of 108 claims for damages suffered by its members. The total amount was 21,267,430.712 Libyan pounds, subdivided according to citizenship:

Libyan citizens	£L15,807,184.787
Italian citizens	£L3,316,964.811
British citizens	£L1,274,228.737
Tunisian citizens	£L861,256.377
Libyan-Egyptian citizens	£L7,846.000

It should be noted that, for various reasons, almost none of the largest property-owners submitted claims.

49. On October 24, 1971, in a letter to the Libyan chargé d'affaires in Rome, the Jews of Libya Association, after recalling its previous contacts with the Libyan authorities, wrote:

"A long time has passed without any solution being reached for our problem. Our situation became the worst possible, after we had been obliged to abandon our homes and were deprived of the necessities of life, even the most modest, so that many of us have been reduced to terrible poverty, despite appearances which some manage to save, through loans or other harmful means, in order to preserve an external decorum corresponding to their accustomed social standing. In fact, most members of our Association do not have any identity or travel documents; thus we find ourselves in a foreign country and devoid of resources. We therefore repeat our petition, and state the following requests:

"(1) that the Revolutionary Command Council make one of its members responsible for talking with our representatives, so that we may promptly reach a realistic solution to our problems, which would save us from the deplorable situation in which we are living and preserve Libya's reputation before justice, law, and history;

"(2) that an emergency payment be made to those who have been expropriated in Libya; this should be in the form of a substantial amount which would help to cover family debts and enable the recipients to begin working to support themselves pending a final solution of the overall problem. Such an advance would be deducted from the total amount to be agreed upon."

50. On January 27, 1972, the Jews of Libya Association sent the following letter regarding the cemeteries to the Libyan minister of the interior:

"We have received very alarming news, to the effect that construction is being done for new roads in the area of the Jewish cemetery of Tripoli, and that some tombs have been damaged by the construction.

"As you no doubt know, the Jewish religion, like all other monotheistic religions, pays great respect and devotion to tombs; it is essential to visit the graves at various times during the year to say special prayers.

"Although we have been away for several years and unable to say the required prayers, we rested assured that since Islam is the official religion of Libya, the cemeteries and graves would be respected, since the constitutional declaration and the principles of the Revolution guarantee religious freedom and allow religious observance.

"The news which has now reached us disturbs us and forces us to write to you, on behalf of all Jews from Libya, to request the following:

"(1) That you investigate with the departments involved in the road construction mentioned above and find out how far the work has proceeded and what is planned in the area of the Jewish cemetery.

"(2) If, as a result of road or other construction—in the area of the cemetery of Tripoli or of any other Jewish cemetery in any town in Libya—tombs would have to be disturbed, we ask you to instruct that the work be temporarily suspended, since the Jewish religion specifically forbids the bones of the dead from being moved without observing precautions of a religious nature.

"(3) In the latter case, we ask you to allow our Association to arrange to appoint rabbinical advisers who will come to Tripoli to give their religious opinion regarding what should be done in such an unfortunate situation, since any decisions in this respect must be taken solely by rabbis of a certain level and according to the observances prescribed by religion.

"(4) That you allow anyone so requesting—even through the Libyan Embassy in Rome—to arrange for transfer of the remains of their family members, when the Jewish religion does not forbid it, and provide these individuals with the necessary assistance. Since this is a religious issue, which for us is of utmost importance, due to its family, humanitarian, and social dimensions, we trust that our requests will be given your closest attention and that you will honor us with a positive reply as soon as possible, as you previously did with your letter of May 25, 1970. Yours respectfully."

51. *Il simposio di Parigi*, pp. 19 ff., 25 ff., 49 ff.

Index of Names

Authors are indicated with first initials, others with full names.

Grunebaum, G. E. von, 76
Guetta, A., 302, 359, 360
Guetta, Ammisciaddai, 98
Guetta, Quintino, 95, 311
Gurgi, Jusuf, 74, 121
Gutierrez, Ernesto, 105, 348

Habib, Abramino, 362
Habib, Clemente, 271, 395
Habib, Jacob, 358
Habib, Joseph, 293, 393
Habib, Leone, 348, 395
Habib, Raffaele, 333
Habib, S. L., 316
Habib, Simone, 293
Habib, Zachino, 191, 193, 198, 199, 210, 217, 376, 377
Haddad, Fortunato, 105
Haddad, Jacob, 318
Haddad, Mosè, 361
Haggiag, Gamila, 158
Haggiag, Liluf Zachi, 198
Haggiag, Rahmin, 359
Haggiag, Simeone, 47, 94, 102, 104, 105, 107, 108, 114, 126, 317, 318, 330–332, 342
Haggiag, Vittorio, 395
Haggiag, Zachi e David, Co., 348
Hahn, Lorna, 213
Hahum di Ididia, Musci, 198
Hakim, S., 380
Hakmon, Y., 360
Hakohen, Mordechai, 298, 301, 363
Halfon, Aron, 41, 312
Halfon, Effraim, 41, 305, 312
Halfon, Hammus, 395
Halfon, Sion, 292
Halfon, Vittorio, 280, 293, 388
Halfon family, 8
Halim, Mustafa ben, 261
Hamik (Vali), 22
Hamuna, Isach, 11
Hannuna, R., and Co., 348
Hannuna, S. di M., 317
Hannuna, Vittorio di M., 317
Hannuna e Meghnagi Co., 348
Harbib, Raffaele, 346

Hassan, Angiolino, 318
Hassan, Aron, 317
Hassan, Felice, 109, 316
Hassan, Gino, 155, 157–158
Hassan, Giulio, 285, 393–394
Hassan, Giuseppe, 395
Hassan, Halfalla, 109
Hassan, Hlafo, 318
Hassan, Isac di Haim, 313, 317
Hassan, Iuda, 22
Hassan, Jacob di Haim, 317
Hassan, Leone, 357
Hassan, M. di J., 316, 317
Hassan, Meborath, 47, 313
Hassan, Messaud, 198, 316, 317
Hassan, Moisè, 43
Hassan, Pace, 317
Hassan, Ruben, 198, 248, 344, 361, 378, 383, 384
Hassan, Umberto, 317
Hassan, Vittorio di M., 317, 348, 395
Hassan family, 8
Hatuma, Davide, 317, 318
Hatuma, Huato, 361
Hazan, Eliau, 21
Hemmali, Kamel el, 197
Herodotus, 1
Herzl, Theodor, 24, 124, 303, 319
Hirschberg, H. Z., 297
Hitler, Adolf, 182, 274
Hoelfer, J., 298
Horwitz, Louis D., 393
Huni, Raid Abdul Munham el, 287, 290

Ibn Saud (nationalist), 214
Idris es-Sanusi, Mohammed, 52, 185, 190, 191, 205, 210, 221, 227, 232, 234, 235, 237, 239, 240, 243, 250, 251, 252, 258–262, 270, 271, 273, 274, 275, 279, 283, 373, 382, 383, 391
Iurnò, Arturo, 358

Jannuzzi, Pio, 131
Jason of Cyrene, 1

Nafa, M. A., 388
Naguib, Muhammad, 259
Nahon, Umberto, 97, 211, 216, 221, 222, 303, 304, 346, 374, 375, 377
Nahum, Abramo, 57, 317
Nahum, Angelo, 271, 395
Nahum, Bondi, 395
Nahum, Clemente, 318
Nahum, David, 348
Nahum, Elia, 317
Nahum, Emilio, 318
Nahum, Eugenio, 47, 73, 121, 122, 123, 318, 341
Nahum, Felice, 95, 332, 354
Nahum, Fiorella, 388
Nahum, Halfalla, 26, 43, 47, 74, 93, 94, 102–105, 108, 109, 113, 126, 154, 187, 197, 198, 199, 313, 315, 317, 318, 319, 324, 327, 328, 330, 337, 348, 361
Nahum, Isach, 47
Nahum, Lydia, 361
Nahum, Maurizio, 318
Nahum, Moshè, 249, 253, 254, 255, 384, 386
Nahum, P., 316
Nahum, Raffaele, 68
Nahum, Ruben, 47
Nahum, Salomone, 316
Nahum, Scialom, 198, 217, 318, 348, 359
Nahum, Vittorio, 109, 114
Nahum family, 8, 68
Naim, Iussef, 11
Naim, Pinhas R., 271, 395
Naman, Iusef, 178
Nasser, Gamal Abdul, 259, 261, 262, 276, 278
Nemni, Linda, 157–158
Nemni, Raffaello, 154, 155, 157, 198, 318, 361
Nemni, Sion, 177, 189, 230, 267, 268, 291, 359, 360, 364, 373, 375, 378, 380, 388
Nessler, Edmond, 388
Nhaisi, Elia, 45–47, 95, 96, 103, 104, 314, 321, 329–330

Nhaisi, Saul, 162, 353
Nuari, Raffaello, 358
Nunes Vais, Abramo, 317
Nunes Vais, Alberto, 364
Nunes Vais, Alfredo, 313, 361
Nunes Vais, Bianca Arbib, 305, 341
Nunes Vais, Ercole, 43
Nunes Vais, Frieda, 395
Nunes Vais, Mario, 26, 104, 105, 119, 313, 361
Nunes Vais, Roberto, 395

Ollivier, G., 299
Ortona, Federico, 46, 47, 105
Otman El Sed, Mohammed, 271
Oulton (Colonel), 193, 198, 199

Pacifici, Alfonso, 333, 346
Paget, Barnard, 208
Paggi, Giannetto, 11, 218, 307, 313
Parsons, Arthur, 370
Pasquinelli, Cesare, 277
Pelt, Adrian, 234, 235, 236, 238, 239, 241, 243, 247, 249, 251–256, 271, 380, 381, 382, 384, 386, 389–390
Perlzweig, Maurizio L., 381
Piccioli, Angelo, 325
Pièche, Giuseppe, 121
Pieri, P., 344
Pinner, Wolfgang, 353
Placido, N., 342
Polacco, Emma, 364
Polacco, Vittorio, 38, 341
Pollio, Alberto, 33
Prato, David, 97, 162, 342, 353
Provenzal, Francesco, 339
Ptolemy I, 1

Qadhdhafi, Muammar, 258, 262, 285, 286, 288, 289, 290, 293, 294, 295, 393, 394, 395
Qaramanli. *See* Karamanli
Quarantelli, F., 35
Queirolo, Ernesto, 126

Rabbinovitz, Anna, 300, 301

DATE DUE